THE PRINCIPLE OF PARTICIPATORY DEMOCRACY IN THE EUROPEAN UNION

This book offers the first complete legal doctrinal map of the principle of participatory democracy enshrined in the EU Treaties.

It traces the principle's origins, its theoretical underpinnings and identifies key legal rights and obligations which follow from it. Against the backdrop of representative democracy in crises, the book unpacks the Treaty promise of citizens participating in the democratic life of the Union including its law and rule-making. Case studies, related to participation in EU law-making, are assessed to determine whether institutional practices adhere to or conflict with the identified legal obligations.

The book explores relevant judicial review and redress mechanisms which exist to give effect to the principle of participatory democracy, as well as recent relevant jurisprudence of the CJEU. Drawing on political theory and empirical methods, while centring the analysis on legal interpretation and methods, suggestions are offered to advance the realisation of the principle of participatory democracy. By consolidating and conceptualising the previously contested content of the Treaty's principle of participatory democracy and coupling this doctrinal clarity with an empirically informed blueprint for applying and enforcing the principle, the volume recasts participatory democracy as a concrete, justiciable norm of EU law.

Volume 144 in the Series Modern Studies in European Law

Modern Studies in European Law

RECENT TITLES IN THIS SERIES:

Actors and Roles in EU Disability Law
Edited by Delia Ferri and Eva S Krolla

The Impact of War (in Ukraine) on the EU
Edited by Inge Govaere, Sacha Garben and Eleanor Spaventa

The European Judiciary: A Community of Law and a Community of Judges
Edited by Alejandro Saiz Arnaiz and Joan Solanes Mullor

Dissensus over Liberal Democracy: Insights from European Judges
Edited by Ramona Coman, Viktor Kazai, Leonardo Puleo and Andrew Bradley

Structural Principles of EU Law
Marcus Klamert

Environmental NGOs and Access to Justice before the CJEU
Mario Pagano

Dealing with Rule of Law Crises in the European Union: Challenges from a Comparative Federalism Perspective
Niels F Kirst

EU Citizenship and Responsibility: The Evolving Roles of the Union, the Individual, and the Member States
Maria Haag

EU Cities Facilitating the Commons: Building Blocks of European Constitutional Law for Local Democracy
Chiara Salati

EU Competence and Power
Hannah Bogaert

Activating Human and Fundamental Rights Before the European Courts
Edited by Elise Muir, Sacha Garben and Inge Govaere

The Hidden Virtues of Discretionary Power in European Migration Law
Jonas Bornemann

Europe's New Frontiers: Law, Crisis, Governance, Constitutional Transformations, Volume 1
Edited by Leone Niglia

The Principle of Participatory Democracy in the European Union
Gloria Golmohammadi

For the complete list of titles in this series see www.bloomsbury.com/uk/series/modern-studies-in-european-law/

The Principle of Participatory Democracy in the European Union

Gloria Golmohammadi

•HART•
OXFORD • LONDON • NEW YORK • NEW DELHI • SYDNEY

HART PUBLISHING
Bloomsbury Publishing Plc
Kemp House, Chawley Park, Cumnor Hill, Oxford, OX2 9PH, UK
1385 Broadway, New York, NY 10018, USA
Bloomsbury Publishing Ireland Limited, 29 Earlsfort Terrace, Dublin 2, D02 AY28, Ireland

HART PUBLISHING, the Hart/Stag logo, BLOOMSBURY and the Diana logo are trademarks of Bloomsbury Publishing Plc

First published in Great Britain 2026

1

A catalogue record for this book is available from the British Library.

Library of Congress Control Number: 2026944632

ISBN: HB: 978-1-50999-594-3
ePDF: 978-1-50999-592-9
ePub: 978-1-50999-593-6

Typeset by Amnet

For product safety related questions contact productsafety@bloomsbury.com

To my wonderful parents, Kristina and Bonian Golmohammadi, whose participatory parenting has laid the groundwork for this work.

ACKNOWLEDGEMENTS

This book is a revised and recalibrated version of my doctoral thesis, defended at Stockholm University. The content has been updated to reflect developments in case law, as well as recent geopolitical shifts and evolving legislative contexts. The focus of the thesis has also been reoriented for a broader audience. The import of the principle of participatory democracy and the 'right of citizens to participate in the democratic life of the Union' is now explored in three Member State legal contexts. This part of the research has been funded by Stiftelsen för Rättsvetenskaplig Forskning from the Wallenberg Foundation, for whose support and flexible arrangements I am very grateful.

At the outset, I would like to thank the dedicated team at Hart Publishing, whose exemplary work has elevated the book. Many continued thanks also to my doctoral supervisor, Antonina Bakardjieva Engelbrekt, for her invaluable support in seeing this endeavour through. Likewise, thank you to my co-supervisor, Mauro Zamboni, for his uplifting encouragement. The contributions and overall experience during the defence of my doctoral thesis were instrumental for the decision to bring this book to fruition. I am most grateful to Deirde Curtin, whose sharp insights, questions and encouragement were crucial to continuing the work. A big thank you to Patricia Popelier for her poignant feedback, Joakim Nergelius for his helpful suggestions, and Joana Mendes for her insights, generous advice post-thesis, and continued support. Also thanks to Patricia Jonasson for her constructive engagement and Alberto Alemanno for his encouragement to pursue this book! During the early stages of writing, a few people were instrumental in advancing the manuscript, in particular Anna W Ghavanini, Jane Reichel and Maria Strömvik, and I am thankful for their input along the way. Likewise, I am thankful to Jim Liebman at Columbia University for exposing me to ideas on governance and learning which steered me in this direction in the first place.

There are many Swedish, Austrian and Irish government and parliamentary staff, as well as NGO staff engaging in strategic litigation, and EU Commission officials to whom I am indebted for answering my many (and likely annoyingly detailed) questions. Two experiences influenced the work which also deserve mention: the participatory Foresight in Lower Austria, facilitated by the Austrian Institute of Technology (thank you Peter Biegelbauer, for allowing me to join) and involvement in the Baha'i junior youth empowerment programme in Husby-Akalla and Vienna, which challenged my assumptions about public participation in political life.

To my colleagues and students at Stockholm University – I am grateful to be able to learn alongside you. Previous colleagues at the Administrative Court of Stockholm and the Court of Appeal who have contributed to the intellectual endeavours of this project, thank you! I am also thankful to colleagues at Ljubljana University for welcoming me as a visiting researcher, and especially to Samo Bardutzky for his generous assistance in navigating the organisational and intellectual landscape of the region and the law faculty at Ljubljana University.

Finally, thank you all for the much-needed intellectual, emotional and practical support: mamma and pappa, *mor- och farföräldrar*, the Golmohammadi, Reyhani, Forghani, Norlin, Bergsmo and Namdar clans; Kati, Adel, Hoda, Dayyan, Naima, Nikan, Kami, Nora, Laetitia, Neshat, Patrick, Leyla, Naim, Indra, Charisse, Joanna, Hilda and Miloš, Monika and Andrej, Pija and Ljubo, Mimoza and family, Ana, Mina, Tina, Nadine; my daughters, Leonora and Liva; and, last but not least, Adib. I am always grateful you decided to join me for that walk 10 years ago – and that we still are walking together.

CONTENTS

ABBREVIATIONS

AG	Advocate General
CFR	Charter of Fundamental Rights of the European Union
CJEU	Court of Justice of the European Union
ECHR	European Convention on Human Rights
ECJ	European Court of Justice
EU-InfoG	EU-Informationsgesetz, Austrian EU Act
FOI-Act	Irish Freedom of Information Act,
GC	European General Court
IA	Impact Assessment
ICCPR	International Covenant on Civil and Political Rights
IFG	Informationsfreiheitsgesetz – Austrian Freedom of Information Act
OECD	Organization for Economic Co-operation and Development
RF	Regeringsformen, Swedish Instrument of Government
TEU	Treaty on the European Union
TFEU	Treaty on the Functioning of the European Union
UN	United Nations

TABLE OF CASES (IN CHRONOLOGICAL ORDER)

CJEU

General Court

AG opinions

National cases

TABLE OF LEGISLATION

European Union

Treaties

Regulations

Directives and Decisions

Commission Decisions

Commission Implementing Regulation

Interinstitutional Agreements

International Treaties

National Legislation

Austria

Ireland

Sweden

UPDATE ON RECENT DEVELOPMENTS

Following the completion of the manuscript, the Court has continued to speak to the constitutional character of the EU legal order, with implications for the analysis developed in the book. In particular, in the landmark case C-769/22 *Commission v Hungary (Values of the Union)* the Court confirmed that the values enshrined in Article 2 TEU constitute binding legal obligations for Member States, and that Article 2 TEU is itself a justiciable provision. The judgment has already generated extensive legal commentary, and I will not venture to elaborate on it here. However, a few observations are warranted regarding its implications for the arguments advanced in this book.

While *Commission v Hungary* does not alter the book's core legal arguments or mapping of the principle of participatory democracy, it does situate the legal argument in a different context, while also adding legitimacy to some of the legal analysis in the book. With *Commission v Hungary*, the goal post on the justiciability of EU democracy has moved. The book's legal arguments have consequently gained in relevance, and can be seen in a new light as 'manifest and particularly serious breaches' of democracy can be brought before the Court as a matter of an Article 2 TEU breach – often most likely in combination with one of the 'Provisions on Democratic Principles' enshrined in Articles 9–12 TEU.

Regarding the justiciability of EU democracy in the national context, the analysis presented in the third chapter of the book stands. In sum: to the degree that Article 10 TEU, including Article 10(3), formulates representative democracy rights, the Court has paved the way for enforcing these, beginning to delineate Member State obligations to ensure these rights. With regard to the principle of participatory democracy, and, in particular, thinking of its import for participation in law-making, it would be important to consider that there is much more diversity and variation amongst Member States with regard to the legislative process, and how participation in law-making is framed and practised, when compared with key representative democracy standards or features such as elections. The same applies when in search of equivalents for the instruments of participatory democracy in Article 11 TEU, such as dialogue, consultation or citizens' initiatives, and so forth. From this standpoint, Article 10(3) TEU does not seem sufficiently clear and precise to have direct effect in relation to these practices, or, as such, grant a stand-alone right to participate in EU law-making at the national level. Similarly, at the EU level, although Article 10(3) TEU should in light of the Court's case law be understood as offering citizens a right to know and directly attempt to influence the EU legislative process, it is not sufficiently clear and precise in this regard to be considered a stand-alone right.

As elaborated further in the third chapter, the democratic life of the Union can effectively be construed as having a core and a periphery, or understood in terms of concentric circles around a crucial centre. At the centre of this 'life' are the electoral practices tied to the principle of representative democracy, the founding democratic principle of the Union. Within the centre are also the citizens' rights of the Treaty, as featured in the citizens' rights catalogue in Articles 20–24 TFEU, and the participatory democracy right of the ECI, as well as the right of access to documents. The right to participate in processes and practices at the heart of the democratic life of the Union has direct effect. This would, for example, be relevant when national measures are required to secure the right to participate in European Parliament elections. It also comes into play when democratic guarantees at the national level – primarily core features of representative democracy – are so jeopardised as to undermine the overall exercise of Article 10(3) TEU. We now know such situations would likely also trigger Article 2 TEU and could be litigated as such.

In addition, there may be instances where the right enshrined in Article 10(3) TEU in relation to the processes and practices at the EU level has a wider berth than the respective framing in the Treaties or secondary legislation. As regards the democratic life of the Union outside 'the centre', this includes more direct forms of engagement with the Union and its institutions and bodies, prominently through participation in EU law-making and rule-making. The right also includes direct forms of engagement with Member State institutions and agencies, to the degree that they are acting in a (quasi-) EU legislative or EU rule-making capacity. Other areas included in the periphery of the democratic life of the Union would include dialogue activities. Similarly, it would relate to the Charter right to participate in social activity and corresponding obligations to promote opportunities for marginalised groups to participate. These are all part and parcel of the right to participate in the democratic life of the Union. However, considering the more ambiguous status and modalities of these practices, Article 10(3) TEU is not sufficiently clear and precise to grant direct effect in relation to them. Important, however, is that the relationship between the core and the periphery should not be seen as fixed, but as possessing a moveable quality whereby processes at the periphery can, over time, gravitate towards the centre. And crucially, through the principle of consistent interpretation, national legal norms should be interpreted in light of the right to participate in the democratic life of the Union, including its participatory democracy element. Overall, this analysis rhymes well with the Court's approach in *Commission v Hungary*, even as the scope of Article 2 TEU and 'manifest and particularly serious breaches' of EU democracy remain ambiguous. As the notion of litigating (EU) democracy gains traction, this book sheds light on a crucial but generally overlooked dimension of EU democracy – the principle of participatory democracy.

1

Introduction

1.1. The participative turn

Public participation in political life has recently been manifesting in ways that are both surprising and difficult to measure.[1] Debates at the European and national level highlight the 'participative turn' or 'deliberative wave'[2] – referring to the traction that more direct or innovative forms of involving citizens and non-state actors in law and policy-making have gained with governments and citizens. At the same time, growing apathy towards different forms of political participation has been observed, as well as challenges to traditional participation mediums.[3] Participation, as such, can naturally serve various functions: it may enhance the quality of legislation or give voice to interests and rights. Its merit may be emphasised based on influence over process or outcome; its value argued in terms of balancing interests or as an expression of human dignity. In complex governance schemes, it can serve as crucial democratic input into decision-making.[4] And whether at the local or global level, it is often viewed as a necessary prerequisite for justice.[5] In both political theory and public law, the centrality of representative democracy as a normative framework has historically led to a focus on political participation viewed through electoral representation.[6] However, challenges facing

[1] Compared with traditional forms of political participation, less is known about non-traditional forms of engagement such as online political participation, which has been noted as specifically unpredictable. Jessica T Feezell, 'Predicting Online Political Participation' (2016) 69 *Political Research Quarterly* 495; Dennis Friess and others, 'Political Online Participation and Its Effects: Theory, Measurement, and Results' (2021) 13 *Policy & Internet* 345.

[2] OECD, 'Innovative Citizen Participation and New Democratic Institutions: Catching the Deliberative Wave (OECD Publishing, 2020).

[3] Tom Gerald Daly, 'Democratic Decay: Conceptualising an Emerging Research Field' (2019) 11 *Hague Journal on the Rule of Law* 9; Simon Oxenham, 'The Rise of Political Apathy in Two Charts' (2017) *Nature*, https://www.nature.com/articles/nature.2017.22106#citeas. See also James Sloam, 'Diversity and Voice: The Political Participation of Young People in the European Union' (2016) 18 *The British Journal of Politics and International Relations* 521.

[4] Deirdre Curtin, Herwig Hofmann and Joana Mendes, 'Constitutionalising EU Executive Rule-Making Procedures: A Research Agenda' (2013) 19 *European Law Journal* 1, 1–10.

[5] This idea is featured prominently in literature on restorative justice: see, eg John Braithwaite, 'Democracy, Community, and Problem Solving' in Gale Burford and Joe Hudson (eds), *Family Group Conferencing* (Routledge, 2000).

[6] Stijn Smismans, 'Regulatory Procedure and Participation in the European Union' in Francesca Bignami and David Zaring (eds), *Comparative Law and Regulation* (Edward Elgar Publishing, 2016) 129–30.

modern governance are compelling the legal discipline to reflect more systematically on participation outside of the parliamentary process and beyond elections.[7]

The principle of participatory democracy, first enshrined in the Lisbon Treaty's 'Democratic Principles', at a glance promotes such participation beyond the ballot box. It obliges EU institutions to enter into dialogue with civil society; to consult, in their legislative and policy-making activities, with 'parties concerned'; and to offer citizens the opportunity to invite legislative action through the European Citizens' Initiative (ECI) – all in light of citizens' 'right to participate in the democratic life of the Union'.[8] Although their import and legal status are often not clear, there are, today, several opportunities for citizens and interested and affected actors to engage with EU law and decision-making.[9] This increasing emphasis on citizens' participation and participatory governance is not an isolated development. Nor is the demand for participatory decision-making unique to the long-standing debates on democracy deficits within the EU. At the national and local level, experimentation and digitalisation are opening up new opportunities for democratic participation beyond the ballot box. The opportunity to exercise influence on decision-making processes has long been regarded as a cornerstone of democracy, and linked to human dignity. However, the ability to participate in and contribute to society has, in recent times, also been linked to our individual wellbeing in medical terms and identified as an integral part of mental health.[10]

Transcending the political science discourse on democracy, participation is now a highly relevant concept in several scientific fields. The legal dimensions of participation are, consequently, also gaining traction. In international law, participation is linked to rule of law and access to justice, where the latter has been defined to include 'the ability to seek and exercise influence on law-making and law-implementing processes and institutions', in particular by poor and marginalised groups.[11] While proponents of a legal right to participate have argued for some time that the right to political participation extends beyond political elections and implies a right to be more directly involved in the legislative process,[12] recent years have seen an evolution of international human rights law and jurisprudence on the scope of the right to participate.[13] Research on the role of civil

[7] ibid.

[8] Consolidated Version of the Treaty on European Union [2012] OJ C326/13. Art 10(3) TEU, Art 11 TEU. The link between Art 10(3) and Art 11 TEU is not clear: this is analysed in ch 3, ss 3.1 and 3.2.

[9] Dominik Hierlemann and others, *Under Construction: Citizen Participation in the European Union* (Verlag Bertelsmann Stiftung, 2022).

[10] World Health Organization, 'Mental Health: Strengthening Our Response', www.who.int/news-room/fact-sheets/detail/mental-health-strengthening-our-response, accessed 6 February 2026; Proposition [Prop] 2002/03:35 Mål för folkhälsan [government bill] 119.

[11] Adriaan Bedner, 'An Elementary Approach to the Rule of Law' (2010) 2 *Hague Journal on the Rule of Law* 48.

[12] Henry J Steiner, 'Political Participation as a Human Right' (1988) 1 *Harvard Human Rights Yearbook* 77.

[13] Office of the United Nations High Commissioner for Human Rights, 'Promotion, Protection and Implementation of the Right to Participate in Public Affairs in the Context of the Existing Human Rights Law: Best Practices, Experiences, Challenges and Ways to Overcome Them' [2015] UN Doc A/HRC/30/26 paras 13–21.

society in international law-making is surging.[14] And at the level of EU law, strong arguments have for some time been put forward for a legal right to participate in EU rule-making.[15]

These developments are arguably occurring against a backdrop of two parallel processes. On the one hand, the opportunities to participate in law and public decision-making have broadened – also connected with the advancement of education. A growing consciousness of the value of universal participation and the rights of previously excluded or marginalised groups (such as women, minorities, youth, children, non-citizens and migrants) to contribute to decision-making in a globalised world has propelled the reconceptualisation of concepts such as democracy, participation and rights.[16] Further affecting this participation awakening are the technological advances of past decades, changing how knowledge is being generated and shared, and influencing how citizens organise and mobilise. Governance adaptation, such as crowdsourcing legislation, is consequently one avenue of legislative experimentation.[17] Regular demonstrations and rallies, co-ordinated at a global level, are an example of how citizens mobilising in new ways can quickly become a mainstream fixture. Through the COVID-19 pandemic, the possibilities of connection through digital spaces, also at scale, have also been elucidated. The capacity and action which civic engagement can unlock have also been highlighted in Europe, with citizen and NGO networks arranging concrete protection for Ukrainians through rapid mutual aid, housing, and service delivery, while deliberative formats such as citizens assemblies have shown how structured participation could unlock rights reforms with broad legitimacy. In the EU law-making context, civil society participation has shifted crisis-era legislative outcomes on key legislative files.

On the other hand, a process of participation fragmentation and decline, and multiplying participation hurdles, can be observed, marked by growing apathy towards different forms of political participation, challenges to traditional participation mediums, and increasingly hostile participation spaces. Major trackers show sustained global democratic decline alongside 'autocratization', driven less by classic coups than by legalistic, incremental erosion featuring polarisation,

[14] See, eg Philip Alston and others, *International Human Rights* (Oxford University Press, 2012) 89; Steve Charnovitz, 'The Relevance of Non-State Actors to International Law' in Rüdiger Wolfrum and Volker Röben (eds), *Developments of International Law in Treaty Making*, vol 177 (Springer, 2005) 543.

[15] See Joana Mendes, *Participation in EU Rule-Making: A Rights-Based Approach* (Oxford University Press, 2011).

[16] Nadia Urbinati and Mark E Warren, 'The Concept of Representation in Contemporary Democratic Theory' (2008) 11 *Annual Review of Political Science* 387; see also Charles F Sabel and William H Simon, 'Democratic Experimentalism' in Justin Desautels-Stein and Christopher Tomlins (eds), *Searching for Contemporary Legal Thought* (Cambridge University Press, 2017); Simon Hix, 'When Optimism Fails: Liberal Intergovernmentalism and Citizen Representation' (2018) 56 *Journal of Common Market Studies* 1595–1613.

[17] Tanja Aitamurto, *Crowdsourcing for Democracy: A New Era in Policy-Making* (Parliament of Finland, 2012).

institutional brinkmanship, and voter disaffection[18] Long-term data suggest that political apathy has risen steadily among Europe's citizens since 1990.[19] Voter turn-out across Europe is at one of its lowest points since suffrage rights were extended to the broader population,[20] and citizens – youth, in particular – express a lack of interest in traditional political participation, as well as in joining political parties, which is seemingly founded, in part, on a scepticism about the value and utility of participation in the current system and an aversion to traditional forms of engagement.[21] The aversion towards traditional fora is important to note, as equating political silence to passivity and exclusion loses sight of its other potentially positive dimensions, encompassing forms of reluctance, and even resistance.[22] As non-participation, political silences are no longer solely attributed to the effects of repression, exclusion or lassitude, but to deliberate refusal to play along in a language game the rules of which seem unacceptable.[23]

Connected with this trend is the shift from government to governance, where spaces of influence move beyond the state or state actors to other arenas, and from corporatism to pluralism.[24] It is, then, perhaps only natural that public participation is becoming less predictable. A polarised and hostile political climate marked by lacking or vulnerable information distribution leaves some decision-makers concerned with curbing detrimental, uninformed or misinformed public participation.[25] Such concern is only reinforced, considering not only the opportunities but also particular

[18] V-Dem Institute, 'Democracy Report 2025: 25 Years of Autocratization – Democracy Trumped?', https://www.v-dem.net/documents/60/V-dem-dr__2025_lowres.pdf; Freedom House, 'Freedom in the World 2025', https://freedomhouse.org/sites/default/files/2025-02/FITW_World_2025_Feb.2025.pdf.

[19] Oxenham, 'The Rise of Political Apathy in Two Charts' (n 3).

[20] ibid.

[21] Viktor Dahl and others, 'Apathy or Alienation? Political Passivity among Youths across Eight European Union Countries' (2018) 15 *European Journal of Developmental Psychology* 284.

[22] Monica Alexandra Brito-Vieira and others, 'Critical Exchange: The Nature of Silence and Its Democratic Possibilities' [2019] *Contemporary Political Theory* 424, 426; See also Vincent Jungkunz, 'The Promise of Democratic Silences' (2012) 34 *New Political Science* 127; Sophia Hatzisavvidou, 'Disturbing Binaries in Political Thought: Silence as Political Activism' (2015) 14 *Social Movement Studies* 509; Justin Gest and Sean WD Gray (eds), *Silent Citizenship: The Politics of Marginality in Unequal Democracies* (Routledge, Taylor & Francis Group 2018); Mónica Brito Vieira, 'Silence in Political Theory and Practice' (2021) 24 *Critical Review of International Social and Political Philosophy* 289.

[23] Brito-Vieira and others, 'Critical Exchange' (n 22).

[24] The governance literature is vast, including in relation to the EU: for an overview of some central issues see, eg Ian Bache, 'Multi-Level Governance in the European Union' in David Levi-Faur (ed), *The Oxford Handbook of Governance* (Oxford University Press, 2012); see also Gary Marks, Liesbet Hooghe and Kermit Blank, 'European Integration from the 1980s: State-Centric v. Multi-Level Governance' (1996) 34 *Journal of Common Market Studies* 341; Fritz Scharpf, *Governing in Europe: Effective and Democratic?* (Oxford University Press, 1999); Thomas Christiansen, 'Intra-Institutional Politics and Inter-Institutional Relations in the EU: Towards Coherent Governance?' (2001) 8 *Journal of European Public Policy* 747; Christian Joerges and Renaud Dehousse (eds), *Good Governance in Europe's Integrated Market* (Oxford University Press, 2002); Joanne Scott and David M Trubek, 'Mind the Gap: Law and New Approaches to Governance in the European Union' (2002) 8 *European Law Journal* 1; B Guy Peters and Jon Pierre, 'Multi-Level Governance and Democracy: A Faustian Bargain?' in Ian Bache and Matthew Flinders (eds), *Multi-level Governance* (Oxford University Press, 2004).

[25] For two relatively recent contributions on the challenge of uninformed or misguided political participation, leading to opposite remedial conclusions, see Jason Brennan, *Against Democracy* (Princeton University Press, 2017); Eitan Hersh, *Politics Is for Power: How to Move Beyond Political Hobbyism, Take Action, and Make Real Change* (Scribner, 2020).

challenges that online and social media spaces face in terms of transparency, accessibility and inclusiveness.[26] Beyond concerns about fake news, rabbit holes or the reduction of complex issues to simple narratives, recent research highlights, at the more fundamental level, the adverse impact on cognitive capacity, democracy and 'human will' brought on by the so-called attention economy.[27] Considering these factors, while public participation has been described as a means for the government to inject knowledge and experience into the law and policy process, and a means to remedy democratic deficits by promoting participatory practices, such practices have also been criticised for being too costly, time-consuming, ineffective or merely symbolic – limiting participation to information-sharing or buy-in exercises.[28]

While the debates surrounding the EU democracy deficit traditionally centre on the challenges posed by the multi-level setting and the specificities of EU governance and democracy, such concerns are now compounded when confronted with a deepened 'crisis' of democracy, leading to a reckoning with representative democracy not just beyond, but within, the nation state.[29] In particular, democratic backsliding within Member States and the rise of populism have been prominent.[30]

Additionally, geopolitical shocks – Russia's war against Ukraine, the energy-security crunch, irregular migration pressures, and a broader 'strategic competition' turn in industrial, technology and defence policy – have pushed EU governance into a more permanent emergency posture where speed, consensus and confidentiality are treated as strategic assets, with predictable democratic side effects: the thinning of participation, scrutiny and reason-giving.[31] Meanwhile, experimentation with 'participatory democracy' practices, including within the EU, has drastically increased.[32]

[26] For an overview of the issues, see Andrew Lih, 'Opinion: Can Wikipedia Survive?' *The New York Times* (New York, 20 June 2015), www.nytimes.com/2015/06/21/opinion/can-wikipedia-survive.html, accessed 6 February 2026.

[27] Adrian F Ward and others, 'Brain Drain: The Mere Presence of One's Own Smartphone Reduces Available Cognitive Capacity' (2017) 2 *Journal of the Association for Consumer Research* 140; See also Tim Wu, *The Attention Merchants: The Epic Scramble to Get Inside Our Heads*, 1st edn (Alfred A Knopf, 2016). On the commodification of childhood, and persuasive design, see Beeban Kidron and others, 'Disrupted Childhood: The Cost of Persuasive Design' (*5Rights Foundation*, Version 2, 2023), https://5rightsfoundation.com/uploads/Disrupted-Childhood-2023.pdf, accessed 6 February 2026.

[28] *cf* Marian Barnes and others, 'Constituting "the Public" in Public Participation' (2003) 81 *Public Administration* 379; Renée A Irvin and John Stansbury, 'Citizen Participation in Decision Making: Is It Worth the Effort?' (2004) 64 *Public Administration Review* 55.

[29] Regarding EU democracy deficit debates, see ch 2, s 2.2. Regarding the broader democracy crises, see, eg Hélène Landemore, *Open Democracy: Reinventing Popular Rule for the Twenty-First Century* (Princeton University Press, 2020).

[30] Nadia Urbinati, *Me the People: How Populism Transforms Democracy* (Harvard University Press, 2019); Laurent Pech and Kim Lane Scheppele, 'Illiberalism Within: Rule of Law Backsliding in the EU' (2017) 19 *Cambridge Yearbook of European Legal Studies* 3; Paul Howe, 'Eroding Norms and Democratic Deconsolidation' (2017) 28 *Journal of Democracy* 15.

[31] Jie Ouyang, 'The Omnibus Comeback of the Neoliberal EU' [2025] *Verfassungsblog: On Matters Constitutional*, https://intrechtdok.de/receive/mir_mods_00021446, accessed 1 February 2026. For a general take, see Christina Eckes, Päivi Leino-Sandberg and Anna W Ghavanini, *The Dynamics of Powers in the European Union*, 1st edn (Bloomsbury, 2024).

[32] Brigitte Geißel and Marko Joas (eds), *Participatory Democratic Innovations in Europe: Improving the Quality of Democracy?*, 1st edn (Verlag Barbara Budrich, 2013); see also OECD, 'Innovative Citizen Participation' (n 2); 'SILE, Silent Agents Affected by Legislation: From an Insufficient Knowledge Base to Inclusive Solutions' (*Hiljaiset toimijat*), www.hiljaisettoimijat.fi/?lang=en, accessed 6 February 2026.

The EU principle of participatory democracy seems well suited for such times, yet for all the potential with which the principle is poised, its legal ramifications have received less attention.[33] Around the time of the ratification of the Lisbon Treaty, the new democratic principles of the Treaty, including the novel feature of participatory democracy, created a stir which generated legal commentary, primarily centred around raising legitimate and interesting questions about the implications of Article 11 TEU, including on whether and how the provisions would and should be fleshed out in secondary law.[34] The ambitious RenEUAL project of drafting binding EU administrative procedural rules concretising, inter alia, the principle of participatory democracy for rule-making, while supported by the European Parliament ('the Parliament'), was met with resistance by the Commission and put on ice.[35] So, a decade later, with some intermittent commentary highlighting the 'limits' of the principle of participatory democracy, many of the questions raised at the outset remain largely unanswered.[36] While legal clarity on many features may be elusive, there is a distinct uptake of 'participatory democracy' as a concept being deployed to define an array of EU institutional-related practices. Participating in citizens' initiatives, organising conferences and breakout events, petitioning the Parliament, complaining to the European Ombudsman, various dialogue activities, and participating in Commission consultation have all been labelled as expressions of participatory democracy in the EU, sometimes accompanied with a brief nod to a Treaty article.[37] However, if participatory democracy, in the broad sense, is suddenly everywhere, it is also nowhere, in any defining or legal sense.[38]

[33] Alberto Alemanno, for example, comments on the lack of categorisation or taxonomy of participatory democracy instruments connected with the legal principle: Alberto Alemanno, 'Towards a Permanent Citizens Participatory Mechanism in the EU, Study Commissioned by the Policy Department for Citizens' Rights and Constitutional Affairs, European Parliament' (2022) PE 735.927 15.

[34] Paul Craig, *The Lisbon Treaty, Revised Edition: Law, Politics, and Treaty Reform* (Oxford University Press, 2013) 66–77; Víctor Cuesta Lopez, 'The Lisbon Treaty's Provisions on Democratic Principles: A Legal Framework for Participatory Democracy' (2010) 16 *European Public Law* 123; Mendes, Participation in EU Rule-Making (n 15) 1849–77.

[35] See European Parliament resolution of 9 June 2016 for an open, efficient and independent European Union administration OJ 2018/C 086/19; see also Alberto Alemanno, 'Levelling the EU Participatory Playing Field: A Legal and Policy Analysis of the Commission's Public Consultations in Light of the Principle of Political Equality' (2020) 26 *European Law Journal* 114, 125.

[36] Acar Kutay, 'Limits of Participatory Democracy in European Governance: Participatory Democracy in Lisbon Treaty' (2015) 21 *European Law Journal* 803. The exception is the European Citizens Initiative (ECI), which was fleshed out in secondary legislation, and on which there is a body of case law as well as more legal literature.

[37] See, eg European Youth Portal, 'Conference on the Future of Europe: Experience Participatory Democracy in Your Class', https://youth.europa.eu/news/conference-future-of-europe-experience-participatory-democracy-your-class_en, accessed 6 February 2026; Alberto Alemanno, 'Strengthening the Role and Impact of Petitions as an Instrument of Participatory Democracy, Study Commissioned by the European Parliament's Policy Department for Citizens' Rights and Constitutional Affairs PE 694.837'; European Parliament resolution of 14 March 2023 on the annual report on the activities of the European Ombudsman in 2021 (2022/2141(INI), P9_TA(2023)0070.

[38] It is telling that, when the Commission, in 2021, presented its landmark legislative package in the area of migration and asylum (the New Migration Pact), no open consultation had preceded the legislative bills (the package was accompanied by a succinct staff working document and not an impact assessment). The legislative process is included as one of the case studies in ch 4.

In the meantime, the CJEU has begun to tentatively adopt the language of participatory democracy, highlighting its complementary role: 'That system of representative democracy was complemented, with the Treaty of Lisbon, by instruments of participatory democracy.'[39] Regarding Article 11(3) TEU, which elaborates on the Commission's consultation duties, there is no direct case law to date, and the legal literature is scant, with opposing views on whether legal obligations can be derived from the principle and are justiciable.[40] While stakeholder consultation is a stable feature of the Commission's policy- and law-making, the Commission consistently refrains from framing its engagement with stakeholders in legal terms.[41] Meanwhile, the rise (and sometimes fall) of participation innovations and practices across Europe and within EU institutions raises the broader question of the role of law in the realisation of participatory democracy and the role of democratic participation in institutional law- and decision-making

The classic challenges that EU governance poses to participation and engagement at the national and local level are well known. In Member States, the transfer of normative and legislative power to Brussels is challenging national models of law-making; established and publicised junctures for participation are, for example, disrupted, with public participation occurring too late in the process of EU law-making, often during the phase of implementation rather than negotiation, while consultation occurring during the negotiation phase is opaque.[42] Similarly, for rule-making, participation is often skewed or lacking.[43] There is plenty of scholarly work on democracy deficits and participation in EU law-making in the social sciences. With the rise of the EU Better Regulation Agenda, some increased attention has also been given to the legal implications of public consultations.[44] However, it is still unclear whether and how the principle of participatory democracy implies legally grounded considerations that need to be taken into account when determining the modalities of consultation, or more broadly for public participation in EU law-making and governance. Does the principle give rise to concrete rights and obligations, and if so, is there any possibility for legal redress in the event of a breach of such rights? Relatedly, how do

[39] Case C-418/18 P *Grégor Puppinck and Others v Commision* EU:C:2019:1113, para 65.

[40] *cf* Anne Meuwese, 'Embedding Consultation Procedures: Law or Institutionalization?' (2011) 17 *European Public Law* 527, 532–33; Joana Mendes, 'Participation and the Role of Law after Lisbon: A Legal View on Article 11 TEU' (2011) 48 *Common Market Law Review* 1849; Smismans, 'Regulatory Procedure and Participation in the European Union' (n 6); Alemanno, 'Levelling the EU Participatory Playing Field' (n 35) 114.

[41] Commission, Communication from the Commission to the European Parliament, The Council, The European Economic and Social Committee and the Committee of the Regions, Better Regulation: Joining Forces to Make Better Laws COM/2021/219 final.

[42] Jörgen Hettne and Jane Reichel, *Att Göra Rätt Och i Tid – Behövs Nya Metoder För Att Genomföra EU-Rätt i Sverige?*, vol 2012:4 (Svenska institutet för europapolitiska studier 2012).

[43] See, eg Mendes, *Participation in EU Rule-Making* (n 15).

[44] Anne Meuwese and Patricia Popelier, 'Legal Implications of Better Regulation: A Special Issue' (2011) 17 *European Public Law* 455; Alberto Alemanno, 'How Much Better Is Better Regulation? Assessing the Impact of the Better Regulation Package on the European Union – A Research Agenda' (2015) 6 *European Journal of Risk Regulation* 344; Meuwese, 'Embedding Consultation Procedures' (n 40); Curtin, Hofmann and Mendes, 'Constitutionalising EU Executive Rule-Making Procedures' (n 4).

the legal imperatives operating on different levels (national and supranational) correspond to each other?

1.2. Aims and approach of the book

This book sheds light on an EU legal foundational principle – the principle of participatory democracy – and offers legal and analytical tools for assessing its implications for EU governance, focusing on multi-level law-making. In doing so, the book aims to contribute to the broader conversation about the potential (and limitations) of law in facilitating democratic participation in multi-level settings and beyond the ballot box.

While various features of the principle of participatory democracy have been explored, this is the first monograph covering the principle and its content. Historically, a challenge in analysing this principle has been unclarity and contention about the normative content and assumptions of participatory democracy itself and, relatedly, diverging labels ascribed to the principle at hand.[45] While it is often referred to as the principle of participatory democracy (and the drafting of the Lisbon Treaty, as well as recent CJEU case law, support this term as well), some refer to it as a principle of democratic participation, while others emphasis different articles in the Treaty which prescribe direct, deliberative and participatory democracy practices. A central aim of the book is, therefore, to consolidate an understanding of the principle of participatory democracy (including its ambiguous label) which is coherent with legal methods, thereby contributing to reinvigorating the principle in the EU legal order.

To meet these aims and challenges, the book is divided into three parts, each guided by a question. The first part is devoted to unpacking the principle of participatory democracy, tracing its origins and theoretical underpinnings, and mapping out the rights and obligations which flow from the principle (chapters two and three). The second part attempts to assess to what degree current practices adhere to or conflict with the principle, focusing on law-making consultation as one important mechanism for giving effect to the principle (chapter four). The third part constructively engages with law-making practices to highlight paths for reinvigorating the principle in the EU legal order (chapter five).

The first part, which makes up a substantial portion of the book, asks 'what are the main elements of the principle of participatory democracy and what key rights and obligations does the principle entail and for whom?' In answering the first question, the theoretical foundations and normative roots of the principle of participatory democracy are explored, as well as its drafting history, all of which underpin the legal analysis of the principle and allow for a proper teleological interpretation of the relevant Treaty articles. It also provides a conceptual framework which serves as a touchstone for the third part of the book. The book also

[45] This is explored in more detail in ch 3.

addresses to what extent the normative content of the principle is justiciable. In mapping the normative and legal framework for participation, which is associated with – and stems from – the EU principle of participatory democracy, key standards and duties are distilled.

Proceeding from the outlining of this normative and legal framework for participation, the second part of the book concerns the practical implementation of the principle of participatory democracy and draws on empirical methods. The main question here is to what degree current EU law-making consultation practices at the EU level adhere to or conflict with the identified key standards and duties, and what implications the principle of participatory democracy has for national legal norms. A case-study method is adopted which examines consultation practices and outcomes for distinct EU legislative proposals and assesses whether Commission consultations in these cases adhere to the key standards and duties set by the principle of participatory democracy. Then – using Sweden, Austria and Ireland as the reference cases – the potential implications of the principle of participatory democracy are explored for national practices relating to how Member States participate in EU law-making. The idea is also to capture insights into how the multi-level nature of EU law-making affects the modalities for participation, and consequently the implementation of the principle of participatory democracy. This part of the book moves from exploring the principle at the abstract level to applying it to concrete instances.

Building on the first two parts of the book, the final chapter (chapter five) asks how EU law-making practices can improve so that the realisation of the principle of participatory democracy in the EU is significantly advanced. In particular, how can the coherence between practices at the supranational and national level contribute to such advancement?

To clarify the scope of the book, it is necessary to define and delineate the main objects of study. As regards the principle of participatory democracy, since the Lisbon Treaty the EU has drawn democratic legitimacy not only from representative democracy but also from participatory democracy.[46] The principle of participatory democracy is primarily enshrined in Article 11 TEU and Article 10(3) TEU.[47] An understanding of this principle forms both the starting point and object of this book.

In terms of the second part of the book, which is focused on EU law-making (or the term *EU legislation* is sometimes used), this refers to legislative acts – that is, acts adopted through the ordinary legislative procedure as defined in Article 294 TFEU. Implementing and delegated acts fall outside this definition of EU law. This is not to say that they could not conceptually be squeezed into the concept of

[46] Art 10(1) TEU; Art 11 TEU; Case 138/79 *Roquette Frères v Council* EU:C:1980:249, para 35; *cf* also *Grégor Puppinck and Others* (n 39).

[47] The Court has found that the right to undertake a European Citizens' Initiative established in Art 11(4) TEU also constitutes an instrument concerning the right of citizens to participate in the democratic life of the Union provided for in Art 10(3) TEU: see Case C-589/15 P *Anagnostakis v Commission* EU:C:2017:663, para 24. This is also analysed in ch 3.

law, or that their prominent position does not merit the study of the application of participatory democracy to these acts. Several authors have argued convincingly that participation in EU rule-making and administrative acts is of particular importance from a democracy perspective.[48] However, the choice is one of focus. The relevance of the principle of participatory democracy for rule-making and EU governance in general is covered in the general mapping of legal rights and obligations. However, in terms of concretely assessing adherence to the principle, focus rests on law-making and its multi-level nature, the procedural guarantees of which may serve as a touchstone for other forms of norm creation.[49]

'EU law-making consultation' is, consequently, an umbrella term which refers both to consultation operated by the Commission at the EU level and that occurring at the national level. Article 11 TEU focuses on the EU institutions (not Member States) and, with regard to consultation, specifically the Commission's obligation to consult. However, from Article 10(2) TEU follows that democratic legitimacy in the Union flows from the Parliament as well as Member States, themselves 'democratically accountable' to their Parliament or citizens. Article 10(3) TEU is framed as a right for citizens to participate in the democratic life of the Union. At the national level, laws and regulations guiding participation in law-making may also interact with the implementation of the principle of participatory democracy.

The Commission operates an elaborate and ambitious consultation regime, with roots dating back to the formation of the Union. Its consultations consist of gathering stakeholder input, for deciding on policy or legislative initiatives; the latter are then potentially presented to the Council and Parliament. The Commission's 'Better Regulation' guidelines state that 'stakeholder consultation is a formal process, by which the Commission collects information and views from stakeholders about its policies'.[50] The Commission has traditionally distinguished between open and targeted consultations. A fragmented picture emerges as to the frequency, modalities and effect of these various types of consultation.[51] While this book is chiefly concerned with the open consultations, an initial analysis reveals that the legal framework is not necessarily tied to the Commission's vocabulary and practice; the legal imperatives and restrictions on discretion apply overall to the practice of consultation, regardless of whether it is open or targeted. This means that the overall practice will be included, with a focus on the open consultations, which are arguably of particular relevance for the principle of participatory democracy.[52]

[48] Curtin, Hofmann and Mendes, 'Constitutionalising EU Executive Rule-Making Procedures' (n 4).

[49] Including implementing and delegated acts would also considerably broaden the scope of the research when considering the national level, and the specific interplay with established consultation procedures at the national level would be muddled.

[50] Commission, Better Regulation Guidelines' SWD(2021) 305 final (SWD Better Regulation Guidelines) 13.

[51] Irina Tanasescu, *The European Commission and Interest Groups: Towards a Deliberative Interpretation of Stakeholder Involvement in EU Policy-Making* (VUB Press/Brussels University Press, 2009) 85.

[52] A mere cursory glance at Art 11(3) TEU, which stipulates the Commission should consult in order to ensure 'transparency' for Union action, is indicative. For an in-depth discussion, see ch 4, s 4.1.

As regards the Member State level, the focus rests on how Member States participate in EU law-making primarily through negotiating EU law. National legal norms are assessed and potentially reinterpreted in light of the principle of participatory democracy.[53] The selected Member States are Sweden, Austria and Ireland (the selection criteria are discussed in section 1.5), although the interactions and tension between the legal imperatives at the EU and national level which are illustrated raise questions more broadly relevant for all Member States.

1.3. Why a book now on legal dimensions of EU participatory democracy?

> There would be much more friction and unevenness in elections . . . if, every two years, supporters of representative democracy had to convince people in every community across the country why voting is desirable and explain how to conduct elections.[54]

The above argument from Archon Fung draws our attention to the fact that there is no common understanding or background agreement, analogous to that of elections, about the proper role of public participation in political life and governance.[55] This lack of common understanding has persisted despite the rise in democratic innovations, as well as increasing pressures on more 'traditional' representative democracies. At the risk of stating the obvious, one of the most interesting things about a legal principle of participatory democracy is that its legal status potentially allows for a conversation on, and practice of, participation which has a completely different starting point from many current debates about the proper role of public engagement. This starting point rather casts positions on the possibilities, limitations and pitfalls of participatory practices in a new light, and opens up a space for different questions about participation, ideally (perhaps over time) allowing for a collective learning process around such questions and related capacities. The assumption that this potential new direction, channelled through law, is desirable is not one that I explicitly defend in this book; nevertheless, it is an assumption which underlies the book and its overall approach.[56]

[53] This builds on the legal analysis in ch 3, which demonstrates that the 'democratic life of the Union' in Art 10(3) TEU also encompasses the Member State sphere, and that 'citizens' right to participate in the democratic life of the Union' has legal implications for national legal norms when Member State actors act as gatekeepers for this democratic life: see ch 3.

[54] Archon Fung, 'Putting the Public Back into Governance: The Challenges of Citizen Participation and Its Future' (2015) 75 *Public Administration Review* 513, 521.

[55] Fung (ibid) continues to argue that the lack of analogous agreement on political participation beyond elections means that, 'Almost every single time, such champions must develop freestanding explanations and justifications anew—explaining to allies, supporters, and opponents alike why increased public engagement might be desirable in itself, might have good consequences, and what it could look like.'

[56] In the framing of the book's main questions, this issue is subsumed by the less controversial supposition that a legal norm carries an implicit demand of its realisation, and that legal methods assist in this regard. The main arguments for participatory democracy are covered in ch 3, s 3.1. Concerns related to juridification and legal adversarialism surface, in relation to the discourse on participation in the EU, in ch 3, s 3.2.

The reasons for focusing on multi-level law-making to more concretely explore the principle of participatory democracy is shaped by the formulation of Article 11 TEU and Article 10(3) TEU, as well as literature on participatory democracy and EU governance. In addition to the clear link between the general duty of EU institutions to enter into dialogue and the Commission's duty to consult according to the principle of participatory democracy and the Commission right of legislative initiative, both political and legal theory establish a clear nexus between participating in law-making and democracy.[57] For the EU legal order, this connection is particularly poignant, considering the crucial role EU law has played in the development of the Union. Law has been a driving force in terms of EU integration and the ensuing empowerment of both the CJEU and domestic courts, as well as global standard-setting externally through EU regulation.[58]

The Commission and Member States are both acting as 'key players'[59] in relation to the same law-making process when they consult, or indeed refrain from consulting. In addition, the Member State is arguably acting in a quasi-legislative capacity in relation to the Commission's proposal for a legislative act, in its negotiation activities in the Council.[60] For citizens and interest groups nested primarily within the national context, participation is also possible in both contexts, sometimes simultaneously. For this reason, it was important to include the Member State perspective in the analysis, considering the multi-level governance structure of the EU and the fragmentation of legislative power and opportunities to participate and influence EU law-making. Rather than consisting of two distinct procedures, EU law-making can be viewed from a composite perspective, where diverse forms of democratic legitimation operate at the EU and Member State level.[61] Similarly, procedures in the context of EU administrative law signify a decision-making process which involves both national and Union administration, with interdependent but distinct functions, requiring their active participation to reach a decision.[62]

As regards the choice of focusing on consultation as a measure to assess adherence with the principle of participatory democracy, the EU Commission's

[57] See ch 3, which explores this connection further.

[58] On integration through law, see Mauro Cappelletti, Monica Seccombe and Joseph HH Weiler, 'Integration Through Law: Europe and the American Federal Experience. A General Introduction' in Mauro Cappelletti, Monica Seccombe and Joseph H Weiler (eds), *Integration Through Law, Volume 1: Methods, Tools and Institutions, Book 1: A Political, Legal and Economic Overview* (De Gruyter, 1986); on the EU's power to unilaterally regulate global markets, see Anu Bradford, *The Brussels Effect: How the European Union Rules the World* (Oxford University Press, 2020).

[59] Adrienne Héritier, 'Composite Democracy in Europe: The Role of Transparency and Access to Information' (2003) 10 *Journal of European Public Policy* 814.

[60] *cf* Art 10(2) TEU.

[61] Héritier, 'Composite Democracy in Europe' (n 59).

[62] Herwig CH Hofmann, 'Composite Decision Making Procedures in EU Administrative Law' in Herwig CH Hofmann and Alexander H Türk (eds), *Legal Challenges in EU Administrative Law* (Edward Elgar Publishing, 2009); see also Christina Eckes and Raffaele D'Ambrosio, 'Composite Administrative Procedures in the European Union' (1 November 2020), https://papers.ssrn.com/abstract=3742384, accessed 6 February 2026; 'ReNEUAL - the Research Network on EU Administrative Law', http://www.reneual.eu/> accessed 6 February 2026.

consultations have been described as the core of the Commission's approach to participatory democracy: with hundreds of consultations per year, this mechanism is the most comprehensive scheme of generally accessible societal participation in EU policy-making.[63] Consultations are also the EU's longest-standing, 'most widely travelled' participatory channel.[64] As such, the legal status of law-making consultation at the EU and national level is interesting in its own right. The chosen approach, therefore, has the advantage of analysing the legal imperatives for both levels and effectively scrutinising the frequent perception that the Commission's public consultations have no legal framework.[65]

Finally, barring Treaty change, a consultative role is the current highest form of influence citizens and stakeholders can hope to advance in terms of direct engagement with policy- and law-making in the EU.[66] As the terms 'consult' and 'participate in the democratic life' are neutral with regard to modalities – they can encompass any form of democratic or citizen innovation which may be considered 'consultative' – the legal language of Article 11(3) TEU and Article 10(3) TEU is relevant and informative for the current efforts of 'mainstreaming' participatory and deliberative democracy practices across the Commission.[67]

1.4. Methods

1.4.1. Legal interpretation and democracy theory

The discussion of participation in the EU often proceeds from the perspective of its potentials and limitations as a source of efficiency and legitimacy of EU decision-making and its capacity to redress EU democracy deficits.[68] This perspective is visible in the increased emphasis and discussion that stakeholder consultation has received within the framework of the EU's Better Regulation Agenda. Another field of studies on participation begins from a legal perspective. While this field has mainly been concerned with participation as a legal substantive right in

[63] Alemanno, 'Levelling the EU Participatory Playing Field' (n 35) 114–17; Christian Marxsen, 'Open Stakeholder Consultations at the European Level—Voice of the Citizens?' (2015) 21 *European Law Journal* 257, 260–62.

[64] Henry Hauser (ed), 'European Union Lobbying Post-Lisbon: An Economic Analysis' [2011] *Berkeley Journal of International Law* 694.

[65] Asserted, eg by Tanasescu: see Tanasescu (n 51). A related line of argument is that, while Art 11 TEU hypothetically entails legal obligations, it is highly unlikely to ever be enforced by the CJEU: see Smismans, 'Regulatory Procedure and Participation in the European Union' (n 6).

[66] By this, is not intended to say that various form of mobilisation, media scrutiny, etc cannot also have a decisive impact.

[67] See, eg citizen panels integrating into the Commission's 2023 Work Programme: 'European Citizens' Panels', https://citizens.ec.europa.eu/index_en, accessed 6 February 2026.

[68] See, eg Olivier De Schutter, 'Europe in Search of Its Civil Society' (2002) 8 *European Law Journal* 198, 198–217; Paul Magnette, 'European Governance and Civic Participation: Beyond Elitist Citizenship?' (2003) 51 *Political Studies* 144; Smismans, 'Regulatory Procedure and Participation in the European Union' (n 6).

decision-making, such legal studies can roughly be divided into two strands: one combines a legal-political approach; the other adopts a strictly legal standpoint of analysis.[69] In the first strand, participation has traditionally been analysed, within the fields of competition or administrative law, as a right to be heard, and has since evolved beyond its general scope of inquiry, for example to include participation in EU rule-making.[70]

As outlined in terms of the book's objectives and questions, the book is oriented towards contributing to a 'hard law' analysis of the principle of participatory democracy. The main method of expounding on the principle of participatory democracy is, therefore, one of legal analysis. The wording of the articles where the principle of participatory democracy is enshrined constitute a central part of the analysis. To support the legal interpretation, the theoretical foundation of the principle is first explored, and the principle is situated in its proper historical and constitutional context in the EU legal and political system. In doing so, the method combines the teleological, historical and systematic methods of legal interpretation.[71] The logic and method for exploring the theoretical foundations of the principle of participatory democracy are further outlined in the section below. In terms of legal sources, the leading cases of CJEU, as well as relevant EU legislative norms, are drawn upon. Assessing the standards raised by participatory democracy for EU law-making also raises the issue of soft law, as the EU Commission's consultation regime is embedded in soft-law regulatory instruments. Indeed, as Van Gestel and Micklitz point out, EU legislation is increasingly turning into a combination of both hard and soft law.[72] While these instruments are not used as a legal source, they are noted in sketching the legal framework for EU law-making consultation, for example in the sense that they might have interpretive value through, for example, raising legitimate expectations. For the analysis of legal norms at the national levels, a combination of EU methods and the Swedish legal dogmatic method, the Austrian civil-law legal method and the Irish common-law legal method is adopted (see below).

Finally, in approaching the third part of the book, which is focused on providing suggestions for reform, the overall approach is reconstructive. According to Möller, a reconstructive approach 'is sensitive to both the moral value and the practice it seeks to reconstruct'.[73] In contrast to many philosophical theories that aim for the morally best option regardless of practice, the reconstructive approach, while necessarily morally coherent, opts for a choice which fits the practice.[74] In the context of this book, the moral value is represented by practices which advance the realisation of the principle of participatory democracy as following from the

[69] The observation is made by Joana Mendes, who formulates the strands and analyses them: Mendes, Participation in EU Rule-Making (n 15) 12.

[70] ibid.

[71] ibid.

[72] Rob Van Gestel and Hans-Wolfgang Micklitz, 'Revitalising Doctrinal Legal Research in Europe: What about Methodology?' in Ulla B Neergaard, Ruth Nielsen and Lynn M Roseberry (eds), *European Legal Method: Paradoxes and Revitalisation* (DJØF Publishing, 2011) 67.

[73] Kai Möller, *The Global Model of Constitutional Rights* (Oxford University Press, 2015) 20.

[74] ibid.

analysis in the book, while the practice to which reform is geared refers to current institutional context and practices of the EU law-making at the EU and national level for the cases explored.

1.4.2. Approaching thick vocabulary in constitutional settings

The principle of participatory democracy requires an in-depth analysis in order to understand and define the legal obligations and practices stemming from this principle. The research, therefore, employs democracy theory to inform its legal analysis. Although these two perspectives are used as a foundational background and secondary tool in a constitutional analysis, and not as legal sources per se, their presence as an analytical lens, and the method through which they will be incorporated, demand further attention.

The democratic principles of the EU (Articles 9–12 TEU) are rife with 'historically thick'[75] vocabulary, such as 'democracy', 'equality' and 'participation'. With this in mind, the legal analysis of the principle of participatory democracy needs to be set in a broader context. One natural direction would be to look at Member States' constitutional law. However, the principle of participatory democracy in the EU context is unique in that it has developed as a consequence of the particularities of the EU multi-level setting, and in response to the long-standing debates and demands related to its democracy deficit.[76] As a constitutional principle, it finds little equivalence in Member States' constitutions.[77] The normative roots of Article 11 TEU, therefore, need to be assessed – and democracy theory is well-suited to inform this understanding. Democratic theory has broadened our understanding of democracy and highlighted the importance of participation in public life and decision-making beyond the ballot box. Thus, it has been essential for the emergence of the principle of participatory democracy. Given that the principle of participatory theory builds on democracy theory, delving deeper into the theory can help clarify the assumptions on which it rests but also unpack its content and critically analyse the practices that seek to promote it.

[75] The term is taken from Koskenniemi: 'constitutional vocabularies do not merely frame the internal world of "moral politicians" conscious of the contingency of their choices. They inform political struggles. Instrumental vocabularies are mastered by technical and administrative bodies and articulate concerns they tend to consider important. By contrast, such constitutional vocabularies as "self-determination", "fundamental rights", "division and accountability of power", and so forth, with all their historical thickness, contest the structural biases of present institutions.' Martti Koskenniemi, 'Constitutionalism as Mindset: Reflections on Kantian Themes About International Law and Globalization' (2006) 8 *Theoretical Inquiries in Law* 34.

[76] For the developments leading up to the principle of participatory democracy, see ch 2. *cf* also Felix Uhlmann and Christoph Konrath, 'Participation' in Ulrich Karpen and Helen Xanthaki (eds), Legislation in Europe: A Comprehensive Guide for Scholars and Practitioners (Hart Publishing, 2017).

[77] While legislative consultation is prevalent in EU Member States, Sweden is one of the few Member States that has constitutionalised law-making consultation (ibid).

1.4.3. Assessing legal adherence and implications through a case-study method

The second part of the book (chapter four) is oriented towards testing key legal obligations identified in the legal analysis against EU law-making practices at the EU and national level. While the case study method seems appropriate for the purposes of the questions guiding the book, its main elements need to be approached cautiously and the cases selected carefully.[78] There are two forms of case studies which the book draws on: the first are cases of Commission law-making consultation practices, and the second are Member State-based cases which exemplify how the EU principle of participatory democracy informs national legal norms relevant to EU law-making.

In considering the case-study method, the objective of the case studies is twofold. In the absence of direct case law, the first aim is to demonstrate how identified procedural guarantees flowing from the principle of participatory democracy could possibly be applied to individual consultation cases. Building on the insights of the legal analysis in chapter two, the case-study method would allow for a demonstration of how the principle can be operationalised, in order to assess whether particular consultation practices adhere to, or are in breach of, the principle, thereby more concretely illustrating the principle's legal implications. For this purpose, two key obligations drawn from the legal analysis, related to transparency as responsiveness and procedural equality, were selected.[79] In relation to the second set of case studies, the second objective was to illustrate, in practice, how legal rules and practices at the national level interact with the principle of participatory democracy and impact on the normative goals pursued by the principle.

As regards Commission consultation, to allow for the necessarily detailed substantive legal evaluation to occur, a qualitative study based on a few processes would be preferable to a large quantitative study. The same logic applies for the Member State-based cases, which require some in-depth analysis of national legal norms and practices. Further, a strength of the method chosen (case study) is its capacity for addressing causal complexity. However, considering that case studies are stronger in assessing arguments about causal relationships in particular cases than they are at generalising the weight of causal factors across a range of cases, developing general propositions and theories based on specific case studies has its limitations.[80] So, while the case-study method allows for conclusions – for

[78] I draw from the main elements outlined by Yin in his seminal work on case-study research, while adapting to accommodate the legal interpretation: Yin's main elements are the development of a research protocol, cautious and justifiable case selection on the basis of repetition, a definition of the unit of analysis, the collection of data from multiple and varied sources, a logical manner of linking data with theoretical propositions through pattern matching and other techniques, and, finally, the interpretation of findings: Robert K Yin, *Case Study Research: Design and Methods*, 5th edn (SAGE, 2014) 27–68.

[79] See ch 4 for more detail.

[80] Aikaterini Argyrou, 'Making the Case for Case Studies in Empirical Legal Research' (2017) 13 *Utrecht Law Review* 95, 103–14.

example, on whether the Commission had adhered to the principle of participatory democracy in the specific cases under study, or whether the legal obligations could be effectively applied to those cases – inferring broader conclusions based on these outcomes must be approached with caution.

Traditionally, the case-study method is accompanied by a warning flag of potential verification bias.[81] Proponents of case-study research, however, convincingly argue that, while the risk of bias may be real, such bias is no greater than bias towards confirming preconceived notions in other forms of research.[82] In selecting only a few cases, the issue of bias is, however, crucially relevant for the selection of case studies and needs to be considered. The selection of cases in this book has followed a purposeful selection logic;[83] that is, the selected cases constitute an a priori strategic selection of certain cases of consultation procedures, as well as Member State law-making norms and practices, which would provide rich insights regarding the application of the principle of participatory democracy.[84]

1.4.4. Criteria for selecting cases

The criteria for the selection of cases regarding Commission consultation will first be discussed, and then the criteria for the Member State-based cases. For Commission consultation, the criteria are diversity of consultation procedures as regards policy issues; constellations of interests; and number of consultation responses. An additional criterion is that the cases should reflect current practice. As regards diversity, legislative proposals from different Commission Directorates-General (DGs) serve as a proxy to achieve a spread on policy issues, with proposals addressing areas with diffuse and broad, as well as high-stake and concentrated, interests. The underlying logic was that contrasting different consultations would allow for a fruitful exploration of their alignment with the relevant legal imperatives. At the same time, the diversity might also allow cautiously (considering the small sample size) inferring some broader implications. The criteria were attended to through screening different EU legislative consultations which have

[81] ibid 102.

[82] ibid 104; see also Stanley Eugene Fish, *Is There a Text in This Class? The Authority of Interpretive Communities* (Harvard University Press, 2003).

[83] Other sampling logic developed in the social sciences discipline includes: extreme or deviant case sampling, intensity sampling, maximum variation sampling, homogeneous sampling, critical case sampling, snowball or chain sampling, confirming and disconfirming sampling, stratified purposeful sampling and purposeful random sampling: see Michael Quinn Patton, *Qualitative Research & Evaluation Methods: Integrating Theory and Practice*, 4th edn (SAGE Publications, 2015). However, most of these methods imply a larger part devoted to the empirical research, which would be at the expense of the legal focus of this book.

[84] *cf* the methods used by Argyrou and others with a slightly larger sample: Aikaterini Argyrou and others, 'An Empirical Investigation of Supportive Legal Frameworks for Social Enterprises in Belgium: A Cross-Sectoral Comparison of Case Studies Concerning Social Enterprises in the Social Housing, Finance and Energy Sector' in Volker Mauerhofer (ed), *Legal Aspects of Sustainable Development* (Springer International Publishing, 2016).

been conducted since 2016, while also surveying literature on Commission consultation practices and published information on legislative areas. The year was selected in order to fit the timeline of this project, as well as to allow for legislative proposals which may have taken more time to negotiate. With regard to the number of consultation responses, this refers to the responses to the Commission's open consultations. Looking at available data, the European Court of Auditors calculated that the annual average number of participants for Commission public consultations was around 500 participants in 2015 and 2016, and 2,000 participants for 2017 and 2018.[85] The criteria were, therefore, chosen in order that the selected cases in their totality should reflect consultation outcomes that were significantly higher and lower than 500 responses. In practice, one challenge that emerged was that it was sometimes difficult to determine what should count as a 'public consultation'. However, in order to avoid an overly formulaic approach, which would not be in line with the relatively limited scope of the case studies and their aims, law-making processes were selected without having to pin down the exact number of responses and determine in advance the number of 'open consultations', but where an overall indication of the numbers were clear. This led, in the end, to the four cases having responses ranging from around 100 replies to over 1,000, with one case seemingly not having conducted any public consultations. In line with the research scope, the selection of the cases was also confined by the requirement of a proposal for a legal act, as well as law-making processes for which the Commission had presented its proposal to the Parliament and Council, and the Council adopting a final negotiating position.

To illustrate how the purposeful selection logic was put into practice, the following example is informative. One area of interest which emerged was the digital policy field, as it represents an area where much is still unregulated at the EU level, and where potential legislation targets specific actors ('tech' actors), while also affecting citizens through shaping everything from the digital environment to public service delivery and potentially having an impact on fundamental rights. At the same time, this is an area of collective action challenges due its broad societal impact. The legislative area was also of interest because of the presence of strong lobby groups. A recent study demonstrated that 612 companies, groups and business associations are currently lobbying the EU's digital economy policies, spending over 97 million euros annually, making 'tech' the biggest lobby sector in the EU, measured by spending levels.[86] After surveying the EU legislative agenda in this field, three candidates emerged: EU law-making consultations on the Digital Services Act, the Digital Markets Act, and the Proposal for a Regulation laying down harmonised rules on Artificial Intelligence. After an initial screening, and

[85] European Court of Auditors, '"Have Your Say!": Commission's Public Consultations Engage Citizens, but Fall Short of Outreach Activities' Special Report 14/2019 (Publications Office, 2019) 13.

[86] Corporate Europe Observatory, 'Big Tech Takes EU Lobby Spending to an All Time High', https://corporateeurope.org/en/2021/08/big-tech-takes-eu-lobby-spending-all-time-high, accessed 6 February 2026.

balancing of the potential with other case-study candidates similarly derived, the latter was highlighted as a prospective candidate for the case study.

Aside from the diversity mentioned, the cases should, according to the selection logic applied, ideally also display insights in respect of theoretical variations of the examined phenomenon,[87] ie consultation practices which display a range of adherence to the principle of participatory democracy. This criterion, however, proved challenging. It would be difficult to establish, a priori, that a consultation exercise was legally procedurally defunct or, conversely, legally aligned. Beyond the obvious practical challenge, case selection based on the perceived legal adherence of the consultation would also arguably undermine the exercise of the case study. This was solved by approaching the criteria through surveying the literature, reaching out to institutional actors such as the Regulatory Scrutiny Board (RSB) and Commission staffers and stakeholders, and having informal conversations, with the aim of finding what in the literature or relevant actors could be perceived as a 'best practice' in terms of consultation. One legislative file which surfaced through this process was the review of the Water Framework Directive. However, because of the COVID-19 pandemic, the legislative process was stalled, and considering the timeline of this research project, this was set aside. A 'worst case' practice also emerged which was included in the study: the New Migration Pact, a legislative package which was proposed by the Commission without any impact assessment (IA), and with no open consultation at all, thus foregoing any scrutiny of the RSB, the Commission's internal and independent review board. The Pact was accompanied by a Staff Working Document, whereas the legislative package included a proposal for establishing, inter alia, detention centres at EU country borders, with the purpose of fast-tracking asylum seekers with the potential of prompt expulsion.[88]

As regards the Member State-based case studies, to achieve the goal of assessing and illustrating the implementation of the principle of participatory democracy on different legal norms across various Member States, as stated, it was clear that it would be helpful if this could be done with Member States with diverse legal orders and traditions. At the same time, practical constraints of language and scope of the book would also determine selection. At the outset, because of the author's first-hand experience and familiarity with the Swedish legal framework and Swedish participation in EU law-making, this was a natural choice.[89] In the end, Sweden, Austria, and Ireland were chosen, representing *sui generis*, civil-law, and common-law legal traditions, respectively. Also, an initial exploration demonstrated variances in existing legal frameworks, influencing Member State participation

[87] Argyrou (n 80) 103–04.

[88] See ch 4 (s 4.6.).

[89] In the original thesis version of this book, the only Member State case study included was an in-depth, expansive Swedish case study encompassing both law-making consultation in relation to the selected Commission case studies and an analysis of implications for legal norms. One of the main changes for this book was to curtail this in-depth case study and instead expand the exploration to other Member States.

in EU law-making.[90] It also aligned with the languages familiar to the author, in order to be able to assess and analyse legal texts in their original language. Other possible choices which were considered but rejected were Germany, Denmark and Finland. In terms of selecting the relevant legal norms or frameworks, the existing legal frameworks of each respective Member State as regards participating in EU law-making, specifically transparency, access and consultation when Member State governments negotiate EU law, were analysed (see chapter four).

1.4.5. Data collection and case analysis

In terms of assessing Commission consultations, the main item for analysis is the IA accompanying each legislative proposal, including its annexes and stakeholder reporting. For the one legislative proposal lacking an IA, the attached staff working document served the same function. In addition, the Roadmaps/Initial Impact Assessments and consultation documents published were surveyed. To a secondary degree, 'raw' consultation data for the open consultations were surveyed, as a light check for the Commission's reporting. In terms of analysis of the case studies, this was predominantly textual and extensive. Some background facts and data, which frame the case and the legislative issue examined, are presented to give a context to the case, and in line with the overall method and objective of the research also relying on legal interpretation.

For the Member State case studies, the legal landscape was assessed, including relevant legal methods, in order to reach a correct conclusion on relevant legal sources and interpretation. At the same time, to the degree that legal norms would be read in light of the principle of participatory democracy, the principle of consistent interpretation under an EU legal method would take precedent over national methods of interpretation.[91] During the data collection, interviews were held with relevant Member State ministry officials, national parliamentary administrative officials and national legal experts. These interviews were not included as any legal or authoritative source but helped ensure that national legal and administrative context was being adequately considered.

1.5. Structure of the book

The book first outlines the background and theoretical foundations of the principle of participatory democracy, including its roots in democracy theory (chapter two). Through distilling important insights from democracy theory, a deeper

[90] This followed from an initial reading of primary and secondary legal sources, as well as interviews with legal experts and government officials in Austria and Ireland.

[91] See Massimiliano Delfino, 'The Court and the Charter: A "Consistent" Interpretation of Fundamental Social Rights and Principles' (2015) 6 *European Labour Law Journal* 86.

understanding of the legal implications which flow from the principle, in relation to consultation, are highlighted.[92] Legal interpretation is then used to analyse the legal contours of the principle of participatory democracy – including through exploring Article 11 TEU in its proper constitutional context, while surveying in detail the opportunities for redress and judicial review (chapter three). The book then turns to examining consultation practices and outcomes for distinct EU legislative proposals and assessing whether consultation in these cases adhered to the key standards and duties set by the principle of participatory democracy (chapter four). Following the legal conclusions in chapter three, three different Member State legal contexts are explored, to assess how the principle of participatory democracy interacts with the legal framework. Finally, based on the findings, the question of how law-making practices can improve so that the realisation of the principle of participatory democracy in the EU is significantly advanced is addressed (chapter five).

[92] This approach and its rationale are discussed in detail in ch 2.

2

Participation in Democratic Theory and the Imperatives of Complementarity

The Lisbon Treaty's democratic principles have, on the one hand, been hailed as a framing of democracy, for institutions beyond the state, which are neither apologetic nor utopian, but plausible and viable.[1] On the other hand, the articles have been criticised for being poorly drafted, without clarity as to the relationship and linkages between them or well-defined links to democratic models, and thus characterised as an 'accidental meeting' between representative and participatory democracy, or as an 'arbitrary smorgasbord' of instruments and mechanisms promoting participation and transparency.[2]

This chapter explores the theoretical foundations and normative roots of the principle of participatory democracy, providing groundwork for a legal analysis of the principle. Given that participatory democracy is an EU constitutional principle, the chapter asks what assumptions it rests on. What normative goals does it pursue? And what approaches does it promote? Furthermore, who are the main protagonists of participatory democracy? Bearing in mind that orthodox participatory democracy theory frequently challenges the foundations of representative democracy as traditionally understood,[3] what assumptions need to be held in order to understand and construe participatory democracy as a complement to representative democracy, which the democratic principles of the Treaty clearly state that the Union is founded upon?[4] While democratic experimentation may be on the rise in the Union, no Member State can arguably be labelled as 'a participatory

[1] For the viable approach emphasising values of transparency, participation, deliberation and flexibility, see Armin Von Bogdandy, 'The European Lesson for International Democracy: The Significance of Articles 9 to 12 EU Treaty for International Organizations' (2012) 23 *European Journal of International Law* 315, 317–23.

[2] The former phrase is from Smismans, and the latter from Ackerman, Egidy and Fawkes: Stijn Smismans, 'The Constitutional Labelling of "the Democratic Life of the EU": Representative and "participatory" Democracy' in Lynn Dobson and Andreas Follesdahl (eds), *Political Theory and the European Constitution* (Routledge, 2006) 131; Susan Rose-Ackerman, Stefanie Egidy and James Fowkes, *Due Process of Lawmaking: The United States, South Africa, Germany, and the European Union* (Cambridge University Press, 2015) 236; see also Joana Mendes, 'Participation and the Role of Law after Lisbon: A Legal View on Article 11 TEU' (2011) 48 *Common Market Law Review* 1849.

[3] Joel D Wolfe, 'A Defense of Participatory Democracy' (1985) 47 *The Review of Politics* 370; Carole Pateman, 'Participatory Democracy Revisited' (2012) 10 *Perspectives on Politics* 7.

[4] Art 10(1) TEU.

democracy'. How, then, does this fact mediate or potentially bias the interpretation of constitutional language elaborating on a principle of participatory democracy operating at the supranational level? Exploring the 'normative roots' in this vein will allow for a constitutional legal interpretation which is transparent with regard to its assumptions and limitations, and ultimately more coherent in its teleological interpretation.

The first aim of this chapter is, then, to address the underlying questions and tensions raised by the principle of participatory democracy and root these in democratic theory and the debates leading up to the drafting of the relevant Treaty articles. This endeavour is both descriptive and normative. The descriptive component is primarily to identify the main logos and arguments of participatory democracy as a theory, and see how it has surfaced in the debates of the democratic legitimacy of the EU. As such, it relies on a literature review aiming to capture the important strands of the debates, as well as to obtain a picture of the path leading up to the drafting of the principle. The normative endeavour lies in the attempt to consolidate an understanding of 'participatory democracy' which can be useful for an analysis of the relevant Treaty articles and grounding the legal label 'participatory democracy'. For instance, the principle of participatory democracy is sometimes referred to as a principle of democratic participation, a principle of citizen participation, or 'Article 11 TEU', and legal scholars include and emphasise different Treaty provisions in relation to the 'principle of participatory democracy'.[5] In general, Article 11 TEU has also been said to combine elements of participatory, deliberative and direct democracy.[6] So, while arguably the mainstream legal label of the principle under study is 'participatory democracy', it is not universal, and there is vagueness as to the normative framework and imperatives suggested by the same label. Finally, filtering insights from democratic theory also contributes to creating the normative touchstone for identifying lines of action in order to advance the realisation of the principle of participatory democracy.

To address these aims, the chapter begins with an overview and brief analysis of the origins and theoretical elaboration of participatory democracy, in the end adopting an inclusive definition of the concept which includes deliberative democracy. This broad reading of participatory democracy helps frame the exploration of theorisation on participatory democracy in the EU context and traces the path leading up to the drafting of the Lisbon Treaty. After having summarised the state of play post-Lisbon, the remainder of the chapter is devoted to elaborating on the entry point for understanding the principle of participatory democracy in the

[5] cf, eg Mendes, 'Participation and the Role of Law after Lisbon' (n 2); Armin von Bogdandy, 'Founding Principles' in Armin von Bogdandy and Jürgen Bast (eds), *Principles of European Constitutional Law*, 2nd rev ed (Hart; CH Beck, 2010) 50–52; Tobias Lock, 'Article 11 TEU' in Manuel Kellerbauer, Marcus Klamert and Jonathan Tomkin (eds), *The EU Treaties and the Charter of Fundamental Rights: A Commentary* (Oxford University Press, 2019); Matthias Ruffert, 'Art. 11 EUV' in Christian Calliess and Matthias Ruffert (eds), *EU-VERTRAG*, 6th edn (Beck, 2022).

[6] Beate Kohler-Koch, 'The Organization of Interests and Democracy' in Beate Kohler-Koch and Berthold Rittberger (eds), *Debating the Democratic Legitimacy of the European Union* (Rowman & Littlefield, 2007) 11–17.

Treaty – as a complement to representative democracy. Building on the insights of the rich debate on democratic legitimacy in the Union, I argue for drawing on the framework of complementarity sketched out by Kohler-Koch and Rittberger, with some adjustment and elaboration, to highlight and analyse the most important normative imperatives which serve as an undercurrent to the legal interpretation of, as well as guide the identification of, the key legal imperatives discussed in later chapters. The selected heuristic tool frames the complementarity of participatory democracy in relation to representative democracy through emphasising the intrinsic value of participation over the instrumental: deliberation instead of voting, and citizens and civil society instead of institutions. However, in applying this heuristic tool of contrasts, I clarify, based on the discussion in this chapter, the possibilities and limitations of participatory democracy as a complement.

Overall, the chapter builds on and adds to existing scholarship which recognises that participation as elaborated in the Treaty's democratic principles goes beyond a functional understanding of participation and consolidates an understanding of 'participatory democracy' in the EU setting.

2.1. An inclusive reading of 'participatory democracy'

The practice of 'participatory' democracy has permeated various political designs since Athenian democracy.[7] Interest in political participation beyond representation has also been a stable feature of modern democratic theory, which traces the importance of citizen participation to the work of Rousseau, Mill and Tocqueville.[8] While the debate and practice of democratic participation is long-standing, the concept of participatory democracy began more intense theorisation in the late 1960s, amidst a broader cultural quest for more social equality and democracy.[9]

Most contemporary accounts have drawn on the contribution made in Carole Pateman's *Participation and Democratic Theory*, which outlines the orthodox position of participatory democracy in contemporary political thought.[10] Pateman's

[7] In the 5th century BC, the Greeks would gather in the public space of the agora and legislate on the basis of an agenda set by a randomly selected assembly of 500 other citizens. In India around the same time, public deliberation was occurring through a variety of local institutions. A few centuries later, Icelandic Vikings would gather every summer in a large field south of Reykjavik, at Thingvellir, their place of parliament, and talk through matters of importance. See Hélène Landemore, *Open Democracy: Reinventing Popular Rule for the Twenty-First Century* (Princeton University Press, 2020) 1–2.

[8] Jean-Jacques Rousseau, *The Social Contract* (Maurice Cranston tr, Penguin Books, 1968); Alexis de Tocqueville, *Democracy in America* (Harvey C Mansfield and Delba Winthrop eds, University of Chicago Press, 2002); John Stuart Mill, *Considerations on Representative Government*, 1st edn (Cambridge University Press, 2010); see also Carole Pateman, *Participation and Democratic Theory* (Cambridge University Press, 1970) 22–44.

[9] Thomas Zittel, 'Participatory Democracy and Political Participation' in Thomas Zittel and Dieter Fuchs (eds), *Participatory Democracy and Political Participation: Can participatory engineering bring citizens back in?* (Routledge, 2007) 9.

[10] Rod Dacombe and Phil Parvin, 'Participatory Democracy in an Age of Inequality' (2021) 57 *Representation* 145, 147.

work, like many of the following accounts, focuses on the educative effects of participation of individuals, as well as the influence on the wider society.[11] The theory extends the idea of participation from politics and the state to other areas, including the workplace, education, and local and national governance structures, as well as the family, giving particular emphasis to deliberation and the 'small-group' model of democracy.[12] Similarly, in his influential work outlining 'strong democracy', Barber defines participatory democracy as 'self-government by citizens rather than representative government in the name of citizens'.[13] This entails depth of participation as well as political equality beyond granting formal opportunities or rights to participate. Many participatory theorists acknowledge the need for leadership or representative institutions, while at the same time agreeing that institutions and practices in modern representative democracies provide neither for sufficient participation nor the transformative kind of space which induces the development of the core capacities for 'self-government'.[14] So, while participatory democracy was initially focused on citizens within democratic structures and expanding participation rights and opportunities, particularly for those populations that have been systematically or structurally excluded from the democratic process because of inequities – such as workers and women[15] – it was, at the same time, deepening and expanding the concept of self-government. As Mills states, 'a political act to be done only once in a few years . . . leaves [the citizen's] intellect and moral disposition very much as it found him'.[16]

This key line of argument held that expanding citizens' rights to affect policy choices needed to be balanced by self-transformation, so that the pursuit of private interests was interwoven with a sense of collective responsibility.[17] It is, therefore, a vision of what a self-ruling individual is or could be which animates participatory democracy; participation itself provides her with the necessary civic capacities as much as her participation contributes to transformative spaces of democratic action which, in turn, induce self-transformation. As early as in Rousseau's work, participatory theorists find the question of how the social order affects the structure of human personality, in particular which aspects of an individual's character institutions develop.[18] Through participation, the individual learns that private and public interests are linked, and 'the logic of the participatory system is such that he is forced to deliberate according to his sense of justice'.[19] This symbiotic

[11] Pateman, *Participation and Democratic Theory* (n 8) 22–44.

[12] ibid; Zittel, 'Participatory Democracy and Political Participation' (n 9).

[13] Benjamin R Barber, *Strong Democracy: Participatory Politics for a New Age*, 20th anniversary ed, with a new preface (University of California Press, 2009) 151.

[14] GDH Cole, *Social Theory*, 1st edn (Routledge, 1920) 103–16; Pateman, *Participation and Democratic Theory* (n 8) 42; Barber, *Strong Democracy* (n 13) 237–42; CB Macpherson, *The Life and Times of Liberal Democracy* (OUP Canada, 2012) 78–79.

[15] Michael T Grevén, 'Some Considerations on Participation in Participatory Governance' in Kohler-Koch and Rittberger, *Debating the Democratic Legitimacy of the European Union* (n 6) 234.

[16] Pateman, quoting Mill: Pateman, *Participation and Democratic Theory* (n 8) 30.

[17] Zittel, 'Participatory Democracy and Political Participation' (n 9) 12.

[18] Pateman, *Participation and Democratic Theory* (n 8) 24.

[19] ibid 25.

relationship and iterative process means that a major function of participation is educative at the individual level, born out of the interrelationship between institutions and the psychological qualities and attitudes of citizens,[20] and justice at the collective level, emphasising equality as expressed in terms of outcome but also through the inclusive participatory process itself.

Justification for greater participation is not confined to its educative potential but also grows out of the broader desire to enhance legitimacy in democratic governance.[21] As such, the overall intrinsic value of participation is emphasised. In considering the intrinsic value of participation, the concept may take on different shades depending on context. Particularly, in legal scholarship and political science, the idea of the inherent value of participation emphasises somewhat diverse things. In highlighting legitimacy as a function of democratic participation, participatory theorists often focus on the personal 'internal' benefits derived from participation.[22] Or they highlight that placing value on participation increases the capacity of the individuals who take part and enhances trust and systemic efficiency – in a way which is separate from instrumental understandings of participation's benefit to public institutions.

The political process is an end in itself: a good, or even the supreme good, for those who participate in it. It may be applauded because of the educative effects on the participants, but the benefits do not cease once the education has been completed. On the contrary, the education of the citizen leads to a preference for public life as an end in itself.[23]

In legal scholarship, the emphasis on the inherent value of participation often has less to do with the personal value of feeling good or gains in consciousness, virtue or political capacity. Instead, participation is seen as a right in itself, the value of which can indeed be associated with personal and societal desirable outcomes, but is not dependent upon them.[24] This thinking is found prominently in the legal rights discourse. For example, the right to not be subjected to cruel and inhuman treatment is regarded as fundamental, regardless of whether torture could be construed in utilitarian terms as beneficial regarding information-gathering

[20] Zittel, 'Participatory Democracy and Political Participation' (n 9).

[21] Joshua Cohen, 'Deliberation and Democratic Legitimacy' in James Bohman and William Rehg (eds), *Deliberative Democracy: Essays on Reason and Politics* (MIT Press, 1997); Beate Kohler-Koch and Berthold Rittberger, 'Charting Crowded Territory: Debating the Democratic Legitimacy of the European Union' in Kohler-Koch and Rittberger, *Debating the Democratic Legitimacy of the European Union* (n 6); Archon Fung, 'Putting the Public Back into Governance: The Challenges of Citizen Participation and Its Future' (2015) 75 *Public Administration Review* 513, 515.

[22] Fung, 'Putting the Public Back into Governance' (n 21).

[23] Elster's passage summarises political activity as an end, drawn from the work of Mill, Tocqueville and Arendt: Jon Elster, 'The Market and the Forum: Three Varieties of Political Theory' in Derek Matravers and Jonathan Pike (eds), *Debates in Contemporary Political Philosophy: An Anthology* (Routledge, 2003) 128.

[24] Moellers helpfully develops this argument in relation to democratic theory: Christoph Moellers, *The Three Branches: A Comparative Model of Separation of Powers* (Oxford University Press, 2013) 51–54.

and possibly preventing collective harm.[25] This is not to say that a purely normative view of legitimacy is not also present in democratic theory,[26] and that there is not significant overlap of the normative foundations of legal rights and democracy. The normative assumption of democratic theory begins with the idea of the natural rights of individuals, primarily equality and autonomy.[27] The linkage between political equality and democracy is important to note, with participation developing out of the 'logic of equality'.[28] This derives in no small measure because democracy, as an overall ideal norm, is a political regime where the ones affected by public decisions can have a say in their formation or act against them,[29] sometimes referred to as the all-affected interests principle.[30] This idea is also mirrored in procedural law, with participation either being framed as defence (*uti singuli*) or collaboration (*uti cives*).[31] However, democratic participation moves beyond a narrow application of the all-affected interests principle or participation as defence and collaboration.[32] In order to be fully democratic, political decisions ought to be the result of a procedure in which every citizen enjoys an equal chance to have a say, be it through the electoral process (through elected representatives) or the policy process (through non-electoral input, such as public consultations).[33] The emphasis on the latter in participatory democracy theory is also explained with

[25] The example is not meant to imply that the utilitarian argument for torture prevails according to its own logic. There is empirical research which points to the ineffectiveness of torture, and scientific insights may naturally inform both utilitarian and deontological arguments on torture: see Nayef Al-Rodhan, 'The Wrongs, Harms, and Ineffectiveness of Torture: A Moral Evaluation from Empirical Neuroscience' [2022] *Journal of Social Philosophy* 565.

[26] Peter Graf Kielmansegg, 'Legitimität Als Analytische Kategorie.' (1971) 3 *Politische Vierteljahresschrift* 12 367, 393.

[27] Despite his own misgivings about natural law, Kessler's outline is instructive: Friedrich Kessler, 'Natural Law, Justice and Democracy--Some Reflections on Three Types of Thinking about Law and Justice' (1944) 19 *Tulane Law Review* 34.

[28] Robert A Dahl, *On Democracy* (Yale University Press, 2020) 10.

[29] ibid.

[30] Dahl explains this as 'all who are affected by a decision should have a right to participate into making it': Robert A Dahl, After the Revolution? Authority in a Good Society, Rev ed (Yale University Press, 1990) 64; see also Iris Marion Young, Inclusion and Democracy (Oxford University Press, 2000); Seyla Benhabib, The Rights of Others: Aliens, Residents, and Citizens (Cambridge University Press, 2004); Robert E Goodin, 'Enfranchising All Affected Interests, and Its Alternatives' (2007) 35 Philosophy & Public Affairs 40; Mark E Warren, 'The All Affected Interests Principle in Democratic Theory and Practice' (Institut für Höheren Studien – Institute for Advanced Studies (IHS), 2017); Habermas' discourse principle can also be construed as one variant of this principle: Jürgen Habermas, Between Facts and Norms: Contributions to a Discourse Theory of Law and Democracy (MIT Press, 1996); on the related all-subjected principle, see Sofia Näsström, 'The Challenge of the All-Affected Principle' (2011) 59 Political Studies 116; Arash Abizadeh, 'On the Demos and Its Kin: Nationalism, Democracy, and the Boundary Problem' (2012) 106 *American Political Science Review* 867.

[31] Joana Mendes, *Participation in EU Rule-Making: A Rights-Based Approach* (Oxford University Press, 2011) 33.

[32] Alberto Alemanno, 'Towards a Permanent Citizens Participatory Mechanism in the EU, Study Commissioned by the Policy Department for Citizens' Rights and Constitutional Affairs, European Parliament' (2022) PE 735.927 14.

[33] Charles R Beitz, 'Procedural Equality in Democratic Theory: A Preliminary Examination' (1983) 25 *Nomos* 69; see also Pamela Pansardi, 'Democracy, Domination and the Distribution of Power: Substantive Political Equality as a Procedural Requirement': (2016) n° 275 *Revue internationale de philosophie* 91.

reference to the weak link that elections and party politics establish to citizens, as delegation of power is not bound to specific issues but very vague and broad. There is also an understanding that when certain groups cannot influence the political agenda or decision-making, or gain relevant information to assess how well policy alternatives serve their needs, for example because they are unorganised or excluded, they are likely to be ill-served by laws and policies.[34] Participation here follows from the demands of justice, flowing from the inherent dignity of the individual potentially affected, as manifested in a claim to participate, and based on the epistemic role that individuals and groups can play in determining just outcomes. Regarding the demands of justice, the thinking on rights sheds light on the intrinsic justification for participation: 'For rights are not merely judicially enforceable claims to various good things. They are, rather, a set of social realities, procedures by which we show respect for self-government by individuals and groups in their pursuit of a good life.'[35]

Naturally, the focus on the intrinsic value of participation in participatory democracy has some overlap with regard to representative democracy, in that the importance of participation is partly based on the normative proposition of the free, equal and autonomous citizen. However, emphasis in participatory democracy theory rests on interdependence; on citizens acting together to regulate their mutual existence.[36] Barber distinguishes the perspective on human nature and identity found in liberal and participatory democracy:

> Liberal democracy's three dispositions . . . are linked in a single circle of reasoning that begins as its ends in the natural and negative liberty of men and women as atoms of self-interest. . . . politics is prudence in the service of homo economicus – the solitary seeker of material happiness and bodily security.[37]

Much of the early theorisation on participatory democracy, between the 1960s and 1980s, was primarily pitched as a critique of the liberal conception of democracy as a competition for political power among responsible elites.[38] During this time, democratic theory was dominated by an empirical democratic school of thought (often applying economic analysis and rational choice theory to political processes)[39] which concluded that citizens did not have the will, incentive

[34] Archon Fung, 'Varieties of Participation in Complex Governance' (2006) 66 *Public Administration Review* 66, 70.

[35] Bruce Frohnen and Kenneth L Grasso, 'Introduction; Rights in a Multicultural Age' in Bruce Frohnen and Kenneth L Grasso (eds), *Rethinking Rights: Historical, Political, and Philosophical Perspectives* (University of Missouri Press, 2009) 31.

[36] Barber, *Strong Democracy* (n 13) 213–61.

[37] ibid 20; participatory theorists have retained this critique and expanded upon alternatives, such as the '*homo cooperativus*': see Patrizia Nanz and Claus Leggewie, *No Representation without Consultation: A Citizens' Guide to Participatory Democracy* (Damian Harrison and Stephen Roche trs, Between the Lines, 2019) 52–62.

[38] Zittel, 'Participatory Democracy and Political Participation' (n 9) 9.

[39] See, eg Joseph A Schumpeter, *Capitalism, Socialism and Democracy* (Routledge, 1976); Anthony Downs, 'An Economic Theory of Political Action in a Democracy' (1957) 65 *Journal of Political Economy* 135.

or capacity to participate, and that democracy was indeed to be founded upon this very assumption.[40] Schumpeter, as one of the main proponents of this line of thinking, argued the 'classical doctrine' of democracy, which held that placing participation of people centre stage was empirically unrealistic in large societies, and that democracy was, in essence, 'that institutional arrangement for arriving at political decisions in which individuals acquire the power to decide by means of competitive struggle for the people's vote'.[41]

Robert Dahl's work was also grounded in empirical observation, and closely considered participation in modern democracies, coming to the conclusion that democracy was more accurately referred to as 'polyarchy' because it was essentially 'a system of decision-making in which leaders are more or less responsive to the preferences of non-leaders', and that this system appeared to function with low levels of citizen participation.[42] Dahl softened the critical stance towards participation and advocated for participation which would allow citizens to have equal and sufficient opportunities to form preferences and influence the public agenda, but he concluded that this was more of a utopian ideal rather than a realistic goal.[43] Against this narrative, participatory democracy theory asserted that that citizens, under the right conditions, could, should and would participate meaningfully in democratic processes.[44] In this context, paving the way for avenues where citizens could not just influence but actually determine the outcome of decisions and democratic processes was a key line of thinking.[45] As individual participation on a larger scale would lead to democratisation beyond the political system, to areas such as education, the private sector and foreign policy-making, participatory democracy was, in this early stage, heralded as a strategy for the gradual, non-violent dismantling of capitalism.[46]

The discourse on participatory democracy then took a turn around the 1980s. On the one hand, the crises of the social and political movements that had fostered it led to the decline of participatory democracy theory.[47] On the other hand, the

[40] Citizens would be unlikely to experience the consequences of their actions or determine outcomes: Schumpeter, *Capitalism, Socialism and Democracy* (n 39) 135; see also Stephen Elstub, 'Deliberative and Participatory Democracy' in Andre Bächtiger and others (eds), *The Oxford Handbook of Deliberative Democracy* (Oxford University Press, 2018) 189.

[41] Schumpeter, *Capitalism, Socialism and Democracy* (n 39) 169.

[42] Robert A Dahl, 'Hierarchy, Democracy and Bargaining in Politics and Economics' in Heinz Eulau, Samuel J Eldersveld, and Morris Janowitz (eds), *Political Behavior: A Reader in Theory and Research* (Free Press of Glencoe, 1956) 87.

[43] Robert A Dahl, *A Preface to Democratic Theory* (University of Chicago Press, 1956) 75; Robert A Dahl, *Democracy and Its Critics* (Yale University Press, 1989) 83–90; On Dahl softening the stance on participation, see also Elizabeth Monaghan, 'Assessing Participation and Democracy in the EU: The Case of the European Citizens' Initiative' (2012) 13 *Perspectives on European Politics and Society* 285, 288.

[44] Pateman, *Participation and Democratic Theory* (n 8); Barber, *Strong Democracy* (n 13); Macpherson, *The Life and Times of Liberal Democracy* (n 14).

[45] Pateman, *Participation and Democratic Theory* (n 8) 70–71; see also Sherry R Arnstein, 'A Ladder Of Citizen Participation' (1969) 35 *Journal of the American Institute of Planners* 216.

[46] Grevén, 'Some Considerations' (n 15) 225.

[47] Antonio Floridia, 'The Origins of the Deliberative Turn' in Bächtiger and others, *The Oxford Handbook of Deliberative Democracy* (n 40) 37.

overly normative stance of participatory democracy was criticised, and a lack of empirical research to substantiate its claims was noted.[48] Scharpf, for instance, critiqued the over-emphasis on normative deductionism and argued that participation and the quality of policy outcomes were equally important normative sources of legitimacy.[49] Acceptance or 'compliance', as well as the quality of outputs, emerged into focus rather than the electorate input side. Grevén elaborates on how this approach established a juncture between two directions.[50] One direction treated inputs and outputs as functional equivalents for legitimising policies, so that a decrease in participation could be counterbalanced by an increase in acceptance. The other connected participation to outputs, with the assumption that participation could increase the problem-solving capacity and performance of policies and laws, and consequently result in greater acceptance.[51] This new trend became related to policy research – which shifted focus from participatory citizens to organisations and collective actors.[52] Connected to this trend was an emphasis, including from theorists who promoted public participation, on the epistemic role that citizens and overall broad public participation could offer.[53]

The transitional phase in participatory democracy discourse was not only towards politics in a participatory mode rather than participatory democracy, but also an increased emphasis on the importance of deliberation and the rise of deliberative democracy.[54] Already, from the very beginning, the participatory democracy ideal demanded that the quality of participation was attended to, with an emphasis on deliberation according to justice and 'strong talk'.[55] However, this element, amongst other systemic questions, remained vague.[56] Deliberative democracy has, since then, provided further elaboration on the normative foundations of deliberations as well as the right conditions and principles for its effective execution, in tandem with a robust body of empirical research on deliberative democratic experiments. A distinct feature of the deliberative strand of the discourse on democracy is its focus on process. The process is itself a source of democratic legitimacy and not just the driver of a (democratically associated) desirable outcome.[57]

Habermas captures this requirement in his democratic principle of legitimacy: 'only those statutes may claim legitimacy that can meet with the assent of all citizens in a discursive process of legislation that in turn has been legally

[48] Grevén, 'Some Considerations' (n 15) 235.
[49] ibid, citing Scharpf.
[50] ibid.
[51] ibid.
[52] ibid.
[53] Joshua Cohen, 'An Epistemic Conception of Democracy' (1986) 97 *Ethics* 26; see also David Estlund and Hélène Landemore 'The Epistemic Value of Democratic Deliberation' in Bächtiger and others, The Oxford Handbook of Deliberative Democracy (n 40).
[54] Floridia, 'The Origins of the Deliberative Turn' (n 47) 37.
[55] See, eg Pateman, *Participation and Democratic Theory* (n 8) 25; Barber, *Strong Democracy* (n 13) 178–98.
[56] Floridia, 'The Origins of the Deliberative Turn' (n 47) 37.
[57] For an elaboration on this point, see Moellers, *The Three Branches* (n 24) 52–54.

constituted'.[58] Central to this claim is that interests and opinions are not static and can be swayed by rational exchange, where participants' social power or status is detached from the conversation.[59] In the theoretical stance of deliberative democracy put forward by Habermas, deliberation is, crucially, occurring in the public sphere and, consequently, also unlinked from actual participants.[60] For example, in dialogue or consultation procedures there is the issue of the link between actors and the concerns they represent (or should represent), and whether they do so on equal terms.[61] This has led to calls for deliberative democracy models to consider equal and representative participation, or, as Dryzek calls it, 'discursive representation'.[62] At the micro level, policy processes need to be of a deliberative quality based on reflexive procedures of mutual justification of arguments; furthermore, equal access to information is a necessary condition for successful deliberations.[63] At the macro level, and related to the issue of transparency, the publicity of the deliberation process is crucial.[64]

There are different types of deliberation proposed by theorists and practitioners.[65] The central idea here is that, if the role of citizens in political decision-making is to be enhanced, there is an expectation that their judgements should not be based on raw preferences but, rather, on an informed and reflective assessment of the matter in hand.[66] This considered judgement does not simply require citizens to learn more 'facts' regarding the matter at hand, although such information is important.[67] It requires them to appreciate the views of others with different social perspectives and experiences. Hannah Arendt offers an argument for this form of enhanced political participation. She terms it 'enlarged mentality', and it requires the capacity to imaginatively place oneself in the position of others, as it

> must liberate us from the 'subjective private conditions', that is, from the idiosyncrasies which determine the outlook of each individual in his privacy and are legitimate as long as they are only privately held opinions, but are not fit to enter the market place, and lack all validity in the public realm.[68]

[58] Habermas, *Between Facts and Norms* (n 30) 110.

[59] ibid.

[60] On this point, see David Friedrich, 'European Governance and the Deliberative Challenge' in Raphaël Kies and Patrizia Nanz (eds), *Is Europe Listening to Us? Successes and Failures of EU Citizen Consultations* (Ashgate, 2013); see also Jurgen Habermas, Sara Lennox and Frank Lennox, 'The Public Sphere: An Encyclopedia Article (1964)' [1974] *New German Critique* 49.

[61] Friedrich, 'European Governance and the Deliberative Challenge' (n 60); Habermas, Lennox and Lennox, 'The Public Sphere' (n 60) 49.

[62] John S Dryzek and Simon Niemeyer, 'Discursive Representation' (2008) 102 *American Political Science Review* 481.

[63] ibid.

[64] ibid 490.

[65] See, eg André Bächtiger and others, 'Disentangling Diversity in Deliberative Democracy: Competing Theories, Their Blind Spots and Complementarities' (2010) 18 *Journal of Political Philosophy* 32.

[66] Graham Smith, *Democratic Innovations: Designing Institutions for Citizen Participation*, 1st edn (Cambridge University Press, 2009) 8–29.

[67] ibid.

[68] Hannah Arendt, *Between Past and Future: Eight Exercises in Political Thought* (Penguin Books, 2006) 220–21.

Whether one names it 'considered judgement', 'enlarged mentality' or the 'quality of deliberation', there are ongoing attempts to measure and evaluate whether this has been achieved through different proxies, such as, for example, whether opinions have changed. Within the framework of what he argues are the three basic values of the deliberative model – political equality, participation and deliberation – Fishkin lists five criteria which define the quality of deliberation.[69] These criteria are *information* (the extent to which participants are given accurate and reliable information), *substantive balance* (the extent to which arguments offered by one side are answered by considerations by those who hold other perspectives), *diversity* (the extent to which major positions in the public are represented by participants), *conscientiousness* (the degree to which participants sincerely weigh the merits of the arguments), and *equal consideration* (the extent to which arguments offered by all participants are considered on their merits regardless of who offered them).[70]

Fishkin's criteria place procedural qualities in focus. Habermas, in turn, relates procedural quality and its legitimising effects directly to the legislative process. For Habermas, decisions about laws typically involve validity claims of both factual and normative character, for instance claims about likely consequences of different legal options, their moral validity, or which alternative is realistic or more efficient.[71] Legitimate laws must, then, pass the different types of discursive tests that come along with each of these validity claims.[72] In most varieties of deliberative democracy, laws need to be publicly justified to those who are subject to them.[73] The emphasis moves from the point of decision or adoption into the earlier formational processes of discussion and communication, where opinions are formed and preferences shaped.[74]

In deliberative democracy as proponed by Fishkin, citizens are central to the deliberative process, but the deliberative element may not only be fulfilled by 'lay' citizens. According to Mansbridge and others, public deliberation is meant to fulfil three functions in a democracy: the epistemic function of ensuring reasonably sound decisions;[75] the ethical function of advancing mutual respect among citizens; and the democratic function of promoting 'an inclusive process of collective

[69] Regarding the trade-off between these three basic values, Fishkin argues that two out of three are generally available but all three at the same time is difficult: James S Fishkin, *When the People Speak: Deliberative Democracy and Public Consultation* (Oxford University Press, 2011) 32–64.

[70] ibid 33–34.

[71] Habermas, *Between Facts and Norms* (n 30).

[72] ibid.

[73] Dacombe and Parvin, 'Participatory Democracy' (n 10) 152; Simone Chambers, 'Deliberative Democracy Theory' (2003) 6 *Annual Review of Political Science* 307, 309.

[74] Chambers, 'Deliberative Democracy Theory' (n 73).

[75] This function is elaborated as to 'produce preferences, opinions, and decisions that are appropriately informed by facts and logic and are the outcome of substantive and meaningful consideration of relevant reasons. … Because the topics of these deliberations are issues of common concern, epistemically well-grounded preferences, opinions, and decisions must be informed by, and take into consideration, the preferences and opinions of fellow citizens.': Jane Mansbridge and others, 'A Systemic Approach to Deliberative Democracy' in John Parkinson and Jane Mansbridge (eds), *Deliberative Systems*, 1st edn (Cambridge University Press, 2012) 11.

choice'.[76] From this perspective, 'expert' participation in political decision-making may contribute to its epistemic quality, as expertise is supposed to be a watershed which ensures 'truth-sensitivity' of policies and legislation, and is linked to the problem-solving and enlightenment function of knowledge use.[77] However, it is clear that all these functions cannot be fulfilled by expert or elite engagement, but require broader participation.

Participatory democracy theory clearly suggests that spaces where opinions and preferences are shaped cannot solely exist at the constitutional level.[78] Social groups appear as one central building block for democracy, as they can function as spaces for socialisation.[79] Workplace and worker co-operatives have been raised as suitable spaces because of their ubiquity and frequent diversity of voices and interests.[80] Neighbourhood groups are similarly stressed as a crucial site for developing necessary participatory capacities, and local democracy in general is one answer participatory theory stresses, with the caveat that such spaces and initiatives need to be connected to federal or national systems, with an emphasis on accessible and meaningful opportunities to participate.[81] Deliberative democracy, in turn, is not necessarily concerned with the economic system as the main site for deliberative politics, but the public sphere, and also, more recently, deliberation through mini-publics located in various sites, within or as an appendage to traditional representative structures, or, more radically, replacing them.[82] The concept of the public sphere, as outlined by Habermas, is marked by the absence of a state-sanctioned hierarchical relationship and market-sanctioned societal inequality, allowing for an exchange based on reason, free of social and political pressures, which in turn leads to public opinion embodying moral authority that can hold political decision-making accountable.[83] While modern democracy, according to Habermas, is shaped by the decay of the public sphere due to, amongst other things, the influence of mass media and the economic imperatives they are run by, emancipatory movements can revitalise the public sphere, and this is often associated with strengthening civil society.[84]

Participatory democracy theory overall, while incorporating elements of direct democracy, frequently emphasises the role of civil society organisations as

[76] ibid 12.

[77] Thomas Christiano, 'Rational Deliberation among Experts and Citizens' in Parkinson and Mansbridge, *Deliberative Systems* (n 75); see also Cathrine Holst and Anders Molander, 'Public Deliberation and the Fact of Expertise: Making Experts Accountable' (2017) 31 *Social Epistemology* 235.

[78] Zittel, 'Participatory Democracy and Political Participation' (n 9) 13.

[79] ibid.

[80] Pateman, *Participation and Democratic Theory* (n 8) 67–102; see also Peter Bachrach and Aryeh Botwinick, *Power and Empowerment: A Radical Theory of Participatory Democracy* (Temple University Press 1992).

[81] Zittel, 'Participatory Democracy and Political Participation' (n 9) 13.

[82] See, eg Cristina Lafont, 'Deliberation, Participation, and Democratic Legitimacy: Should Deliberative Mini-Publics Shape Public Policy?: Deliberation, Participation & Democratic Legitimacy' (2015) 23 *Journal of Political Philosophy* 40.

[83] Habermas, *Between Facts and Norms* (n 30) 383ff.

[84] ibid 383; On this point, see also Zittel, 'Participatory Democracy and Political Participation' (n 9) 14.

mediators or as schools of democracy.[85] It is often stressed that the participation of a few has positive effects on the many, and society overall: it contributes to a democratic culture; it has educational and socialisation functions, and is not a zero-sum game.[86] Participation in one forum likely spills over to participation in another. Stronger participation may also facilitate the voice of socially excluded communities. Participatory democracy can, therefore, be said to advance a principle of empowerment of civil society, including facilitating participation of citizens belonging to minority groups, to make their voices heard.[87] Reinforcing this idea and taking it further is associational democracy centred on the premise that as many of the affairs of a society as possible are managed by voluntary and democratically self-governing associations.[88]

There is a lively debate about the relationship between participatory democracy and deliberative democracy, as well as about what practices and thresholds should distinguish participatory governance from 'participatory democracy'.[89] The debate has been fuelled by a perceived crisis of democracy at the national level, reflected in low voter turn-out, as well as disaffection with partisan politics and the political class, the rise of populism, democratic backsliding, and the rise of inequality.[90]

This chapter adopts an inclusive approach to participatory democracy, going forward. I borrow here from Zittel's encompassing definition, in which he argues that participatory democracy should 'neither be reduced to those critical authors writing in the 1960s and 1970s who coined the original concept, nor simply to particular strands in this debate'.[91] The argument is for an understanding of participatory democracy which incorporates various strands of democratic theory, including direct democracy, as well as the theory of deliberative democracy.[92] This inclusive reading of participatory theory comprises a mosaic of concepts and empirical models of democracy; and while relying on different scientific methods and oriented towards varying degrees of conceptualisation, these share the

[85] Zittel, 'Participatory Democracy and Political Participation' (n 9) 13–14; for fundamentals of the associative model of participatory democracy, see Cole, Social *Theory* (n 14); Paul Q Hirst, *Associative Democracy: New Forms of Economic and Social Governance* (Polity Press, 2003).

[86] Pateman, *Participation and Democratic Theory* (n 8) 7–10; see also Jane J Mansbridge, *Beyond Adversary Democracy* (University of Chicago Press, 1983); for a European perspective, see Paul Magnette, 'European Governance and Civic Participation: Beyond Elitist Citizenship?' (2003) 51 *Political Studies* 144, 144; TWG (Tom) Van Der Meer and EJ (Erik) Van Ingen, 'Schools of Democracy? Disentangling the Relationship between Civic Participation and Political Action in 17 European Countries' (2009) 48 *European Journal of Political Research* 281.

[87] Elodie Fazi and Jeremy Smith, 'Civil Dialogue: Making It Work Better, Study Commissioned by the Civil Society Contact Group' (Civil Society Contact Group, 2006) 15.

[88] Hirst, *Associative Democracy* (n 85).

[89] For an argument at the intersection of both these questions, see Pateman, 'Participatory Democracy Revisited' (n 3). The *Journal of Deliberative Democracy*'s issue dedicated to discussing Christina Lafont's *Democracy Without Shortcuts* provides a helpful overview of some of the recent salient debates. See André Bächtiger, Julien Vrydagh and Nicole Curato, 'Democracy without Shortcuts: Introduction to the Special Issue' (2020) 16 *Journal of Deliberative Democracy* 1.

[90] These trends are also nested in broader developments of technological change and globalisation: see Landemore, *Open Democracy* (n 7) 26–32.

[91] Zittel, 'Participatory Democracy and Political Participation' (n 9) 10–11.

[92] ibid.

basic tenet that participation can be increased through institutional reform, and that this is a worthy goal.[93] It is, therefore, helpful to view them as elements of one conversation. Zittel explains participatory democracy theory along the lines of three democratising strategies: integrative democratisation (focusing on the relationship between institutions and individuals, and fostering the civic-minded citizen); expansive democratisation (increasing the utility of participation through expanding participation rights); and efficiency-oriented democratisation (emphasising political institutions as incentive systems with an emphasis on lowering the costs of participation, rather than on its benefits).[94] Zittel takes this 'common debate' and reconstructs it in order to serve as a theoretical basis to evaluate and inform strategies of participatory engineering, emphasising the importance of 'local democracy'. I leave aside his democratising strategies and use his overall broad reading to further explore the meaning of participatory democracy as it surfaces in the debates surrounding the democratic legitimacy of the EU, which has indeed drawn on various strands of democratic theory.

However, before turning to participatory democracy as it has surfaced in the EU context, a couple of issues remain to be untangled, under the broad reading of 'participatory democracy' adopted. The first pertains to the potential contradiction of including deliberative democracy in an understanding of participatory democracy. Because claims to legitimacy of deliberative democracy do not necessarily reside in participation or participants, but in the logic of reason-giving argumentation and discursive representation,[95] some theorists, including Pateman, have contrasted participatory democracy, as a theory of change with a revolutionary political ideal, with the focus in deliberative democracy literature on participatory forums which involve few citizens and/or hold little actual decision-making power.[96] One question being asked here is whether deliberative democracy and its proponents are committed to broader participation.[97]

A main response from prominent deliberate democracy theorists has been to emphasise that deliberative democracy is committed not just to the quality of participation but also the number of citizens engaged in deliberation, even though such reforms have sometimes, at the practical level, remained elusive.[98] Indeed, a recurring question in the debates on deliberative democracy has been how more people can be engaged in democratic deliberation, as well as how the effects of such deliberation can be scaled up.[99] Looking at the research field in general, the

[93] ibid 11.

[94] ibid 9–26.

[95] Elster, 'The Market and the Forum' (n 23) 1.

[96] Pateman, *Participation and Democratic Theory* (n 8). The argument for their conceptual distinctness can be framed as an 'aggregative participatory democracy' that does not value deliberation, and a 'liberal deliberative democracy' that that does not require mass citizen participation in deliberation: Elstub, 'Deliberative and Participatory Democracy' (n 40) 188.

[97] See, eg Simone Chambers, 'Rhetoric and the Public Sphere: Has Deliberative Democracy Abandoned Mass Democracy?' (2009) 37 *Political Theory* 323.

[98] Nicole Curato and others, 'Twelve Key Findings in Deliberative Democracy Research' (2017) 146 *Daedalus* 28, 30–33.

[99] ibid.

mainstream analysis has been that deliberative democracy has passed through an initial normative phase, moving on to an empirical one where conditions and effects of deliberations have been scrutinised and refined, to – finally – the most recent 'systemic' turn, which explores the possibility of deliberative systems as well as issues of scale.[100] Regarding the ambitions for change, several prominent deliberative democracy theorists emphasise that deliberative democracy calls for fundamental changes in political decision-making and requires more egalitarian political, social and economic conditions, as deep inequities and privileges upset the communicative equality that deliberation requires.[101] In essence, this signifies that subscribing to the main assumptions and theory of deliberation implies a commitment to having more, or as many as possible, involved in such deliberation, ie deliberation should not just be happening in a microcosm involving a few citizens or elites, no matter how representative, deliberative or empowered such microcosms may be. However, discursive representation may, in this context, be a useful stepping-stone.

In view of the other possible contradiction regarding varieties of participation, participatory democracy theory is open to various forms of political activity and not just deliberation. Dialogic approaches that induce preference reflection have, however, in most elaborations of the theory since its inception, retained a privileged position.[102] And scholarship has also expanded the notion of what it means to deliberate.[103] This inclusive reading, therefore, joins the position of scholars who place deliberative democracy within the broader frame of participatory democracy or see it as its continuation, defence or saviour,[104] as well as those theorists who claim that the normative and explanatory potential of the deliberative and participatory approach is not contradictory but enhanced through the presence of each other.[105] Participatory democracy facilitates the inclusion of pertinent reasons and assent from all those affected, as a deliberative interpretation of legitimacy

[100] Mansbridge and others, 'A Systemic Approach to Deliberative Democracy' (n 75). For a critical appraisal of the 'turn', see Smith, *Democratic Innovations* (n 66); for a more detailed analysis of how the deliberative field came to be in different stages, see Floridia, 'The Origins of the Deliberative Turn' (n 47) 36.

[101] Archon Fung, 'Deliberation before the Revolution: Toward an Ethics of Deliberative Democracy in an Unjust World' (2005) 33 *Political Theory* 397, 397–98; see also Curato and others, 'Twelve Key Findings' (n 98) 30–33.

[102] See, eg Pateman, *Participation and Democratic Theory* (n 8) 25; Barber, *Strong Democracy* (n 13) 178–98. For an opposing view, Mouffe emphasises the agonistic value of participation, while Mutz argues it is doubtful that political activism and deliberation go together: see Chantal Mouffe, 'Deliberative Democracy or Agonistic Pluralism?' (1999) 66 *Social Research* 745; Diana Carole Mutz, *Hearing the Other Side: Deliberative versus Participatory Democracy* (Cambridge University Press, 2006).

[103] Iris Marion Young, 'Six: Communication and the Other: Beyond Deliberative Democracy' in Seyla Benhabib (ed), *Democracy and Difference* (Princeton University Press, 1996) 120–36; Robert B Talisse, *Deliberation* (Oxford University Press, 2012) 204–22.

[104] Denise Vitale, 'Between Deliberative and Participatory Democracy: A Contribution on Habermas' (2006) 32 *Philosophy & Social Criticism* 739; Donatella Della Porta, *Can Democracy Be Saved? Participation, Deliberation and Social Movements* (Polity Press, 2013) 7; James Bohman, *Public Deliberation: Pluralism, Complexity, and Democracy* (MIT Press, 1996) 238.

[105] Joshua Cohen, 'Reflections on Deliberative Democracy' in Thomas Christiano and John Christman (eds), *Contemporary Debates in Political Philosophy* (Wiley-Blackwell, 2009); Elstub, 'Deliberative and Participatory Democracy' (n 40).

requires.[106] A special role for deliberation, in turn, makes participatory democracy less vague, contributes to the transformative effects hailed as the dominant paradigm of participatory democracy, and has the potential to reduce inequalities by promoting public reasoning.[107]

The second issue relates to institutional design and its role in scaling participation as well as ensuring equality. The exposition thus far has been concerned with elaboration of participatory democracy theory, including its deliberative democracy strand, mainly at the normative and abstract level. However, the last couple of decades have seen participatory democracy practices and innovations systematically gathered on a large scale and made accessible to practitioners, researchers, interested parties and the wider public through accessible databases, networks and crowdsourcing platforms. Notable examples include Participaedia[108] and the LATINNO[109] databases – both of which include thousands of various public participation and democratic innovations – as well as robust reports compiling best-practice participatory or deliberative exercises, for example by the OECD,[110] regional democratic research networks with a long-standing record of participatory action research,[111] and new entities such as the European Union Competence Centre on Participatory and Deliberative Democracy.[112]

This growing emphasis on the operation of participation – including, in particular, deliberation – has been an important driver for shaping the basis of institutional reform.[113] This literature also offers a range of measurement tools that can be used to demonstrate the effectiveness of deliberative democratic reforms through empirical work. As a consequence, the design of participatory democratic institutions has been able to address issues of scale and equality.[114] Regarding scale, there are now empirically grounded observations of participatory democracy practices involving millions of citizens regularly engaged in deliberation at the local level, tied to the government policy apparatus, leading to substantive policy and legislative outcomes at the national level.[115] The leading practices involving

[106] Elstub, 'Deliberative and Participatory Democracy' (n 40) 199.

[107] ibid.

[108] A global network and crowdsourcing platform which functions as a sort of Wikipedia for democratic innovation: 'Participedia', https://participedia.net/, accessed 6 February 2026.

[109] 'LATINNO: Innovations for Democracy in Latin America', https://www.latinno.net/en/, accessed 6 February 2026.

[110] OECD, 'Innovative Citizen Participation and New Democratic Institutions: Catching the Deliberative Wave' (OECD Publishing, 2020).

[111] 'Participatory Research in Asia', https://www.pria.org/, accessed 6 February 2026.

[112] European Commission, 'Community of Practice of the Competence Centre on Participatory and Deliberative Democracy', https://cop-demos.jrc.ec.europa.eu/, accessed 6 February 2026.

[113] Floridia, 'The Origins of the Deliberative Turn' (n 47) 36–45; Elstub, 'Deliberative and Participatory Democracy' (n 40) 192.

[114] See, eg Smith, *Democratic Innovations* (n 66).

[115] For example, in Brazil, 7 million individuals participated in at least one national public policy conference on health between 2003 and 2011. The conferences, which are jointly organised by civil society and the relevant ministry, begin with widely dispersed thousands of conferences held simultaneously at the municipal level, open to all, each deliberating and producing a final report and electing delegates to the state-level conference, where the process is repeated, culminating in a national

deliberative mass participation are outside Europe and exist in a different context; however, they substantiate the possibility of such participation, as well as how it can be complementary to representative democracy.

Regarding equality, many innovations seek to address inequalities and achieve diversity by selecting participants through random sampling ('mini-publics' are primarily organised through such sampling) or involving underrepresented groups in policy deliberations.[116] A common concern is that the process is not dominated by a few powerful voices; avoiding this can be facilitated through institutional design and facilitation.[117] In this context, there is a close relationship between equality and inclusion, as 'collective agendas and decisions are democratic to the degree that those affected by collective outcomes are empowered to influence them'.[118]

Equality, as understood here, is in essence about two values.[119] The first is the value of universal moral equality, referring to the fundamental common humanity and moral worth, which requires abstracting from social circumstances.[120] The second is the value of equity, which refers to fair distributions of power and resources, in turn requiring attending to social circumstances.[121] Justice, then, refers not only to redistribution when, for example, economic inequality distorts empowerment, but also refers to advancing the conditions which enable social-group members to develop and exercise their individual and collective capacities.[122] For those participatory democrats who also emphasise the epistemic or problem-solving function of democracy, the principle of abstraction is frequently counterbalanced, either by diversity focusing on 'cognitive diversity'[123] or know-how in terms of specific access to knowledge and realities, for example local conditions.[124] Two points are

---

conference with distilled recommendations for policy, legislative or even constitutional reform. See Thamy Pogrebinschi and David Samuels, 'The Impact of Participatory Democracy: Evidence from Brazil's National Public Policy Conferences' (2014) 46 *Comparative Politics* 313; the constitutionally enshrined Gram Sabha village council in India counts every individual eligible to vote as a member, affecting 840 million people living in approximately 1 million villages in rural India. Significant deliberative and substantive impacts have been noted. See Ramya Parthasarathy and Vijayendra Rao, 'Deliberative Democracy in India' in Bächtiger and others, *The Oxford Handbook of Deliberative Democracy* (n 40).

[116] On consulting through random sampling, see James S Fishkin, 'Consulting the Public through Deliberative Polling' (2003) 22 *Journal of Policy Analysis and Management* 128; on including underrepresented groups in policy deliberation, see Archon Fung and Erik Olin Wright, 'Deepening Democracy: Innovations in Empowered Participatory Governance' (2001) 29 *Politics & Society* 5.

[117] Dacombe and Parvin, 'Participatory Democracy' (n 10) 153.

[118] Young, 'Six: Communication and the Other' (n 103); Goodin, 'Enfranchising All Affected Interests' (n 30); Fung, 'Putting the Public Back into Governance' (n 21).

[119] André Bächtiger and Edana Beauvais, 'Taking the Goals of Deliberation Seriously: A Differentiated View on Equality and Equity in Deliberative Designs and Processes' (2020) 12 *Journal of Deliberative Democracy*, Article 2.

[120] ibid.

[121] ibid.

[122] Young, Inclusion and Democracy (n 30) 39.

[123] Hélène Landemore, 'Deliberation, Cognitive Diversity, and Democratic Inclusiveness: An Epistemic Argument for the Random Selection of Representatives' (2013) 190 *Synthese* 1209.

[124] Joshua Cohen and Charles Sabel, 'Directly-Deliberative Polyarchy' (1997) 3 *European Law Journal* 313, 326–28.

worth noting with regard to the question on institutional design and equality: the first is that, in terms of participation selection, empirical research strongly suggests that self-selection as a stand-alone recruitment method often produces more homogeneous groups that reflect social inequality;[125] and second, that this lack of diversity may also negatively impact on the epistemic goals of a participatory practice.[126]

Finally, my inclusive reading of participatory democracy is not quite as ecumenical as Zittel's, in terms of the normative imperatives of participatory democracy. Under Zittel's 'big tent', what is commonly understood as 'participatory governance', as well as the 'orthodox' view of participatory democracy, both reside. The lowest common denominator here is the promotion of public participation by institutions, with a reference to equality. While an inclusive reading of participatory democracy should be attentive to what is often highlighted in empirical accounts of participatory democracy, i.e. that 'success' in terms of democratic participation or participatory democratic innovations is context-specific,[127] I contend that, for a practice or model to be connected to participatory democracy, it must retain some tangible connection to the ideal outlined in this section, namely democracy by the people. An inclusive reading of participatory democracy, therefore, still entails strengthening participation through increasing the opportunities for, and meaningfulness of, citizens' participation beyond elections, or at the very least providing meaningful forms of discursive representation for citizens (through, for example, civil society or interest groups) which sufficiently attend to the value of equality. Some ambiguity is purposefully left here, as these very questions lie at the heart of the debate on political participation in the EU.

2.2. Participatory democracy in the debates on the democratic legitimacy of the European Union

Participation by non-state actors has, to varying degrees, been a feature of the Union since its very inception. During the early years of the Union, participation was institutionalised through the creation of advisory bodies (Consultative Committee on European Coal and Steel Community, and the Economic and Social Committee common to the European Economic Community and the European Atomic Energy Community) – an example of this is how citizens 'are called upon to cooperate in the functioning of the Community', as referenced in *Van Gend*

[125] Smith, *Democratic Innovations* (n 66) 21; see also Nadia Urbinati and Mark E Warren, 'The Concept of Representation in Contemporary Democratic Theory' (2008) 11 *Annual Review of Political Science* 387, 403–06.

[126] Dryzek and Niemeyer, 'Discursive Representation' (n 62).

[127] Smith, *Democratic Innovations* (n 66).

en Loos in support of the uniqueness of the Community legal order.[128] However, doubts regarding the feasibility and desirability of participation, in the mainstream empirical accounts of democracy post-World War II, were also seemingly reflected in the attitudes of EU leaders, with leading figures such as Monet being wary of democratic and participatory politics.[129]

Mendes has shown that participation, in the form of interest representation, has been a been a constitutive feature of EU decision-making.[130] This can be traced across the practices of committees, agencies, regulatory networks and the Commission throughout the foundational period of the Union, leading up to the establishment of the Single Market.[131] Such participation was, however, primarily promoted and viewed as a remedy for administrative deficits rather than democracy ones, with its main aim being to address the limited resources and enforcement capacities of EU administration.[132] Additionally, participation was viewed as a strategy to further expand the reach of Union action, and to compensate for lack of competence through soft law and governance.[133]

The early steps towards economic integration were thus framed in terms which, de facto, if not always deliberately, bypassed citizen participation, and the approach to integration was not one where democracy was a central factor.[134] A popular 'permissive consensus' was said to legitimise integrative action.[135] It was following the legitimacy crises brought by the Maastricht Treaty that political participation at the EU level first prominently emerged on the political and public agenda.[136] The Danish rejection, the French *'petit oui'*, and the Irish challenges in ratifying the Treaty indicated an end to the 'permissive consensus' on European integration and brought to the fore the argument that the EU was suffering from a democratic legitimacy deficit. This section will, consequently, focus on the ways in which 'participatory democracy' surfaced after the Maastricht Treaty, leading up to the drafting of the Lisbon Treaty.

[128] Case C-26/62 *Van Gend en Loos* EU:C:1963:1.

[129] Monaghan, 'Assessing Participation and Democracy in the EU' (n 43) 289. See also Featherstone, who argues that Monet's technocratic and elitist conception of the High Authority contributed to the Commission's lack of democratic legitimacy up until the Maastricht Treaty: Kevin Featherstone, 'Jean Monnet and the "Democratic Deficit" in the European Union' (1994) 32 *Journal of Common Market Studies* 149, 165.

[130] Mendes, *Participation in EU Rule-Making* (n 31) 80–120.

[131] ibid. The 'Foundational Period', according to Weiler, begins in the 1950s and runs up until the mid-70s: JHH Weiler, 'The Transformation of Europe' (1991) 100 *Yale Law Journal* 2403, 2410–50.

[132] Mendes, *Participation in EU Rule-Making* (n 31) 119.

[133] See, eg Fabien Terpan, 'Soft Law in the European Union–The Changing Nature of EU Law: Soft Law in the European Union' (2015) 21 *European Law Journal* 68.

[134] Characterising the EU as a technocracy, lacking in transparency and political accountability and marked by bargaining between sectarian interests, see, eg Erik Oddvar Eriksen and John Erik Fossum (eds), *Democracy in the European Union* (Routledge, 2002).

[135] Leon N Lindberg and Stuart A Scheingold, *Europe's Would-Be Polity: Patterns of Change in the European Community* (Prentice-Hall, 1970) 249–62.

[136] Sabine Saurugger, 'The Social Construction of the Participatory Turn: The Emergence of a Norm in the European Union' (2010) 49 *European Journal of Political Research* 471.

The debate and literature on the EU's democracy deficit is sprawling and vast, and from the very beginning, the deficit's nature, extent and very existence were contested.[137] Much of this disagreement can be attributed to the different theories of democracy that are used as normative criteria to assess the EU, and their diverging underlying assumptions.[138] The main strands of the deficit argument are many, and refer to the disjunction between power and electoral accountability; concerns of executive dominance; delegation of powers to non-democratic spaces and actors; the geographical and psychological distance between Brussels and citizens; the lack of a European demos; complexity and transparency concerns relating to multi-level governance; as well as the substantive imbalance between economic and social issues, with the former unduly prioritised at the expense at the latter.[139]

The debate in academic and political spheres up until the 1990s focused on enhancing the role and powers of the Parliament.[140] This discussion was gradually complemented by other discourses – including participatory democracy – attempting to address a crisis of legitimacy observed not just at the European level because of its specific institutional configurations and multi-level nature, as well as literal and psychological distance from citizens, but also in challenges with parliamentary democracy at the national level, with its low voter turn-out and an overall disillusionment with political parties and the political class.[141] While this led some scholars to stress the existence of a democratic deficit on both the national and the European level, as well as in the relationship between these levels,[142] others argued there was little reason to speak of a EU democratic deficit when the same deficit was de facto present in national democracies, whereas the EU should be considered as a regulatory body rather than a federal superstate.[143]

Most scholars, however, agreed that there was a democracy deficit, though opinions naturally diverged as to how it could be resolved. Dahl argued that, in order to match levels of democratic accountability and control in modern democracies,

[137] For an overview, see Paul Craig and Gráinne De Búrca, 'Integration, Democracy, and Legitimacy' in Paul Craig (ed), *The Evolution of EU Law* (Oxford University Press, 2021) 12–45; see also Giandomenico Majone, 'Europe's "Democratic Deficit": The Question of Standards' (1998) 4 *European Law Journal* 5, 5; Fritz Scharpf, *Governing in Europe: Effective and Democratic?* (Oxford University Press, 1999); Andrew Moravcsik, 'Reassessing Legitimacy in the European Union' (2002) 40 *Journal of Common Market Studies* 603, 603; Christopher Lord, *A Democratic Audit of the European Union* (Palgrave Macmillan UK, 2004); Andreas Follesdal and Simon Hix, 'Why There Is a Democratic Deficit in the EU: A Response to Majone and Moravcsik' (2006) 44 *Journal of Common Market Studies* 533, 533; Vivien A Schmidt, *Democracy in Europe: The EU and National Polities*, 1st edn (Oxford University Press, 2006).

[138] Kohler-Koch and Rittberger, 'Charting Crowded Territory' (n 21).

[139] The overview is primarily drawn from Craig and De Búrca, 'Integration, Democracy, and Legitimacy' (n 137) 31; see also Joseph HH Weiler, Ulrich Haltern and Franz Mayer, 'European Democracy and Its Critique Five Uneasy Pieces' EUI Working Paper RSC No 95/11; Follesdal and Hix, 'Why There Is a Democratic Deficit in the EU' (n 137).

[140] Saurugger, 'The Social Construction of the Participatory Turn' (n 136); see also Paul Magnette, 'Democracy in the European Union: Why and How Combine Representation and Participation' in Stijn Smismans (ed), *Civil Society and Legitimate European Governance* (Edward Elgar, 2006) 24.

[141] Saurugger, 'The Social Construction of the Participatory Turn' (n 136).

[142] Follesdal and Hix 'Why There Is a Democratic Deficit in the EU' (n 137).

[143] Moravcsik, 'Reassessing Legitimacy' (n 137).

'political leaders would have to create political institutions that would provide citizens with opportunities for political participation, influence and control'.[144] Others pointed to the lack of a proper demos and an all-encompassing political identity in the Union, which would make it possible to delegate majority rule which could be consented to.[145] Follesdal and Hix questioned whether a European demos was necessary, suggesting more democratic competition, enabled through constitutional engineering.[146]

The debate could be characterised in terms of theorists focusing their attention on the quality of what occurs inside EU governance, including questions of representation and accountability, and those addressing the quality of what inputs and outputs EU governance delivered, assessing legitimacy primarily on the basis of legislative and policy outcomes or on citizens' active participation and deliberation.[147] The latter has long been discussed – first by Scharpf, who, drawing on system theory, divided democratic legitimacy into output, judged by the effectiveness of the EU's policy outcomes for the people, and input, judged by the EU's responsiveness to citizen concerns as a result of participation by the people.[148] Schmidt added to this the normative criteria of 'throughput', consisting of governance processes with the people, defined in terms of efficacy, accountability, transparency and inclusiveness.[149] Schmidt demonstrates the challenges the EU has in providing citizens with government by and for the people while performing better in providing government for and with the people.[150]

Kohler-Koch identifies three different overarching problem-solving approaches that emerged to address the European democratic deficit. The first was institutional reform to strengthen representative democracy; the second was participation of stakeholders in an EU governance system centred on efficiency; and the third was a turn to civil society with demands for enhanced civil society participation, which to a lesser degree also included demands for broader public and citizen engagement.[151]

The question of what role citizen- and interest-group participation should play in the political process paved the way for a normative body of literature which prominently included the role of civil society.[152] Saurugger argues that, following

[144] Dahl, *On Democracy* (n 28) 115.

[145] Weiler, Haltern and Mayer, 'European Democracy and Its Critique' (n 139); Scharpf, *Governing in Europe* (n 137).

[146] Follesdal and Hix, 'Why There Is a Democratic Deficit in the EU' (n 137) 533; see also Simon Hix, 'The Study of the European Union II: The "New Governance" Agenda and Its Rival' (1998) 5 *Journal of European Public Policy* 38, 50–54.

[147] Vivien A Schmidt, 'Democracy and Legitimacy in the European Union Revisited: Input, Output, and "Throughput"' (2013) 61 *Political Studies* 2, 2–5.

[148] Scharpf, *Governing in Europe* (n 137).

[149] Schmidt, 'Democracy and Legitimacy in the European Union Revisited' (n 147).

[150] ibid.

[151] Beate Kohler-Koch and Christine Quittkat, *De-Mystification of Participatory Democracy: EU Governance and Civil Society*, 1st edn (Oxford University Press, 2013) 22.

[152] Sabine Saurugger, 'Interest Groups and Democracy in the European Union' (2008) 31 *West European Politics* 1274, 1275.

the purposeful activities of several political, bureaucratic and academic actors, the 'participatory norm' in the EU emerged, which led to the acceptance, inter alia, of the importance of civil society involvement in decision-making processes.[153] The turn towards participation, Heidbreder elaborates in the same vein, was linked to three interrelated dynamics.[154] First, the debate surrounding the EU's democratic legitimacy contributed to the EU decision-making context becoming more politicised, which put the spotlight on civil society as a new actor in EU policy processes.[155] Second, academics shifted their attention from overarching integration dynamics to issues of governance, which raised the interest in the role of interest organisations to enhance decision-making from both a democracy and effectiveness perspective, through 'stakeholder inclusion'.[156] Third, practitioners in Brussels became attuned to the potential of civil society as a possible solution to address legitimacy, accountability and efficiency challenges in a constantly enlarging Union.[157] There is also wide agreement that 'the Commission was to be credited with paving the way for civil society's entrance into the European system'.[158] By the 1990s, scholars and EU institutions had taken up the concept of participatory democracy, as well as democratic participation beyond the ballot box, to analyse the strengths and weaknesses of public- and interest-group participation present at the EU level.[159] This analysis primarily occurred through the lens of an associative version of democracy and deliberative democracy.[160]

According to the associative variant, the enhancement of the democratic legitimacy at EU level through the contribution of interest groups was based on the assumption that interest groups can contribute to efficient and legitimate decision-making as they have greater resources at their disposal, compared with individual citizens.[161] Drawing from comparative empirical research focused on neo-corporatism and consociationalism at the national level, several flaws with the associative perspective were, however, identified, including the questionable democratic credentials of civil society and interest groups, as well as the asymmetries in citizens' and interest groups' capacities to organise, privileging institutionalised and professionalised actors.[162] The involvement of groups in the public policy processes could be justified for reasons of system effectiveness, but the democratic quality from the perspective of both representative and participatory models of

[153] Saurugger, 'The Social Construction of the Participatory Turn' (n 136).

[154] Eva G Heidbreder, 'Civil Society Participation in EU Governance' (2012) 7 *Living Reviews in European Governance* 8.

[155] ibid.

[156] ibid.

[157] ibid.

[158] Kohler-Koch and Quittkat (n 151) 24.

[159] Saurugger, 'Interest Groups and Democracy' (n 152); Gautier Busschaert, *Participatory Democracy, Civil Society and Social Europe: A Legal and Political Perspective*, 1st edn (Intersentia, 2016) 21–34.

[160] Busschaert, *Participatory Democracy* (n 159) 21–34; Saurugger, 'Interest Groups and Democracy' (n 152).

[161] Saurugger, 'Interest Groups and Democracy' (n 152) 1278.

[162] ibid.

democracy were put into question.[163] Calls for stronger representativity criteria for organisations were put forward.[164] The professionalisation of interest groups, as well as their frequent seeming lack of genuine link to citizens or constituents, called into question their role in promoting the public sphere or representing their constituents.[165] From the associative model, Saurugger distils the arguments developed by participatory democracy into three guiding lines for analysis at the EU level.[166] The first is the emphasis, by participatory theorists, on the regulation of civil society access; the second is the enhancement of resources among various groups lacking the means to participate; and the third is the degree to which citizens are represented and can participate in decision-making processes, prominently through grass-roots civil society mobilisation.[167]

Related to the associative democracy model, but more influential, was the influence of deliberative democracy, to which European integration scholars turned.[168] Participatory theorisation in the EU based on deliberation can be categorised as macro, micro or meso, expressed particularly through the contribution of civil society.[169] The macro perspective focuses on the enhancement of the public sphere and the idea of citizenship. The micro-theories instead relied on the participatory turn to possess deliberative qualities which would advance the problem-solving capacity of the EU.[170] Deliberative democracy, in this setting, served as a theoretical foundation for moving beyond aggregation and bargaining of preferences, to processes that would support a discursive structure of forming opinions – a range of different and competing views that would receive 'fair' treatment.[171] Central was not giving dues to representatives of general interests but, rather, procedures that require reason-giving and justification for the problems at stake.[172] The theory of 'Deliberative Supranationalism' stressed the contribution of European law for 'transforming strategic action into deliberative problem-solving'.[173] European law rules and principles would structure the decision-making processes so that they

[163] ibid.

[164] Fazi and Smith, 'Civil Dialogue' (n 87) 24–29.

[165] Beate Kohler-Koch, 'Civil Society and EU Democracy: "Astroturf" Representation?' (2010) 17 *Journal of European Public Policy* 100; see also Darren Halpin and Peter McLaverty, 'Legitimating INGO Advocacy: The Case of Internal Democracies' in Jens Steffek and Kristina Hahn (eds), *Evaluating Transnational NGOs: Legitimacy, Accountability, Representation* (Palgrave Macmillan UK, 2010).

[166] Saurugger, 'Interest Groups and Democracy' (n 152) 1277.

[167] ibid.

[168] Busschaert, *Participatory Democracy* (n 159) 25–35.

[169] ibid.

[170] Cohen and Sabel, 'Directly-Deliberative Polyarchy' (n 124) 313; Mark A Pollack, 'Theorizing EU Policy-Making' in Helen Wallace, Mark A Pollack and Christilla Roederer-Rynning (eds), *Policy-making in the European Union*, 8th edn (Oxford University Press, 2020) 35–46; Philippe C Schmitter, 'Governance in the European Union: A Viable Mechanism for Future Legitimation? 1' in Arthur Benz and Yannis Papadopoulos (eds), *Governance and Democracy* (Routledge, 2006) 161–63.

[171] Kohler-Koch, 'The Organization of Interests and Democracy' (n 6).

[172] Christian Joerges, '"Good Governance" Through Comitology?' in Christian Joerges and Ellen Vos (eds), *EU Committees: Social Regulation, Law and Politics* (Hart, 1999) 334.

[173] Christian Joerges and Jürgen Neyer, 'From Intergovernmental Bargaining to Deliberative Political Processes: The Constitutionalisation of Comitology' (1997) 3 *European Law Journal* 273.

would 'narrow down the range of arguments that are admissible within debate so that only generally reproducible and justifiable grounds or concerns . . . can be used', while also promoting the presentation of all relevant interests, and refining arguments with an eye to the legitimate concerns and interests of those who did not directly participate within the committee system.[174] The theory was substantiated through empirical observation of the committee system (comitology), but its application to other forms of EU decision-making processes are questionable.[175] For example, with regard to law-making consultations, the final decision will be taken in another arena, so participants are not as incentivised to 'deliberate' and arrive at a common understanding.[176]

The overall thrust of the micro-theories is that, by holding decision- and law-making processes to a standard of fairness and increasing accountability and responsiveness through abiding by principles of transparency, openness and participation,[177] these arrangements would be provided with procedural legitimacy.[178] This procedural legitimacy was primarily framed as a complement to democratic legitimacy flowing from parliament.[179] As Closa notes, participation would contribute to deliberation of high quality when the engaged actors 'avoid arguments based on vested interest and seek persuasion based on strong arguments appealing to superior moral reason'.[180] Prominent in these debates was the role of transparency for enabling deliberation in the public sphere, in laying the foundation for participation in decision-making, and for overall accountability.[181] As regards the micro-theories, there was criticism that they either were too focused

[174] Christian Joerges and Michelle Iverson, 'Challenging the Bureaucratic Challenge' in Erik Oddvar Eriksen and John Erik Fossum (eds), *Democracy in the European Union: Integration through Deliberation* (Routledge, 2000) 182; regarding the relevant interests, see Joerges and Neyer, 'From Intergovernmental Bargaining to Deliberative Political Processes' (n 173).

[175] Kohler-Koch, 'The Organization of Interests and Democracy' (n 6) 261–62.

[176] ibid.

[177] Renaud Dehousse, 'European Governance in Search of Legitimacy: The Need for a Process-Based Approach' in Olivier De Schutter, Notis Lebessis and John Paterson (eds), *Governance in the European Union* (Forward Studies Series, Office for Official Publications of the European Communities, 2001) 177, 182; Joerges, '"Good Governance" Through Comitology?' (n 172).

[178] Giandomenico Majone, *Regulating Europe* (Routledge, 1996) 291–94.

[179] Adrienne Heritier, 'Elements of Democratic Legitimation in Europe: An Alternative Perspective' (1999) 6 *Journal of European Public Policy* 269, 271–73; Dehousse, 'European Governance in Search of Legitimacy' (n 177) 186–87; Christopher Lord and David Beetham, 'Legitimizing the EU: Is There a "Post-Parliamentary Basis" for Its Legitimation?' (2001) 39 *Journal of Common Market Studies* 443, 452–53; Christopher Lord, 'Parliamentary Representation in a Decentered Polity' in Kohler-Koch and Rittberger, *Debating the Democratic Legitimacy of the European Union* (n 6) 146–50.

[180] Carlos Closa, 'Deliberative Constitutional Politics and the Turn towards a Norms-Based Legitimacy of the EU Constitution' (2005) 11 *European Law Journal* 411, 421.

[181] Deirdre M Curtin, 'Betwixt and Between: Democracy and Transparency in the Governance of the European Union' in Alfred E Kellermann and others (eds), Reforming the Treaty on European Union (Brill/Nijhoff, 1996); see also Weiler, 'The Transformation of Europe' (n 131) 2453–747; Carol Harlow, 'Accountability in the European Union' (2002), https://cadmus.eui.eu/handle/1814/2895, accessed 6 August 2023; Deirdre Curtin and Albert Jacob Meijer, 'Does Transparency Strengthen Legitimacy?' (2006) 11 *Information Polity* 109.

on collective actors, jeopardising equality, or that participation was formulated in a rather abstract way, or was sidestepped by other theoretical concerns.[182]

The meso-theories often focus on the democratic 'transmission belt' and participation-catalyst role that interest groups and civil society could play, arguing that the EU as a political system is in need of direct legitimacy, given the wide range of legislation, rules and policies it produces.[183] These theories mostly assessed the democratising potential of participation of civil society according to the ideal of public deliberation.[184] This thinking held that the European governance would need to meet democratic norms of public control and political equality,[185] looking beyond functional holders and addressing the citizen as the 'ultimate stakeholder' of governance, in order to address the existing democracy deficit.[186] The concepts of representation and accountability which characterised the middle-ground theories, however, arguably do not properly convey the ideal of participatory democracy, as they do not ensure that citizens will participate in European governance beyond elections.[187] Still, one strand of this literature, however, implies a commitment to participatory democracy, in that it sees deliberative democracy as implying a commitment to wide public participation, where citizens and civil society contribute decisively, and civil society is regarded as a civic space between the state and market.[188] Civil society, in this context, facilitates participation from the grass roots through a framework of governance.[189]

Regarding the term 'participatory democracy' and its appearance in EU official documents, it can be traced to efforts to enhance non-governmental organisations'

[182] Busschaert, *Participatory Democracy* (n 159) chs 2–3; Smismans, 'The Constitutional Labelling of "the Democratic Life of the EU"' (n 2) 128–29.

[183] Jens Steffek and Patrizia Nanz, 'Emergent Patterns of Civil Society Participation in Global and European Governance' in Jens Steffek, Claudia Kissling and Patrizia Nanz (eds), *Civil Society Participation in European and Global Governance* (Palgrave Macmillan UK, 2008) 7–8; Busschaert, *Participatory Democracy* (n 159) 36–37.

[184] Steffek and Nanz, 'Emergent Patterns' (n 183) 7–8; Busschaert, *Participatory Democracy* (n 159) 36–37.

[185] Lord and Beetham, 'Legitimizing the EU' (n 179) 435–55; B Guy Peters and Jon Pierre, 'Multi-Level Governance and Democracy: A Faustian Bargain?' in Ian Bache and Matthew Flinders (eds), *Multi-level Governance* (Oxford University Press, 2004); on governance and democracy challenges, see Arthur Benz and Yannis Papadopoulos (eds), *Governance and Democracy: Comparing National, European and International Experiences*, Reprint (Routledge, 2007); Deirdre Curtin, Peter Mair and Yannis Papadopoulos (eds), *Accountability and European Governance* (Routledge, 2012).

[186] Steffek and Nanz, 'Emergent Patterns' (n 183) 6–9; Dawid Friedrich, 'Old Wine in New Bottles? The Actual and Potential Contribution of Civil Society Organisations to Democratic Governance in Europe' RECON Online Working Paper 2007/08.

[187] Busschaert, *Participatory Democracy* (n 159) 36–37.

[188] ibid.

[189] See Deirdre Curtin, '"Civil Society" and the European Union: Opening Spaces for Deliberative Democracy?' in Academy of European Law (eds), *Collected Courses of the Academy of European Law*, vol VII, book 1 (Kluwer Law International, 1999); Kenneth A Armstrong, 'Rediscovering Civil Society: The European Union and the White Paper on Governance' (2002) 8 *European Law Journal* 102, 102; Alex Warleigh, 'Civil Society and Legitimate Governance in a Flexible Europe: Critical Deliberativism as a Way Forward' in Stijn Smismans (ed), *Civil Society and Legitimate European Governance* (Edward Elgar, 2006) 71.

involvement in European policy-making.[190] The Commission argues, in its 2000 discussion paper on partnership with non-governmental organisations, that although 'the decision making process in the EU is first and foremost legitimized by the elected representatives of the European people, NGOs can make a contribution fostering a more participatory democracy'.[191] The European Economic and Social Committee (EESC), in its opinion on the paper, replied that

> participatory democracy requires that parties who are affected by legal provisions should be involved in the opinion-forming process at the earliest possible stage and should be given the opportunity to bring their wishes to bear in this process and put forward their proposals.

It added that, 'this principle, in particular, chimes with the participatory model of civil society'.[192]

Smismans argues that 'participatory democracy', to a large extent, emerged in the discourse on civil society and civil dialogue developed by both the European Commission and the EESC since the end of the 1990s.[193] This discourse then broadened to other sectors and became a part of the Commission's efforts for administrative reform, and of its governance debate.[194] In the Commission's White Paper on European governance, participation through civil society organisations held an important place to ensure 'good governance', while the concept of 'civil society organisations' in the Paper was interpreted more broadly to also include economic actors, professional associations and business.[195]

The connection between 'participatory democracy' and the involvement of civil society organisations in European policy was also made by the EESC,[196] which defined its own role as guaranteeing the implementation of a participatory model of civil society, enabling civil society to participate in the decision-making process, and thereby contributing to reducing the democracy deficit.[197] In relation to the

[190] Smismans traces the concept and discusses its evolution: Smismans, 'The Constitutional Labelling of "the Democratic Life of the EU"' (n 2) 127.

[191] This phrase is under the title 'Fostering participatory democracy': European Commission, Commission discussion paper 'The Commission and non-governmental organisations: building a stronger partnership' COM/2000/0011 final indent 3.1.4.

[192] ibid.

[193] Smismans, 'The Constitutional Labelling of "the Democratic Life of the EU"' (n 2) 127.

[194] ibid.

[195] Smismans comments on the Commission using the discourse on civil society involvement and participation to legitimate a variety of (existing) structures of interaction with various actors, 'including private lobbyists' (ibid); on the influence between academics, experts and stakeholders in relation to the drafting of the White Paper, see Saurugger, 'The Social Construction of the Participatory Turn' (n 136).

[196] The EESC was created through the Treaty of Rome and has advisory powers across a wide range of areas. It is composed of representatives from national employers' organisations, trade unions and 'various interests' (eg professional associations, small and medium enterprises, consumers and social economy organisations): see European Union, 'European Economic and Social Committee', https://european-union.europa.eu/institutions-law-budget/institutions-and-bodies/search-all-eu-institutions-and-bodies/european-economic-and-social-committee-eesc_en.

[197] Smismans, 'The Constitutional Labelling of "the Democratic Life of the EU"' (n 2) 128.

issue of a European public sphere and 'peoples', the EESC argued that its consultative role, enshrined in the Treaty and composed of representatives of intermediary organisations, could act as a representation of the people's way of identifying with civil society organizations and complement the legitimacy of the parliament, while also not monopolising this role, because the European democratic model will contain many 'elements of participatory democracy'.[198]

The cementing of the participatory norm also meant that the 1990s saw a shift in participation, as dialogue with civil society increased. Stakeholders were identified and the Commission supported the creation of forums for exchange.[199] Along with the older consultative bodies of the EESC, as well as social dialogue, European institutions were working with a wide range of consultative committees.[200] During this period, a few quasi-political rights were accorded to European citizens, including the right to petition before the European institutions and the right to complain to the European Ombudsman.[201] A legal duty to consult was also established through the Amsterdam Treaty, enshrined in Protocol number 2 on the application of the principles of subsidiarity and proportionality: 'The Commission should . . . consult widely before proposing legislation and, wherever appropriate, publish consultation documents.'[202]

Significantly, with the Amsterdam Treaty, the co-decision procedure was extended across 15 existing legal bases, cementing the European Parliament (EP)'s role as a policy- and law-making institute/institution.[203] With the evolution of lobbying towards new and restructured European peak associations, a growing number of firms and civil society groups led to the overall interest group population becoming denser – EU officials talked of interest-group overload, and of bottleneck effects on policy-making.[204] Following this overcrowding, as well as the overall democracy and governance debate, EU officials started to explore the

[198] European Economic and Social Committee, Opinion of the Economic and Social Committee on 'Organised civil society and European governance: the Committee's contribution to the drafting of the White Paper' (2001/C 193/21) indent 3.3.1.

[199] Smismans, 'The Constitutional Labelling of "the Democratic Life of the EU"' (n 2).

[200] See, eg Mendes, Participation in EU Rule-Making (n 31) 94–102.

[201] The right to petition the European Parliament and complain to the Ombudsman were added through Art 8d Maastricht Treaty: 'Consolidated Version of the Treaty on European Union [2012] OJ C326/13', art 8d. The European Ombudsman was first established by the Maastricht Treaty, yet the idea of a European Ombudsman had already circulated in the 1970s, with a resolution by the European Parliament calling for the establishment of a 'Community Ombudsman': see Dominik Hierlemann and others, *Under Construction: Citizen Participation in the European Union* (Verlag Bertelsmann Stiftung, 2022) 112.

[202] Treaty of Amsterdam amending the 'Consolidated Version of the Treaty on European Union [2012] OJ C326/13' (n 201) para 9.

[203] For a discussion of this shift, see Lord and Beetham, 'Legitimizing the EU' (n 179) 453–55; Peters and Pierre, 'Multi-Level Governance and Democracy' (n 185); on the democracy challenges raised by European governance, see Benz and Papadopoulos, *Governance and Democracy* (n 185); Erik O Eriksen, Christian Joerges and Jürgen Neyer (eds), 'European Governance, Deliberation and the Quest for Democratisation' Arena Report 2/03 (2003); Curtin, Mair and Papadopoulos, *Accountability and European Governance* (n 185).

[204] See, eg David Coen, 'The European Business Lobby' (1997) 8 *Business Strategy Review* 17, 21; Sonia Mazey and JJ Richardson (eds), *Lobbying in the European Community* (Repr, Oxford University Press, 1998).

regulation of lobbyists and (better) ways to manage access to the policy process. This final phase crystallised in conjunction with the publication of the Commission's White Paper on governance, in 2001, which in turn influenced the debates leading up to the drafting of the Constitutional Treaty.[205]

2.3. The path leading to the Lisbon Treaty and a 'principle' of participatory democracy

Based on the analysis of a 'widening gulf between the European Union and the people it serves', the White Paper marked a change of paradigm for the EU.[206] The White Paper defined the EU policy process as the result of different influences and mechanisms of participation beyond the institutional triangle, and also acknowledged the need to foster citizens' involvement in the EU process, promote new forms of contact between EU institutions and different interest groups, and increase openness in different phases of the decision-making process.[207] The five good governance principles of this new direction were openness, participation, efficiency, accountability and coherence.[208] The White Paper signified a broader qualitative change in the EU's approach, which to a degree could be expressed in terms of a shift from government to governance.[209] The role played by interest groups evolved as EU institutions shifted from a straightforward, hierarchical style of policy-making to a looser, more horizontal, and more decentralised one.[210] In turn, this created a variation in legitimacy demand – between input and output – among different EU institutions, and even between different elements within the Commission.[211] The White Paper intended to address, at least to some degree, how to advance the legitimacy of EU law and decision-making.[212] An important subtext, however, was the corruption scandal leading to the retirement of the preceding Santer Commission, and the desire to distance the new Commission from the

[205] Commission, European Governance, 'A White Paper', COM (2001) 428 final, 25 July 2001; on the Paper's influence on these debates, see Neil Walker, 'The White Paper in Constitutional Context' [2001] Jean Monnet Chair, Jean Monnet Working Papers.

[206] White Paper 8; on the paradigm shift, see, eg Fazi and Smith, 'Civil Dialogue' (n 87) 24.

[207] Christine Quittkat and Barbara Finke, 'The EU Commission Consultation Regime' in Beate Kohler-Koch, Dirk de Bièvre and William Maloney (eds), 'Opening EU Governance to Civil Society: Gains and Challenges' (Connex Report Series 05 2008); Fazi and Smith, 'Civil Dialogue' (n 87) 24.

[208] White Paper indent II.

[209] David Coen, Alexander Katsaitis and Matia Vannoni, *Business Lobbying in the European Union*, 1st edn (Oxford University Press, 2021) 32–38.

[210] ibid.

[211] See, eg Scharpf, *Governing in Europe* (n 137); David Coen and Alexander Katsaitis, 'Chameleon Pluralism in the EU: An Empirical Study of the European Commission Interest Group Density and Diversity across Policy Domains' (2013) 20 *Journal of European Public Policy* 1104; Vivien Schmidt and Matthew Wood, 'Conceptualizing Throughput Legitimacy: Procedural Mechanisms of Accountability, Transparency, Inclusiveness and Openness in EU Governance' (2019) 97 *Public Administration* 727.

[212] Mendes, *Participation in EU Rule-Making* (n 31) 129. It was also framed in terms of promoting new forms of European governance, and unveiled as one of four key strategic objectives of the 2000–2005 Commission: Walker, 'The White Paper in Constitutional Context' (n 205) 44.

practices and attitudes that had characterised the corruption and mismanagement of the old one.[213]

The White Paper and its principles became the starting point for a series of reforms in the Commission's working methods, including the 'General principles and minimum standards for consultation and impact assessments'.[214] In the minimum standards, the Commission also took a clearly articulated strong stance against any legal mandate to participate, arguing that binding rules would unnecessarily bureaucratise the work and become an obstacle to in-house learning; there was an explicit statement that the Commission did not want decisions on consultation challenged before the courts.[215] The White Paper and the following reforms sparked further discussion on the nature of participation and Europe's civil society. There was a sense that the Commission had acknowledged, albeit sometimes tacitly, that output legitimacy must be complemented by input legitimacy, and that participatory democracy could complement and not compete with representative democracy.[216] Even with the White Paper drawing attention to civil society participation, the instrumental focus of participatory governance largely remained: consultation was conceived primarily to ameliorate limited resources and regulatory challenges – its main raison d'etre was improving the quality of decision-making and facilitating compliance, and in some spheres it served as a strategy to expand the EU's role and influence through dialogue.[217] The Commission's approach of including economic actors in its definition of civil society also seemed to support the functional approach to participation.[218]

Even so, the EU supported the mobilisation of (non-business) civil society organisations, prominently through providing financial subsidies in targeted areas – and this likely contributed to the population of such organisations growing dramatically across the mid-2000s.[219] The lobbying and participation landscape in Brussels changed, in one decade, from a business club to a diverse ecosystem which included think tanks, representatives of regions, consultancies, law firms, civil society groups and other non-state actors.[220] This shift also meant a continuous

[213] Walker, 'The White Paper in Constitutional Context' (n 205) 44.

[214] Commission, Communication from the Commission 'Towards a reinforced culture of consultation and dialogue - General principles and minimum standards for consultation of interested parties by the Commission', COM(2002) 704 final, 11 December 2002. These standards and the framework of the impact assessment formed a touchstone for Commission consultation up until current practices emerged.

[215] ibid 14 'Nature of the document'.

[216] Walker, 'The White Paper in Constitutional Context' (n 205).

[217] It seemed that the turn to 'European civil society' did little more than 'to give new appearance and structure to the forms of interest representation that the Commission had since long promoted': Mendes, 'Participation and the Role of Law after Lisbon' (n 2) 1855–57; continuity with previous practices could also be seen in the Commission's own statements, in relation to its principle of participation, in the White Paper (n 205), focusing on efficiency; see also Armstrong, 'Rediscovering Civil Society' (n 189).

[218] Smismans, 'The Constitutional Labelling of "the Democratic Life of the EU"' (n 2) 127.

[219] Coen, Katsaitis and Vannoni, *Business Lobbying* (n 209) 33; Andreas Broscheid and David Coen, 'Lobbying Activity and Fora Creation in the EU: Empirically Exploring the Nature of the Policy Good' (2007) 14 *Journal of European Public Policy* 346.

[220] Coen, Katsaitis and Vannoni, *Business Lobbying* (n 209) 33.

contact between policy-makers and interest groups.[221] There was, however, a sense, at least in hindsight and in some corners, that the Commission had taken a wrong turn by focusing too much on organised civil society and interest groups.[222]

As participatory democracy entered the discourse surrounding the democratic legitimacy more prominently, the term 'participatory democracy' was used somewhat ambiguously, as was the term 'civil society'. The principal ambiguity hinged on who the main protagonists of participation were.[223] Direct citizen involvement in European policy-making now attracted more attention in the academic debate.[224] Yet the governance debate, as we have seen, however, remained mainly focused not on direct citizen participation, but on an alternative form of representation: functional representation, or representation via associations and interest groups.[225] However, this divide was sometimes not clear, and the White Paper itself indicated that it was simultaneously reaching out to interest groups and the broader public, albeit with an emphasis on the former.[226] As several scholars noted, European integration literature often equated participatory democracy with civil society involvement rather than direct citizen involvement.[227] The Commission, in turn, as well as some scholars, equated civil society with all forms of interest groups, leading to accusations of epistemological sliding and 'lip-service' to participatory democracy and the role of civil society.[228] Despite this, direct citizen participation was invoked, especially with regard to legislative process: for example, Lenaerts argued that, in 'its broadest interpretation "participatory democracy" is used for "the direct involvement in decision-making of those that are most affected by it"'.[229] Smismans notes that such a conception could imply the decentralisation of decision-making to ensure direct citizen participation, but was mainly used by scholars to structure participation in 'central' European decision-making, via e-democracy or through the involvement of civil society organisations.[230]

[221] ibid; see also George Christou and Seamus Simpson, 'The Internet and Public–Private Governance in the European Union' (2006) 26 *Journal of Publicy Policy* 43.

[222] Daniela Obradovic and Jose M Alonso Vizcaino, 'Good Governance Requirements Concerning the Participation of Interest Groups in EU Consultations' (2006) 43 *Common Market Law Review* 1049.

[223] Grevén, 'Some Considerations' (n 15).

[224] Michael Nentwich, 'Opportunity Structures for Citizens' Participation: The Case of the European Union', European Community Studies Association Austria vol. 0 (1996) ; see also Joseph Weiler, The Constitution of Europe: 'Do the New Clothes Have an Emperor?' And Other Essays on European Integration (Cambridge University Press, 1999) 324–58; Deirdre Curtin, *Postnational Democracy: The European Union in Search of a Political Philosophy* (Kluwer Law International 1997).

[225] Smismans, 'The Constitutional Labelling of "the Democratic Life of the EU"' (n 2) 128.

[226] ibid; this approach has persisted, as the Commission still frequently targets 'citizens' in its public consultations. The minimum standards also refer to the advantage of consultations engaging the general public more: see Commission, General Principles and Minimum Standards; Commission, Better Regulation Guidelines' SWD(2021) 305 final (SWD Better Regulation Guidelines) 14–15.

[227] Olivier De Schutter, 'Europe in Search of Its Civil Society' (2002) 8 *European Law Journal* 198; Grevén, 'Some Considerations' (n 15).

[228] Smismans, 'The Constitutional Labelling of "the Democratic Life of the EU"' (n 2) 137; Saurugger, 'Interest Groups and Democracy' (n 152).

[229] Smismans, 'The Constitutional Labelling of "the Democratic Life of the EU"' (n 2) 137; Saurugger, 'Interest Groups and Democracy' (n 152); Smismans citing Lenaerts.

[230] Smismans, 'The Constitutional Labelling of "the Democratic Life of the EU"' (n 2) 137; Saurugger, 'Interest Groups and Democracy' (n 152); see also Curtin, *Postnational Democracy* (n 224).

The developments leading up to the drafting of the Lisbon Treaty reflected a turn in the approach to, and rationales for, participation, which had previously been instrumental and focused on participation as a means to enhance efficiency.[231] Participation as a means of connecting the EU with its citizens was widely used by all EU institutions at the time of the Laeken Convention (drafting of the European constitution).[232] The Laeken European Council adopted a new Declaration on the Future of Europe, which insisted on addressing the democratic challenge facing Europe, and maintained that EU institutions must be brought closer to their citizens.[233] The Laeken Declaration convened a Convention with a mandate to pursue the democracy debate and intended to openly pave the way for the next Intergovernmental Conference. The Convention was conceived as a public forum of deliberation which included representatives of national governments, members of national parliaments, members of the EP, and Commission representatives.[234] Moreover, the forum set up by the Laeken Declaration allowed civil society organisations and non-institutional interest groups to provide inputs into the Convention deliberations.[235]

The 1,264 contributions presented came from 160 different registered organisations, ranging from academic institutions, social partners, churches and religious communities to business associations, professional organisations and other non-governmental organisations.[236] Safeguarding and promoting a 'more participatory democracy' featured in many statements, as did the inclusion of a regular dialogue with civil society, which should lead to consultation of the relevant organisations at an early stage in the framing of Union legislation.[237] The process brought to the fore questions relating to the purpose and nature of participation: was it instrumental or intrinsic? Was the input, the process or the outcome the focus?[238] During the proceedings, for instance, it could be heard that what mattered 'is not that the eventual decision can be formally attributed to the will of the citizenry, but rather that those who so wish be given a chance to express their views'.[239]

[231] See, eg Presidency Conclusions of the Laeken European Council (14 and 15 December 2001) SN 300/1/01 REV 1 ANNEX 1; see also Víctor Cuesta Lopez, 'The Lisbon Treaty's Provisions on Democratic Principles: A Legal Framework for Participatory Democracy' (2010) 16 European Public Law 123, 125–27; Mendes, *Participation in EU Rule-Making* (n 31) 1858.

[232] Cuesta Lopez, 'The Lisbon Treaty's Provisions on Democratic Principles' (n 231) 126.

[233] Presidency Conclusions of the Laeken European Council (14 and 15 December 2001) SN 300/1/01 REV 1 ANNEX 1. Preceding the Laeken Declaration, a declaration attached to the Treaty of Nice also highlighted that transparency and democratic legitimacy would need to be addressed: Treaty of Nice amending the Treaty on European Union, the Treaties establishing the European Communities and certain related acts - Declarations Adopted By The Conference, declaration on the future of the Union [2001] OJ 080, 10/03/2001 P. 0085 - 0086 point 6.

[234] Cuesta Lopez, 'The Lisbon Treaty's Provisions on Democratic Principles' (n 231) 126.

[235] ibid 126–27.

[236] European Convention, 'Report from the Presidency of the Convention to the President of the European Council', CONV 851/2003, 3.

[237] Cuesta Lopez, 'The Lisbon Treaty's Provisions on Democratic Principles' (n 231); Nicolas Beger, 'Participatory Democracy: Organised Civil Society and the "New" Dialogue' [2004] Federal Trust Constitutional Online Paper No 09/04.

[238] Luis Bouza Garcia, *Participatory Democracy and Civil Society in the EU: Agenda-Setting and Institutionalisation* (Palgrave Macmillan, 2015) 62–69.

[239] Renaud Dehousse, 'Beyond Representative Democracy: Constitutionalism in a Polycentric Polity' in JHH Weiler and Marlene Wind (eds), *European Constitutionalism beyond the State*, 1st edn (Cambridge University Press, 2001) 135–56.

A *principle* of participatory democracy first surfaced when the Secretariat of the Convention presented a series of articles on the democratic life of the Union, which included an article on participatory democracy,[240] and linked this proposal to the ongoing debate on how to bring the EU closer to its citizens.[241] The first draft of the Constitution suggested an article that would set out the principle of participatory democracy, stating that 'the Institutions are to ensure a high level of openness, permitting citizens' organizations of all kinds to play a full part in the Union's affairs',[242] which led to the formulation of '[t]he principle of participatory democracy', which consisted of three points. The first was that '[e]very citizen shall have the right to participate in the democratic life of the Union', now placed under Article 10(3) TEU. This was followed by two articles stating that the Union institutions should allow 'citizens and representative associations the opportunity to make known and publicly exchange their opinions on all areas of Union action' and maintain 'an open, transparent and regular dialogue with representative associations and civil society'.[243] Initially, this article was placed under the title 'The democratic life of the Union', which included articles on the principle of equality, the European Ombudsman, political parties, transparency, protection of personal data, and the status of churches and non-confessional organisations.[244]

At this stage, no mention was made of a principle of representative democracy, although representative democracy followed naturally from constitutional provisions on the Parliament and voting rights recognised under the title of citizenship.[245] Many amendments were, however, tabled which asked for a specific reference to representative democracy, either as a part of the same article or as a separate one under the same title.[246] When the article was first presented, no debate arose on any of the fundamentals of the principle of participatory democracy, and it was generally well received.[247]

The social partners welcomed the enhanced participation of civil society but prioritised consolidation and protection of the special position of the social dialogue.[248] Business groups were also enthusiastic, with the European umbrella organisation of the chambers of commerce even declaring that participatory democracy constituted a 'cornerstone of European integration'.[249] Civil society organisations and other groups were also very active, also reflected in the number

[240] Document from the Praesidium: Draft Title VI of the Constitutional Treaty relating to the democratic life of the Union (2 April 2003) art 34.

[241] Bouza Garcia, *Participatory Democracy and Civil Society* (n 238) 80.

[242] European Convention, 'Report from the Presidency of the Convention to the President of the European Council', CONV 851/2003, 3.

[243] ibid.

[244] Document from the Praesidium: Draft Title VI of the Constitutional Treaty relating to the democratic life of the Union (2 April 2003).

[245] On this point, see Smismans, 'The Constitutional Labelling of "the Democratic Life of the EU"' (n 2) 133.

[246] ibid.

[247] Kohler-Koch and Quittkat (n 151) 31.

[248] ibid 33.

[249] ibid; see also Geir Ove Kværk, 'Organised Civil Society in the EU Constitution-Making Process' in John Erik Fossum, Philip Schlesigner and Geir Ove Kværk (eds), *Public Sphere and Civil Society? Transformations of the European Union* (ARENA REPORT 2/2007: 141–223) 179.

of their petitions, which was 'second to none'.[250] Different civil society groups and coalitions also contributed to different articles: for example, the insertion of the European Citizens' Initiative (ECI) was the result of a differentiated mobilisation; most of the civil society organisations that demanded the recognition of consultation were not involved at all in activism for the ECI.[251]

Despite the lack of overall opposition to the principle, some reservations likely existed, partly reflected in the many demands that a principle of representative democracy be explicitly and clearly mentioned; and in terms of participation overall, it 'would have been difficult to publicly challenge a notion that is so normatively charged'.[252] Civil society actors also made clear calls for the provision of a stronger legal basis for the ongoing Commission consultation practices.[253] More specifically, one request was for the article to be more concrete, and the general recognition of dialogue was then supplemented by a particular reference to 'broad consultations with concerned parties'.[254]

Differences of opinion also emerged between organisations and members of the Convention, regarding the notion of civil society, including the role of citizens in the civil dialogue.[255] On one end, the opinion was expressed that the dialogue should be expanded to 'literally everyone' – in particular, citizens – and on the other end, the opinion was that dialogue with organised civil society (often structured) was to be favoured.[256] However, even for those advocating the latter, the expectation was expressed that the EU would advance engagement of citizens in associations – repeatedly stressing that civil society organisations must be entrenched in citizenship and themselves be open and representative.[257]

During the later stages of the drafting of the articles, mobilisation to support the insertion of the ECI (currently Article 11(4) TEU) was successful, despite the somewhat grudging assent of the Commission, who worked to make sure that its sole right to initiate legislation remained intact.[258] As the drafting evolved, two articles, labelled the principle of representative democracy and the principle of participatory democracy, respectively, were included. The titles were later removed, but the articles remained in the Lisbon Treaty. When the European Council later, in 2007, called for an intergovernmental conference to draft a new treaty which was to avoid constitutional references, the overall question of

[250] Kohler-Koch and Quittkat (n 151) 32. Despite this, civil society participation in many ways remained a one-sided exchange: see Kværk, 'Organised Civil Society' (n 249) 159; Eleanor Lombardo, 'The Participation of Civil Society in the Constitution-Making Process' (CIDEL Workshop Constitution Making and Democratic Legitimacy in the EU, 2004) 154.

[251] Bouza Garcia, *Participatory Democracy and Civil Society* (n 238) 19–70.

[252] Kohler-Koch and Quittkat (n 151) 31.

[253] Bouza Garcia, *Participatory Democracy and Civil Society* (n 238) 44.

[254] ibid 17.

[255] Kohler-Koch and Quittkat (n 151) 33–35; Bouza Garcia, *Participatory Democracy and Civil Society* (n 238) 105.

[256] The substantial positions were influenced by institutional links and the political party affiliation: see Kohler-Koch and Quittkat (n 151) 36–37.

[257] ibid.

[258] Bouza Garcia, *Participatory Democracy and Civil Society* (n 238) 89; see also Smismans, 'The Constitutional Labelling of "the Democratic Life of the EU"' (n 2).

democracy, however, was not to be avoided. The reform Treaty replicated several of the provisions of the Constitutional Treaty, but under a new title: 'Provisions on Democratic Principles'.[259]

Although 'the Constitutional Convention was not a body that engages in theoretical reasoning',[260] the Lisbon Treaty undeniably constitutionalised a participatory norm oriented towards bringing the citizens closer to the Union. Both the discourse on participation and the debates leading up to the drafting, as well as later iterations, demonstrated a notion of participatory democracy as clearly rooted in an understanding of participation beyond a narrow functional purpose, and more aligned with the ideals of participatory democracy, even while placing it as a complement to representative democracy.

2.4. Participatory democracy post-Lisbon: The legal road not taken

Since the ratification of the Lisbon Treaties, the new title of democratic principles, and particularly the novel principle of participatory democracy, have prompted some normative and legal evaluations assessing the strength of the EU's participatory mechanisms.[261] It also generated analysis of democracy as featured in the Lisbon Treaty, in relation to the diverse theories found in the normative literature on the EU's democratic deficit.[262]

Early on, scholars noted that, while the democratic principles, including Article 11 TEU, seemed to fall short of any aspirational expectations of institutionalising citizen participation,[263] participation was now, for the first time, explicitly linked

[259] Cuesta Lopez, 'The Lisbon Treaty's Provisions on Democratic Principles' (n 231) 127.

[260] Beate Kohler-Koch, 'Does Participatory Democracy Hold Its Promises?' in Beate Kohler-Koch and Fabrice Larat (eds), *Efficient and Democratic Governance in the European Union* (Connex Report Series 09 2008) 266.

[261] See, eg Cuesta Lopez, 'The Lisbon Treaty's Provisions on Democratic Principles' (n 231); Mendes, 'Participation and the Role of Law after Lisbon' (n 2); Juan Antonio Mayoral, 'Democratic Improvements in the European Union under the Lisbon Treaty: Institutional Changes Regarding Democratic Government in the EU' [2011] *SSRN Journal*; Acar Kutay, 'Limits of Participatory Democracy in European Governance: Participatory Democracy in Lisbon Treaty' (2015) 21 *European Law Journal* 803; Alberto Alemanno, 'Levelling the EU Participatory Playing Field: A Legal and Policy Analysis of the Commission's Public Consultations in Light of the Principle of Political Equality' (2020) 26 *European Law Journal* 114; Craig and De Búrca, 'Integration, Democracy, and Legitimacy' (n 137).

[262] Stephen C Sieberson, 'The Treaty of Lisbon and its Impact on the European Union's Democratic Deficit' (2007), available at SSRN: https://ssrn.com/abstract=1628869, accessed 9 February 2026; Cuesta Lopez, 'The Lisbon Treaty's Provisions on Democratic Principles' (n 231); Kohler-Koch and Quittkat (n 151); Kutay, 'Limits of Participatory Democracy (n 261).

[263] Carlos Closa, 'Constitutional prospects of European citizenship and new forms of democracy' in Giuliano Amato, Hervé Bribosia and Bruno de Witte (eds), *Genèse et destinée de la Constitution européenne: commentaire du traité établissant une constitution pour l'Europe à la lumière des travaux préparatoires et perspectives d'avenir* (Bruylant, 2007); Smismans, 'The Constitutional Labelling of "the Democratic Life of the EU"' (n 2); Jo Shaw, 'Citizenship: Contrasting Dynamics at the Interface of Integration and Constitutionalism' in Paul Craig and Gráinne De Búrca, *The Evolution of EU Law* (Oxford University Press, 2021) 638.

to democracy.[264] Participation was no longer only to be viewed as solely serving efficiency- or output-oriented goals, or with reference to its previous role in EU governance.[265] Instead, it was an aspect of democratic legitimacy, closely tied to transparency and equality.[266] While it was clear that this shift would have normative implications, it remained less clear how these implications were to be given effect in light of how the democratic principles were framed.[267]

The adoption of secondary legislation to operationalise the ECI helped flesh out this instrument and its workings, also promoting judicial review, by the Court, of the administration of citizens' initiatives.[268] However, secondary legislation clarifying other institutional obligations or clearly elaborating other participation rights was never adopted. Nevertheless, relying only on the democratic principles as normative yardsticks including the principle of participatory democracy, the EU governance approach to participation was deemed lacking: for instance, lack of transparency of participant selection or consultation format, or lack of (and lacking) feedback to participants.[269]

The role of the Court was highlighted in determining to what extent failure to uphold procedural practices with regard to dialogue and consultation could be challenged by relevant actors, as infringements of the principles of participatory democracy.[270] Furthermore while the democratic principles did speak to the citizen as a political actor within the EU, the connection between the citizens and the exercise of their political rights and the 'democratic life of the Union' seemed tenuous.[271]

There was, however, clear agreement – echoed by scholars; the German Constitutional Court, in its verdict on the German ratification of the Lisbon Treaty; and the CJEU, in adjudicating the Commission's discretion in its handling of ECIs[272] – that the participatory democracy as formulated in the Treaty was meant as a complement to representative democracy. In the debates following the drafting of the Lisbon Treaty, Kohler-Koch and Rittberger argued that democratic legitimacy in the EU can be viewed alongside three dimensions, each of which juxtaposes features which can be associated with liberal representative democracy

[264] Mendes, 'Participation and the Role of Law after Lisbon' (n 2) 1850.

[265] ibid 1850–59.

[266] ibid.

[267] See, eg Cuesta Lopez, 'The Lisbon Treaty's Provisions on Democratic Principles' (n 231); Gregorio Garzón Clariana, 'Les droits politiques des citoyens de l'Europe : les vingt premières années' (2013) 13 *ERA Forum* 545.

[268] Regulation (EU) 2019/788 of the European Parliament and of the Council of 17 April 2019 on the European citizens' initiative [2019] OJ L130/55.

[269] See, eg Fazi and Smith, 'Civil Dialogue' (n 87); Quittkat and Finke, 'The EU Commission Consultation Regime' (n 207); Alemanno, 'Levelling the EU Participatory Playing Field' (n 261) 126–27.

[270] Garzón Clariana, 'Les droits politiques des citoyens de l'Europe' (n 267); Mendes, 'Participation and the Role of Law after Lisbon' (n 2); Alberto Alemanno, 'Unpacking the Principle of Openness in EU Law: Transparency, Participation and Democracy' (2014) 39 *European Law Review* 72.

[271] Closa, 'Constitutional prospects of European citizenship' (n 263) 1052; Shaw, 'Citizenship: Contrasting Dynamics' (n 263) 638.

[272] VerfG, 2 BE 2/08 of 3062009; Case C-418/18 P *Grégor Puppinck and Others v Commission* EU:C:2019:1113, para 65.

in relation to more participatory forms of democracy, emphasising intrinsic participation, deliberation and civil society as the new complementary features.[273] While scholars such as Grevén highlighted that citizens had been lost as the main protagonists in the understanding of participatory democracy, others, drawing on empirical observation, drew the 'obvious conclusion' that participatory democracy in the EU must primarily be expressed through interest-group participation.

The tumultuous years following the ratification of Lisbon Treaty also did little to lessen the debates on democracy in the Union. A number of developments, often related to the legitimacy of EU procedures, occurred in direct response to a series of (real or perceived) crises: the euro crisis, the refugee crises, Brexit, the COVID pandemic, rule-of-law and political crises in Member States, a climate crisis, and, finally, a war once again on European soil, followed by a trade war and a weakening of the international rules-based order. Against this background, four specific developments post-Lisbon relating to the debates on democracy in the Union have a specific bearing on an understanding of 'participatory democracy' in the Union.

The first is that the rule-of-law crises in Hungary and Poland spurred on debates which emphasised how the rule of law and democracy are mutually supportive, and not only how the rule of law and fundamental rights constitute essential prerequisites for democracy, but also how the rule of law flows from democratic practices and relies on democratic rotation.[274] In this context, the interdependent nature of democracy at the EU level and democracy at the nation-state level was once again highlighted and emphasised.[275] This also prompted discussion on the potential to bring the EU values, such as democracy, including through the Treaty's democratic principles, before the Court.

The second development is that, despite a strong focus, pre-Lisbon, on configuring democratic participation in the EU through the lens of collective actors and through civil society and interest representation, citizens have emerged more strongly into focus as participation protagonists. One part of this development was, naturally, the ECI, which attracted some scholarly, activist and citizen attention, coupled with a small but distinct body of case law.[276] In addition, calls were renewed for including citizen perspectives into the law- and policy-making apparatus, including, inter alia, engaging more citizens or groups through the Commission consultation regime; including 'citizen narratives' for unregulated areas; and expanding upon direct engagement with citizens through citizen

[273] Kohler-Koch and Rittberger, 'Charting Crowded Territory' (n 21) 14–17.

[274] See, eg András Jakab, 'Three Misconceptions about the EU Rule of Law Crisis' (*Verfassungsblog: On Matters Constitutional*, 17 October 2022), https://verfassungsblog.de/misconceptions-rol/, accessed 16 March 2026

[275] Armin von Bogdandy and Luke Dimitrios Spieker, 'Transformative Constitutionalism in Luxembourg: How the Court Can Support Democratic Transitions' (2022) 29 *Columbia Journal of European Law* 65.

[276] See also ch 4.

dialogues and consultation, as well as the practice of mini-publics.[277] The latter featured prominently during the Convention on the Future of Europe and, most recently, were integrated by the Commission into its law- and policy-making.[278] The literature on these last developments has been somewhat sceptical of their current potential for enhancing democratic legitimacy, while at the same time underlining that further experimentation and improvements over time might allow this form of participation to make a participatory democracy contribution.[279]

The third development relates to lobbying in the EU and the developments post-Lisbon to attempt to regulate it, as well as the connection to the role of lobbying in EU 'participatory democracy'. The important role that interest groups play for governance outcomes in the EU, in terms of knowledge contribution, is widely recognised. Considering the complex task of EU regulation, and the relatively limited resources of the Commission, historically and currently, interest groups offer specialised knowledge and insights into the fields in which they operate.[280] In offering a reaction to intended legislative measures, they also function as a litmus test of their broader impacts and implementation.[281] Scholars have also argued, post-Lisbon, that 'participatory democracy' in the EU must find expression through participation and advocacy by business firms and economic actors. Aside from the output potential of their contribution, their general role in the deliberative arena, in offering contrasting positions to other actors and raising issues for debate, is highlighted. Furthermore, the assumption that non-profit groups or civil society act in the public interest is also contested, with the public interest, as such, being open to interpretation.[282]

However, some systemic imbalances of access and influence highlight the problem with ascribing to lobbying the virtue of democratic participation, and the challenge of finding its place in a participatory democracy framework. Despite the noted diversification of interest groups, more than half of the estimated 30,000 permanent lobbyists based in Brussels still represent business interests,[283] and current empirical research suggests that earlier assessments of the EU's system of interest representation as a form of 'elite pluralism' still hold true.[284] Empirical

[277] See, eg Sofia Ranchordás, 'Consultations, Citizen Narratives and Evidence-Based Regulation: The Strange Case of the Consultation on the Collaborative Economy' (2017) 19 *European Journal of Law Reform* 52; European Court of Auditors, '"Have Your Say!" : Commission's Public Consultations Engage Citizens, but Fall Short of Outreach Activities' (Publications Office, 2019) 14; Alberto Alemanno and James Organ, 'The Case for Citizen Participation in the European Union: A Theoretical Perspective on EU Participatory Democracy' (HEC Research Papers Series 1376, 2020).

[278] See, eg 'European Citizens' Panels', https://citizens.ec.europa.eu/index_en, accessed 6 February 2026.

[279] Hierlemann and others, *Under Construction* (n 201).

[280] See, eg Mendes, *Participation in EU Rule-Making* (n 31) 111–12.

[281] ibid.

[282] Kohler-Koch, 'Civil Society and EU Democracy' (n 165).

[283] This number excludes lobbyists that travel in and out of Brussels daily to engage with EU policy-makers: Coen, Katsaitis and Vannoni, *Business Lobbying* (n 209) 9.

[284] ibid.

research also suggests that it is rare for business interests, although diverse, to face off against each other in terms of lobbying,[285] and business interests and citizen groups predominantly take unified positions against each other in policy debates, while those groups that are 'lobbying outsiders' remain as such across different levels of governance.[286] Business associations also tend to be more Europeanised than other groups.[287] The dominance of business interests and elitism is not all-embracing or without nuance in the EU: business interests are not monolithic, and, beyond resources, it is well known that the types of interests that mobilise around policy areas depend on sociological and historical institutional factors. However, concerns about business lobbying are not just a question of an imbalance of influence and voice from a democracy perspective, reflecting a broader understanding of the limits of pluralism. Crucially, the unethical practices of lobbying pose challenges to the democratic process. The OECD, in a recent study on lobbying, paints a rather gloomy picture in surveying industry lobbying practices and their effects, especially on major global challenges.[288] Several such practices have, in recent years, been observed in regard to lobbying in the EU, and lobbying by firms in the EU is also on the rise.[289] This has, in turn, also led to the mobilisation, and sometimes birth, of coalitions and interest groups who address the concerns about the influence of lobbying in the EU decision-making process.[290] Such practices are also dealt with directly in literature on regulatory capture, and it is arguably also from this area that language calling for 'ethical' interest representation[291] has migrated to the Agreement on a Transparency Register.

Efforts to address and regulate interest mediation in EU affairs also led to the establishment of the Transparency Register – an open database listing interest representatives, organisations, associations, groups and self-employed individuals who carry out activities to influence the EU policy- and decision-making process.[292] After several years of negotiations and public consultations, and iterations of a register

[285] Andreas Dür and Gemma Mateo, *Interest Group Politics in Multilevel Europe*, 1st edn (Oxford University Press, 2016).

[286] Marie Hojnacki and others, 'Assessing Business Advantage in Washington Lobbying' (2015) 4 *Interest Groups and Advocacy* 205; Andreas Dür, Patrick Bernhagen and David Marshall, 'Interest Group Success in the European Union: When (and Why) Does Business Lose?' (2015) 48 *Comparative Political Studies* 951.

[287] Morten Egeberg, Günther Schaefer and Jarle Trondal, 'The Many Faces of EU Committee Governance' (2003) 26 *West European Politics* 19.

[288] OECD, *Lobbying in the 21st Century: Transparency, Integrity and Access* (OECD, 2021), www.oecd-ilibrary.org/governance/lobbying-in-the-21st-century_c6d8eff8-en, accessed 6 February 2026.

[289] See, eg Adam Satariano and Matina Stevis-Gridneff, 'Big Tech Turns Its Lobbyists Loose on Europe, Alarming Regulators' *The New York Times* (New York, 14 December 2020), www.nytimes.com/2020/12/14/technology/big-tech-lobbying-europe.html, accessed 6 February 2026.

[290] Corporate Europe Observatory (CEO) and ALTER-EU are two examples: Corporate Europe Observatory, https://corporateeurope.org/en, accessed 6 February 2026; 'ALTER-EU –Europe's Campaign for Lobbying Transparency', www.alter-eu.org/, accessed 6 February 2026.

[291] 'Ethical participation' is not a common phrase in democratic theory (although deliberating according to a sense of justice is arguably the same thing). However, the basic requirements for deliberation outlined in deliberative democracy theory clearly preclude 'unethical' lobbying, as it distorts deliberations.

[292] 'Transparency Register', https://ec.europa.eu/transparencyregister/public/homePage.do, accessed 6 February 2026.

which was neither mandatory nor inclusive of the Council, an agreement between the Council, Commission and the Parliament was reached, in 2021, on a mandatory transparency register.[293] The agreement sets out what interest representation or lobbying activities are covered, the type of information registrants are expected to provide, and a code of conduct for registrants and a procedure for complaints about registered organisations.[294] In accordance with the agreement, the three institutions adopt 'conditionality' measures when they decide to make certain interest representation activities conditional upon prior registration in the Transparency Register. In the agreement, a link is made to the dialogue elements of the principle of participatory democracy in Article 11(2) TEU; the agreement states that 'the transparency of that dialogue, is enhanced by having a common register of the organizations and individuals engaged in EU policymaking and policy implementation'.[295]

The fourth and final development relates to how the EU legislative process has evolved. On the one hand, the tendency has persisted to delegate – to either the Commission, committee bodies, regulatory agencies or standardization entities – difficult, controversial or significant features of legislation on which no clarity or consensus exists between the main legislative actors. On the other hand, in empowering the Parliament – the attempt to make up for what was conceived as the main reason for the EUs democratic deficit – the increase in Parliament powers was paralleled by an overall decreasing interest by the electorate in participating in the European electoral process.[296] This challenge also played into the turn to alternative modes of democratic legitimisation that included an increased emphasis on participation instruments within the EU and allowed direct engagement of citizens alongside other stakeholders.[297] Increasingly, institutional deal-making within the ordinary legislative procedure also took place in the so-called trilogues: informal arenas where the institutional actors hammered out legislation based on proposals presented by the Commission. The combination of the trilogues' opaque nature and their dominant position in EU law-making – an overwhelming majority of EU legislation processed through the ordinary procedure was adopted through the use of trilogues[298] – called into question the democratic legitimacy of

[293] See Justin Greenwood and Joanna Dreger, 'The Transparency Register: A European Vanguard of Strong Lobby Regulation?' (2013) 2 *Interest Groups and Advocacy* 139; Kim Fyhr, 'The Reform of the EU Transparency Register' (2021) 17 *Croatian Yearbook of European Law and Policy* 177.

[294] Interinstitutional Agreement of 20 May 2021 on a mandatory transparency register [2021] OJ L207/1.

[295] ibid 1, 2.

[296] Cuesta Lopez, 'The Lisbon Treaty's Provisions on Democratic Principles' (n 231) 123–24; JHH Weiler, 'Does Europe Need a Constitution? Demos, Telos and the German Maastricht Decision' (2010) 1 *European Law Journal* 219. This trend was reversed in the 2019 elections, which saw a turnout of 50.66%: see European Parliament resolution of 26 November 2020 on stocktaking of European elections (2020/2088(INI)) OJ L C425/11.

[297] Such instruments include European Citizens' Consultations, as well as Citizens' Dialogues: see Hierlemann and others, *Under Construction* (n 201) 148–72.

[298] There is also a stated commitment between EU institutions to secure agreement at first reading, wherever possible, within the ordinary legislative procedure: Joint Declaration (EC) on Practical Arrangements for the Co-decision Procedure (Art 251 EC Treaty) [2007] OJ C145/2, para 11.

these proceedings. Through pressure from various corners, including litigation at the CJEU,[299] critical academic scholarship, and pressure from the Ombudsman,[300] the transparency of the process increased. Meanwhile, the system of comitology[301] – the multitude of expert committees which had been influential leading up to the Lisbon Treaty – somewhat decreased, with regulatory networks playing an increasing role, whereby Member States delegated policy-making to the Commission, which in turn delegated the crafting of detailed regulatory policy to European regulatory networks. The arrangement was one of 'double delegation': Member States delegated policy-making to the Commission, which in turn delegated the crafting of detailed regulatory policy to European regulatory networks.[302] Within the regulatory network, the Commission could push for common regulation through policy co-ordination without directly infringing on national sovereignty (while business could potentially undermine policy through the selective provision of information).[303] This network governance approach came as a precursor to the later strategy of agencification.[304] The shift towards a 'single regulatory space' brought about the crystallisation of what were originally regulatory networks and expert groups.[305] Through agencies, experts were selected and given authority to shape a regulatory space.[306]

These developments coincided with the Commission's increased focus on 'smart' and then 'better' law-making (currently under the label 'The Better Regulation Agenda'), which stressed evidence-based law-making, part of a broader global regulatory trend of the late twentieth century.[307] Consultations

[299] Case T-540/15 *Emilio De Capitani v European Parliament* [2018] ECLI:EU:T:2018:167.

[300] Regarding the latter, see, eg European Ombudsman, 'European Ombudsman Strategic Inquiry on the Transparency of Trilogues: Follow-up and First Results', www.ombudsman.europa.eu/en/doc/correspondence/en/88698, accessed 6 February 2026.

[301] On comitology, see, eg Joerges and Neyer, 'From Intergovernmental Bargaining to Deliberative Political Processes' (n 173); Renaud Dehousse, 'Comitology: Who Watches the Watchmen?' (2003) 10 *Journal of European Public Policy* 798; Charles F Sabel and Jonathan Zeitlin, 'Experimentalism in the EU: Common Ground and Persistent Differences: Experimentalism in the EU' (2012) 6 *Regulation & Governance* 410; see also Paul Craig, *EU Administrative Law* (Oxford University Press, 2012) ch 5.

[302] Martino Maggetti and Fabrizio Gilardi, 'The Policy-Making Structure of European Regulatory Networks and the Domestic Adoption of Standards' (2011) 18 *Journal of European Public Policy* 830; Berthold Rittberger and Arndt Wonka, 'Introduction: Agency Governance in the European Union' (2011) 18 *Journal of European Public Policy* 780.

[303] Coen, Katsaitis and Vannoni, *Business Lobbying* (n 209) 47.

[304] Rittberger and Wonka, 'Introduction: Agency Governance in the European Union' (n 302).

[305] David Lewi-Faur, 'Regulation and Regulatory Governance' in David Lewi-Faur (ed), *Handbook on the Politics of Regulation* (Edward Elgar, 2011).

[306] Coen, Katsaitis and Vannoni, *Business Lobbying* (n 209) 47. Currently, more than 40 such entities exist: see Lewi-Faur, 'Regulation and Regulatory Governance' (n 305). Agencification has also been viewed as an attempt to deal with collective action problems or regulatory challenges in a specific field, such as the European securities market: see Andreas Eriksen and Alexander Katsaitis, 'Accountability through Mutual Attunement: How Can Parliamentary Hearings Connect the Elected and the Unelected?' (2023) 38 *Public Policy and Administration* 352.

[307] On the expansive subject of better regulation, see Carol Harlow and Richard Rawlings, *Law and Administration*, 3rd edn (Cambridge University Press, 2009) 251ff; Carol Harlow and Richard Rawlings, *Process and Procedure in EU Administration* (Hart, 2014) 55 ff.; Rick Haythornthwaite, 'Better Regulation in Europe' in Stephen Weatherill (ed), *Better Regulation* (Hart, 2007).

were integrated into the impact assessment (IA) analysis, in many ways a technocratic process centred on evidence collection and evaluation.[308] Additionally, consultation access points throughout the legislative cycle increased, and to a certain degree were streamlined, primarily through a digital access point – the Commission's 'have your say' consultation website. Different actors have been established to review the quality of IAs, including their participatory element of consultations – the Commission's internal Regulatory Scrutiny Board (RSB), the Court of Auditors, and the European Ombudsman – with the latter two initiating (ad hoc) quality control on their own initiative.[309] With these developments and shifts of influence in legislative and policy-making matters – to new (and old) arenas, channels and agencies – non-state actors seeking to access and influence EU action gravitated along. Unsurprisingly, such gravitation often occurred at unequal paces – and while participation in the form of lobbying may not have suffered, participation grounded in democratic legitimacy, it has been argued, remains elusive.[310] Connected to this is the Commission's right of legislative initiative and framing, even if the underlying impulse for EU legislation is not always, de facto, the Commission.[311] The development of the EU legislative process has also been marked by a distinct recent trend: the rise of 'simplification' and Omnibus legislation. This development is elaborated on in the section below

2.5. The rise of crises law-making: Simplification and Omnibus

In the first von der Leyen Commission, law-making remained anchored in the Better Regulation Agenda, even while governance in crises mode normalised fast preparation and narrowed the time and channels through which affected publics and groups could participate.[312] This tension became concrete in a set of high-profile files that were criticised specifically on participation grounds because the Commission had treated urgency as a justification for derogating from core

[308] Anne Meuwese, 'Embedding Consultation Procedures: Law or Institutionalization?' (2011) 17 *European Public Law* 527; see also Alemanno, 'Levelling the EU Participatory Playing Field' (n 261) 117.

[309] For an in-depth analysis of different review bodies, see Anne Meuwese, 'Regulatory Review of European Commission Impact Assessments: What Kind for Which Better Regulation Scenario?' (2017) 19 *European Journal of Law Reform* 16.

[310] See, eg Kohler-Koch and Quittkat (n 151); Alemanno, 'Levelling the EU Participatory Playing Field' (n 261).

[311] A study from 1998 found that the impetus for only 5% of Commission proposals came from the Commission itself. Rather, the drivers were international obligations; requests from EU institutions, Member States, or other actors; or adaptation of EU law to 'new social, technological, and economic data': Damian Chalmers, 'The Democratic Ambiguity of EU Law Making and Its Enemies' in Damian Chalmers and Anthony Arnull (eds), *The Oxford Handbook of European Union Law* (Oxford University Press, 2015) 321.

[312] European Parliament, 'Simplified Sustainability Reporting and Due Diligence Rules for Business', https://www.europarl.europa.eu/pdfs/news/expert/2025/12/press_release/20251211IPR32164/20251211IPR32164_en.pdf, accessed 19 February 2026.

preparatory steps. During the second von der Leyen term, simplification moved from an auxiliary objective to a leitmotif; simplification emerged as an overriding condition for Europe's capacity to act in a harsher geopolitical economy, and the Commission framed competitiveness as requiring systematic burden reduction.[313]

Following the Draghi Report on EU Competitiveness, the Commission announced a simplification agenda targeting a 25 per cent reduction in administrative burdens for all businesses, and 35 per cent for small and medium-sized enterprises (SMEs), by 2030, saving 37.5 billion euros in recurring costs.[314] At the outset of 2025, the Commission's new roadmap, the *Competitiveness Compass*, established the framework for these targets, and systematic regulatory simplification through Omnibus legislation.[315] An Omnibus regulation or directive is a single legislative instrument that simultaneously amends multiple existing legal acts across different policy domains. The Omnibus method itself met with widespread criticism, as it was noted that the Omnibus enabled 'rapid, large-scale policy redirection while circumventing the deliberative safeguards and evidentiary requirements that would apply to discrete amendments pursued through ordinary legislative procedures'.[316]

Omnibus I, presented in February 2025, became the emblematic file because it targeted the flagship Green Deal corporate accountability architecture. Civil society organisations and academics argued that the Commission had weakened laws without proper public consultation or IA, while the Commission defended the approach in competitiveness terms and pointed to stakeholder exchanges it considered sufficient.[317]

In this political and legal environment, the Commission increasingly situated consultation and IA inside a more volatile political economy: rising trade coercion and tariff threats, pressure to 'match' deregulation elsewhere, and anxiety about a weakening rules-based order. In what appears to be a doubling down on this approach, the Commission has announced its aim to revise its Better Regulation framework, with a focus on simplification.[318] Following complaints by civil society

[313] See, eg Philip Blenkinsop and Kate Abnett, 'EU Points Way to Competitive Future to Catch US, China Rivals' (*Reuters*, 29 January 2025), https://www.reuters.com/business/eu-points-way-competitive-future-catch-us-china-rivals-2025-01-29/, accessed 2 February 2026.

[314] European Commission, 'A Simpler and Faster Europe: Communication on Implementation and Simplification' (European Commission 2025) COM (2025) 46 final.

[315] European Commission, 'Competitiveness of the European Economy: Annual Competitiveness Report 2025 - The Competitiveness Compass' COM (2025) 30 final; European Commission, 'Commission Proposes to Cut Red Tape and Simplify Business Environment' (26 February 2025), https://commission.europa.eu/news/commission-proposes-cut-red-tape-and-simplify-business-environment-2025-02-26_en, accessed 19 February 2026.

[316] Alberto Alemanno, 'The Legality of Omnibus Legislation Under EU Law: A Preliminary Analysis of Omnibus I Simplification Directive of CSRD and CSDD and Its Legal Consequences on the EU Legal Order' (*SSRN*, 2025), https://www.ssrn.com/abstract=5727822, accessed 2 February 2026.

[317] See, eg Kate Abnett, 'EU Commission Faces Complaint over Easing of Sustainability Rules' (*Reuters*, 18 April 2025), www.reuters.com/sustainability/climate-energy/eu-commission-faces-complaint-over-easing-sustainability-rules-2025-04-17/, accessed 2 February 2026.

[318] European Commission, 'Commission Work Programme 2026: Europe's Independence Moment' COM (2025) 870 final.

organisations, the Ombudsman found, in late 2025, that the Commission had, in three legislative acts, lacked sufficient grounds to justify skipping an IA and public consultation (and, in some cases, a climate-consistency assessment).[319]

Against this background, calls to formalise, proceduralise and juridify the law- and policy-making process have persisted.[320] Meanwhile, sceptics of judicialization point to the cost and time investments and the adversarial nature brought on by litigation, making it an inefficient and detrimental choice.[321] Closely related is the question as to whether (over-)judicialization of a certain issue decreases the opportunity to formulate meaningful approaches.[322] Furthermore, there have been concerns, in the context of policy- and law-making, that extending participation rights would further exacerbate inequality and favour the well-funded and well-organised.[323] On the opposing side, it has been argued that judicial review of *ex ante* evaluations could constrain regulatory decision-making, ensuring that decision-makers would not benefit from stretching the meaning of soft-law instruments, legal ambiguities and junk scientific evidence in their preferred direction, and would insulate decision-making processes from the fickle sway of politics.[324] It has also been promoted as necessary for the EU law-making process based on its specificities, noting that, given the diminishing role of parliaments in the multilevel setting and the multiplicity of law-makers, the substantive and procedural requirements of legitimate law become even more important.[325]

Review of legislation by courts emerges here as a democratic asset, as principles of better law-making reveal democratic guarantees.[326] Furthermore, parties who are underrepresented in the institutional framework of decision-making can thus be assisted to obtain a motivated answer to the question whether the presumed

[319] European Ombudsman, 'Recommendation on the European Commission's Failure to Comply with Its Better Regulation Guidelines in Preparing Several Legislative Proposals'.

[320] See, eg Alemanno, 'Levelling the EU Participatory Playing Field' (n 261) 125.

[321] For a general argument, see Neil K Komesar, *Imperfect Alternatives: Choosing Institutions in Law, Economics, and Public Policy* (University of Chicago Press, 1997) 3; for an EU specific one, see Busschaert, *Participatory Democracy* (n 159) 118–19; as stated, the Commission has itself expressed that judicial review of its consultation activities would make the regulatory process too rigid and cumbersome. There are also old standing general concerns with juridification: that, rather than promoting co-operation among actors in the system, judicialisation tends to encourage defensive action, where parties use courts to make inflexible demands: see Robert A Kagan, *Adversarial Legalism: The American Way of Law*, 2nd edn (Harvard University Press, 2019).

[322] For a classic case, see Kagan, *Adversarial Legalism* (n 321); for a more recent example, see Anette Bringedal Houge and Kjersti Lohne, 'End Impunity! Reducing Conflict-Related Sexual Violence to a Problem of Law' (2017) 51 *Law & Society Review* 755, 755–89.

[323] Busschaert, *Participatory Democracy* (n 159) 119–25.

[324] Cass R Sunstein, 'Cost-Benefit Analysis, Who's Your Daddy?' (2016) 7 *Journal of Benefit-Cost Analysis* 107, 107.

[325] Anne Meuwese and Patricia Popelier, 'Legal Implications of Better Regulation: A Special Issue' (2011) 17 *European Public Law* 455, 465; see also Joana Mendes, 'The Democratic Foundations of the Union: Representative Democracy, Complementarity and the Legal Challenge of Article 11 TEU' in Adam Lazowski and Steven Blockmans (eds), *Research Handbook on EU Institutional Law* (Edward Elgar Publishing, 2016).

[326] Meuwese and Popelier, 'Legal Implications of Better Regulation' (n 325) 465.

neglect of their interests was justified.[327] The protection of legally protected interests that may be neglected in the political process also supports juridification of participation in a rights-based fashion.[328] Similarly, it has been argued that, while juridification is not a panacea for the actual lacunae in the overall openness of the EU machinery, it is necessary to secure effectiveness and democratic empowerment of society.[329]

Regardless of the appeal of, or distaste for, the juridification of participation, the fact remains that, through the Lisbon Treaty, participation, including in the form of consultation, is now constitutionalised. The question then is, rather, in what way the legal framing deals with the difficult questions that have followed the gradual opening of EU governance and how this impacts on existing and future channels for participation.

2.6. The imperatives and limits of complementarity

The review of the evolution of participatory democracy as a normative goal in the Union, cemented in the Treaties and followed by a range of institutional practices and democratic experimentation, suggests that any relevant analytical approach to understanding complementarity needs to be inclusive enough to capture the varied and rich insights of the debate on the role of democratic participation, including deliberation, without losing sight of some of the key goals of participatory democracy theory which inspired the participatory norm and its constitutionalisation. The literature review and the analysis of how participatory democracy is featured in the debates on the democratic legitimacy of the EU also highlighted that participatory democracy as featured in EU democracy discourse is used to signify different but related things, often depicted as representing either a functional or a principled understanding of participation. Some of the normative yardsticks for participatory democracy-related activities in the EU, including the Commission's consultations, when construed as such, are inclusion, equality, effectiveness and public review.[330] Yet these values are all also associated with representative democracy.[331] As participatory democracy in the EU legal framework is complementary to representative

[327] Meuwese and Popelier, 'Legal Implications of Better Regulation' (n 325); commenting on the relationship between the RSB and Courts, Popelier suggests that, while administrative regulatory oversight is recommendable, it does not make up for a lack of judicial review: see Patricia Popelier, 'A Legal Perspective on Regulatory Impact Assessments' (International Symposium: Regulatory Impact Analyses, Luxembourg 23–24 November 2017).

[328] Mendes argues that participation rights are arguably the 'appropriate means' to give citizens and representative associations an opportunity to make their views known according to Article 11 TEU: see Mendes, 'Participation and the Role of Law after Lisbon' (n 2) 1862.

[329] Alemanno, 'Unpacking the Principle of Openness in EU Law' (n 270).

[330] Kohler-Koch and Quittkat (n 151) 175.

[331] ibid.

democracy (the 'founding' democratic feature, according to the legal text), focus should rest on what distinguishes participation from representation.[332]

Kohler-Koch and Rittberger's model, then, emerges as helpful tool for filtering the insights from democracy theory, using the legal imperative of complementarity as a starting point. The heuristic frame of contrasts is broad enough to capture the different strands of the participatory democracy debate in relation to the EU without sacrificing core concerns. One elaboration, as well as one adjustment to the framework, is, however, in order. First, the adopted framework must naturally be seen in light of the specific nature of the EU, which is that the EU is a multi-level polity. This view is in line with the overall approach of this book in approaching law-making.

Second, in adopting this frame, I do not take on Kohler-Koch and Rittberger's assumption that the normative goal of citizen participation in EU policy- and law-making must be fulfilled squarely through the intermediary of civil society. This dimension of their framework is, therefore, broadened to include citizens, as the sole reliance on civil society appears too constrictive. It is clear from the debates on the democratic legitimacy of the EU that the question of direct or even indirect participation of citizens in the EU is contested.[333] To a certain degree, adding citizens to the framework may be an issue of semantics. Kohler-Koch and Rittberger, in discussing how participatory democracy as a legal and moral norm should be understood in the EU, articulates that civil society must contain certain qualitative features to contribute to democratic legitimacy, ultimately deriving its value from what they label 'enlightened' participatory citizens within civil society.[334] In this sense, civil society which is entrenched in citizen participation attends to the democratic value of citizen participation. Over a decade ago, Kohler-Koch argued that, when looking at the way EU institutions function, as well as the level of citizen interest in participation opportunities, 'the obvious conclusion' is that participatory democracy in the foreseeable future must be given expression primarily through interest-group representation, highlighting how an empirical approach is crucial.[335]

In this context, it must be said that the possibility of something resembling regular mass citizen deliberation in policy- and law-making with tangible results has, as has been discussed, already been empirically observed, albeit the prominent examples lie outside of Europe. In the European context, it is true that citizens play

[332] Art 10 TEU clearly states the Union is founded upon representative democracy. See also Case C-418/18 P *Grégor Puppinck and Others* (n 272), para 65.

[333] De Schutter, 'Europe in Search of Its Civil Society' (n 227); Stijn Smismans, *Law, Legitimacy, and European Governance: Functional Participation in Social Regulation* (Oxford University Press, 2004); Beate Kohler-Koch and Berthold Rittberger, 'Review Article: The "Governance Turn" in EU Studies' (2006) 44 *Journal of Common Market Studies* 27; Grevén, 'Some Considerations' (n 15); Stijn Smismans, 'New Modes of Governance and the Participatory Myth' (2008) 31 *West European Politics* 874; Stephan Bredt, 'Prospects and Limits of Democratic Governance in the EU: European Law Journal' (2011) 17 *European Law Journal* 35; Curtin, Mair and Papadopoulos, *Accountability and European Governance* (n 185); Mendes, *Participation in EU Rule-Making* (n 31); Mendes, 'Participation and the Role of Law after Lisbon' (n 2); Busschaert, *Participatory Democracy* (n 159).

[334] Kohler-Koch and Rittberger, 'Charting Crowded Territory' (n 21).

[335] Kohler-Koch and Quittkat (n 151) 11.

a minor role in participatory governance processes compared with interest groups, civil society, and so on. However, different forms of direct citizen engagement in the EU have increased over the last decade.[336] Furthermore, clearly spelling out citizens as the emphasis of participatory democracy means explicitly paying close attention to the value of equality. It also calibrates the perspective to attend to citizenship and relevant geographical concerns and multi-level EU governance; civil society and the key actors operating within such groups may primarily be located at the European level, whereas citizens are often set in their local or national social and legal contexts. Finally, including citizens in the framework allows for better capture of the developments in democratic theory and practice where political participation beyond the ballot box is clearly not geared towards civil society. Such practices include consulting directly with citizens online, through activism and social movements not confined to civil society, as well as the continued and recently deepened experimentation with mini-publics at the EU and Member State level. The following, then, briefly restates what each of these dimensions mean for a normative foundation of the principle of participatory democracy.

2.6.1. The intrinsic value of participation: Participation as the end justifying the means?

As is clear from the analysis thus far, participation, as a democratic principle, implies a normative shift from an instrumental to an intrinsic view of participation.[337] This perspective sees participation and the participatory process as ends and not just as means. Connected to this view is the promotion of more direct participation because of its educative role, serving the self-development and civic virtues of the individual, indispensable to the individual's wellbeing, and providing them with social capital.[338] But beyond this, the intrinsic view on participation, similar to a rights-based one, is grounded on the inherent dignity and equality of each individual, with participation expressing this reality. In the EU setting, the institutionalisation of a participatory norm has particularly focused on the opportunity to participate of affected individuals, groups and actors, and the intrinsic perspective adds to this practice that the equality of individuals and groups is central to attend to, and that participation is valuable because it respects and expresses the dignity of persons affected.[339]

[336] See, eg Hierlemann and others, *Under Construction* (n 201) 74–172.

[337] Mendes also argues that the link established by Art 11 TEU, between participation and democracy, is a normative yardstick against which to assess the participation practices: Mendes, 'Participation and the Role of Law after Lisbon' (n 2) 1860.

[338] This is discussed in ch 3, s 3.1. See also Robert D Putnam, *Bowling Alone: The Collapse and Revival of American Community*, Revised and updated (Simon & Schuster Paperbacks, 2020).

[339] This is discussed in ch 3, s 3.1. See also David Feldman, 'Constitutionalism, Deliberative Democracy, and Human Rights' in John Morison, Kieran McEvoy and Gordon Anthony (eds), *Judges, Transition, and Human Rights* (Oxford University Press, 2007).

As a complementary feature, emphasis on the intrinsic value of participation does not imply that functional perspectives of rationality and efficiency, or indeed the overall epistemic function of participation, including deliberation, are abandoned. Rather, such considerations must be balanced with, and, crucially, sometimes also defer to, the inherent value of participation by those affected. This signifies paying close attention to both inclusion and equality in the participation process. It implies mindfulness of the importance of reaching out to many, but also the value of including voices which are, for various reasons, traditionally excluded in the representative democracy framework, marginalised, or just not present – particularly in cases when they are affected by EU action. For participation in EU law-making, it could imply selection of participants or targeting that is not just based on interest groups or the perceived need of the legislator for expertise or regulatory efficiency.

One established insight from democracy theory and practice – which has largely been confirmed in the EU setting – is that self-selection processes on their own carry great risks for exacerbating imbalances and inequalities in terms of access, regardless of the participation medium. This means, for example, that in many situations the duty to consult might also require tailoring the consultation practice to such groups or efforts to facilitate inputs from local actors and non-organised civil society.

2.6.2. Deliberation as a complement to voting

In the context of the EU, deliberative democracy has framed legitimacy as possibly flowing from deliberation in several contexts, including the comitology system, the open method of co-ordination, civil dialogue, social dialogue, and the Commission's consultation regime.[340] Frameworks were also deployed to view EU governance as a holistic deliberative system. Acknowledgement of, and responsiveness to, difference, adherence to the principle of justification, as well as transparency and publicity of deliberation, consequently meant an emphasis on learning processes that provided central inputs for theorisation drawing on deliberation for democratic legitimacy in the EU setting.[341]

In terms of complementarity, the inherent tension between representative and participatory democracy is highlighted in both theoretical and empirical accounts

[340] See ch 3, s 3.2; also Cohen and Sabel, 'Directly-Deliberative Polyarchy' (n 124); Joerges and Neyer, 'From Intergovernmental Bargaining to Deliberative Political Processes' (n 173).

[341] Kohler-Koch and Fink summarily argue that, from the standpoint of deliberative democracy, participation must be evaluated by investigating the plurality of voices, the quality of communication, and the emergence of a European public space: Beate Kohler-Koch and Barbara Finke, 'The Institutional Shaping of EU–Society Relations: A Contribution to Democracy via Participation?' (2007) 3 *Journal of Civil Society* 205, 216.

with regard to deliberation.[342] As touched upon in the discussion of the origins and elaboration of participatory democracy, some empirical research suggests that partisan political participation and deliberation do not go together:

> either people will be willing to engage with dissenting others and enjoy the epistemic benefits of exposure to diverse or conflicting views, or they will be willing to vote, campaign for candidates and generally be engaged as partisans in the political arena.[343]

Some scholars go further and suggest that representative democracy is not conducive to deliberation.[344] Acknowledging this tension without accepting foreclosure suggests that participation instruments which are based on the principle of participatory democracy should promote a complementary yet distinct vision of democracy, moving away from the methods of contestation, which so often are sought for in debates on EU democracy. Such methods might better find their place in the parliamentary setting. As Mark Warren puts it:

> because representatives function within a context that combines public visibility with adversarial relations, they must weigh the strategic and symbolic impact of speech. Thus, representative institutions have limited capacities for deliberation, which requires a suspension of the strategic impact of communication in favour of persuasion and argument.[345]

Drawing legitimacy from the participation process would, then, potentially translate into procedural guarantees,[346] or in establishing participation arenas or channels which emphasise deliberation or create an environment which is more conducive to deliberation. This means the decision-maker weighing contributions based on substance and not affiliation. Arguably, it also highlights how certain principles of equality and objectivity play out when placing them in a deliberative rather than an interest-based framework characterised by, for instance, diversity and inclusion as well as equal consideration.

To give effect to qualitative features of the participation process, the law-making spaces of deliberation would, in any case, need to include equal consideration of potential participants, as well as equality of access, including 'active' transparency and access to information, as well as meaningful exchange. This may include transparency in criteria for participant selection. Crucially, procedural requirements in the spirit of deliberation mean that there is some form of exchange which implies, at minimum, adequate feedback mechanisms. This may include recording

[342] At least the way representative democracy is most frequently construed and practised.
[343] Landemore, *Open Democracy* (n 7) 37–38; see also Mutz, *Hearing the Other Side* (n 102).
[344] Landemore, *Open Democracy* (n 7) 35–39.
[345] Landemore cites Warren on parliaments' deliberative capacity: see ibid 132.
[346] For arguments in this direction, see Mendes, 'Participation and the Role of Law after Lisbon' (n 2) 1863–72; Alemanno, 'Levelling the EU Participatory Playing Field' (n 261) 120–32; see also 'ReNEUAL – the Research Network on EU Administrative Law', www.reneual.eu/, accessed 6 February 2026.

how participatory input has or has not impacted on a decision-making process, and why.[347] This procedural element would thus fulfil some minimum level of substantive balance while also accounting clearly for choices to provide opportunity, select, attract, or empower potential participants.

In terms of the decision-making power with which deliberative bodies or processes may be endowed, the complementary role of participatory democracy arguably excludes co-decision and direct law-making power.[348] And herein lies an important limitation to the idea of complementarity in the EU setting: deliberation can inject legitimacy into the democratic processes through either input, throughput or output, but must always be viewed in light of the institutional balance in the EU system. This means that participation in the form of, for example, deliberative spaces can be dispersed in a multi-government setting, but it cannot be configured towards displacement of the role of EU institutions or Member States in, for example, the ordinary legislative process.[349]

The function of deliberation, in addition to advancing the ideals associated with the intrinsic value of participation discussed, is also epistemic. We sometimes see that the epistemic orientation in deliberative democratic theory leads to a focus on 'expert' participation, as expert participation can be seen as promoting 'truth-sensitivity' and the function of knowledge use, in line with the idea of evidence-based practices and legislation. Consulting those affected is construed in terms of the knowledge they possess, as well as the role they might play in the implementation of policies, decisions and legislation. The same orientation may, however, also lead to focusing on citizen and lay deliberation, as 'only the man who wears the shoe knows where it pinches', implying that ordinary citizens possess information that experts lack.[350]

The debates on participatory democracy and the focus on deliberation have emphasised the centrality of interdependence. In EU deliberative supranationalism, interdependence is seen as reflected through European integration and the EU project itself, as well as being something that EU policy-makers and legislators (including when representing their Member States) advance and generate through deliberative interaction occurring at different levels.[351] One can also think of interdependence in terms of the relationship between, for example, Commission or

[347] This stands in contrast to current practices, where one of the most frequent critiques of the EU Regulatory Scrutiny Board has been the persistent tendency of the Commission to not faithfully represent the outcome of law-making consultation in its impact assessments: see 'Regulatory Scrutiny Board: Annual Report 2022' 21, https://commission.europa.eu/system/files/2023-05/RSB_2022_1.pdf, accessed 7 August 2023.

[348] As we have seen from the debates, this is a matter of contention between some participatory and deliberative democrats, and between deliberative democrats, within and beyond the EU context.

[349] This is somewhat tricky to untangle but would have to be configured based on a constitutional-legal interpretation, which includes attending to institutional balance: see ch 4.

[350] Sabel and Simon, citing Dewey on this point: Charles F Sabel and William H Simon, 'Democratic Experimentalism' in Justin Desautels-Stein and Christopher Tomlins (eds), *Searching for Contemporary Legal Thought* (Cambridge University Press, 2017) 486.

[351] Joerges and Neyer, 'From Intergovernmental Bargaining to Deliberative Political Processes' (n 173).

the Parliament in relation to stakeholders and civil society, in terms of knowledge exchange for influence. However, in terms of the democratic value of deliberation, which serves as a counterpoint to pluralism and lobbying, interdependence is one underlying assumption which allows for deliberation towards the common good, rather than bargaining and negotiation.[352] In general, however, one of the dilemmas of consociation is that it may entrench divisions rather than produce a common commitment to the welfare of the whole, because, as David Feldman puts it, 'it penalizes people who do not define their identities by reference to one of the separate constituent peoples'.[353]

Finally, participation and 'consultation' can be redefined through the lens of deliberation. The range and depth of democratic innovations over the past decade have demonstrated that participation or consultation should not be interpreted with reference to past practices of EU institutions or Member States but, rather, the opportunity of potential practices to contribute to democratic legitimacy. This means that deliberative spaces such as citizens' panels and citizens' assemblies, as well as other practices, can be viewed through the lens of the procedural practices discussed.

2.6.3. Bringing in citizens and civil society

The third function of participatory democracy as a complement to representative democracy is in its focus on participation by citizens and civil society in contrast to institutions. The question as to the extent to which the lay citizen is, or should, be involved in EU participatory democracy and governance is a matter of debate.

One reason why involving more individuals in democratic participation is crucial, according to participatory democracy, is the broader educative role of participation. Democratic participation requires democratic competence, which must be learned through the exercise of active responsibility.[354] Participation itself is seen as fostering this capacity-building process in an iterative cycle.[355] Finally, increased citizen participation has also been promoted for its epistemic advantages; this was touched upon earlier in the discussion of the functions of deliberation. Such research argues that citizens' narratives, containing situated knowledge through lived experiences, if rightly contextualised, are not only coherent with evidence-based law-making standards, but can make valuable contributions to law-making.[356] More crucially, the broad public participation involving many citizens is valuable and tied to the understanding that when certain groups cannot

[352] Much of the literature of interest-based representation and lobbying is either pluralist, rational-choice-oriented or grounded in deliberative democracy.

[353] Feldman, 'Constitutionalism, Deliberative Democracy, and Human Rights' (n 339) 453.

[354] See John Braithwaite, 'Democracy, Community, and Problem Solving' in Gale Burford and Joe Hudson (eds), Family Group Conferencing (Routledge, 2000) 132–33.

[355] Pateman, *Participation and Democratic Theory* (n 8).

[356] For instance, in unregulated areas: see Ranchordás, 'Consultations, Citizen Narratives and Evidence-Based Regulation' (n 277).

influence the political agenda or decision-making, or gain relevant information to assess how well policy alternatives serve their needs, for example because they are unorganised or excluded, they are likely to be ill-served by laws and policies.[357] The value of equality of citizens can be fulfilled either through direct citizen participation or through (new) forms of representation, including prominently through civil society.

Distinct conceptions of civil society in the EU were identified: civil society has been construed as the representation of different voices and interests in society, or as the autonomous participation of organisations in the public sphere.[358] It has been defined as organisations mediating between spheres of society, or simply organisations orientated towards the public good.[359] In analysing civil society in the EU, many scholars have opted for the 'organised civil society' approach, defined mainly as voluntary organisations – distinct from state and market actors – which aim to influence these spheres through activism and activities in a European segmented public sphere.[360] It is also argued that this approach is better suited to analysing the reality of the EU political system and the way in which interests are organised.[361]

There are other legitimate reasons for wanting to differentiate market interest from civil society. One of the main goals of participatory democracy is to infuse corporate actors with its rationales and practices – and such change has largely not occurred.[362] There is also no doubt that the prevalence, or dominance, of market actors in the EU policy process deserves appropriate attention. It is also worth noting that the conceptual divide between market actors and non-profit organisations in certain areas appears increasingly blurry.[363] This being said, it should be kept in mind that the notion of civil society in participatory democracy emphasises organisations which are oriented towards the common good. This chimes well with the definition of civil society which the EU institutions in their own view subscribe to, as 'social action carried out by individuals or groups who are neither connected to nor managed by state authorities', and the definition of a civil society organisation as an 'organisational structure whose members serve the general interest through a democratic process and which plays the role of mediator between public authorities and citizens'.[364] Central to the democratic legitimacy of civil society in the EU is its mediator role, its ability to channel the voice of citizens

[357] Fung, 'Varieties of Participation in Complex Governance' (n 34) 70.

[358] Beate Kohler-Koch, 'The Three Worlds of European Civil Society—What Role for Civil Society for What Kind of Europe?' (2009) 28 *Policy and Society* 47.

[359] ibid.

[360] De Schutter, 'Europe in Search of Its Civil Society' (n 227) 198–217.

[361] It accounts for the above-mentioned multiplicity of access points and fundamental plurality of interests in the EU. It also acknowledges the difficulty of drawing a clear line between organisations advocating sectoral and general interests, and better suits the way in which the EU has defined civil society. It thus has a better analytical correspondence with the object that will be analysed: Kohler-Koch and Quittkat (n 151) 8–9.

[362] See Pateman, 'Participatory Democracy Revisited' (n 3) 7–10; Mansbridge, *Beyond Adversary Democracy* (n 86).

[363] Consider, for instance, the issue of regulating the shared economy.

[364] European Union, 'EUR-Lex, Civil_society_organisation', https://eur-lex.europa.eu/EN/legal-content/glossary/civil-society-organisation.html, accessed 6 February 2026.

and certain groups, its overall connection to citizens, and its orientation towards the common good.

2.7. Summary

After exploring the theoretical origins of participatory democracy, an inclusive understanding of the concept of 'participatory democracy' was adopted which allowed for capture of democracy debates at the European level incorporating contributions written in deliberative, associative and direct democracy traditions. The review also demonstrated how participatory democracy surfaced directly and indirectly in the debates leading up to the drafting of the principle, as well as EU institutional documents. In analysing how an understanding of a 'more participatory democracy'[365] emerged in the debates on democracy in the Union, it was clear that participation in EU governance was viewed from both a functional and a principled perspective, with the latter gaining ascendancy in the events leading up to drafting of the Constitution. The participatory norm which was constitutionalised did not just represent a functional understanding but a principled one. Establishing links and contacts to citizens was emphasised.

Participatory democracy as featured in the EU democracy discourse prominently came across as a right of those affected by a decision to be able to participate in its formation. However, in the academic literature and the documents of the EU institutions, and in the drafting process of the democratic principles of the Lisbon Treaty, it was clear that the role of participatory democracy was complementary to that of representative democracy. And this complementarity would have to play out in a multi-level polity, as well as in the political and legal context which followed the Lisbon Treaty. Against this background, in order to distil some of these insights into a normative framework which could undergird an understanding of the principle of participatory democracy, I drew on Kohler-Koch and Rittberger's framework juxtaposing elements of representative democracy in the EU with elements of participatory democracy, emphasising the intrinsic value of participation, deliberation and an emphasis on citizens and civil society as participation protagonists. The elaboration on the meaning of these core elements, combined with an overall reading of participatory democracy as an inclusive concept that is still committed to government by the citizens, provides the grounding for the legal analysis in the following chapter.

[365] European Commission, Commission discussion paper 'The Commission and non-governmental organisations: building a stronger partnership' COM/2000/0011 final, indent 3.1.4.

3

The Principle of Participatory Democracy: Instruments, Obligations, Rights

The principle of participatory democracy represents a turning point in the constitutional framing of democracy on the European continent. Europe has a strong tradition of democracy, but one that, in legal terms, has been almost exclusively expressed through representative democracy. Noting, for instance, that the European Convention on Human Rights (ECHR) is completely silent on non-electoral participation, Steiner argues that the Convention suggests that 'the tradition of liberal democracy from which it developed insists *firmly but solely* upon a government's commitment to an open political process culminating in periodic contested elections'.[1] The Lisbon Treaty's Democratic Principles, therefore, demonstrate an evolution of the European tradition of democracy in ways beyond its supranational configuration.

The aim of the preceding chapter was to gain a deeper understanding of the underlying theoretical foundations and history of the principle of participatory democracy, distilling insights on its purpose. The analysis highlighted the multilevel character of the EU, which should inform an understanding of participatory democracy. It arrived at a framing which stressed how the intrinsic value of participation should complement the instrumental perspective on participation and deliberation complement voting, all secured through strong emphasis on participation by civil society and citizens. Proceeding from these core elements, some possible procedural imperatives were also identified. Based on this understanding, this chapter now explores the principle of participatory democracy, drawing on the method of legal interpretation, and asks what key obligations and rights the principle entails.

After exploring the wording and constitutional context of the principle of participatory democracy enshrined in Article 11 TEU and Article 10(3) TEU, associated rights featured in Articles 20–24 TFEU and 15 TFEU are discussed. The analysis then turns to the relationship between the constitutional underpinnings of consultation and administrative law more broadly.

[1] Henry J Steiner, 'Political Participation as a Human Right' (1988) 1 *Harvard Human Rights Yearbook* 77, 96 (emphasis added).

Based on these insights, the analysis explores if, and in what way, the legal principle of participatory democracy can constitute the ground for judicial review by the CJEU. It also analyses Article 11 TEU and Article 10(3) TEU as potentially embedded in the procedural review of the Court. Taken together, these insights form the basis for mapping out the substance of the principle of participatory democracy and determining key procedural requirements flowing from the principle of participatory democracy.

This section begins by analysing Article 11 TEU, as the main Treaty provision relating to participatory democracy, and this is followed by an in-depth analysis of Article 10(3) TEU in the next section, before it moves on to other related rights.

3.1. Voice, dialogue, consultation and citizens' initiative: A textual analysis of Article 11 TEU

The provisions of Article 11 TEU establish normative standards binding on the institutions,[2] and can be headlined, in the order they appear there, as voice, dialogue, consultation, and citizens' initiative. These four points deal with different forms or mechanisms of participation in EU governance with different addressees.[3] The first requires the institutions to, 'by appropriate means, give citizens and representative associations the opportunity to make known and publicly exchange their views in all areas of Union action', the second that the institutions maintain 'an open, transparent and regular dialogue with representative associations and civil society', and the third that the Commission 'carry out broad consultations with parties concerned in order to ensure that the Union's actions are coherent and transparent'.[4] The last point provides citizens with the right to prompt the Commission to submit a proposal for legislation, provided that the citizens number at least 1 million.[5]

While these mechanisms differ in their immediate aims, as participatory democracy instruments they should all be viewed as serving to enhance citizen engagement with the Union and its institutions.[6] This is clearly spelled out in the preamble of the regulation laying out the functioning of the Europeans Citizens'

[2] Joana Mendes, 'Participation and the Role of Law after Lisbon: A Legal View on Article 11 TEU' (2011) 48 *Common Market Law Review* 1860.

[3] Lock labels these different 'elements' of participatory democracy: Tobias Lock, 'Article 11 TEU' in Manuel Kellerbauer, Marcus Klamert and Jonathan Tomkin (eds), *The EU Treaties and the Charter of Fundamental Rights: A Commentary* (Oxford University Press, 2019).

[4] Art 11 TEU.

[5] Art 11(4) TEU.

[6] 'The aim of the concept is, therefore, to achieve greater integration of citizens and civil society in the Union's decision-making process': see Ricardo Jesús García Macho, 'Article 11 [Participatory Democracy]' in Hermann-Josef Blanke and Stelio Mangiameli (eds), *The Treaty on European Union (TEU): A Commentary* (Springer, 2013).

Initiative, stressing how the initiative must be viewed in light of all the mechanisms 'by which citizens may bring certain issues to the attention of institutions of the Union and which consist notably of dialogue with representative associations and civil society, consultations with parties concerned, petitions and applications to the Ombudsman'.[7]

Each of these mechanisms will be analysed in turn.

3.1.1. Voice and dialogue – a framework for 'ethical' and transparent interest representation

To begin with, who are the duty-bearers and addressees of Article 11(1) and 11(2) TEU? The fact that the two articles bind not just the Council, Parliament and Commission, but all the EU institutions, including the European Central Bank, the European Court of Auditors and the Court of Justice, to a standard of voice and dialogue may indeed reflect an oversight on the part of the drafters.[8] The application of Article 11(1) and 11(2) TEU would, in any case, need to be applied in a tailored way, depending on the relevant institution.[9] Regarding the legal subjects addressed in the paragraphs, different segments of the public are mentioned in the different points of the article.[10] In Article 11(1) and 11(2) TEU, citizens, representative associations and civil society are mentioned.[11] Citizens, in this context, refers to EU citizens as outlined in Article 9 TEU.[12] Representative associations are not defined in the Treaties but feature in EU institutional documents and generally have the aim of influencing policy-making at the European level.[13] As such,

[7] Regulation (EU) 2019/788 of the European Parliament and of the Council of 17 April 2019 on the European citizens' initiative [2019] OJ L130/55 preamble para 1.

[8] Mendes, 'Participation and the Role of Law after Lisbon' (n 2) 1869.

[9] ibid.

[10] Finding the article unclear, Closa asks who the addressees are; years later, scholars are still asking the same question. See Carlos Closa, 'Constitutional prospects of European citizenship and new forms of democracy' in Giuliano Amato, Hervé Bribosia and Bruno de Witte (eds), *Genèse et destinée de la Constitution européenne: commentaire du traité établissant une constitution pour l'Europe à la lumière des travaux préparatoires et perspectives d'avenir* (Bruylant, 2007); Hanneke van Eijken, *EU Citizenship & the Constitutionalisation of the European Union* (Europa Law Publishing, 2015); Lock, 'Article 11 TEU' (n 3).

[11] Art 11(1) and (2) TEU.

[12] Art 9 TEU. See also Lock, 'Article 11 TEU' (n 3). Schrauwen notes that Art 9 refers to 'its' citizens, ie Union citizens, and concludes that Art 10(3) TEU has the same *rationae personae*: Annette Schrauwen, 'European Union Citizenship in the Treaty of Lisbon: Any Change at All?' (2007) 15 *Maastricht Journal of European and Comparative Law* 55, 56.

[13] Matthias Ruffert, 'Art. 11 EUV' in Christian Calliess and Matthias Ruffert (eds), *EU-VERTRAG*, 6th edn (Beck, 2022) para 12. Lock, for example, includes trade unions and industry groups: Lock, 'Article 11 TEU' (n 3). Blanke and Mangiameli assert that the reference to representative associations is essentially a reference to organised pressure groups and lobbying: García Macho, 'Article 11' (n 6); Bouza demonstrates that the term was not really defined or discussed during the drafting of the Convention. Although there was a notion that representativeness of sorts was important for an institutionalised civil dialogue, discussions were focused on the broad contribution of civil society to European integration. Civil society organisations and NGOs left the debate about the definition and the characteristics of

the openness and transparency of the process demanded by Article 11(1) 'is an important step towards controlling these associations and avoiding opacity'.[14] The separate mention of representative associations and civil society can also be attributed to the special role representative associations have had in social dialogue within the European Economic and Social Committee, (EESC) as well as being taken to indicate that civil society should be conceived of as groups whose aim is the public good in some form.[15] As was discussed in the previous chapter, there is no single or accepted definition for civil society in EU affairs. However, Advocate General Wahl argues that the EU recognises the special role that charitable and voluntary associations play in contributing to a just society through, inter alia, 'the dialogue between EU institutions and civil society required by Article 11 TEU and Article 15 TFEU'.[16] This role is indirectly confirmed by the CJEU in recognising the special status of non-profit organisations in EU internal market law.[17] The above makes it sufficiently clear that civil society, in Article 11(2) TEU, does not refer to for-profit economic actors or associations.

At first glance, the demands towards EU institutions to, 'by appropriate means give citizens and representative associations the opportunity to make known and publicly exchange their views in all areas of Union action', as well as maintaining 'an open, transparent and regular dialogue with representative associations and civil society', appear broad and vague. The two points of Article 11 TEU have been explained in lay terms as referring to *vertical and horizontal* dialogue – one occurring between citizens and representative associations, and the other between institutions and representative associations and civil society.[18] There has been some recent rejection of this somewhat confusing terminology.[19] What is important is that Article 11(1) TEU calls for an opening of channels for engagement towards citizens and representative associations in all areas of Union action, and Article 11(2) TEU for a *dialogue* in all these areas. The latter goes beyond a listening exercise, requiring reciprocity and response.[20]

Civil society organisations, as well as the EESC, have long called for a specific implementation of Article 11(1) and (2) TEU and a 'structured' dialogue,[21] to give permanency and governance to dialogue, similar to the Commission

legitimate partners on 'stand-by', in order to concentrate on the principles and recognition: Luis Bouza Garcia, *Participatory Democracy and Civil Society in the EU: Agenda-Setting and Institutionalisation* (Palgrave Macmillan, 2015) 55–64.

[14] García Macho, 'Article 11' (n 6).

[15] Lock, 'Article 11 TEU' (n 3).

[16] Case C-113/13 *Azienda sanitaria locale n 5 'Spezzino' and Others v San Lorenzo and Croce Verde Cogema cooperativa sociale Onlus* [2014] Opinion of AG Wahl, EU:C:2014:291, para 2.

[17] ibid.

[18] Johannes W Pichler, Stephan G Hinghofer-Szalkay and Paul Pichler, *Civil Dialogue and Participatory Democracy in the Practice of the European Union Institutions* (NWV Verlag GmbH, 2016) 36.

[19] ibid.

[20] Víctor Cuesta Lopez, 'The Lisbon Treaty's Provisions on Democratic Principles: A Legal Framework for Participatory Democracy' (2010) 16 *European Public Law* 123, 135; Lock, 'Article 11 TEU' (n 3).

[21] Civil Society Europe, 'A Roadmap to Civil Dialogue in the EU' (20 June 2019), https://civilsocietyeurope.eu/a-roadmap-to-civil-dialogue-in-the-eu/, accessed 6 February 2026.

consultation regime, although less ambitious in scope.[22] The Council, Parliament and Commission have resisted any attempt for any overall structured or permanent direct civil dialogue related to Article 11 TEU. What exists are specific dialogue practices grounded in other Treaty provisions, primarily the social dialogue and the dialogue with churches and religious communities.[23] The Commission, for its part, maintains civil dialogue groups sectorally for several fields, where the civil dialogue frontier has been led by a few Directorates-General (DGs), including established rules for how to manage such groups and requirements on their balanced composition, in legally binding decisions.[24] There are also many different citizen consultation and dialogue activities, which have occurred in waves, with some occurring regularly. The Parliament has primarily channelled civil dialogue through informal public hearings, with dialogue activities of the Council being more limited. While there are periodic activities and ad hoc forums, Cuesta-Lopez argues that these are 'far from the idea of maintaining a regular dialogue'.[25] While the Conference on the Future of Europe, which included pan-European mini-publics, could be viewed as an application of Article 11(1) and 11(2) TEU (and Article 10(3) TEU, for that matter), the conference is arguably not a regular feature of EU institutional operations. The Commission's consultations could be understood as an expression of Article 11(1) and 11(2) TEU, and as such, would constitute the exception, with their ubiquity for legislative and major initiatives.[26] However, in order to see consultations as a dialogue, there need to be measures of reciprocity and feedback. In any case, while the mode of the dialogue is not fixed, the demands of its regularity imply a minimum level of structure and continuity.

Beyond mandating positive actions to create dialogue opportunities, Article 11(1) and 11(2) TEU provide impetus for a general frame for EU institutional contacts with non-state actors. The General Court's reference to Article 11 TEU enshrining 'a fundamental principle of transparency' also points to this overarching purpose.[27] Similarly, Advocate General Emiliou notes 'the requirements of openness and transparency of the public administration' as envisioned in Article 10(3) and Article 11(2) TEU.[28] The instruments of voice and dialogue now provide the constitutional underpinning for the mandatory Transparency Register, which

[22] See also European Economic and Social Committee, 'Action Plan for the implementation of Articles 11(1) and 11(2) of the Treaty on European Union' (European Economic and Social Committee, 4 July 2018), www.eesc.europa.eu/en/documents/action-plan-implementation-articles-111-and-112-treaty-european-union, accessed 6 February 2026.

[23] On social dialogue, see Art 153 TFEU and Art 154 TFEU. See also Art 17 TFEU.

[24] For an overview of the legal framework, the Commission's relevant website is instructive: Commission 'Selection of Civil Dialogue Groups' (13 April 2023), https://agriculture.ec.europa.eu/common-agricultural-policy/cap-overview/committees-and-expert-groups/civil-dialogue-groups/2014-22-agricultural-cdgs/selection-civil-dialogue-groups_en, accessed 6 February 2026.

[25] Cuesta Lopez, 'The Lisbon Treaty's Provisions on Democratic Principles' (n 20) 126; see also Nicolas Beger, 'Participatory Democracy: Organised Civil Society and the "New" Dialogue' [2004] Federal Trust Constitutional Online Paper No 09/04 4–5; Lock, 'Article 11 TEU' (n 3).

[26] Mendes, 'Participation and the Role of Law after Lisbon' (n 2) 1852.

[27] Case T-306/12 *Darius Nicolai Spirlea and Mihaela Spirlea v Commission* EU:T:2014:816, para 52.

[28] Case C-883/19 P *HSBC Holdings and Others v Commission* [2023], Opinion of AG Emiliou, para 148.

contributes to shaping the overall exchange between the EU institutions and interest groups. The 2021 Interinstitutional agreement on a mandatory transparency register ('Agreement on a Transparency Register') frames the establishment of the register as flowing from the principle of participatory democracy, referencing the European Parliament's, Council's and Commission's duties according to Article 11(1) and (2) TEU.[29] The Agreement on a Transparency Register further elaborates that the dialogue enshrined in Article 11(2) TEU 'enables stakeholders to present their views on decisions that may affect them and hence to contribute effectively to the evidence base on which policy proposals are made'.[30] Furthermore, the agreement states that engaging with stakeholders enhances 'the quality of decision-making by providing channels for external views and expertise to be given'.[31] It also states that transparency and accountability are essential for 'maintaining the trust of Union citizens in the legitimacy of the political, legislative and administrative processes of the Union',[32] while transparency regarding interest representation is crucial 'in order to allow citizens to follow the activities and be aware of the potential influence of interest representatives'.[33] In accordance with the Agreement, the three institutions adopt 'conditionality' measures when they decide to make certain interest representation activities and access conditional upon prior registration in the Transparency Register.[34]

With reference to the Agreement, the rules of procedure of the Parliament now state that MEPs should adopt the systematic practice of only meeting interest representatives that are registered in the Transparency Register, publicise online all scheduled meetings falling under the Agreement.[35] The Commission, in turn, has communicated its commitment to conditionality with regard to high-level Commissioner officers, as well as taking two decisions on disclosure of meetings. In these two decisions (one in relation to Commissioners and Cabinet members, and the other in relation to Directors-General), the Commission elaborates on the constitutional underpinnings of the limits of its discretion: more precisely, its obligations to publicise contacts with interest representatives. Meetings with organisations and self-employed individuals are framed in the context of fulfilling the Commission's dialogue duties according to Article 11(1) and 11(2) TEU, as well as its duties to consult widely before proposing legislative acts in accordance

[29] Interinstitutional agreement of 20 May 2021 on a mandatory transparency register [2021] OJ L207/1 preamble, points 1 and 2.

[30] ibid.

[31] ibid preamble, point 2.

[32] ibid preamble, point 3.

[33] ibid.

[34] On the possibility of the Agreement being binding, see Art 295 TFEU.

[35] The rules also lay out the obligation for rapporteurs, shadow rapporteurs and committee chairs to publish online, for each report, all scheduled meetings with interest representatives. See European Parliament, 'Rules of Procedure' 9th parliamentary term, July 2023, Rule 11.

with Article 2 Protocol No 2 and Article 11(3) TEU.[36] In the first decision, relating to Commissioners and Cabinet members, this is followed by:

> In accordance with Article 10(3) TEU, in order to facilitate the participation of European citizens in the democratic life of the Union and to ensure that decisions are taken as openly as possible, it is important to enable citizens to know what contacts the Members of the Commission and members of their Cabinets have with organizations or self-employed individuals.[37]

These duties and obligations for Members of Parliament and the Commission concretise the demands of the principle of participatory democracy to give voice to citizens and representative associations, and, crucially, to maintain a transparent dialogue, emerging in part as citizens' right to know about the interactions between EU institutions and interest representation, which includes active disclosure and publicising practices. Overall, the mandatory register gives effect to a constitutional obligation enshrined in Article 11(1) and 11(2) TEU, in that it provides 'a framework and operating principles for a coordinated approach . . . as regards transparent and ethical interest representation'.[38] Regardless of whether the institutions would revoke or amend the inter-institutional agreement, the fundamental imperative, flowing from Article 11(1) and 11(2) TEU, to provide a structure would remain.

The understanding of 'active transparency' is important to note, as the historically dominant EU legal approach is one of 'passive transparency', centred on EU institutions providing access to documents – assuming that citizens possess certain legal, financial and epistemic resources.[39] Scholarly debates have highlighted the limitations of this approach, including in light of the democratic function that transparency serves.[40]

[36] Commission, Decision of 25 November 2014 on the publication of information on meetings held between Members of the Commission and organisations or self-employed individuals [2014] 2014/839 /EU para 1 preamble; Commission, Decision of 25 November 2014 on the publication of information on meetings held between Directors-General of the Commission and organisations or self-employed individuals [2014] 2014/838/EU, para 1 preamble.

[37] Commission, Decision of 25 November 2014 on the publication of information on meetings held between Members of the Commission and organisations or self-employed individuals [2014] 2014/839/EU para 3 preamble; Art 10(3) TEU is only referenced indirectly in the decision on Directors-General, likely reflecting that the decision to disclose, for Directors-General, only applies to 'issues relating to policy-making and implementation in the Union', and not any kind of meeting, as it does for Commissioners and Cabinet members: see Commission, Decision of 25 November 2014, para 3 preamble.

[38] Interinstitutional agreement of 20 May 2021 on a mandatory transparency register [2021] OJ L207/1, art 1.

[39] Eógan Hickey and Maria Weimer, 'The Transparency of EU Agency Science: Towards a New Proactive Approach' (2022) 59 *Common Market Law Review* 673, 675.

[40] Alberto Alemanno, 'Unpacking the Principle of Openness in EU Law: Transparency, Participation and Democracy' (2014) 39 *European Law Review* 72; Päivi Leino-Sandberg, 'Transparency, Participation, and EU Institutional Practice: An Inquiry into the Limits of the "widest Possible"' EUI Dept of Law

The already-established link between democratic participation and transparency in the EU courts' case law,[41] and the more recent comments by the General Court and Advocate General on the principle of transparency enshrined in Article 11 TEU, as well as on the Agreement on a Transparency Register and related Commission decisions, linking Article 10(3) TEU and 11 TEU, all imply an expansive view of transparency; that is, that transparency as mandated by the principle of participatory democracy includes an 'active' component.

3.1.2. The Commission's obligation to consult (Article 11(3) TEU)

The explicit duty to consult enshrined in Article 11(3) TEU is central to participation in EU law-making, as well as EU rule-making. The complementary role of participatory democracy in relation to representative democracy[42] means that the principle should also be viewed in light of the specific constitutional principles which exemplify the particular way that representative democracy in the EU has developed, including the principles of subsidiarity and proportionality.[43] For consultation as outlined in Article 11(3), these principles help flesh out its substance in a concrete way. Article 5 TEU, which holds that the use of Union competences shall respect the principles of subsidiarity and proportionality, has been further concretised in Protocol No 2 on the Application of the Principles of Subsidiarity and Proportionality annexed to the Treaty ('Protocol No 2').[44] Protocol No 2 states that, before proposing legislative acts, 'the Commission shall consult widely'.[45] The Protocol also specifies that, in carrying out such consultations, the Commission has to take into account the regional and local dimension of any action envisaged, and that the duty to consult broadly always applies, except in cases of 'exceptional urgency'. Even then, the Commission has to explain its

Research Paper No 2014/03; Deirdre Curtin and Päivi Leino-Sandberg, 'Openness, Transparency and the Right of Access to Documents in the EU' (2016) No RSCAS 2016/63 Robert Schuman Centre for Advanced Studies; Päivi Leino-Sandberg, 'Disruptive Democracy: Keeping EU Citizens in a Box' in Inge Govaere, Sascha Garben and Paul Nemitz (eds), *Critical Reflections on Constitutional Democracy in the European Union* (Hart Publishing, 2019); Hickey and Weimer, 'The Transparency of EU Agency Science' (n 39) 675.

[41] See, prominently, Joined Cases C-39/05 P and C-52/05 P *Sweden and Turco v Council* ECLI:EU:C:2007:721; Joined Cases C-92-93/09 *Schecke and Eifert* EU:C:2010:662 [68]; Case C-280/11 P *Info Access Europe* EU:C:2013:325; Case C-57/16 P *ClientEarth v European Commission* [2018] EU:C:2018:660; Case T-540/15 *Emilio De Capitani v European Parliament* [2018] ECLI:EU:T:2018:167.

[42] Art 10(1) TEU states that representative democracy is the founding principle of the Union.

[43] Art 5(3) TEU and Consolidated version of the Treaty on the Functioning of the European Union Protocol (No 2) on the application of the principles of subsidiarity and proportionality [2007] OJ C202/206.

[44] ibid.

[45] The duty to consult can be linked to specific Treaty obligations to conduct cost–benefit analysis, for instance with regard to environmental and social policy (Art 191(3) TFEU). However, such obligations are subsumed in the context of law-making, where the duty to consult applies to all Commission legislative proposals irrespective of policy area.

decision to forego consultation.[46] This means that, in general, substantive issues such as controversial legislation or urgency may not serve as a legitimate reason to forego consultation obligations.

It follows from Article 11 TEU that there is a clear legal mandate to consult in EU rule- and law-making. This mandate, considering Protocol No 2, is even stronger for law-making. The language of Article 11 TEU is also sharper in terms of a consultation duty when compared with previous EU legal texts, such as the protocol to the Amsterdam Treaty. 'Should' has been replaced by the more prescriptive 'shall', and consultation is now featured much more prominently in the current subsidiarity Protocol.[47] While, in some respects, the language of Article 11(3) seems to refer back to existing practices of the Commission during the last decade,[48] inserting consultation under the Treaty's catalogue of democratic principles, as has been discussed, is new. By virtue of a participatory democracy practice, the Commission does not have unlimited discretion on whom, when and how to consult.[49] In interpreting Article 11(3) TEU, the Commission is bound by Article 11(1) and (2) TEU, which establish general obligations of giving voice and facilitating open and transparent dialogue, thereby signifying participation with normative grounds that are different from functional rationales.[50] This connection is reinforced by Article 10(3) TEU, which establishes the right of Union citizens to participate in the democratic life of the Union. The ECJ has held that this right to participate goes beyond electoral rights. In *ClientEarth*, the Court granted an environmental organisation access to early legislative preparatory documents, in light of Article 10(3) TEU.[51] The Court thereby put forward an understanding of democratic participation as framed in 10(3) TEU that encompasses direct forms of engagement with the legislative process.[52]

The emphasis by the Court on Article 10(3) TEU in relation to the legislative process suggests, again, that Articles 11(1) and 11(2) TEU are more geared towards creating a dialogue climate rather than reflecting an obligation to respond to items raised for debate on individual legislative or policy files.[53] A notable difference regarding consultation is that the obligation to consult rests with the Commission,

[46] Protocol No 2 Article 2.

[47] Treaty of Amsterdam amending the Treaty on European Union, the Treaties establishing the European Communities and certain related acts – Protocol on the application of the principles of subsidiarity and proportionality, [1997] OJ C 340 P. 0105, para 9; Irina Tanasescu, *The European Commission and Interest Groups: Towards a Deliberative Interpretation of Stakeholder Involvement in EU Policy-Making* (VUB Press/Brussels University Press, 2009) 58.

[48] It has been argued that Art 11 TEU constitutionalises parts of the Commission's White Paper on Governance: Lock, 'Article 11 TEU' (n 3). See also Neil Walker, 'The White Paper in Constitutional Context' [2001] Jean Monnet Chair, Jean Monnet Working Papers.

[49] Making this point in relation to consultation on non-legislation procedures, see Mendes, 'Participation and the Role of Law after Lisbon' (n 2) 1871.

[50] ibid 1852.

[51] *ClientEarth* (n 41) para 84.

[52] ibid.

[53] ibid.

and is invariably tied to the Commission's right of initiative.[54] The distinction and interplay between the duty to promote voice and social dialogue in general, and consultation in particular, is indirectly touched upon by the Court in *ClientEarth*, where the Court acknowledges that, while 'consultations are also intended to ensure the openness of the Commission's decision-making process and the participation of citizens in that process', it is also clear that consultations 'are not necessarily to be open to the public as a whole. They do not replace the possibility for those citizens to be granted access to the legislative process through e.g. impact assessment reports'.[55] The Court here acknowledges that there can be different kinds of consultations. However, considering the clear legal duty to consult openly for legislation, also enshrined in Protocol No 2, the Court's statement can arguably not be understood to mean that an open public consultation can generally or lightly be foregone. Finally, while representative associations are mentioned in the first and second paragraphs of Article 11 TEU, they are not mentioned in relation to the third, where they are replaced by 'parties concerned', suggesting that 'representative associations' play a particular role in ensuring wider public debate but have no privileged role in the specific consultation mechanisms of the Commission.[56]

3.1.2.1. Concerning the 'parties concerned': Who to consult?

Considering the above analysis, the question of how Article 11(3) TEU can be understood can be framed as how a consultation exercise can be structured in alignment with its participatory ideal while adhering to the necessary dimensions and procedural goals that flow from the purpose of a consultation medium. Keeping this in mind is helpful when interpreting 'broad consultation with parties concerned', as featured in Article 11(3) TEU. The term 'broad' excludes one-sided consultation. For law-making, Protocol No 2 adds the duty to take into account the regional and local dimensions.[57] Broad consultations, as featured in Article 11 TEU, also stand in relation to the term 'parties concerned'. The latter term is frequently featured in regulatory policy and legislative theory and appears in several variations: 'affected and interested parties', 'significantly affected and potentially interested parties', as well as 'citizens and interested parties'.[58] The concept of 'parties concerned' also finds some parallel in the right to be heard, established in procedural law.[59]

[54] Art 17 TEU. See also Lock, 'Article 11 TEU' (n 3).

[55] *ClientEarth* (n 41) para 94.

[56] On this point, see Stijn Smismans, 'The Constitutional Labelling of "the Democratic Life of the EU": Representative and "participatory" Democracy' in Lynn Dobson and Andreas Follesdahl (eds), *Political Theory and the European Constitution* (Routledge, 2006) 138.

[57] Art 2 Protocol No 2.

[58] OECD, Best Practice Principles on Stakeholder Engagement in Regulatory Policy Draft (OECD 2008) 26.

[59] Case 17/74, *Transocean Marine Paint Association v Commission* EU:C:1974:106; Case C-135/92 *Fiskano v Commission* EU:C:1994:267, para 39; Case 234/84, *Belgium v Commission*, EU:C:1986:302, paras 27 and 48; Case T-260/94 *Air Inter v Commission* ECLI:EU:T:1994:265, para 60; see also Charter of Fundamental Rights of the European Union [2012] OJ C 326/391, art 41.

The Commission's internal guidelines indicate how the Commission – in its own view – should approach the issue: whom the policy or law will affect, who will have to implement it, and who has a stated interest in it.[60] Although the Commission avoids directly linking this suggested approach to the terminology of Article 11 TEU (or any legal obligation, for that matter), it seems to correspond with what Article 11 TEU implies. Such determinations, however, are prone to a great deal of subjectivity, considering how democracy theory and practice highlight that 'who will show an interest' is linked to access to information and capacity to respond. In this context, it is unfortunate that the Commission, in its updated Better Regulation Guidelines and Toolbox, consistently focuses on the term 'interested parties'[61] as the relevant standard, rather than 'parties concerned', as the latter phrase (which is in the Treaty text, and is the legally relevant one) is not dependent on awareness of the Commission's activities and proposals. The guidelines even go so far as to misrepresent the content of Article 11 TEU, which is quoted verbatim, except for the replacement of that one phrase:

> Under Article 11 of the Treaty on European Union (TEU), the Commission has a duty to carry out broad consultations with *interested parties* to ensure Union action is coherent and transparent (emphasis added).[62]

This seemingly trivial distinction, however, conceals a larger problem, as the Commission then commits to 'prioritizing stakeholder categories to engage with according to their level of interest in, expertise about, or influence on the initiative'.[63] This approach, then, clearly moves away from the meaning of the Treaty text, which is centred on who is affected by the legislation instead of their level of interest in it.[64] Although the latter certainly can be indicative of the former, assuming such equivalence goes against the Treaty text and the empirical insights of democratic theory elaborated on in the previous chapter. By comparison, in the Aarhus Convention, the phrase 'the public concerned' is defined as 'the public affected or likely to be affected by, or having an interest in, the environmental decision-making'.[65] Considering that alternative available terminology with a narrower field of application, such as 'directly affected' or 'significantly affected', has been discarded for the more open-ended 'parties concerned', the term should

[60] Commission, 'Better Regulation Guidelines' SWD(2021) 305 final (SWD Better Regulation Guidelines) 19.

[61] ibid 13.

[62] ibid.

[63] ibid 19.

[64] There seems to be no legal problem with the Commission's approach to prioritising stakeholders, proportionally related to the strength of their connection to the proposed legislation, only its method of placing 'interest in' the legislation as a main metric/factor to determine their status as 'parties concerned', which is at odds with the wording of the Treaty text, as well as its underlying telos.

[65] Convention on Access to Information, public participation in decision-making and access to justice in environmental matters (adopted on 25 June 1998), United Nations, 2161 UNTS 447 (UNECE) art 2,5.

be understood to have a wide-ranging application, and arguably be understood as a principle of inclusion.

The Commission's own minimum standards on consultation identify the consultation target groups as 'those affected by the policy, those who will be involved in implementation of the policy, or bodies that have stated objectives giving them a direct interest in the policy'.[66] This, then, seems like a definition more in line with Article 11 TEU than the unwarranted focus on 'interest'. The constitutional grounding of the participation of those affected is important, considering the complementary role that participatory democracy can play in relation to representative democracy, in that it would include parties concerned which may not easily find a voice through traditional means of representation.

Two additional dimensions are worth mentioning. As the link between Article 10(3) TEU and access to law-making has been confirmed by the CJEU, the right enshrined in Article 10(3) TEU for all citizens to participate in the democratic life of the Union informs the understanding of 'parties concerned', emphasising the importance of a genuine link to citizens and the necessary depths of the consultation process. Additionally, the logic underlying consulting 'concerned parties' is not limited to the concept of citizenship – highlighting necessary width in the circle of parties consulted. The language of Article 11(3) TEU draws no distinction between whether parties concerned are citizens of the Union or so-called third-country nationals, and where they reside, just as there is no distinction as to whether parties are individuals, businesses, organisations, or other legal persons.[67] However, it should be noted that the *right* to democratic participation is afforded exclusively to citizens.[68]

3.1.2.2. How to consult: Principles and practices

Article 11(3) TEU does not prescribe any specific consultation modalities, which allows for flexibility and adaptability. However, the democratic standards which flow from the principle of participatory democracy must be maintained: primarily, consultations must be conducted in an open and transparent way.[69] As a general rule, this means that Article 11(3) TEU requires open Internet-based consultation

[66] Commission, Communication from the Commission 'Towards a reinforced culture of consultation and dialogue - General principles and minimum standards for consultation of interested parties by the Commission', COM(2002) 704 final, 11 December 2002.

[67] On parties from third countries' lobbying being affected by legislation, see Emilia Korkea-Aho, '"Mr Smith Goes To Brussels": Third Country Lobbying and the Making of EU Law and Policy' (2016) 18 *Cambridge Yearbook of European Legal Studies* 45; Anu Bradford, *The Brussels Effect: How the European Union Rules the World* (Oxford University Press, 2020).

[68] *cf* Schrauwen, 'European Union Citizenship' (n 12) 56.

[69] This follows, inter alia, from the stated purpose of consultations in Art 11(3) TEU – transparency – and is also spelled out in the Interinstitutional Agreement on Better Law-Making: see Interinstitutional Agreement of 13 April [2016] on Better Law-Making OJ L123/1, point 19. For an in-depth analysis, see ch 4, s 4.1.2.1.

for legislative proposals, which is also spelled out in the Interinstitutional Agreement on Better Law-Making.[70]

The phrase 'broad consultations with parties concerned' implies that parties should not be limited in expressing their opinions on a proposal at hand. 'Broad', then, does not mainly refer to the scope of participants – on which the term 'parties concerned' primarily operates – but to the substantive scope of the consultation. This adds a legal emphasis to the question of 'framing' relevant issues, as highlighted in participatory democracy theory, and the importance of which behavioural research in the last decades has robustly evidenced.[71] Practices which run contrary to this obligation include when consultation occurs at a late stage in legislative drafting or there is overreliance on closed-question multiple-choice questionnaires.[72] However, the term 'broad consultations with parties concerned' in no way excludes consultations at different stages of the drafting process, reaching out to different actors depending on their ties to the potential legislation, for instance as a target or implementor of legislation. Actors involved with implementation could, for instance, be more suited to consultation on technical or legal features at a later stage in the law-making process.[73] There is also no explicit statement with regard to the choice of the consultation medium: Internet-based, hearings, conferences, workshops, deliberate polling or citizen panels, field visits, and so on. For areas outside the Union's exclusive competence, Protocol No 2 places an additional duty on the Commission to consult as widely as possible in preparing legislative proposals, referring, presumably, to both the circle of participants and the scope of the proposal.[74]

While Article 11 TEU strengthens the opportunities of potential participants in law-making consultation, it does not (and neither does Protocol No 2) place any direct obligation on the Commission to follow the outcome of a consultation or any specific content generated through a consultation procedure. This is also an important feature of the complementary function of the principle of participatory democracy, as it cannot impinge on representative democracy in the EU and the crucial institutional balance which is one of its main features.[75] The obligation to consult, while leaving the Commission with final discretion to decide, implies the consultation process generating perspectives and knowledge providing a basis for taking an informed decision, or perhaps even new approaches. Arguably, this can often be achieved when consultation occurs in the early stages of drafting. Whether Article 11 TEU implies any outer limits of substantive discretion is

[70] Although implicit in Art 11 TEU, especially in light of Art 2 Protocol No 2, this obligation is codified in the Interinstitutional Agreement on Better Law-Making (ibid). Furthermore, the courts have begun to engage with the Agreement and its provisions (see following sections).

[71] Alberto Alemanno, Anne-Lise Sibony and Cass R Sunstein (eds), *Nudge and the Law: A European Perspective* (Hart Publishing, 2015).

[72] At the time of writing, such questionnaires are quite frequent.

[73] See, eg OECD, Best Practice Principles on Stakeholder Engagement in Regulatory Policy Draft (n 58).

[74] Art 2 Protocol No 2.

[75] See, eg Case 138/79, *Roquette Frères v Council* EU:C:1980:249. See also ch 4, s 4.6 and cited case law in relation to institutional balance as a feature of representative democracy in the EU.

questionable. Rather, the overall duty of the Commission, with its sole right of legislative initiative to act in the 'best interest of the Union', would, rather, be guiding.[76] Considering that the stated purpose of consultations is to ensure coherence and transparency, this requires clarity in the process, whether or not consultation input has been received and has been taken on.[77]

The question of equal opportunity and the obligation of equal treatment is tied to the principle of equality. Equality of citizens is a fundamental EU value and a democratic principle of the EU, by force of Article 9 TEU. Giving voice to, and equal treatment of, participants comes through in a consultation setting as procedural equality – meaning that potential participants should be able to have equal procedural opportunities to influence decision-making procedures.[78] Overall, Article 9 TEU underscores the political dimension of EU citizenship. While such an understanding is supported by Article 10(3) TEU, the application of equality in the context of participatory democracy is not without complications. Legitimacy, in a participatory democracy framework, is not necessarily achieved through traditional notions of representativeness, and it is not clear how procedural equality should be measured, considering the range of actors potentially participating in a consultation exercise and their respective links to citizens.[79] All this considered, the Commission must take into account that Charter rights require consultation design to attend to the following: ensuring equality between women and men;[80] non-discrimination of people belonging to minorities and other vulnerable and marginalised groups;[81] and the obligation to respect cultural, religious and linguistic diversity[82] and ensure reasonable accommodation for the needs of persons with disabilities.[83] Relatedly, the Interinstitutional Agreement on Better Law-Making clearly spells out and codifies two procedural requirements implicit for Article 11 TEU: 'ensuring that the modalities and time-limits of those public consultations allow for the widest possible participation', and that 'results of public

[76] Art 17 TFEU.

[77] See s 3.3 on transparency.

[78] Mendes, 'Participation and the Role of Law after Lisbon' (n 2) 1862; Alberto Alemanno, 'Levelling the EU Participatory Playing Field: A Legal and Policy Analysis of the Commission's Public Consultations in Light of the Principle of Political Equality' (2020) 26 *European Law Journal* 120; see also Michael T Grevén, 'Some Considerations on Participation in Participatory Governance' in Beate Kohler-Koch and Berthold Rittberger (eds), *Debating the Democratic Legitimacy of the European Union* (Rowman & Littlefield, 2007) 236–40.

[79] See, eg Case T-135/96 *UEAPME v Council* EU:T:1998:128.

[80] Art 23 CFR.

[81] Art 21 CFR. The Commission has also recently acknowledged the need to address existing hurdles limiting democratic participation and representation for groups susceptible to marginalisation, such as people with a minority racial or ethnic background: see Commission, 'Communication from the Commission to the European Parliament, the Council, The European Economic and Social Committee and the Committee of Regions: A Union of equality: EU anti-racism action plan 2020–2025', COM(2020) 565 final, 18 September 2020.

[82] Art 22 CFR.

[83] Convention on the Rights of Persons with Disabilities and Its Optional Protocol (Adopted 12 December 2006) (A/RES/61/106), 9.

and stakeholder consultations shall be communicated without delay to both co-legislators and the public'.[84]

Regarding the more innovative or unconventional participatory practices at the EU level, such as citizens' consultations, citizens' dialogues and citizen panels, these have occurred outside the main policy- and law-making apparatus, and either with noted limited impact or no documentation on their impact.[85] It is too early to assess the developments following the Conference on the Future of Europe and the Commission commitment to streamlining so-called citizens' panels, as well as this nascent practice itself, which began in spring 2023.[86] While the rhetoric surrounding these citizens' panels certainly has evoked their importance for EU democracy – with (perhaps inadvertent) references to Article 10(3) TEU, labelling them as 'vital to the democratic life' of the Union – so far it is too early to see whether they are used for policy direction or as law-making consultation (see also section 3.5).

3.1.2.3. *The purpose of consulting: Transparency, coherence and participation of those affected*

It is clear that the duty to consult could encompass a wide range of practices, where procedural equality or representativeness would be expressed in different ways. The way in which the Commission is obligated to pursue broad consultations and implicitly ensure procedural equality should further be informed by how participation is gauged in relation to the stated purpose of the consultations in the Treaty, ie coherence and transparency.[87]

Beginning with the former, the 'coherence' of Article 11 TEU, in the absence of further clarification, has broad application, and in the Treaty it functions as an umbrella term. 'Consistency' appears as a constitutional principle in several places in the Treaty of Lisbon, elaborated as a fundamental legal obligation of EU institutions.[88] The principle of consistency is featured most prominently in Article 7 TFEU, which refers to consistency between the Union's 'policies and activities . . . and its objectives . . . in accordance with the principle of conferral of powers'.[89]

Although the English word used in Article 7 TEU is 'consistency', a number of language versions refer to consistency as coherence (for example, German

[84] Interinstitutional Agreement of 13 April [2016] on Better Law-Making OJ L123/1, point 19.
[85] See, eg Dominik Hierlemann and others, *Under Construction: Citizen Participation in the European Union* (Verlag Bertelsmann Stiftung, 2022).
[86] Commission, 'European Citizens' Panels', https://citizens.ec.europa.eu/index_en, accessed 6 February 2026.
[87] There is little analysis of these stated goals. The few existing comments stop at taking note: 'Interestingly, the aims of these consultations are limited to effecting transparency and coherence—both of which are of course important for good governance—but it is no express aim to make "good" law.': see Lock, 'Article 11 TEU' (n 3); see also, noting that Art 11(3) TEU and broad consultations are vaguely defined, García Macho, 'Article 11' (n 6).
[88] Christian NK Franklin, 'The Burgeoning Principle of Consistency in EU Law' (2011) 30 *Yearbook of European Law* 42.
[89] Art 7 TFEU.

(*'Kohärenz'*), French (*'cohérence'*), Spanish (*'coherencia'*); and in Article 11 TEU – *'Kohärenz'*, *'coherencia'*).[90] This has led to academics interchangeably referring to the principle of consistency and the principle of coherence in EU law.[91] In the literal sense, however, in English, consistency is not equivalent to coherence. Consistency is often defined as the absence of contradictions, whereas coherence refers to positive connections.[92] Herlin-Karnell and Konstantinides argue that, while EU policies shall be both consistent and coherent, 'consistency' – used in the English-language version of the Treaty of Lisbon – is better viewed as an all-encompassing principle rather than a precondition to coherence. The rationale for consistency encompassing or being equivalent to coherence (although the literal meaning works the other way around) is to avoid making 'a false allegation out of linguistic pedantry' – that is to say, the Treaty drafters omitted to pay lip-service to the principle of coherence by referring to consistency.[93]

Accepting this rationale means understanding that 'ensuring coherence', as found in Article 11 TEU, is helped by an understanding of the principle of consistency (here implying a wider berth than consistency in the literal sense). In providing that the EU institutional framework 'shall aim to promote its values, advance its objectives, serve its interests, those of its citizens and those of the Member States, and ensure the consistency, effectiveness and continuity of its policies and actions' (Article 13(1) TEU), consistency can be viewed as a systemic principle embedded in the constitutional text of a legal system as an element of the rule of law, helping to ensure legal certainty.[94] The connection between consultation and coherence in Article 11 TEU mirrors a legal anchoring of the overall Better Regulation Agenda (of which consultation was a part, prior to the Lisbon Treaty) to the rule of law, which, according to Article 2 TEU, acts as one of the EU's founding principles.[95] In a legal system founded on the rule of law, the legislative process in its totality is rule-bound. Consistency or coherence also expresses MacCormick's argument that the law should make sense, when considered as a whole, through being rational and orderly.[96] This goes beyond 'bare consistency' and moves closer to Dworkin's description of 'a single vision of justice'.[97] Consistency/coherence is, consequently,

[90] Art 11 TEU in Spanish reads 'Con objeto de garantizar la coherencia y la transparencia', and in German, 'Um die Kohärenz und die Transparenz des Handelns der Union zu gewährleisten'.

[91] See Ester Herlin-Karnell and Theodore Konstadinides, 'The Rise and Expressions of Consistency in EU Law: Legal and Strategic Implications for European Integration' (2013) 15 *Cambridge Yearbook of European Legal Studies* 139.

[92] ibid 141.

[93] ibid.

[94] ibid 142.

[95] Garben and Govaere argue the Better Regulation Agenda's constitutional legitimacy is supported by Art 2 TEU, which refers to the rule of law as a EU founding principle: Sacha Garben and Inge Govaere, 'The Multi-Faceted Nature of Better Regulation' in Sacha Garben and Inge Govaere (eds), *The EU Better Regulation Agenda: A Critical Assessment* (Hart Publishing, 2018) 6.

[96] Neil MacCormick, *Legal Reasoning and Legal Theory* (Oxford University Press, 1994).

[97] Ronald Dworkin, *Taking Rights Seriously* (Harvard University Press, 2001); Von Bogdandy also sees coherence as a justification for the conceptualisation and elaboration of constitutional principles; it is a principle underlying the grand plan of the constitutional universe. See Armin von Bogdandy, 'Founding Principles' in Armin von Bogdandy and Jürgen Bast (eds), *Principles of European Constitutional Law*, 2nd rev ed (Hart; CH Beck, 2010) 11–54.

expressed in a web of legal obligations in EU law, through loyalty and primacy (vertical consistency), as well as in the principles of good administration and good governance connected to openness and transparency (horizontal consistency).[98] Regarding the latter, the English-language version of 'coherence', for Article 11(3), also provides a bridge to the EU governance principle of 'coherence' as elaborated by the Commission in its White Paper on European Governance. The Paper highlights the need for coherence in the face of EU enlargement, increasing diversity, current challenges crossing boundaries of Union sectoral policies, and the fact that regional and local authorities are increasingly involved in forming and implementing EU policies.[99]

In sum, Article 13(1) TEU, read together with Article 7 TFEU as well as the values laid out in Articles 1 and 2 TEU, express the single-vision notion of coherence while also featuring distinct horizontal, vertical and formal facets of coherence.

In the context of participation in law-making, coherence as featured in Article 11 TEU can, then, be construed as three main lines of action or considerations which should inform consultation design: (a) coherence between a legislative proposal and the values and objectives of the Union, including the Commission's duty to initiate legislation that is in the best interest of the Union;[100] (b) consistency between the proposal at hand and existing legislation at the Union and national level;[101] and (c) coherence between the stated objective of a piece of legislation and the way that it materialises that objective. Regarding the last point, the Commission, in its own elaboration of coherence in good governance, has placed an emphasis on the challenge of cross-sectoral issues (which pose challenges to evidence-gathering and participation), as well as the importance of regional and local authorities as implementors of EU legislation and action.[102] The lack of cross-sectoral approaches has also been brought to light by civil society actors as a challenge with regard to consultation and dialogue with the EU institutions.[103] Considering the imperatives of participatory democracy theory, the legal emphasis placed on coherence can, then, best be viewed as a call to a systematic approach to avoid potential structural biases: for example, proactively reaching out to parties beyond the usual suspects, and an emphasis on diversity in participation selection, particularly with regard to a diversity of perspectives.[104] Conversely, it may also imply more tailored consultations to avoid the domination of certain actors

[98] Herlin-Karnell and Konstadinides, 'The Rise and Expressions of Consistency in EU Law' (n 91) 142–43.

[99] Commission, European Governance, 'A White Paper', COM(2001) 428 final, 25 July 2001, title II.

[100] See Art 17 TEU.

[101] Herlin-Karnell and Konstadinides, 'The Rise and Expressions of Consistency in EU Law' (n 91).

[102] White Paper (n 99).

[103] Elodie Fazi and Jeremy Smith, 'Civil Dialogue: Making It Work Better, Study Commissioned by the Civil Society Contact Group' (Civil Society Contact Group, 2006) 39–49.

[104] Dawson highlights the gatekeeper problem with consultations: Mark Dawson, 'Better Regulation and the Future of EU Regulatory Law and Politics' (2016) 53 *Common Market Law Review* 1209, 1219. Alemanno discusses the problem of 'the usual suspects': Alberto Alemanno, 'How Much Better Is Better Regulation? Assessing the Impact of the Better Regulation Package on the European Union – A Research Agenda' (2015) 6 *European Journal of Risk Regulation* 344, 349.

or interests. Throughout these three expressions of coherence, the principles of subsidiarity and proportionality either represent constitutional elements with which EU legislation must be coherent, or tools which themselves promote coherence in the multi-legislative setting.[105]

In understanding how the other stated purpose of broad consultation – namely, transparency – informs consultation design, the Treaties' reference to transparency serves as a baseline. Transparency is featured primarily in Articles 15(1), 15(3) and 298(1) TFEU. The obligation placed on EU institutions to be open is established in Article 1 TEU, under which 'decisions are taken as openly as possible and as closely as possible to the citizen', and Article 15(1) TFEU ('In order to promote good governance and ensure the participation of civil society, the Union institutions, bodies, offices and agencies shall conduct their work as openly as possible.'), underlining the connection between participation and openness, as enshrined in the Treaty. While there are no single definitions of the principles of openness and transparency in EU law, these terms are often used interchangeably.[106] Openness, as both a principle and practice, it has been argued, encompasses two dimensions: transparency and participation.[107] From this perspective, the main element and precondition of participation is transparency, with the most concrete manifestation being access to information and, correspondingly, the right to documents of the EU institutions.[108]

The Commission is also, according to the Interinstitutional Agreement on Better Law-Making, obligated to communicate the results of public and stakeholder consultations, without delay, to both co-legislators, and to make them public.[109] In understanding the connection between participation and transparency outlined in Article 11(3) TEU, transparency, as recorded in Article 15 TFEU, serves as means to ensure that civil society participates in the work of the Union.[110] In a preliminary draft of the Constitutional Treaty, openness also appeared as a condition of the principle of participatory democracy:

> The Institutions are to ensure a high level of openness, permitting citizens' organizations of all kinds to play a full part in the Union affairs.[111]

[105] The links between subsidiarity and proportionality and the principle of participatory democracy will be further elaborated on in exploring the opportunities of judicial review of Article 11(3) TEU: see below.

[106] Deirdre Curtin, *Executive Power of the European Union: Law, Practices, and the Living Constitution* (Oxford University Press, 2009) 205; Joana Mendes, *Participation in EU Rule-Making: A Rights-Based Approach* (Oxford University Press, 2011) 113; Juliet Lodge, 'Transparency and EU Governance: Balancing Openness with Security' (2003) 11 *Journal of Contemporary European Studies* 95.

[107] Alemanno, 'Unpacking the Principle of Openness in EU Law' (n 40).

[108] The right of access to documents (Art 15(3) TFEU) is concretised by Regulation 1049/20019 and formulated as a fundamental right ('freedom of information') in Art 41 CFR. Regulation (EC) No 1049/2001 of the European Parliament and of the Council of 30 May 2001 regarding public access to European Parliament, Council and Commission documents OJ L145.

[109] Interinstitutional Agreement of 13 April [2016] on Better Law-Making OJ L123/1, point 19.

[110] Art 15 TFEU; see also *ClientEarth* (n 41).

[111] Secretariat of the Convention, 'Cover Note from Praesidium to the Convention', Conv 369/02, Brussels, 28 Oct 2002, 15.

The right of access to documents is the most developed legal dimension of EU institutional openness.[112] It is enshrined in Article 15(3) TFEU and fleshed out in Regulation 1049/2001, and, as a key element of the principle of transparency, which itself is a subset of the principle of openness, also finds support in Articles 1, 10, and 11 TEU.[113] Finally, it is also established in Article 42 of the Charter.[114] Access to documents has been expressed as the ontological precondition for citizen participation in the Union and the most concrete expression of the principle of openness, as expressed in Article 10(3) TEU, and its corollary, transparency.[115] Transparency and openness are recognised as having the potential to enhance democratic legitimacy, in that they serve the ability of citizens and affected parties to participate in governance and allow the same citizens and other relevant actors, such as the media, to hold elected leaders and government officials accountable.[116] Article 11(3) TEU can, then, reflect the understanding that, just as transparency promotes participation, so too does participation foster transparency – in the sense that information and knowledge is diffused, and possibly generated, through participation. In the two-way corridor of participation and transparency, consultation's secondary function is one of active transparency.

In particular, through Article 11(3), focus is placed on the underlying logic and reasoning behind norm creation being brought to light through consultation exercises.[117] Transparency here refers to both the logic and the input of norm creation – that is, not just the stated intent of the legislator but also those voices seeking to inform and influence the legislator and norm-creation process. The duty to hold broad consultation in order to 'ensure that Union action is transparent' is, then, a duty that acts as an exclusionary factor.[118] It excludes a central role being given to practices of opaque forms of stakeholder and advisory input or closed-door lobbyism. If transparent consultations are on the periphery of decision-making, or merely a secondary medium of input and influence, it is very difficult to see how

[112] Alemanno, 'Unpacking the Principle of Openness in EU Law' (n 40) 16–17.

[113] Explicitly, Art 10(3) TEU, Art 11(2) TEU and Art 11(3) TEU.

[114] Art 42 CFR.

[115] On this point, see Alberto Alemanno, 'Towards a Permanent Citizens Participatory Mechanism in the EU, Study Commissioned by the Policy Department for Citizens' Rights and Constitutional Affairs, European Parliament' (2022) PE 735.927; for an overview of the principle of transparency, see Matthew Levitt, 'Access to the File: The Commission's Administrative Procedures in Cases Under Articles 85 and 86' (1997) 34 *Common Market Law Review* 1413; Deirdre M Curtin, 'Citizens' Fundamental Right of Access to EU Information: An Evolving Digital Passepartout' (2000) 37 *Common Market Law Review* 7; Morten Petersen Broberg, 'Access to Documents - A General Principle of Community Law?' (2002) 27 *European Law Review* 195.

[116] Cornelia Moser, *How Open Is 'Open as Possible'? Three Different Approaches to Transparency and Openness in Regulating Access to EU Documents, vol 80* (Institut für Höhere Studien (IHS), 2001); for a more critical appraisal, see Deirdre Curtin and Albert Jacob Meijer, 'Does Transparency Strengthen Legitimacy?' (2006) 11 *Information Polity* 109.

[117] Deirdre Curtin, Herwig Hofmann and Joana Mendes, 'Constitutionalising EU Executive Rule-Making Procedures: A Research Agenda' (2013) 19 *European Law Journal* 1, 17; David Stasavage, 'Open-Door or Closed-Door? Transparency in Domestic and International Bargaining' (2004) 58 *International Organisation* 667.

[118] Different language versions place equally strong emphasis: 'Con objeto de garantizar'; 'En vue d'assurer'; 'zu gewährleisten'.

broad consultations could ever ensure transparency in EU governance or law-making – the stated purpose of Article 11(3) TEU would then be unachievable. This also speaks for a broad interpretation of the kind of activities which fall under the label of 'consultation'. The exclusionary nature of Article 11(3) TEU is reinforced by the legislator's choice of word: 'ensure' is an absolute, as opposed to more declamatory verbs, such as 'promote' or 'foster'. Naturally, this also implies that the Commission's consultation process itself has to live up to such a high transparency standard, implying proactive measures of publication, notice and feedback.

Finally, an additional purpose of consultation is also revealed through the addressees of consultation, namely the already analysed 'parties concerned'. Consulting 'parties concerned' encompasses both the instrumental and intrinsic values of participation. It aims to cover those affected parties with relevant knowledge and insights, and to protect the inherent value of the participation.

3.1.3. The European Citizens' initiative (Article 11(4) TEU)

Article 11(4) TEU situates the European Citizens' Initiative (ECI) inside the Union's constitutional architecture as a channel through which citizens may try to shape the agenda of Union action. The Court has repeatedly framed the ECI as a right to invite the Commission, within the framework of its powers, to submit an appropriate proposal for a Union legal act, and as a participatory democracy instrument that grants citizens a structured form of direct access to the Commission.[119] At the same time, the Court has made explicit that the mechanism does not convert the Commission's power of initiative into a duty to legislate: the ECI is designed to 'invite', not to oblige, and the Commission remains free not to submit a proposal, provided that it gives reasons in line with the regulatory framework.[120] In this sense, the ECI functions less as a device of direct legislation and more as a potential agenda-setting part of the infrastructure of participatory democracy: it proceduralises access, requires an institutional hearing of citizen claims, and produces a reasoned institutional stance that can be subjected to judicial scrutiny.

Against that constitutional baseline, the Court's case law on registration has pushed the instrument towards a 'registration-friendly' reading that protects its practical usefulness. In *Stop TTIP*, the General Court rejected a narrow understanding of what citizens may propose, holding that an ECI may concern Commission proposals for acts relating to the conclusion of an international agreement, and may seek to prevent the conclusion of such an agreement; more broadly, it underlined that the ECI is meant to strengthen citizen participation, and that participation can include intervening before an act is adopted, not only reacting afterwards.[121]

[119] Case C-589/15 P *Anagnostakis v Commission* ECLI:EU:C:2017:663, paras 23–24.
[120] Case C-418/18 P *Puppinck and Others v Commission* ECLI:EU:C:2019:1113, para 57; paras 61–63.
[121] Case T-754/14 *Efler and Others v Commission* ECLI:EU:T:2017:323, paras 31–33; 41–43.

More recently, the Court has clarified that the registration stage must not become a substantive prejudgement of the initiative's merits: in *Romania v Commission* it endorsed the Commission's power to proceed with partial registration, as a way to preserve the effectiveness of citizen participation where only part of a proposed initiative falls within the Commission's powers.[122] These lines of authority treat registration as a gateway that should be policed for clear inadmissibility, not used to insulate the Commission from politically inconvenient mobilisation.

The ECI secondary legislation provides a clear framework for its functioning – allowing 1 million EU citizens to invite the Commission to propose legislation.[123] Additionally, online signature collection is specified by means of a Commission implementation regulation,[124] and the Parliament's Rules of Procedure include a number of rules relating to the Parliament engaging with citizens' initiatives, for example through public hearings and debates on the initiatives, as well as rules inviting certain bodies to ascertain to what the degree the Commission has fulfilled its obligations.[125] When a citizens' initiative is registered, organisers have six months to schedule the launch of their signature-collection campaign.[126] Once the collection starts, there is a one-year deadline to collect a total of 1 million signatures and reach the designated signature thresholds (which emerge in secondary legislation) in at least seven EU countries.[127] Upon receiving the necessary certificates from competent national authorities, a six-month examination period begins: organisers are invited for a meeting with the Commission within a month, and are invited to participate in a public hearing in the Parliament within three months.[128] At the end of this examination procedure, the Commission issues a response to a 'successful' initiative, in the form of a communication explaining 'the action it intends to take, if any, and its reasons for taking or not taking action'.[129]

The instrument has, over time, become more accessible as secondary legislation and Commission practice has been reformed, propelled in part by the CJEU finding the Commission mistaken in its initial approach, for example in refraining from registering initiatives,[130] as well as vocal pressure from the Parliament and the European Ombudsman, and the findings of the Commission in its own

[122] Case C-54/22 P *Romania v Commission* ECLI:EU:C:2024:164, paras 62–64.

[123] Regulation (EU) 2019/788 of the European Parliament and of the Council of 17 April 2019 on the European citizens' initiative [2019] OJ L130/55.

[124] Commission, Implementing Regulation (EU) 2019/1799 of 22 October 2019 laying down technical specifications for individual online collection systems pursuant to Regulation (EU) 2019/788 of the European Parliament and of the Council on the European citizens' initiative OJ L 274/3, 28 October 2019.

[125] EP RoP rr 222, 230.

[126] Regulation (EU) 2019/788 (n 123), arts 8 and 16.

[127] ibid, arts 8 and 16.

[128] After this hearing, the European Parliament will hold a debate in plenary: EP RoP rr 222, 230.

[129] Regulation (EU) 2019/788 (n 123), art 15.

[130] In the case of the Stop TTIP ECI, for example, the Commission initially refused to register the ECI, based on the institutional grounds that negotiations were ongoing with the Council. The Court argued in reply: 'far from amounting to an interference in an ongoing legislative procedure, ECI proposals constitute an expression of the effective participation of citizens of the European Union in the democratic life thereof' (*Efler and Others* (n 121)).

review (after consulting interest groups) of the original legislation implementing Article 11(4) TEU.[131] While the ECI has attracted much attention due to its strong citizen participatory dimension and potential for influence and agenda-setting, its impact is debated.[132] Even though the ECI was seen as one of the few elements of Article 11 TEU which increased the stakes attached to citizen participation, there are clearly differing expectations, with, for example, its role explained in terms of fostering debate or providing an opportunity to be heard, rather than influencing the outcome.[133] In terms of ECI initiation and organising, civil society organisations, rather than individual citizens, are the dominant actors. That being said, the ECI remains one of the most visible, tangible and justiciable elements of the principle of participatory democracy.

3.2. Citizens' right to participate in the democratic life of the Union in view of multi-level law-making

The potentially central link between Article 10(3) TEU and Article 11 TEU has already been touched upon in the analysis of Article 11 TEU. However, in order to properly assess this link, a more in-depth analysis is required. How, then, can we understand the citizen's right to participate in the democratic life of the Union?

Looking more closely at Article 10(3) TEU, it is drafted in the same style as the citizenship rights listed in Articles 20–24 TFEU, which further highlights the strong legal foundation for democratic participation: 'every citizen shall have the right to participate in the democratic life of the Union' and 'decisions shall be taken as openly and as closely as possible to the citizen' (Article 10(3) TEU).[134] While Article 10(3) TEU is situated under the Treaty article associated with representative democracy, clearly spelled out in Article 10(1) TEU, the formulation of Article 10(3) TEU indicates that the right of participation referred to here is not just one of voting – an interpretation which has been confirmed by the Court, linking it to the right to attempt to influence the EU legislative process.[135] Indeed, it has been noted that the wording of Article 10(3) TEU can be given substance in various ways, implying both representative and participatory democracy.[136] In the Treaty establishing a Constitution for Europe, this right was set out in Article I-46, entitled

[131] See Hierlemann and others, *Under Construction* (n 85) 74–92.

[132] For an overview, see Hierlemann and others, *Under Construction* (n 85).

[133] Elizabeth Monaghan, 'Assessing Participation and Democracy in the EU: The Case of the European Citizens' Initiative' (2012) 13 *Perspectives on European Politics and Society* 285.

[134] Kris Grimonprez makes this connection, noting that Art 10(3) TEU is often neglected as a citizenship right by scholars, as well as EU citizen reports, and deserves much more attention: Kris Grimonprez, *The European Union and Education for Democratic Citizenship: Legal Foundations for EU Learning at School* (Nomos Verlagsgesellschaft mbH & Co KG, 2020) 469.

[135] *ClientEarth* (n 41) para 84.

[136] Grimonprez, *The EU and Education for Democratic Citizenship* (n 134) 470–71.

'The principle of representative democracy', leading to its current placement in the Treaty.[137] However, as discussed in the previous chapter, in the initial proposal of the Praesidium on 'the democratic life of the Union', the right was included in Article 34, 'The principle of participatory democracy'. This history, and its textual formulation, suggest that Article 10(3) TEU should best be interpreted as an overarching right relating to both representative and participatory democracy.[138] This view has now been cemented through the case law of the Court. Apart from its assessment in *ClientEarth*, the Court has stated that the ECI is 'an instrument concerning the right of citizens to participate in the democratic life of the Union, provided for in Article 10(3) TEU',[139] also now expressed in the regulation fleshing out the ECI.[140]

This overlapping function of participation, as expressed through different modes of participation relating to participatory or representative democracy, is similar to that of transparency. The application of the principle of transparency to the EU legislative process is, for instance, on the one hand, grounded in the system of representative democracy – in that citizens need to be able to understand how and why legislative choices are made, as well the substance of legislation, in order to hold their elected leaders accountable for those choices.[141] On the other hand, to the degree that transparency is intended to allow the public to engage more directly in the legislative and policy process, the principle of transparency serves participatory democracy purposes.[142]

The active link between transparency and democratic participation has been recognised by the CJEU in a string of cases, including *ClientEarth*, where the Court held that access to documents was prompted, in part, by the right that transparency was intended to secure, namely the right to participate in the democratic life of the Union according to Article 10(3) TEU – which, as interpreted by the Court, gives citizens the opportunity to learn of Union action and attempt to influence it.[143]

[137] Document from the Praesidium: Draft Title VI of the Constitutional Treaty relating to the democratic life of the Union (2 April 2003), art 34.

[138] Recital U states that 'a common European voting day would better reflect common participation by citizens across the Union, [and] reinforce participatory democracy': European Parliament, Resolution of 11 November 2015 on the reform of the electoral law of the European Union [2017] OJ C366/7; on an overarching *'demokratisches Grundrecht'*, see Ruffert, 'Art. 11 EUV' (n 13); associating the right 'primarily' with voting, see Koen Lenaerts and José A Gutiérrez-Fons, 'Epilogue on EU Citizenship: Hopes and Fears' in Dimitry Kochenov (ed), *EU Citizenship and Federalism*, 1st edn (Cambridge University Press, 2017); associating it with representative democracy, see Smismans, 'The Constitutional Labelling of "the Democratic Life of the EU"' (n 56).

[139] *Anagnostakis* (n 119), para 24.

[140] Regulation (EU) 2019/788 (n 123).

[141] This line of thinking is developed clearly by the AG: Case C-280/11 P *Info Access Europe* EU:C:2013:671, Opinion of AG Cruz Villalón, paras 61–72; see also Deirdre M Curtin and Päivi Leino-Sandberg, 'In Search of Transparency for EU Law-Making: Trilogues on the Cusp of Dawn' (2017) 54 *Common Market Law Review* 1673, 1679–80.

[142] Alemanno, 'Unpacking the Principle of Openness in EU Law' (n 40).

[143] *ClientEarth* (n 41), para 94; Paul Craig, *EU Administrative Law* (Oxford University Press, 2012) 341; transparency here is thus tied to accountability and allows for judicial review. *cf* with the obligation to give a statement of reasons for all legal acts, according to Art 296 (2) TFEU; see also Jürgen Schwarze, *European Administrative Law* (Office for Official Publications of the European Communities; Sweet & Maxwell, 1992) 1400–01; Case C-367/95 *Sytraval and Brink's France v Commission* EU:C:1997:249 341.

From the substantial body of case law on transparency, relevant to the intersection of the principle of participatory democracy and EU law-making is the Court's established link between democratic participation and transparency.[144] According to the Public Access to EU Documents Regulation, the documents held by the EU institutions are subject to the principle of 'widest possible access', subject only to certain specific and strictly interpreted exceptions to disclosure.[145] Furthermore, the Regulation provides that even wider access should be granted to 'legislative documents', and that these documents should, subject to the discrete enumerated exceptions to disclosure, be made directly accessible by the institutions.[146]

The Treaties provide that, according to the ordinary legislative procedure, the holders of the legislative function, to whom the Commission addresses its proposals, are jointly the Council and the Parliament,[147] and the obligations to provide reasons for legislative acts, now enshrined in Article 296 TFEU, has been a part of Community law since the very beginning.[148] However, the Court has further clarified that the key role the Commission plays, due to its right to initiate legislation, means that the documents it produces as part of its right of initiative – as well as the Council negotiating its position on a legislative file – are all legislative activities, and as such cannot rely on any general presumption of secrecy.[149] The same goes for documents relating to trilogue negotiations.[150] In commenting on the right of access to documents by the institutions during the legislative preparatory phase, the General Court comments that 'the expression of public opinion with regard to a particular legislative proposal forms an integral part of the exercise of Union citizens' democratic rights'.[151] The General Court also clarifies that the reality of the risk of external pressure, which may constitute a legitimate ground for restricting access to documents related to the decision-making process, needs to be established with certainty through 'tangible evidence'.[152] In these ways, transparency and participation are inextricably intertwined, and together may contribute to enhancing democratic legitimacy while increasing accountability through, inter alia, Article 10(3) TEU.[153]

[144] See, prominently, *Sweden and Turco* (n 41); *Schecke* (n 41), para 68; *Info Access Europe* (n 41); *ClientEarth* (n 41); *De Capitani* (n 41).

[145] Regulation (EC) No 1049/2001 of 30 May 2001 regarding public access to European Parliament, Council and Commission documents [2001] OJ L145.

[146] ibid, preamble para 6, Art 2(4), and Art 12(2); see also *Info Access Europe* (n 41).

[147] Art 14(1) and Art 16(1) TEU.

[148] Armin von Bogdandy, 'The European Lesson for International Democracy: The Significance of Articles 9 to 12 EU Treaty for International Organizations' (2012) 23 *European Journal of International Law* 315, 330.

[149] *Info Access Europe* (n 41), paras 74 and 75. For the Council, its Rules of Procedure help to determine when it is acting in a legislative capacity. See also mandated openness of the Council's voting record on legislative measures according to Art 16(8) TEU.

[150] *De Capitani* (n 41), para 84; see also Curtin and Leino-Sandberg, 'In Search of Transparency' (n 141).

[151] *De Capitani* (n 41), para 84.

[152] ibid, para 85.

[153] von Bogdandy, 'The European Lesson for International Democracy' (n 148).

3.2.1. The democratic life of the Union – unlocking the vertical component of Article 10(3) TEU

The analysis has revealed that the right to participate in the democratic life of the Union refers to practices and rights associated with the principles of representative and participatory democracy. However, the boundaries of the 'democratic life of the Union' are not spelled out in the text. Is the scope of the right limited to activities at the EU level? This question has not received much attention in literature.[154] The overall sparse legal commentary on this right may be linked to the observation that it is often forgotten or omitted by scholars and practitioners, perhaps owing to its absence in the citizens' rights catalogue in Articles 20–24 TFEU.[155] This omission is not in any way decisive, as the adjustments to this list brought by the Lisbon Treaty clarified that the list is not exhaustive (the phrase 'inter alia' was included), and the introductory paragraphs emphasise that the listing of the rights is without prejudice to other rights and prerogatives enumerated in the Treaty.[156] The question, then, remains whether and to what extent Article 10(3) TEU can inform the interpretation and application of national laws relating to participating in the democratic life of the Union, implicitly implying a right to participate in EU law-making, including related transparency standards. Can substantive and procedural national legislation – and, indeed, also EU secondary legislation relating to the democratic life of the Union – then 'activate' Article 10(3) TEU? And, relatedly, is it sufficiently clear, precise or unconditional to qualify as a stand-alone participation right?

As to the former question, it is possible to construe Article 10(3) TEU as targeting EU institutions and, therefore, not being applicable to Member States or other EU agencies or bodies. The context of existing (albeit limited) CJEU case law on Article 10(3) TEU also concerned EU institutions. However, a legal interpretation which takes into account the text and position of the article, its normative underpinnings, and related case law, highlights that Article 10(3) TEU should be interpreted as having a broader reach. Four arguments are developed in this regard.

Firstly, Article 10(3) TEU specifically refrains from pointing out EU institutional actors as duty-holders, in stark contrast to Article 11 TEU. In Article 11 TEU, as has been discussed, different institutional actors are pointed out as responsible for, for example, dialogue and consultation, which clearly delineates, directs and limits institutional obligation at the EU level. This leaves the clear impression that, for Article 10(3) TEU, the citizen's relationship to the democratic life of the Union is central.

Secondly, other elements of Article 10 TEU are directed at actors beyond the EU institutions. For instance, in referencing citizens' rights to participate and be

[154] See, however, Armin von Bogdandy and Luke Dimitrios Spieker, 'Transformative Constitutionalism in Luxembourg: How the Court Can Support Democratic Transitions' (2022) 29 *Columbia Journal of European Law* 65; Ruffert, 'Art. 11 EUV' (n 13).

[155] Grimonprez, *The EU and Education for Democratic Citizenship* (n 134) 469–71.

[156] Art 20 TFEU.

elected in European Parliament elections, Article 10(2) TEU is referencing rights which are realised primarily through institutions at the national and local level when organising European elections. The Court has also clarified in its case law that EU law imposes obligations on Member States with respect to the participation of EU citizens in the governance of the EU, notably by guaranteeing the right to vote in elections to the (European) Parliament in the Member State of which the EU citizen is a national.[157] Similarly, Article 10(2) TEU establishes the role of Member States and their peoples in the democratic legitimacy of the EU. Referring to Article 10(3) TEU, Lenaerts comments that such

> participation is *primarily* carried out by means of electing the members of the Parliament who are democratically entrusted with the representation of the interests of EU. In order to facilitate such democratic participation and representation, EU law imposes obligations on both the EU institutions and the Member States.[158]

The last sentence highlights the composite nature of EU democracy, which leads to the third argument. The phrase 'the democratic life of the Union' should be understood in a citizen-oriented way consistent with its rights-based formulation and the following reference to subsidiarity in the same article.[159] It is not just, then, that the democratic life and functioning of the Union depend upon the democratic life in the Member States, which scholars have recently emphasised in the context of Member State democratic backsliding, but that the 'democratic life of the Union' is not just occurring in Brussels or in relation to EU institutions. Following the discussion in the previous chapter, 'the democratic life of the Union' is best understood as a multi-level, composite phenomenon. The second sentence of Article 10(3) TEU, which references the principle of subsidiarity, and that decisions should be taken as open and closely as possible to citizens, promotes the understanding that EU democracy is occurring close (or as close as possible) to citizens. Member State governments, as well as national and local authorities, are also, in their different capacities, a part of the democratic life of the Union, specifically with regard to shaping, implementing and applying EU law. It is, therefore, clear that, in dealing with shaping EU law, this element of the principle of participatory democracy should inform the interpretation of pertinent legal norms at the national level. Given the Court's elaboration, a right to know and influence the EU legislative process flows from Article 10(3) TEU, and this could potentially inform national legal provisions related to both transparency and/or participation.

Fourthly, such an understanding of the principle of participatory democracy in the Union also closes an existing coherence gap between relevant international law obligations, primarily Article 25 of the International Covenant on Civil and

[157] Case C-650/13 *Delvigne v Commune de Lesparre Médoc and Préfet de la Gironde* EU:C:2015:648; Case C-814/21 *Commission v Poland* ECLI:EU:C:2024:963; Case C-808/21 *Commission v Czechia* ECLI:EU:C:2024:962.

[158] Lenaerts and Gutiérrez-Fons, 'Epilogue on EU Citizenship' (n 138) (emphasis added).

[159] Art 10(3) TEU – 'as closely as possible'.

Political Rights (ICCPR), but also other relevant international law instruments.[160] In this case, EU Member States' obligations, according to international law, to grant citizens the right of political participation, which includes a non-electoral dimension, have mutated due to the transference of legislative power and competence to the EU level.

Article 25 of the ICCPR and respective General Comments and jurisprudence of the UN Human Rights Committee define the obligations of States Parties regarding the right to participate in public and political life. Any restrictions on direct and indirect political and public participation are allowed under international human rights law only when these are based in law and are objective, reasonable and non-discriminatory.[161] Article 25 ICCPR entails not only a right to participate – the UN Human Rights Committee's guidelines clarify that the right of participation includes the opportunity to participate in the legislative processes, and that the state has a duty to facilitate citizens' enjoyment of this right.[162] Recent years have also seen a progressive evolution of international human rights law and jurisprudence on the scope of this right.[163] The UN High Commissioner for Human Rights now asserts that public participation rights following from ICCPR encompass the right 'to be consulted at each phase of legislative drafting and policymaking; to voice opinions and criticism; and to submit proposals aimed at improving the functioning and inclusivity of all State bodies'.[164] Article 25 is understood to require positive measures to create inclusive and meaningful processes and mechanisms,[165] including reaching out to underrepresented and marginalised groups[166] and avoiding cases where private corporations and lobby groups take precedence over other less-resourced and less-organised voices.[167] Finally, states should also guarantee full and effective access to justice and redress mechanisms to

[160] International Covenant on Civil and Political Rights 1966 (999 UNTS 171 (ICCPR)), art 25; The United Nations Declaration of Human Rights, and other specific human rights conventions, contain provisions on participation, albeit not to the same strong effect as the ICCPR: see Aditi Aparajita and others, 'A Comparative Survey of Procedures for Public Participation in the Lawmaking Process' (Oxford Pro Bono Publico, 2011).

[161] United Nations Human Rights Committee, General Comment no 25: The right to participate in public affairs, voting rights and the right to equal access to public service, UN Doc CCPR/C/21/Rev.1 /Add.7 (1996), para 4.

[162] ibid. Linking participation as a legal right with direct participation in law-making is not a new phenomenon in international human rights law: see, eg Steiner, 'Political Participation as a Human Right' (n 1).

[163] Office of the United Nations High Commissioner for Human Rights, 'Promotion, Protection and Implementation of the Right to Participate in Public Affairs in the Context of the Existing Human Rights Law: Best Practices, Experiences, Challenges and Ways to Overcome Them' [2015] UN Doc A/HRC/30/26, para 6.

[164] ibid, para 10; see also Convention on the Rights of Persons with Disabilities and Its Optional Protocol (n 83).

[165] United Nations Human Rights Committee, General Comment no 25 (n 161), paras 12, 26, and 27.

[166] Office of the United Nations High Commissioner for Human Rights, 'Promotion, Protection and Implementation' (n 163), paras 19–22.

[167] ibid, para 22; Special Rapporteur on extreme poverty and human rights, 'Report of the Special Rapporteur on extreme poverty and human rights', UN Doc A/HRC/23/36 (2013), para 72.

those unduly deprived of their right to participate in political and public affairs.[168] National constitutional courts have, for example, disqualified legislation on the basis of lacking participation, explicitly basing their argument (in part) on Article 25 ICCPR.[169]

Moreover, relevant provisions in the specific Conventions of the United Nations outline participatory obligations and rights in relation to specific groups.[170] The Convention on the Rights of the Child enshrines a child's right to express his or her views freely in all matters, including law-making, affecting him or her.[171] The Convention on the Elimination of All Forms of Discrimination against Women also guarantees women's rights to participate in the formulation of government policy, while the International Convention on the Elimination of All Forms of Racial Discrimination regulates the right of all people to take part in government and the conduct of public affairs at any level.[172] The International Convention on the Protection and Promotion of the Rights and Dignity of Persons with Disabilities involves the duty of the state to guarantee participatory rights to persons with disabilities.[173] Finally, the Declaration on the Rights of Indigenous Peoples of the United Nations also includes the right of indigenous peoples to public participation in matters that could affect their rights.[174]

The application of international law, and particularly the ICCPR, in the EU context is interesting, as it not only raises the issue of the EU courts upholding international law obligations made by Member States prior to joining the Union, but also what happens when those very obligations have mutated due to membership of the Union and a transference and fragmentation of legislative and public power. Through its vertical component, Article 10(3) TEU would contribute to addressing this mutation and fragmentation in a sustainable way, allowing for a coherent interpretation of EU and international law.

Finally, the vertical understanding of Article 10(3) TEU is not only consistent with a textual analysis of the article and the discussed statements of the CJEU. Crucially, it is grounded in an overall telos of the principle of participatory democracy – of enhancing democratic legitimacy and complementing representative democracy through emphasising and realising citizen-grounded participation. In unveiling these vertical dimensions of Article 10(3) TEU, there also lies a potential

[168] Special Rapporteur on extreme poverty and human rights, 'Report of the Special Rapporteur' (n 167), para 72.

[169] *Doctors for Life International v Speaker of the National Assembly and Others* [2006] Constitutional Court of South Africa ZACC 11, 2006 12 SA (CC) 2006 BCLR 1399 (CC); *Merafong Demarcation Forum & Others v President of the Republic of South Africa & Others* [2008] Constitutional Court of South Africa ZACC 10, 2008 5 SA 171 (CC) 2008 10 BCLR 968 (CC).

[170] See, eg Hanna Hämäläinen and Janne Salminen, 'Inclusive Participation in Law-Making: Good Governance or a Constitutional Obligation?' (2025) 13 *The Theory and Practice of Legislation* 213.

[171] Convention on the Rights of the Child 1989 (UNTS), Art 12.

[172] Convention on the Elimination of All Forms of Discrimination against Women 1979 (UNTS), Art 7b; International Convention on the Elimination of All Forms of Racial Discrimination 1965 (UNTS), Art 5.

[173] Convention on the Rights of Persons with Disabilities and Its Optional Protocol (n 83).

[174] United Nations Declaration on the Rights of Indigenous Peoples 2007 (UNGA Res 61/295).

pragmatically appealing prospect for stimulating a greater burden-sharing for the realisation of the principle of participatory democracy in the Union, through EU law refining this right in national contexts and activating Member States, national and local authorities and courts in its implementation – thereby giving practical effect to the right.[175]

3.2.2. The right to participate in the democratic life of the Union – a stand-alone participation right?

The question, then, remains whether direct effect may be attributed to Article 10(3) TEU. A few scholars, such as constitutional scholar Matthias Ruffert, contend that Article 10(3) TEU does indeed have direct effect.[176] However, in terms of delineating the content of this right, the citizens' catalogue in the Treaty is referred to, with the claim that Article 10(3) TEU would only be invoked on a stand-alone basis in exceptional cases.[177] This interpretation of Article 10(3) TEU has been picked up in the context of bringing the EU values, including democracy, before the Court, in response to the anti-democratic developments in certain Member States. Departing from the assumption that the democratic legitimacy at the EU level depends on the situation in each Member State, von Bogdandy and Spieker argue that:

> Article 10(3) TEU fulfils even the most demanding conception of direct effect, which requires a provision to contain a right that can be invoked by an individual before courts. Such a right concerns democratic standards at the EU, but also at the national level.[178]

In this way, they argue that Article 10(3) TEU can translate the value of democracy into justiciable obligations at the Member State level. To the degree that Article 10(3) TEU encompasses the value of representative democracy and associated rights, it is more plausible that Article 10(3) TEU has direct effect.[179] Von Bogdandy and Spieker, addressing the argument that Article 10(3) TEU might be too vague to be justiciable or directly effective, refer to a common European democratic core developed by standard-setters such as the Venice Commission, suggesting that the Court can take a case-by-case approach or a regression test to hammer out

[175] Art 19 TEU.
[176] Ruffert, 'Art. 11 EUV' (n 13); see also Marcel Haag, 'Art. 10 EUV' in Hans von der Groeben, Jürgen Schwarze and Armin Hatje (eds), *Europäisches Unionsrecht*, 7th edn (Nomos, 2015); on the opposing side, however, see Thomas Kröll and Georg Lienbacher, *EU-Kommentar*, 4th edn (Ulrich Becker and others (eds); Nomos; Facultas; Helbing Lichtenhahn Verlag, 2019).
[177] Ruffert, 'Art. 11 EUV' (n 13).
[178] von Bogdandy and Spieker, 'Transformative Constitutionalism in Luxembourg' (n 154).
[179] John Cotter, 'To Everything There Is a Season: Instrumentalising Article 10 TEU to Exclude Undemocratic Member State Representatives from the European Council and the Council' (2022) 47 *European Law Review* 69.

the exact content of the right in question.[180] Because their argument is developed in the context of what arguably constitutes rather severe democratic backsliding at the Member State level, the reasoning is primarily geared towards traditional democratic norms associated with representative parliamentary democracy and the rule of law. The Court is also increasingly concretising whether and how the overall principle of democracy is justiciable, in a string of cases which emphasise the political dimensions of EU citizenship.

For instance, in *Commission v Poland* and *Commission v Czechia*, the Court ruled on two infringement actions launched by the European Commission against Czechia and Poland, which both reserve the right to become a member of a political party to their own nationals. The European Commission argued that this constituted a violation of Article 22 TFEU, which

> guarantees all EU citizens residing in a Member State of which they are not nationals the right to vote and to stand as a candidate in municipal and European Parliament elections in that Member State under the same conditions as its nationals.[181]

In finding Czechia and Poland in violation of Article 22 TFEU, the Court interpreted Article 22 TFEU 'in the light of Articles 20 and 21 TFEU, Article 10 TEU and Article 12 of the Charter'. The Court linked free movement rights and equal treatment to EU citizens' political rights, including the right to participate in the democratic life of the Union, and also expressed how Article 10 TEU gives concrete expression to democracy as a founding EU value:

> Under Article 10(1) TEU, the functioning of the European Union is to be founded on representative democracy, which gives concrete expression to democracy as a value. Democracy is, under Article 2 TEU, one of the values on which the European Union is founded . . . Article 10(2) and (3) TEU confers on EU citizens the right to be directly represented in the European Parliament and to participate in the democratic life of the European Union. . . . Article 10 underscores, as regards elections to the European Parliament, the connection between the principle of representative democracy within the European Union and the right to vote and to stand as a candidate in European Parliament elections attached to citizenship of the Union . . . Political parties, one of whose functions is to field candidates in elections . . . thus fulfil an essential function in the system of representative democracy, on which the functioning of the European Union is founded, in accordance with Article 10(1) TEU.[182]

Similarly, in the highly publicised *Malta citizenship case*, the Court emphasises that 'citizens have political rights which ensure their participation in the democratic life of the European Union, as referred to in Articles 10 and 11 TEU and given concrete expression in Articles 20, 22 and 24 TFEU', and that 'in exercising

[180] von Bogdandy and Spieker, 'Transformative Constitutionalism in Luxembourg' (n 154).
[181] *Commission v Poland* (n 157) para 66.
[182] *Commission v Czechia* (n 157), paras 114–21; *Commission v Poland* (n 157) paras 112–19.

the political rights conferred on them by Articles 10 and 11 TEU, Union citizens participate directly in the democratic life of the European Union'.[183]

Following this line of thought, the Court in *Malta* further connects the exercise by the Member States of their power to lay down the conditions for granting citizenship with consequences for the functioning of the EU as a common legal order.[184] It is therefore clear that, to the degree that Article 10 TEU, including Article 10(3), formulates representative democracy rights, the Court has paved the way for enforcing these, beginning to delineate Member State obligations to ensure these rights.[185]

With regard to the principle of participatory democracy, and, in particular, thinking of its import for participation in law-making, it would be important to consider that there is much more diversity and variation amongst Member States with regard to the legislative process, and how participation in law-making is framed and practised, when compared with key representative democracy standards or features such as elections.[186] The same applies when in search of equivalents for the instruments of participatory democracy in Article 11 TEU, such as dialogue, consultation or citizens' initiatives, and so forth. From this standpoint, Article 10(3) TEU does not seem sufficiently clear and precise to have direct effect in relation to these practices, or, as such, grant a stand-alone right to participate in EU law-making at the national level. Similarly, at the EU level, although Article 10(3) TEU should be understood as offering citizens a right to know and directly attempt to influence the EU legislative process, it is not sufficiently clear and precise in this regard to be considered a stand-alone right. The question of whether Article 10(3) TEU may have direct effect in other respects does not fall directly within the research scope of this book. However, a brief elaboration is in order, to ground a coherent understanding of the 'democratic life' of the Union.

The democratic life of the Union can effectively be construed as having a core and a periphery, or, alternatively, understood in terms of concentric circles around a crucial centre. At the centre of this 'life' are the electoral practices tied to the principle of representative democracy, the founding democratic principle of the Union. Within the centre are also the citizens' rights of the Treaty, as featured in the citizens' rights catalogue in Articles 20–24 TFEU, and the participatory democracy right of the ECI, as well as the right of access to documents.[187] The right to participate in processes and practices at the heart of the democratic life of the Union has direct effect. This would, for example, be relevant when national

[183] Case C-181/23 *Commission v Malta* ECLI:EU:C:2025:283, para 43.

[184] *Commission v Malta* (n 183).

[185] See also Timothée Ceurremans and Elisabeth David, 'Article 10(3) TEU: Unlocking untapped potential to safeguard muted citizens' democratic rights' in Denis Duez and Cecilia Rizcallah (eds), *Standing up for the voiceless? Exploring the EU's capacity for rights protection* (Presses universitaires Saint-Louis Bruxelles, 2025) 147–70.

[186] Felix Uhlmann and Christoph Konrath, 'Participation' in Ulrich Karpen and Helen Xanthaki (eds), *Legislation in Europe: A Comprehensive Guide for Scholars and Practitioners* (Hart, 2017).

[187] See the next section for an in-depth analysis of the relationship between Art 10(3) TEU and catalogue rights.

measures are required to secure the right to participate in European Parliament elections.[188] It also comes into play, in line with the arguments of von Bogdandy and Spieker, when democratic guarantees at the national level – primarily core features of representative democracy – are so jeopardised as to undermine the overall exercise of Article 10(3) TEU.[189]

In addition, similarly to the argument made by Matthias Ruffert, there may be instances where the right enshrined in Article 10(3) TEU in relation to the processes and practices at the EU level has a wider berth than the respective framing in the Treaties or secondary legislation. In these circumstances, Article 10(3) TEU would gain particular relevance.[190] Now, as regards the democratic life of the Union outside 'the centre', this includes more direct forms of engagement with the Union and its institutions and bodies, prominently through participation in EU law-making and rule-making. The right also includes direct forms of engagement with Member State institutions and agencies, to the degree that they are acting in a (quasi-)EU legislative or EU rule-making capacity.[191] Other areas included in the periphery of the democratic life of the Union would include dialogue activities and, for example, the citizen panels which the president of the Commission has recently referred to as becoming a regular feature of the democratic life of the Union.[192] Similarly, it would relate to the Charter right to participate in social activity and corresponding obligations to promote opportunities for marginalised groups to participate. It would also correlate to the Charter rights in relation to rights to participate in social activity.[193]

These are all part and parcel of the right to participate in the democratic life of the Union. However, considering the more ambiguous status and modalities of these practices,[194] Article 10(3) TEU is not sufficiently clear and precise to grant direct effect in relation to them. Important, however, is that the relationship between the core and the periphery should, arguably, not be seen as fixed, but as possessing a moveable quality whereby processes at the periphery can, over time, gravitate towards the centre.

[188] *cf Delvigne v Commune de Lesparre Médoc and Préfet de la Gironde* (n 157); *Commission v Czechia* (n 157); *Commission v Poland* (n 157).

[189] von Bogdandy and Spieker, 'Transformative Constitutionalism in Luxembourg' (n 154).

[190] *cf* Ruffert, 'Art. 11 EUV' (n 13).

[191] That is, to the degree that they act as gatekeepers or holders of public power which may enable or encumber the exercise of citizens' and other parties' democratic rights in relation to these processes.

[192] 'The citizens' panels that were central to the Conference will now become a regular feature of our democratic life.': 'State of the Union Address by President von Der Leyen' (*European Commission*, 14 September 2022), https://ec.europa.eu/commission/presscorner/detail/en/speech_22_5493, accessed 6 February 2026.

[193] Art 24 CFR regulates the rights of the child, according to which, children may express their views freely, and their views shall be taken into consideration on matters that concern them in accordance with their age and maturity. Arts 24–26 CFR concern the right of the elderly to participate in social life, and aim to integrate people with disabilities, enabling their participation in the life of the community.

[194] In particular, with regard to how this right may be given effect: through direct participation, representation, or sortition.

In sum, as argued above, Article 10(3) TEU can and should, through the principle of consistent interpretation, inform legal norms at the national level as they relate to participation in EU law-making. Although Article 10(3) TEU does not possess direct effect in relation to participatory democracy practices such as directly participation in EU law-making, the effects of the application of Article 10(3) TEU, through consistent interpretation, to other norms at the EU and national level need not be trivial.

3.3. Transparency as the infrastructure of participatory democracy

While transparency features as a consultation goal in the Treaty text, it serves an overall much more crucial role in the Treaties, as the infrastructure for participation. As a crucial element in achieving the purpose of an 'ever-closer Union', Article 1 TEU characterises a core feature of this Union as one in which 'decisions are taken as openly as possible and as closely as possible to the citizen'. Article 10(3) TEU then reiterates this commitment and situates democratic participation alongside openness ('decisions are taken as openly and as closely as possible to the citizen'). Article 15(3) TFEU then constitutionalises access to documents as a general condition for democratic life, while Article 42 of the Charter confirms document access as a fundamental right.[195]

As stated, the Court has repeatedly connected the right of access to democratic participation in the legislative sphere. In *Sweden and Turco*, the Court anchored transparency in the democratic character of EU institutions and stressed the heightened importance of openness where institutions act legislatively; in *Access Info Europe*, it rejected attempts to anonymise Member State positions in ongoing legislative discussions when the justification was essentially 'pressure' or discomfort rather than a concrete, foreseeable harm.[196]

What this jurisprudence adds is the idea of traceability as a participatory condition: participation is weakened where citizens can neither see the legal reasoning shaping drafts nor attribute positions to identifiable actors. *Turco*'s insistence that legal advice can, in appropriate cases, be disclosed in legislative contexts speaks to a participatory model where critique is expected and 'reason-giving' is part of legitimacy, not a threat to it.

Transparency challenges become most acute where law-making is informal. The trilogue setting illustrates how 'early agreement' practices risk relocating real bargaining away from public view; the Court has rejected the idea that trilogues sit outside the transparency logic of legislation, and the European Ombudsman's trilogue inquiry pressed for systematic, proactive publication practices.[197] Recent

[195] Arts 10(3) and 11 TEU; Art 15(3) TFEU; Charter, Art 42.
[196] *Sweden and Turco v Council* (n 41); Case T-233/09 *Access Info Europe v Council* EU:T:2011:105.
[197] European Ombudsman, 'Decision in OI/8/2015/JAS on the Transparency of Trilogues'.

litigation has also pushed that point further into the Council's internal ecology. In *De Capitani v Council* (2023), and the subsequent 2025 judgment, the General Court treated working-party material as part of the normal legislative process and reiterated that sensitivity, informality or the 'preliminary' character of documents does not, by itself, justify secrecy; refusal still demands a specific, actual, reasonably foreseeable risk, not an abstract invocation of decision-making space.[198]

A complementary (and institutionally different) transparency track comes from the Ombudsman's strategic work on the Council's preparatory bodies. The Ombudsman framed insufficient recording and failure to make timely publication of Member State positions, and extensive use of 'LIMITÉ' practices, as impairing citizens' ability to hold legislators to account – an accountability deficit that directly undercuts participatory democracy in multi-level law-making. The Ombudsman's work complements the Court by shifting the focus from 'reactive disclosure on request' to structural conditions for democratic oversight. In the trilogues inquiry, the Ombudsman argued for proactive publication of key documents to make inter-institutional law-making intelligible and accountable to the public.[199]

A parallel line concerns the Council's preparatory bodies, where opacity can systematically weaken participatory democracy, even if final votes are public. The Ombudsman has scrutinised working parties and Committee of Permanent Representatives (COREPER) practices and treated insufficient visibility of Member State positions as a democratic problem in legislative law-making.[200] Case law shows how transparency disputes often target the epistemic backbone of proposed legislation. This link between transparency and participation is crucial; participation without access to the underlying knowledge base can easily become performative.

Transparency as participation also extends beyond documents to the visibility of influence. The previously discussed 2021 interinstitutional agreement on a mandatory transparency register, and the Commission's decisions on publishing meetings with interest representatives, institutionalise 'ethical and transparent' interest representation as a structural condition for meaningful dialogue, reducing (in theory, at least) informational asymmetries between repeat-player lobbyists and diffuse publics.[201]

EU transparency has long been criticised for being reduced to a narrow, legalistic 'documents model' (passive transparency), even though democratic participation often requires proactive disclosure, intelligible narratives, and timely traceability (active transparency).[202] This literature also cautions against a simplistic

[198] Case T-163/21 *Emilio De Capitani v Council of the European Union* ECLI:EU:T:2023:15; Case T-590/23 *Emilio De Capitani v Council of the European Union* ECLI:EU:T:2025:1001.

[199] European Ombudsman, strategic inquiry on trilogue transparency, OI/8/2015/JAS.

[200] European Ombudsman recommendation and special report, OI/2/2017/TE.

[201] See, eg Interinstitutional agreement of 20 May 2021 on a mandatory transparency register [2021] OJ L 207/1; Commission, Decision of 25 November 2014 on the publication of information on meetings held between Members of the Commission and organisations or self-employed individuals [2014] 2014/839/EU.

[202] Maarten Hillebrandt, 'EU Transparency as "Documents": Still Fit for Purpose?' (2021) 9 *Politics and Governance* 292.

'more transparency is always better' claim. One strand emphasises potential trade-offs: publicity may harden positions, reduce willingness to compromise, and push deliberation into even more informal channels; another strand challenges the inevitability of that trade-off and argues that certain forms of transparency (for example, reliable legislative records) can improve bargaining and accountability simultaneously.[203]

The overall legal implication is that transparency, understood as participatory infrastructure, in line with the Treaty references and CJEU case law, translates into enforceable entitlements for citizens and correlative procedural duties for EU institutions. For citizens, this means a justiciable right to request and obtain documents.[204] For institutions, the same framework entails obligations to register and manage documents so that access rights can be exercised in practice, and to justify refusals with concrete, foreseeable harm.

At the level of participatory democracy, these rights and obligations connect directly to the Treaty's participation duties: citizens' ability to 'participate in the democratic life of the Union' and 'publicly exchange views' presupposes timely access to the evidentiary and political record of law-making, while the Commission's obligation to consult widely and to maintain open, transparent dialogue presupposes not just inviting input but making it possible to follow the decision-making process – who was consulted, on what text, on what timetable, and with what follow-up?[205] Concretely, this entails that EU actors should design consultations and impact assessments (IAs) as traceable processes, and that citizens and civil society can invoke the access-to-documents framework and Ombudsman oversight to contest opacity and procedural shortcuts as democratic, not merely administrative, failures.[206]

3.4. Additional rights flowing from the principle of participatory democracy

In addition to the explicitly mentioned rights and obligations that emerge from a closer analysis of Article 11 TEU and Article 10(3) TEU and the embedded link to transparency, the principle of participatory democracy is frequently said to encompass the right to petition the Parliament and the right to complain to the European Ombudsman. The link between these instruments and the principle of participatory democracy is, at an initial glance, however, somewhat murky. As

[203] See, eg Stéphanie Novak and Maarten Hillebrandt, 'Analysing the Trade-off between Transparency and Efficiency in the Council of the European Union' (2020) 27 *Journal of European Public Policy* 141.

[204] Subject to strictly interpreted exceptions under Regulation 1049/2001, read in light of Art 15(3) TFEU and Art 42 CFR with a heightened public-interest weight where documents relate to legislative activity; Art 15(3) TFEU; Art 42 CFR; *Sweden and Turco v Council* (n 41).

[205] Arts 10(3) and Art 11 TEU; see also Interinstitutional Agreement of 13 April [2016] on Better Law-Making OJ L123/1.

[206] ibid. See also ss 3.1. and 3.2.

has been mentioned, the instruments predate the Lisbon Treaty and do not correspond neatly to any of the practices outlined in Article 11 TEU. At the national level, although appealing to an ombudsman or petitioning a national parliament is certainly a citizen's participation instrument unrelated to voting, it is often associated with representative democracy, for example as an instrument to enhance parliamentary accountability, or centred on addressing maladministration, and is a feature of many modern constitutional democracies. Despite this, and while noting that the two instruments are not confined to EU citizens, the right to petition Parliament, as well as to address the Ombudsman, give expression to the citizen's right to participate in the democratic life of the Union in Article 10(3) TEU. As such, these rights are now explicitly linked to democracy in the Union, and, through Article 10(3) TEU, arguably to both its representative and participatory pillars. This interpretation finds support in the Court's case law, which connects the right to petition the EU institutions as both 'an instrument of citizen participation in the democratic life of the European Union' and 'one of the means of ensuring direct dialogue between citizens of the European Union and their representatives'.[207]

Articles 20–24 TFEU, which catalogue citizen rights, reinforce and structure the connection between the Democratic Principles in Title II TEU and citizens' rights. Article 20 TFEU summarily lists all the citizens' rights covered in the rights catalogue; Articles 21–23 TFEU then outline citizen rights related to representative democracy (for example, the right to stand in elections, as well as freedom of movement); while Article 24 TFEU expounds on citizen rights which could also relate to participatory democracy. Article 24 TFEU begins with a legal basis for legislating on the ECI,[208] followed by the right to petition the Parliament in accordance with Article 227 TFEU,[209] the right to write to any of the institutions or bodies and receive a reply,[210] and the right to complain to the European Ombudsman.[211] These rights are also mirrored in Article 41 of the Charter.[212] In order to understand how these instruments serve as elements of participatory democracy, as well as to assess the import for EU law-making, each will be surveyed in turn.

Regarding petitions, while they have historically had a relatively low visibility and impact in EU institutional decision-making,[213] petitioning Parliament remains the oldest all-purpose participation option available to anyone wishing to interact

[207] Case C-261/13 P *Peter Schönberger v European Parliament* EU:C:2014:2423, para 17.

[208] Art 24(1) TFEU states: 'The European Parliament and the Council, acting by means of regulations in accordance with the ordinary legislative procedure, shall adopt the provisions for the procedures and conditions required for a citizens' initiative within the meaning of Article 11 of the Treaty on European Union, including the minimum number of Member States from which such citizens must come.'

[209] 'Every citizen of the Union shall have the right to petition the European Parliament' in accordance with Article 227 TFEU.

[210] 'Every citizen of the Union may write to any of the institutions or bodies' in one of the languages mentioned in Article 55(1) of the Treaty on European Union and have an answer in the same language.

[211] 'Every citizen of the Union may apply to the Ombudsman established in accordance with Art 228 TEU.'

[212] See Art 41 CFR.

[213] Hierlemann and others, *Under Construction* (n 85) 92–110.

with the EU institutional framework of their own accord.[214] According to 227 TFEU, any citizen of the Union, and any natural or legal person residing or having its registered office in a Member State, shall have the right to address, individually or in association with other citizens or persons, a petition to the Parliament on a matter which comes within the Union's fields of activity, and which affects him, her or it directly.[215] This broadly framed right gives EU citizens and residents a convenient way to address issues that escape the notice and attention of Parliament committees or EU institutions.[216] Over the last few years, there have been between 1,000 and 1,500 petitions per year, of which roughly two-thirds have been declared admissible.[217] However, during the 2014–19 legislative term,[218] the Petitions Committee only addressed questions for oral answer to the Commission or the Council 15 times, on nine different topics, five of which were followed up by a resolution.[219] Meanwhile, the Petitions Committee has been recognised as the least popular committee in the Parliament, with little political currency.[220] This may be beginning to change, with the Petitions Committee and its secretariat attempting to reform its work and raise its profile, in part emphasising its role for participatory democracy in the EU.[221] Indeed, the right to petition can serve a variety of complementary roles, including setting the legislative agenda and providing administrative and political oversight over the EU Commission and Member States. It may also provide a tool for enhancing representation for people and groups that do not currently have one, such as non-EU citizens, immigrants, and minorities. In terms of its current import for EU law-making, its visibility and impact are low. While very rare, it is, however, possible for the Parliament to follow up on a citizen's petition by requesting the Commission to take legislative action relating to the substance of a petition.[222] Its flexibility, accessibility and low threshold for participation – citizens can, on their own accord, and in their own time, file a petition on an array of matters, and also do so together with other citizens – make it an underutilised participatory democracy tool with potential for democratising, both in terms of participation in EU affairs more broadly and participation in EU law-making specifically. The Court has emphasised the role that petitions play in fulfilling dialogue, as mandated by Article 11(2) TEU.[223]

As regards the European Ombudsman, its profile and impact have steadily increased since its inception, while its independence has been cemented.[224] The

[214] Alberto Alemanno, 'Strengthening the Role and Impact of Petitions as an Instrument of Participatory Democracy, Study Commissioned by the European Parliament's Policy Department for Citizens' Rights and Constitutional Affairs PE 694.837' 63.

[215] Art 227 TFEU.

[216] Alemanno, 'Strengthening the Role and Impact of Petitions' (n 214) 34–37.

[217] ibid.

[218] ibid 25.

[219] Hierlemann and others, *Under Construction* (n 85) 92–110.

[220] ibid.

[221] Alemanno, 'Strengthening the Role and Impact of Petitions' (n 214) 34–37.

[222] ibid 32.

[223] *Peter Schönberger v European Parliament* (n 207), para 17.

[224] Hierlemann and others, *Under Construction* (n 85) 110–30.

right to complain against maladministration is well established in the Treaties and Charter. Article 15 TFEU states that the EU should conduct its work as openly as possible, so that any citizen has the right to documents of the Union's institutions. Relatedly, Article 41 of the Charter establishes that 'every person has the right to have his or her affairs handled impartially, fairly and within a reasonable time'. These provisions constitute the EU citizen's fundamental right to good administration. To uphold that right, any citizen or legal person lawfully residing in the EU has the right to refer cases of maladministration to the European Ombudsman, and the Ombudsman has the duty to receive and to deal with those complaints.[225]

The legal foundation for the work of the Ombudsman is found in Article 228 TFEU, which stipulates, inter alia, that, in accordance with her duties, the Ombudsman shall conduct inquiries for which she finds grounds, either on her own initiative or on the basis of complaints submitted to her directly or through a Member of the Parliament.[226] Over the years, the Ombudsman has increasingly broadened its approach by shifting its focus from a narrower notion of maladministration to the wider and more encompassing idea of good administration. More recently, an increased focus on strategic inquiries has extended the office's influence. Despite the lack of a binding nature, the acceptance rate of proposals of the European Ombudsman is high (between 70 and 90 per cent, depending on the institution).[227] It is widely recognised that various individual and recent strategic inquiries, as well as its ongoing work, have substantially impacted on the workings of the EU's public administration.[228] The European Ombudsman has highlighted her dual role, on the one hand, as a citizen's instrument, and, on the other, as a specific obligation to 'protect participatory democracy', referencing Article 10(3) TEU.[229] Viewed through this lens, the right to appeal to the Ombudsman rather emerges as a redress mechanism for Article 10(3) TEU and Article 11 TEU (see section 3.7. below). The Ombudsman herself would seem to subscribe to this interpretation, with several of the recent key strategic initiatives, which have been initiated *ex officio*, being linked to Article 10 TEU and Article 11 TEU.[230]

[225] Arts 24 and 25 TFEU; Art 43 Charter and Art 228 TFEU.

[226] Art 228(1) TFEU.

[227] Hierlemann and others, *Under Construction* (n 85) 110.

[228] ibid 119–21.

[229] See, eg European Ombudsman, '25 Years of the European Ombudsman. Strengthening the role of the European Ombudsman in challenging times for citizens' (Speech, Brussels, 25 October 2020, https://www.ombudsman.europa.eu/en/speech/en/134202, accessed 6 February 2026.

[230] Citing Arts 1(2) TEU and 10(3) TEU, the Ombudsman, for example, states that 'The Commission expressed the concern that full transparency as regards the work of expert groups might impact negatively on their smooth functioning. The Ombudsman notes however that the Treaty on European Union requires that decisions are taken as openly as possible and as closely as possible to the citizen. The Commission utilises its expert groups as part of its internal decision-making process. The Commission's rules governing expert groups must therefore comply with the Treaty provisions.': European Ombudsman, 'Recommendation of the European Ombudsman in her strategic inquiry OI/6/2014/NF concerning the composition of Commission expert groups, 29 January 2016', indent E 52.

3.5. Participatory democracy innovation: Commission citizen panels

The European Commission's European Citizens' Panels emerged as a direct institutional legacy of the Conference on the Future of Europe: a deliberate move to normalise deliberative participation inside the Commission's policy cycle rather than treating it as an exceptional constitutional moment. The Commission presents the panels as a standing feature of 'European democratic life' and links them explicitly to the post-Conference 'new push for European democracy', ie to a strategy of widening participatory access beyond elections and party representation.[231] Operationally, panels convene a demographically and geographically stratified sample of citizens drawn from all Member States, with typically around 150 participants, working across several sessions with facilitation and expert input, producing recommendations that are formally transmitted into Commission workstreams.[232] The Commission has used this format on concrete policy files (for example, food waste, learning mobility, and virtual worlds), and it has explicitly cited panel input as part of its evidence and participation base for subsequent policy communications, and for one legislative initiative (food waste).[233]

Legally, these panels are not a Treaty-based right in the way that the ECI is. They are an administrative instrument created and run by the Commission; the binding rules are mainly those that attach to Commission procedure, and to the handling of participants, rather than a justiciable 'right to a panel'. However, the panels are framed and constrained, not only by the Commission's Better Regulation and general EU public-law constraints such as data protection, non-discrimination, and good administration, but also by Article 10(3) TEU and Article 11(3) TEU on consultation. Because the panels, due to their very nature, enhance procedural equality as well as bringing in citizens, with transparent processes and output, they seem to fulfil the procedural requirements of the principle of participatory democracy. The remaining obligation which flows from the principle would be the obligation of the Commission to detail whether and how the recommendations made by the panel have been taken on.

In the emerging scholarship, the panels are generally assessed as a meaningful procedural innovation with limited weight unless their outputs are more tightly coupled to decision-making, and to duties of institutional justification. Indeed, it has been noted that the panels are not yet embedded institutionally in the Commission, as there is significant internal scepticism within the Commission

[231] European Commission, 'Conference on the Future of Europe: Putting Vision into Concrete Action' (2022) COM(2022) 404 final.

[232] European Commission, 'European Citizens' Panels' (Factsheet, 2023), https://citizens.ec.europa.eu/european-citizens-panels_en, accessed 25 February 2026.

[233] See European Commission, 'Proposal for a Directive of the European Parliament and of the Council Amending Directive 2008/98/EC on Waste' (2023) COM(2023) 420 final.

about the utility of consulting citizens, and the panels in general.[234] A recurring diagnosis is that the panels strengthen the participatory infrastructure, but that the terms of engagement (topic choice, framing, expert curation, and the institutional pathway for uptake) remain controlled by the Commission.[235] Policy-facing evaluations welcome the method, but argue for greater ambition on follow-up, clearer institutional responsibilities for responding to recommendations, and more robust transparency around how panel outputs are filtered into policy.[236]

Finally, empirical and evaluation work on the earlier Conference panels tends to find high participant satisfaction and solid deliberative quality but mixed evidence of policy incidence, reinforcing the core point that deliberation's democratic value in the EU depends less on the internal quality of discussion than on the legal and procedural conditions that govern uptake, reason-giving, and traceability of influence.[237]

3.6. Good administration and participatory democracy

The connection between good administration and participatory democracy, as highlighted by the role of the Ombudsman, has several linkages.[238] Necessary for realising the principle of participatory democracy are rules related to the gathering, application and dissemination of information and knowledge.[239] Procedural principles ensuring the functions of participatory democracy (and necessary flow of information upon which meaningful participation rests) are tied to the principle of rule of law, and to good administration. It is clear from Articles 9–12 TEU that the Union's executive or administrative arm contributes to the realisation of democratic ideals through its preparation of legislation and its implementational activities.[240] Viewed through this lens, parts of EU procedural administrative law may be seen as a concretisation of the principle of democratic participation.[241] Good administration appears in EU law as a right developed through the case law of the EU courts, derived from general principles on the basis of the rule of law, and partially codified in Article 41 of the Charter.[242]

[234] Andrey Demidov, Johannes Greubel and Perle Petit, 'Assessing the European Citizens' Panels: Greater Ambition Needed' Observatory Report (EU Democracy Reform Observatory, 2023).

[235] Emilie Gjaldbæk-Sverdrup, Kalypso Nicolaïdis and Nicolás Palomo Hernández, '"Technocratic Democratisation": What Can We Learn from the European Commission's New Generation European Citizens' Panels?' (European University Institute) RSC Working Paper 2023/65.

[236] Demidov, Greubel and Petit, 'Assessing the European Citizens' Panels' (n 234).

[237] European Commission, 'Study on the Citizens' Panels as Part of the Conference on the Future of Europe' (Technopolis Group, 29 March 2024).

[238] Curtin, Hofmann and Mendes, 'Constitutionalising EU Executive Rule-Making Procedures' (n 117) 13–14.

[239] ibid.

[240] Herwig Hofmann, Gerard C Rowe and Alexander Türk, *Administrative Law and Policy of the European Union* (Oxford University Press, 2011) 148.

[241] Curtin, Hofmann and Mendes, 'Constitutionalising EU Executive Rule-Making Procedures' (n 117) 14–15.

[242] ibid 15.

For EU rule-making, as well as in the administration of individual cases, there is a strong connection between the principle of participatory democracy and the right to good or sound administration.[243] However, the application and force of administrative law for legislative consultation is complex and more limited. While there are strong arguments for good administration principles – including the right to be heard, statements of reasons, and the duty of care – to be applied to EU executive rule-making, these cannot be immediately transposed to the Commission's actions as a legislator in law-making.[244] This dilemma is demonstrated in the pre-Lisbon case *Atlanta*, where the CJEU draws a clear distinction between the right to be heard in the context of individual determinations, and norms of a legislative nature.[245]

The right to good administration in the Charter includes, for instance, the right of every person to be heard before any individual measure that would affect him or her adversely is taken. Article 41 primarily applies to individual measures; however, its content is somewhat ambiguous, and there are interpretations suggesting that it may also apply when an individual's rights or interests may be adversely impacted by a procedure.[246] However, the standard interpretation, also informed by the Court, is that it does not apply to norms of a general or legislative nature, ie rule-making. For rule-making, the Commission obligation to consult according to Article 11(3) TEU, in combination with Article 10(3) TEU, would instead apply.

The Court has, however, in other contexts stressed that the principle of good administration applies generally to the actions of the EU in its relations with the public.[247] For actions the Commission takes in relation to consultation, some portions of good administration may consequently apply. Furthermore, EU administrative law concretises other constitutional principles which are applicable broadly to the Commission.[248] The duty of care (also known as the duty of diligent and impartial examination) is one manifestation of the Commission's constitutional obligation to promote the general interest of the Union in its legislative mandate, as well as the Treaty-bound duty to be completely independent in its actions.[249] Similarly, the general obligation to give reasons, according to Article 296 TFEU, applies to all legal acts, allowing for judicial review.[250]

It is also clear that the Commission is obliged to promote the values articulated in the Treaty (human dignity, freedom, democracy, equality, the rule of law and

[243] Mendes, *Participation in EU Rule-Making* (n 106).

[244] Case C-104/97 *Atlanta v Commission* EU:C:1999:498.

[245] ibid.

[246] Itai Rabinovici, 'The Right to Be Heard in the Charter of Fundamental Rights of the European Union' (2012) 18 *European Public Law* 149; Hämäläinen and Salminen, 'Inclusive Participation in Law-Making' (n 170).

[247] Case C-337/15 P *Ombudsman v Staelen* EU:C:2016:823.

[248] See, eg Frietz Werner, 'Verwaltungsrecht Als Konkretisiertes Verfassungsrecht' [1963] Mensch und Verwaltung.

[249] Art 17 (1)(2), and (3) TEU, and Art 1 TEU.

[250] The Court elaborates that the duty to give reasons, 'which is justified in particular by the need for the Court to be able to exercise judicial review, must apply to all acts which may be the subject of an action for annulment': Case C-370/07 *Commission of the European Communities v Council of the European Union* EU:C:2009:590, para 42.

respect for human rights).[251] The values of pluralism and non-discrimination also find expression in the democratic principle of equality of Article 9 TEU, which all Union institutions and bodies are obliged to adhere to in all their activities; through Article 8 TFEU, obliging the Union to eliminate inequalities in all of its activities;[252] and finally also through Article 18, which prohibits any discrimination on the grounds of nationality, within the scope of application of the Treaties.[253]

In addition, the Treaties also established a duty for the EU institutions to ensure consistency, effectiveness and continuity in their policies and actions.[254] These constitutional imperatives are not confined, in their application, to administrative cases – they apply broadly to the Commission's work. Consequently, the parts of administrative law and good administration that are manifestations of constitutional obligation are relevant to EU institutions as they apply Article 11 TEU and 10(3) TEU, including the Commission in its role in the legislative process, and including for consultation work. As previously discussed, the Treaty's 'democratic principles' and EU administration also overlap insofar as openness is concerned – this comes clearly into focus through Article 15 TFEU, noting that, 'in order to promote good governance and ensure the participation of civil society, the institutions, bodies, offices and agencies of the Union shall conduct their work as openly as possible'.[255]

In considering the strong links (concretisation) and sometimes overlapping responsibilities prompted by participatory democracy and good administration, as well as other Treaty obligations, it has been demonstrated that case law on good administration needs to be assessed in order to examine which parts may apply to the Commission's consultation work with regard to law-making. While the duty of careful and impartial examination (as well as statements of reasons, which are also a Treaty obligation) would in many respects be applicable, the right to be heard would, for instance, not on its own apply directly to the Commission's legislative work (setting EU rule-making aside).[256] Because case law on EU administrative law is primarily concerned with administrative cases, attention must also be given to the degree to which the Court's formulation of administrative law principles applies solely to that case format. The Court generally tends to be stricter in its review of administrative acts, compared with legislative ones.[257] Further, within the framework of the Court's judicial review of Commission preparation of legislative acts, good governance obligations are commonly framed neither as good administration principles nor generally as obligations derived from democracy in the broad sense, but as requirements in

[251] Art 2 TEU. On the obligation of the Union to have 'an institutional framework which shall aim to promote its values', see Art 13 TEU.

[252] Art 8 TFEU.

[253] Art 9 TEU, Art 8 TFEU and Art 18 TFEU.

[254] See Art 181 TFEU, Art 21(3) TEU and Art 212(1) TFEU.

[255] Art 15 TFEU.

[256] *cf* Alexander H Türk, 'Oversight of Administrative Rulemaking: Judicial Review: Judicial Review' (2013) 19 *European Law Journal* 126.

[257] Case C-18/62 *Barge v High Authority* EU:C:1963:56; Schwarze, *European Administrative Law* (n 143) 1406, 1412.

order to fulfil the requirements of proportionality and subsidiarity, or for the Court to fulfil its obligation of judicial review.[258]

3.7. Rights and obligations – a snapshot

The legal analysis thus far has shed light on the rights and obligations which flow from the principle of participatory democracy, of which a summary catalogue overview is presented below.[259] The rights are delineated from obligations and listed according to their addressees and duty-bearers, followed by a brief comment.[260] The overall aim is to capture, as a form of snapshot, the rights and obligations outlined and discussed in the analysis thus far, in order to provide an overview. The rights are formulated at a rather high level with a reference to the key legal source underlying the formulated right or obligation. At the end of this section, two tables (Tables 1 and 2) capture the overall picture.

3.7.1. Participatory democracy citizen rights

The legal analysis has revealed key *citizen and resident rights* flowing from the principle of participatory democracy.[261] These are as follows:

- The right of citizens to participate in the democratic life of the Union.[262]
- The right of citizens to know about the EU legislative process, and to attempt to meaningfully inform or influence it. This includes the right to:
  - Scrutinise legislative documents and information relating to EU law-making 'in good time' in order to attempt to influence that process.[263]
  - Scrutinise 'all the information which has formed the basis of a legislative act'.[264]

[258] See, eg Case C-310/04 *Spain v Council* EU:C:2006:521 (paras 122 and 130); this is analysed in the section on enforcement.

[259] In highlighting that no taxonomy of legally grounded participatory democracy instruments in the EU exists or has even been attempted, Alemanno suggests as a starting point to organise them according to their rationale, ie agenda-setting tools, input mechanisms, administrative actions, and ex post review channels. I take a different approach in this section. Categorising participatory democracy instruments according to their purpose may have the advantage of clarity and overview for the potential participatory protagonists and assist in constructing a framework for citizen participation in the EU. Such a classification, however, is arguably less helpful in attempting to pin down legal rights and obligations flowing from the principle. In addition, several of the instruments and actions discussed in relation to the principle of participatory democracy seem to serve multiple purposes, and the strict EU-level approach is a bad fit for the multi-level approach to law-making taken in this research. *cf* Alemanno, 'Towards a Permanent Citizens Participatory Mechanism in the EU' (n 115) 15–16.

[260] For each right, I cite the main legal source, or a combination of the most relevant sources, based on the overall legal analysis in the chapter thus far.

[261] Art 10(3) TEU.

[262] ibid.

[263] *Sweden and Turco v Council*, (n 41), paras 44–45; *ClientEarth* (n 41), para 84; See also Regulation No 1049/2001, recital 6.

[264] *Sweden and Turco v Council* (n 41), paras 44, 45 and 68. This includes, in principle, an obligation to

  - Effectively make their views known before legislative choices have been definitively adopted, so far as both the Commission's decision to submit a legislative proposal and the content of that proposal are concerned.[265]
- The right of citizens and residents to petition the Parliament.[266]
- The right of citizens and residents to complain (refer complaints) to the European Ombudsman.[267]
- The right of citizens to initiate and participate in European Citizenship Initiatives, and:[268]
  - The right to a reasoned reply from the Commission (in the event of successful registration).[269]
  - The right to a hearing in Parliament (in the event of successful registration).[270]
- The right of citizens and residents to access documents of the Union institutions, bodies, offices and agencies.[271]
- Related key rights: the right of every person to good administration;[272] the right to write to an EU official and get a reply.[273]

It is clear that the principle of participatory democracy provides a right for citizens to engage with EU law-making at various stages, but with a focus on the early stages of the legislative process – starting from its early stages, when the Commission prepares an IA. The right to know about, and to attempt to inform and influence, the EU law-making process applies to all EU institutions acting in a 'legislative' or 'key player'[274] capacity, notably the Parliament, the Council and the Commission. While there is no overarching general right for citizens to participate in consultations, when consultation opportunities are presented, for example because they are mandated for legislative proposals, citizens have a right to be treated equally, including with regard to access. While the right to petition, in its current modus operandi, is not particularly directed at EU law-making, it holds potential to further realise the principle of participatory democracy in the Union. The right to complain to the Ombudsman, while a citizen's instrument, should, crucially, be seen as an overarching 'soft' redress or enforcement mechanism for participatory democracy rights.

---

disclose the opinions of the Council's legal service relating to a legislative process; see also Curtin and Leino-Sandberg, 'In Search of Transparency' (n 141).

[265] *ClientEarth* (n 41) para 84.

[266] This includes any natural or legal person residing or having its registered office in a Member State: see Art 24 TFEU, Art 227 TFEU and Art 44 CFR.

[267] Art 24 TFEU, Art 228 TFEU and Art 43 CFR.

[268] Art 11(4) TEU and Art 24 TFEU. See also Regulation No 1049/2001.

[269] Regulation (EU) 2019/788 (n 123), art 6(4).

[270] ibid, art 14.

[271] Art 15 TFEU.

[272] Art 41 CFR.

[273] Art 24 TFEU.

[274] A 'key player' is how Court labels the Commission's role in the legislative process, with legal effects for its obligations and discretion: *ClientEarth* (n 41), paras 88 and 94.

3.7.2. Participatory democracy obligations

Several obligations of the EU institutions were noted, and these are outlined below.

EU institutions, bodies, offices and agencies:

- Shall observe the principle of the equality of the EU's citizens, who shall receive equal attention from them.[275]
  - shall promote equal access to participation opportunities and channels of communication.[276]
- Shall take decisions as openly and as closely as possible to the citizen,[277] and conduct their work as openly as possible, to ensure the participation of civil society.[278]

EU institutions[279]

- Give 'citizens and representative associations the opportunity to make known and publicly exchange their views in all areas of Union action'.[280]
- Maintain 'an open, transparent and regular dialogue with representative associations and civil society'.[281]

The Council, Parliament and Commission

- Establish a framework for ethical and transparent interest representation.[282]
  - Limit the discretion of engagement with interested parties to that framework; currently, to those who are registered in the Transparency Register, according to the principle of conditionality.[283]
  - Disclosure obligations for the Commissioners, their Cabinet members and Directors-General, as well as MEPs, with regard to contact with interest representatives.[284]

[275] Art 9 TEU.
[276] Art 9 TEU, Art 11 TEU, Art 2 Protocol No 2.
[277] Art 10(3) TEU.
[278] Art 15 TFEU.
[279] The following obligations apply overall to EU institutions, but the level and form of their applicability, in particular in relation to the Court and ECB, must be assessed on a case-by-case basis. For a discussion of the Court's obligations, see Alberto Alemanno and Oana Stefan, 'Openness at the Court of Justice of the European Union: Toppling a Taboo' (2014) 51 *Common Market Law Review* 97.
[280] Art 11(1) TEU.
[281] Art 11(2) TEU.
[282] Art 11(1), (2) TEU.
[283] Art 11(1) TEU, Art 11(2) TEU, and Interinstitutional agreement of 20 May 2021 on a mandatory transparency register [2021] OJ L207/1.
[284] Commission, Decision of 25 November 2014 on the publication of information on meetings held between Members of the Commission and organisations or self-employed individuals [2014] 2014

The Commission

- Shall conduct broad consultations with parties concerned, in order to ensure that Union action is coherent and transparent.[285]
    - Shall consult with parties concerned in its rule-making activities.
    - Shall consult widely before proposing a legislative act. This includes taking into account the regional and local dimension of the action envisaged, except in cases of exceptional urgency, in which case the Commission shall give reasons for this in its proposal.[286]
    - Before adopting a proposal, conduct public consultations in an open and transparent way, ensuring that the modalities and time limits of those public consultations allow for the widest possible participation.[287]
    - Conduct open Internet-based consultations for legislative proposals.[288]
    - Communicate the results of public and stakeholder consultations, without delay, to both co-legislators and the public.[289]
    - Shall provide consultation feedback which details the reasoning on whether and how contributions have impacted on the proposal.[290]
    - Is obliged to actively promote equality of access to consultation opportunities.[291]

The duty to consult for EU law-making is clearly and unequivocally enshrined in Article 11(3) TEU and, as such, is a central element of the principle of participatory democracy. Article 2 Protocol No 2 further clarifies that, except for areas of exclusive competence, consultation is a must for law-making, and provides the only exception to this duty as 'exceptional urgency', while adding an obligation to state the reason whenever this exception is used. Article 11(3) TEU should also be interpreted in light of Article 10(3) TEU. Other constitutionally enshrined principles, such as transparency, in Article 15 TFEU, and equality, in Article 9 TEU, and the stated goal of consultation in 'ensuring' transparency and coherence, in combination with Article 11 TEU and 10(3) TEU, establish an

/839/EU; Commission, Decision of 25 November 2014 on the publication of information on meetings held between Directors-General of the Commission and organisations or self-employed individuals [2014] 2014/838/EU.

[285] Art 11(3) TEU.

[286] Art 2 Protocol No 2, with the exception for areas in which the EU has exclusive competence.

[287] This would generally imply a 12-week standard and minimum amount of time: see Commission, General Principles and Minimum Standards (n 66).

[288] This follows from the obligation to consult openly and broadly for legislative proposals in Art 11(3) TEU and Art 2 Protocol No 2. It also provides the floor for the exercise of citizens' rights to know and attempt to make their views known in relation to legislative proposals. It is also spelled out in the Interinstitutional Agreement on Better Law-Making: Interinstitutional Agreement of 13 April [2016] on Better Law-Making OJ L123/1, para 19.

[289] 2016 Interinstitutional Agreement on Better Law-Making, operationalising Art 10(3) TEU, Art 11(1) TEU and 15 TFEU.

[290] Arts 11(3) TEU, 11(2) TEU; Art 15(1) TEU; Art 10(3) TEU. This also follows from principles of proportionality and subsidiarity.

[291] Art 11(3) TEU, Art 10(3) TEU, Art 9 TEU, Art 2TEU; Treaty and Charter articles on non -discrimination and equality; also Art 25 ICCP.

obligation to provide consultation feedback, and also to actively promote equality of access to consultation opportunities.

Table 1 The Principle of Participatory Democracy: Citizens' Rights

The right of citizens to participate in the democratic life of the Union.
The right of citizens to know about the EU legislative process, and to attempt to meaningfully inform or influence it. This includes the right to: *Scrutinise legislative documents and information relating to EU law-making 'in good time' in order to attempt to influence that process.* *Scrutinise 'all the information which has formed the basis of a legislative act'.* *Effectively make their views known before legislative choices have been definitively adopted, so far as both the Commission's decision to submit a legislative proposal, and the content of that proposal, are concerned.*
The right of citizens and residents to petition the Parliament.
The right of citizens and residents to complain (refer complaints) to the European Ombudsman.
The right of citizens to initiate and participate in European Citizenship Initiatives. *The right to a reasoned reply from the Commission (in the event of successful registration).* *The right to a hearing in Parliament (in the event of successful registration).*
The right of citizens and residents to access documents of the Union institutions, bodies, offices and agencies.
Related key rights: the right of every person to good administration; the right to write to an EU official and get a reply.

3.7.3. Participatory democracy obligations for Member State actors

The overall key obligation for Member State actors is to interpret national law in light of citizens' right to participate in the democratic life of the Union.[292] Relevant actors include national and local institutions and courts, which potentially could be informed by the principle of participatory democracy, and could relate to transparency, participation in law-making (for example, for negotiation and implementation), good administration, and digital rights.[293] One area which

[292] Art 10(3) TEU.

[293] Although outside the ambit of this book, it is also foreseeable that legislation which relates to the right to know, such as the right to education, could be informed by the principle; the enjoyment of the right is dependent on some basic understanding of the EU. See Grimonprez, *The EU and Education for*

Table 2 The Principle of Participatory Democracy: Obligations

<table>
<tr><td rowspan="5">EU institutions</td><td rowspan="3">EU bodies, offices and agencies</td><td>Shall observe the principle of the equality of the EU's citizens, who shall receive equal attention from them.</td></tr>
<tr><td>Shall promote equal access to participation opportunities and channels of communication.</td></tr>
<tr><td>Shall take decisions as openly and as closely as possible to the citizen, and conduct their work as openly as possible, to ensure the participation of civil society.</td></tr>
<tr><td colspan="2">Give 'citizens and representative associations the opportunity to make known and publicly exchange their views in all areas of Union action'.</td></tr>
<tr><td colspan="2">Maintain 'an open, transparent and regular dialogue with representative associations and civil society'.</td></tr>
<tr><td rowspan="4">Commission</td><td rowspan="3">Council and Parliament</td><td>Establish a framework for ethical and transparent interest representation.</td></tr>
<tr><td>Limit the discretion of engagement with interested parties to that framework: currently those who are registered in the Transparency Register, according to the principle of conditionality.</td></tr>
<tr><td>Disclosure obligations for the Commissioners, their Cabinet members and Directors-General, as well as MEPs, with regard to contact with interest representatives.</td></tr>
<tr><td colspan="2">Shall conduct broad consultations with parties concerned, in order to ensure that Union action is coherent and transparent.</td></tr>
<tr><td rowspan="6"></td><td colspan="2">Shall consult widely before proposing a legislative act. This includes taking into account the regional and local dimension of the action envisaged, except in cases of exceptional urgency, in which case the Commission shall give reasons for this. Shall consult with parties concerned in its rule-making activities.</td></tr>
<tr><td colspan="2">Before adopting a legislative proposal, conduct public consultations in an open and transparent way, ensuring that the modalities and time limits of those public consultations allow for the widest possible participation.</td></tr>
<tr><td colspan="2">Conduct open Internet-based consultations for legislative proposals.</td></tr>
<tr><td colspan="2">Communicate the results of public and stakeholder consultations, without delay, to both co-legislators and the public.</td></tr>
<tr><td colspan="2">Shall provide consultation feedback which details the reasoning on whether and how contributions have impacted on the proposal.</td></tr>
<tr><td colspan="2">Obligation to promote equality of access to consultation (to reach 'parties concerned').</td></tr>
<tr><td>Member State Actors</td><td colspan="2">Interpret national law in light of citizens' right to participate in the democratic life of the Union.</td></tr>
</table>

stands out as particularly relevant is legal norms which impact on citizens' foundational democratic capacities, including, for example, education (including EU education). However, for all such cases, this would largely depend on the formulation of national law, the domestic scope of judicial review, and the space for consistent interpretation.[294]

In sum, the principle of participatory democracy affects citizens by providing them with an opportunity to participate directly and indirectly in the democratic life of the Union (primarily the latter, through representative organisations, civil society, and interest representation more broadly). To democratic legitimacy, participatory democracy adds participation and representation of citizens, stakeholders and interests.[295]

Having identified and analysed the instruments, rights and obligations that flow from the principle of participatory democracy for EU law- and rule-making broadly, the next section will focus in more depth on to what degree the rights and obligations associated with law-making consultation are justiciable, and the path to such review. Article 11 TEU, combined with Article 10(3) TEU and Protocol No 2, charts a path for consultation, but in several respects leaves the door open for interpretation over its reach and the question of binding character. While the principle of participation enshrined in Article 11 TEU, in the absence of secondary legislation, does not translate into a specific and enforceable subjective right to participate in law-making consultation,[296] the discussion so far emphasises that it entails legal duties and obligations on the Commission, and that neglect of these obligations could or should entail opportunities for redress, which will be explored in the following section.[297]

Because there is a lack of jurisprudence dealing directly with Article 11(3) TEU, any understanding of the scope of the duties laid down by participatory democracy cannot be separated from the EU courts' comments on the overarching principle of democracy, as well its stance on judicial review, including standing. The following section teases out and discusses these various strands of case law as they relate to the principle of participatory democracy and law-making consultation obligations specifically.

Democratic Citizenship (n 134). Furthermore, participation is increasingly mediated by digital rights, which would also be informed by Article 10(3) TEU.

[294] For Swedish law-making consultation, this will be explored in the next chapter.

[295] Grimonprez, *The EU and Education for Democratic Citizenship* (n 134) 501.

[296] On this point there is generally broad agreement, although it is unclear whether a complete lack of consultation could amount to any legal consequence: see, eg Closa, 'Constitutional prospects' (n 10) 128–29; Mendes, 'Participation and the Role of Law after Lisbon' (n 2) 1866; García Macho, 'Article 11' (n 6); Lock, 'Article 11 TEU' (n 3).

[297] Although often indicative of each other, subjective rights and opportunities for redress are not always synonymous.

3.8. Legal Redress at the EU level for breaches of the principle of participatory democracy

While the analysis so far has outlined some key legal obligations flowing from Articles 11 and 10(3) TEU, and demonstrated some specific duties and rights stemming from the principle of participatory democracy, the question remains as to what degree these imperatives can be realised through judicial review.

First, the relatively straightforward review framework for the ECI and transparency as it relates to access to documents will be discussed. The analyses will then turn towards breaches of law-making consultation duties. Here, the pathway to redress at the EU level will be assessed, looking at the legal opportunities and obstacles relating to standing, annulment and reparations.

In the legal analysis, attention is drawn to how the Court's jurisprudence reflects the Treaty's framing of consultation as a feature of democracy and consultation, and as a tool to enhance rational and effective law-making,[298] in particular through facilitating the principles of subsidiarity and proportionality.[299] The question is then explored of to what degree the principle of participatory democracy can be enforced as a stand-alone claim, and how it may influence the Court's proportionality review.

After exploring the possibilities for judicial review, alternative paths to materialise consultation and other participatory democracy rights and obligations are analysed, focusing on the investigative powers of the European Ombudsman.

3.8.1. Review of the rights related to the ECI, access to documents and petitions

EU participatory democracy rights are enforceable mainly through judicial review of procedural duties and transparency duties, plus a smaller set of Treaty-based complaint channels. The hard-law route is Articles 263 and 265 TFEU: applicants challenge refusals or procedural defects in instruments that operationalise participation (and they challenge secrecy that blocks participation through access-to-documents law.[300] The courts treat openness as legally relevant to democratic legitimacy, especially in legislative contexts.[301]

[298] I use the terms 'rational' and 'effective' here in a broad sense, referring generally to the Commission's Treaty obligations to be effective in their duties, as well as their stated good governance principle of effectiveness. In other situations, more clarity is required relating to the value and difference between efficacy, efficiency and effectiveness of legislation: Maria Mousmouti, 'Making Legislative Effectiveness an Operational Concept: Unfolding the Effectiveness Test as a Conceptual Tool for Lawmaking' (2018) 9 *European Journal of Risk Regulation* 445.

[299] To a lesser degree, coherence as well. Meanwhile, it should be noted that the link to subsidiarity and proportionality does not apply equally for domains where the EU has exclusive competence.

[300] Regulation No 1049/2001 Art 15 TFEU, Art 42 CFR.

[301] *Sweden and Turco v Council* (n 41); *De Capitani v European Parliament* (n 41).

Soft-law enforcement is carried out by two Treaty mechanisms that create institutional obligations even when courts are slow, deferential, or procedurally hard to access. Petitions to the European Parliament can force a file or an issue into a public parliamentary process, and can trigger inquiries, hearings and political pressure.[302] This is not a binding remedy, but it is a structured accountability tool. Complaints to the European Ombudsman[303] target maladministration that typically undermines participation in practice: opacity, failure to give reasons, delay, and unfair handling. Ombudsman findings and recommendations are non-binding, but they frequently produce corrective administrative changes and generate standards of good administration that complement judicial review.[304] "Having determined there exists straightforward legal redress mechanisms for breaches of such rights; i.e. access to documents, the ECI and petitions," the analysis will now explore to what degree there is legal redress for breaches of participation or consultation duties.

3.8.2. Breaches of participation and consultation duties: Standing

In general, it is clear the CJEU is disinclined to establish participation rights,[305] and this is clear in its approach to standing. The Court has limited the scope of participation rights to not include acts of a general nature. It has drawn a clear distinction between access to individual determinations, and norms of a legislative nature – the leading case being *Atlanta*.[306] There, the applicant sought compensation for costs incurred though a Community regulation on the banana market. The argument was that the right to be heard in an administrative procedure affecting a person could be transposed to the process leading to a regulation: from the perspective of the party, it was irrelevant whether their legal situation was affected as a result of an administrative or legislative process.[307] The CJEU rejected this argument and held that case law involving a right to be heard related only to acts of direct and individual concern to the applicant. It also held that the only obligations of consultation on the EU legislator were those laid down by the Treaty article in question.[308] This approach has been confirmed in a string

[302] Art 227 TFEU; Art 44 CFR.

[303] Art 228 TFEU; Art 43 CFR.

[304] Arts 227–28 TFEU; Arts 43–44 CFR "See also section 3.9."

[305] Case T-521/93 *Atlanta AG and others v Council and Commission* ECLI:EU:T:1996:184, para 71; Case C-104/97 P *Atlanta AG and Others v Commission and Council* EU:C:1999:498, para 38; Case C-258/02 P *Bactria Industriehygiene-Service Verwaltungs GmbH v Commission*, para 43; Paul Craig and G De Búrca, *EU Law: Text, Cases, and Materials*, 7th edn (Oxford University Press, 2020) 521; for a critical appraisal, see Mendes, *Participation in EU Rule-Making* (n 106) ch 5.

[306] Case C-104/97 P *Atlanta AG and Others v Commission and Council* (n 305).

[307] As argued by the appellant (ibid 31).

[308] The Court noted that 'the only obligations of consultation incumbent on the Community legislature are those laid down in the article in question' (ibid 38).

of cases, including *Pfizer* and *Bactria*.[309] In *Pfizer*, even though the plaintiff was directly and individually concerned by the norm, the Court found that the right to access did not apply. Also, the courts have been unwilling to draw legal consequences from participation in the legislative process.[310] However, years earlier, in *UEAPME*,[311] the General Court accepted that lack of democratic legitimation was a relevant argument to support a claim for enhanced consultation duties on the part of the Commission and Council (the legislative procedure in question did not provide for full involvement of the Parliament). Although the case led to an unsuccessful outcome for the applicants in terms of standing, the Court accepted that standing could be granted to stakeholders in such cases, even if they were appealing against 'legislation'. The wider applicability of this case is, however, tenuous. *UEAPME* played out within the realm of social dialogue, where social partners are co-creators of the law, and the Court did not analyse the democratic legitimacy of the Union.[312]

Throughout this case law, the Courts repeatedly emphasise an absence of stated Treaty rights. It is telling that in *Atlanta*, the General Court stated:

> In its judgment in Case 138/79 *Roquette Frères v Council* [1980] ECR 3333, the ECJ held that the obligation to consult the Parliament, as laid down in various places in the Treaty, reflects at Community level the fundamental democratic principle that the people should take part in the exercise of power through the intermediary of a representative assembly.

Representation of the various groups of economic and social life also takes place in the Community's legislative process, in the form of consultation of the Economic and Social Committee. In the *Atlanta* action, both the Parliament and that committee were, in fact, consulted before Regulation No 404/93 was adopted, as provided for in the Treaty.[313] Current Treaty provisions requiring consultation in relation to law-making – and anchoring the right to democratic participation – therefore cast this case law in a different light, prompting rather a reflection on the current different constitutional and legal status of consultation.

How, then, might the Court view participatory democracy's import and place within the overarching principle of democracy? Looking at the Court's case law on democracy, it cautiously began to use the concept of democracy as a legal

[309] Case T-13/99 *Pfizer v Council* ECLI:EU:T:2002:209; *Bactria Industriehygiene-Service Verwaltungs GmbH v Commission* (n 305).

[310] In *Asocarne*, participation in legislative process leading to a directive did not grant standing, whereas in *Jégo-Quere* law-making participation did not imply that the party was individually concerned: see Case C-10/95 *Asocarne v Council* EU:C:1995:406; Case C-263/02 *Commission v Jégo-Quére* EU:C:2004:210; see also Case C-321/95 P *Greenpeace v Commission* EU:C:1998:153; Case T-60/96 *Merck v Commission* ECLI:EU:T:1997:81.

[311] *UEAPME* (n 79).

[312] On this point, see Joana Mendes, 'The Democratic Foundations of the Union: Representative Democracy, Complementarity and the Legal Challenge of Article 11 TEU' in Adam Lazowski and Steven Blockmans (eds), *Research Handbook on EU Institutional Law* (Edward Elgar, 2016).

[313] Case T-521/93 *Atlanta* (n 305), paras 71–72.

principle in the 1980s, initially primarily to enable judicial review.[314] In its case law, the Court has commented on both traditional and novel features of democracy, with representative democracy standing as the bedrock, while transparency and 'democratic' governance reflect the evolution of the concept.[315] Commenting on representative democracy, the Court has emphasised the fundamental democratic principle that people should take part in the exercise of power through the intermediary of a representative assembly, elaborating on institutional balance.[316] It has also acknowledged the complexities of the supranational context, which may imply unconventional structures of authority and decision-making, for instance in order to supply constitutional goods and fundamental rights.[317]

Moving beyond representative democracy, in the aforementioned *UEAPME* case, the General Court explored how participatory democratic mechanisms could complement representative democracy within the context of social dialogue.[318] The Court found that direct participation of interest representatives of sufficiently broad spectrum and representativity would be required to compensate for a lack of Parliament participation, and that such a party could be granted standing. This would require some built-in mechanisms which guarantee that those parties are sufficiently representative. The applicability of *UEAPME* to an understanding of the principle of participatory democracy and giving it effect, as discussed, is limited. Although it confirmed the courts' endorsement of complementary forms of democracy, the case deals with a legislatively distinct situation: the negotiation stage of social dialogue which has its own legal base, and where social partners share legislative power with the EU institutions.[319] The General Court's reasoning has been criticised in that it lacked reference and reasoning to the Member States as a source of democracy, and that criteria for representativity was not really examined.[320] Finally, it should be noted that the case also predates the Lisbon's Treaty's current constitutional outline of democracy.

In more recent case law, however, the courts have found reason to elaborate on Article 11(4) and Article 10(3), in cases regarding the ECI and transparency, respectively. As has been analysed, as regards the ECI, the courts are guided by specific secondary legislation envisioned in Article 24 TEU which fleshes out the process of the ECI. The current regulation, to a large degree, codifies what the CJEU established through review of the Commission's management of the ECIs. In the existing cases dealing with appeals of Commission decisions to refuse to register

[314] *Roquette Frères* (n 75), para 33; C-300/89 *Commission v Council* EU:C:1991:244, para 20; Case C-392/95 *Parliament v Council* EU:C:1997:289, para 14.

[315] Lenaerts categorises these developments as 'continuity' and 'change': Koen Lenaerts, 'The Principle of Democracy in the Case Law of the European Court of Justice' (2013) 62 *International and Comparative Law Quarterly* 271.

[316] *Roquette Frères* (n 75); Case 294/83 *Les Verts v Parliament* EU:C:1986:166; *Commission v Council* (n 314); *Parliament v Council* (n 314).

[317] Case C-133/88 *Martinez v Parliament* EU:C:1989:124.

[318] *UEAPME* (n 79).

[319] See Arts 154 and 155 TEU.

[320] This lack of reasoning was noted: see Lenaerts, 'The Principle of Democracy' (n 315) 299.

an initiative, the courts navigate procedural guarantees enshrined in the (previous) regulation and its foundation in the Treaty while outlining the boundaries of the Commission's discretion.[321] Looking at the CJEU's interpretation of the democratic foundations of the ECI, there is some indication of how Article 11(3) TEU could be applied as well. In *Efler and Others v Commission*, the General Court concluded that the interpretation of the concept of 'legal act' found in Article 11(4) TEU must be done in view of the broader principle of democracy, as well as the improvement of the democratic functioning of the EU aimed for through Article 11 TEU:

> On the contrary, the principle of democracy, which, as it is stated in particular in the preamble to the EU Treaty, in Article 2 TEU and in the preamble to the Charter of Fundamental Rights of the European Union, is one of the fundamental values of the European Union, as is the objective specifically pursued by the ECI mechanism, which consists in improving the democratic functioning of the European Union by granting every citizen a general right to participate in democratic life.[322]

The General Court's reasoning implies that the duties enshrined in Article 11 TEU should not be interpreted in a narrow sense, so as to undermine their democratising objectives or, in the General Court's words, 'the objective of participation in the democratic life of the European Union'.[323] In a similar line of reasoning, the General Court refuted the Commission's argument that the right for citizens to participate in the ECI was of lower value than rights enshrined in the Charter, reminding the parties that Article 11 TEU, being primary Union law, enjoyed the same legal value as the Charter, and consequently should not enjoy a lesser degree of judicial protection.[324] As noted, the Court has also interpreted the right to undertake an ECI as 'an instrument concerning the right of citizens to participate in the democratic life of the Union, provided for in Article 10(3) TEU'.[325] The EU courts, in their ECI case law, also emphasise the importance of participatory mechanisms in raising items for democratic debate.[326]

The link between participation, democracy and transparency has been explicitly commented on by the EU courts. In *Schecke*, the Court expressed that transparency 'enables citizens to participate more closely in the decision-making process and guarantees that the administration enjoys greater legitimacy and is more effective and more accountable to the citizens in a democratic system'.[327] In *MyTravel*, the Court held that the application of the principle of openness is not limited to the legislative process, although it is more central

[321] T-646/13 *Minority SafePack - one million signatures for diversity in Europe v Commission* EU:T:2017:59; *Anagnostakis* (n 119); Case T-561/14 *One of Us and other v Commission* EU:T:2018:210; *Efler and Others* (n 121).

[322] *Efler and Others* (n 121), paras 36 and 38.

[323] ibid 42.

[324] *One of Us and other* (n 321), paras 99 and 100.

[325] *Anagnostakis* (n 119), para 24.

[326] See, eg *Efler and Others* (n 121), para 43.

[327] *Schecke* (n 41), para 68; Lenaerts argues that this case law implies that, in certain cases, it is appropriate to entrust independent agencies with the adoption of policy or individual decisions that take a broader range of stakeholders into consideration: Lenaerts, 'The Principle of Democracy' (n 315) 277.

for law-making than in the context of administrative procedures.[328] In balancing the principle of transparency against other legitimate considerations, the General Court highlighted in *Access Info Europe* that transparency enables citizens to participate more closely in the decision-making process, and that public access to the entire content of Council documents constitutes the general rule, subject to exceptions which must be interpreted and applied strictly, while generally the Court of Justice has also emphasised that openness contributes to strengthening democracy by enabling citizens to scrutinise all the information and considerations which have formed the basis for a legislative act.[329] The Court has specifically established, as formulated in *Turco*, that the possibility for citizens to find out the considerations underpinning legislative action is a precondition for the effective exercise of their democratic rights.[330] In *Client Earth*, the Court solidified this relationship and established a clear legal link between citizens' right to participate in the democratic life of the Union and related rights, such as transparency, that allow the realisation of this right.[331] This understanding was, for example, reinforced in *De Capitani v Parliament*,[332] *in relation to trilogue documents*.[333]

These determinations are, in a sense, an interpretation of transparency in the light of the democratic objective pursued by the principle.[334] The analysis of Article 11 TEU and the linkages established in jurisprudence between access to the legislative process and an evolving conception of democracy, therefore, suggest that the EU courts, at this juncture, are well placed to intervene where consultation duties are breached (see section 3.8.3. below).

However, the procedural path leading to judicial review for such determinations would be cumbersome, to say the least.[335] First, there is the courts' case law favouring both limited standing and judicial review in direct challenges, as well as for claims to reparations.[336] Hypothetically, a breach of Article 11(3) TEU – possibly in combination with Article 10(3) TEU – would trigger liability with regard to infringement of the Treaties or essential procedural requirements for law-making. For access to a direct challenge, the claim would either have to be brought

[328] Case C-506/08P *Sweden v Commission and MyTravel* EU:C:2011:496.

[329] *Access Info Europe v Council* (n 196); *Sweden and Turco v Council* (n 41).

[330] *De Capitani* (n 41), para 80; *Info Access* (n 41), para 33; *Sweden and Turco v Council* (n 41), para 46; see also Case T-755/14 *Herbert Smith Freehills LLP v Commission* EU:T:2016:482.

[331] *ClientEarth* (n 41).

[332] *De Capitani* (n 41).

[333] Curtin and Leino-Sandberg, 'In Search of Transparency' (n 141).

[334] Alemanno, 'Unpacking the Principle of Openness in EU Law' (n 40).

[335] It may be incorrect to draw the conclusion that the courts are hesitant to enforce the various elements of Art 11 TEU, as there has been no litigation. See also Mendes, 'The Democratic Foundations of the Union' (n 312).

[336] Takis Tridimas and Sara Poli, 'Locus Standi of Individuals under Article 230(4): The Return of Euridice?' in Anthony Arnull, Piet Eeckhout and Takis Tridimas (eds), *Continuity and Change in EU Law*, 1st edn (Oxford University Press, 2008); Steve Peers and Marios Costa, 'Court of Justice of the European Union (General Chamber), Judicial Review of EU Acts after the Treaty of Lisbon; Order of 6 September 2011, Case T-18/10 *Inuit Tapiriit Kanatami and Others v. Commission* & Judgment of 25 October 2011, Case T-262/10 *Microban v. Commission*' (2012) 8 European Constitutional Law Review 82, 82–104.

by one of the privileged actors (Member States et al.) or the courts' current view on standing for private parties, rooted in *Plaumann* and solidified through *Inuit*, where the Court specifically held that the Lisbon Treaty did not alter its established case law on standing, would have to shift as a result of the principle of participatory democracy.[337] Some commentators have noted that the Court's position on standing is probably untenable in light of the constitutionalising of participation, while others remain highly sceptical of the Court's willingness to intervene at all in such cases.[338]

Another argument in favour of a shift in the Court's jurisprudence on standing, which surfaced in the previous section, and which is largely overlooked, is that of international law. The right to participate in public affairs, according to Article 25 ICCPR, encompasses the right 'to be consulted at each phase of legislative drafting and policymaking; to voice opinions and criticism',[339] with an emphasis on guaranteeing full and effective access to justice and redress mechanisms to those unduly deprived of their right to participate in political and public affairs.[340] The interpretive demands of viewing EU law and international law through a lens of coherence could prompt the Court to interpret Article 11(3) and its stance on standing in light of the international law obligations made by Member States prior to joining the Union, since these obligations have been transferred to the Union to the degree that legislative power now rests with the Union.

In this context, it is relevant to note that, in a recent case, the AG seemed to indicate that a right to be heard could follow from the principle of participatory democracy – specifically with regard to lapse of consultation or information-gathering among stakeholders. The case emerged in the context of tariff threats and concerned whether a company affected negatively by a Commission implementing regulation which added customs duties on certain products from the United States had a right to be heard before the adoption of the regulation in question. One of the enforcement regulations had its own clause mandating information-gathering from stakeholders. Referencing Article 11(2) and (3) TEU, AG Capeta wrote:

[337] Case 25-62 *Plaumann v Commission* EU:C:1963:17; Case C583/11 P *Inuit Tapiriit Kanatami and Others v European Parliament and Council of the European Union* EU:C:2013:625.

[338] The potential for review in this regard is contested. For views favouring the view that the Court would or should grant standing and intervene, see Alberto Alemanno, 'The Better Regulation Initiative at the Judicial Gate: A Trojan Horse within the Commission's Walls or the Way Forward?' (2009) 15 European Law Journal 382, 392–94; Ymre Schuurmans and Wim Voermans, 'Better Regulation by Appeal' (2011) 17 *European Public Law* 507; Mendes, 'Participation and the Role of Law after Lisbon' (n 2) 1873–75; Anne Meuwese, 'Embedding Consultation Procedures: Law or Institutionalization?' (2011) 17 *European Public Law* 527; on the opposing side regarding the outlook, see eg Smismans, 'The Constitutional Labelling of "the Democratic Life of the EU"' (n 56); Lock, 'Article 11 TEU' (n 3); García Macho, 'Article 11' (n 6); as well as – more ambiguous regarding feasibility and desirability – Gautier Busschaert, *Participatory Democracy, Civil Society and Social Europe: A Legal and Political Perspective*, 1st edn (Intersentia, 2016) 110–20.

[339] Office of the United Nations High Commissioner for Human Rights, 'Promotion, Protection and Implementation' (n 163) para 10.

[340] ibid, para 22; see also Special Rapporteur on extreme poverty and human rights, 'Report of the Special Rapporteur' (n 167), para 72.

> That being said, in a system based on the principle of participatory democracy, where subjects who may be affected by measures of general application adopted by the administration must be given the opportunity to express their interests and explain their concerns, that opportunity may be given by means of some sort of information gathering procedure before the adoption envisaged in Article 9 of the Enforcement Regulation.[341]

The AG noted that, in the case at hand, the Commission had indeed organised consultations, whereas the plaintiff had not participated in these. The AG further noted:

> In the judgment under appeal, the General Court did not find any issue relating to the transparency and openness of that procedure, in so far as it was organised in relation to the contested regulation. Nor has Zippo challenged that finding by means of a cross-appeal. It may thus be concluded that, in the present case, the right to be heard in procedures leading to the adoption of measures of general application, to the extent that such a right may be deemed to exist independently from Article 41(2)(a) of the Charter, was satisfied.[342]

It is unclear, at this point, to what degree the AG framed the right to be heard as solely based on the principle of participatory democracy as exemplified in Article 11 TEU, and specifically in the context of delegated and implementing acts, ie rule-making. It is also unclear whether the AG was indicating that the right to be heard is triggered when non-legislative acts contain some form of consultation provisions. Considering rule-making in the EU setting presents a specific democratic challenge; the case has long been made that participation and consultation play a significant democratic legitimacy purpose.[343] In any case, the AG found that, even if such a right were to exist based on participatory democracy reasons, circumstances in the present case did not speak to such a right being triggered. Crucially, the Court did not engage with this reasoning, finding in late January 2026 that the General Court had erred in law when granting a right to be heard to the company in question.[344] The Court basically confirmed its settled case law, relying on the classic arguments of acts of a general vs individual nature, while clearly stating that Article 41 of the Charter neither grants a right to be heard towards acts of a general nature nor changes the previous determinations of the Court in this regard.[345] Considering the Court's current stance, a major shift on standing currently seems unlikely. However, this case, as well as the statements of the AG, signify that there may be room in the future for the principle of participatory democracy to play a larger role in determinations of standing, specifically as it relates to non-legislative acts.

[341] Case C-811/23 *European Commission v Zippo* [2025] P Opinion of AG Capeta ECLI:EU:C:2026:48, para 96.
[342] ibid, paras 97–102.
[343] See, eg Mendes, *Participation in EU Rule-Making* (n 106).
[344] Case C 811/23 P *Commission v Zippo* ECLI:EU:C:2026:48, paras 51–77.
[345] ibid.

According to Article 263(2) TFEU, the Court shall have jurisdiction in actions brought either by a Member State, the Parliament, the Council or the Commission on grounds of lack of competence; infringement of an essential procedural requirement; infringement of the Treaties, or of any rule of law relating to their application; or misuse of powers. This means that the possibility nevertheless remains for the privileged parties to bring a claim to the Court, or for other parties to seek redress through an indirect claim.

3.8.3. Annulment

A direct or indirect challenge of a legal act based on Article 11(3) TEU could be directed at several of the grounds of annulment, such as the absence of a procedural requirement, or infringement of the Treaties, since the legal basis for consultation is now clearly written into primary law.

Overall, the analysis, in the previous sections, of the relevant Treaty articles, as well as Protocol No 2, revealed strong and clear language in primary law on the obligation to consult. A direct or indirect challenge of a legal act based on Article 11(3) TEU – for example, flawed or absent legislative consultation – could constitute a breach of a procedural requirement, or infringement of the Treaties. Such cases may involve situations where there has been no consultation, significant groups/parties concerned have not been consulted, consultation time frames have clearly been inadequate, or there has been a serious deficiency in transparency and feedback (for example, if the Court has failed to share how participatory input has impacted on its legislative work). References to, inter alia, Article 10(3) TEU, Article 9 TEU and Article 15 TFEU, as well as Article 11(1) and Article 11(2) TEU, and, to a lesser extent, the Interinstitutional Agreement on Better Law-Making and Article 25 ICCPR, could support such claims.

In fact, the EU courts have now also recently begun to tentatively engage with the provisions of the Interinstitutional Agreement on Better Law-Making, in cases brought by Member States for the annulment of an act.[346] In two such cases, the relevant plea invoking the Interinstitutional Agreement related either to an allegedly flawed IA (for a directive) or the lack of proper consultation in relation to a non-legislative act.[347] Even though the pleas were not successful, the way the courts engaged with the provisions of the Interinstitutional Agreement, assessing the discretion the provisions in question afforded, alternatively determined whether the party in question had lived up to the relevant requirements of the agreement, thus indirectly confirming the status of the inter-institutional agreements in mandating procedural requirements for consultation.[348]

[346] Case C-128/17 *Republic of Poland v European Parliament and Council of the European Union* EU:C:2019:194; Case T-626/17 *Republic of Slovenia v European Commission* EU:T:2020:402.

[347] *Poland v European Parliament and Council* (n 346), paras 21–29; *Slovenia v European Commission* (n 346), paras 240–50.

[348] The principle of participatory democracy or related provisions were not mentioned: *Poland v*

It is helpful, in this regard, not to conflate EU institutions' and bodies' participatory democracy obligations, including the Commission's obligation to consult, with the general practice and obligation to carry out an IA. The Court has, in the context of IAs, clearly stated that the failure of EU institutions to carry out an IA in the preparation of EU legislation is not, by itself, a breach of its principle of proportionality.[349] The Court has also stated that the obligation to carry out an IA in every circumstance does not follow from the wording of the Interinstitutional Agreement – even if preparation of IAs, as a rule, must take place if a legislative initiative is liable to have significant social, environmental or economic implications.[350] The obligation to govern as openly and closely as possible, as well as for the Commission to consult with parties concerned, has a different legal basis and foundation from the obligation to conduct an IA. The mention and elaboration in the Interinstitutional Agreement of, for example, legislative consultation, therefore, cannot be equated with the mention of IAs, which only feature indirectly in the Treaties, through demands of assessments on proportionality and subsidiarity (see below for an analysis of the Court's review in this regard). Participation, featured prominently as consultation, in the EU legislative process has a separate and explicit mention in the Treaties, with a separate pedigree and drafting history, and – as has been extensively argued – is inextricably intertwined with an understanding of democracy in the EU, as well as being a constitutive feature of EU law- and rule-making.

However, considering that the principle of participatory democracy is a relatively untested legal concept, it is still unclear which breaches would be considered grave, and what the boundaries of the Commission's discretion are, although there does seem to be some tentative agreement that a very serious direct breach of Article 11(3) TEU – such as no consultation at all – might amount to a ground for annulment. While this might initially seem to highly limit the potential of Article 11(3) TEU, it should be remembered that a stocktaking exercise between 2015 and 2018, of all proposals linked to the Commission work programme Annex and II, showed that 28 per cent were not accompanied by an IA and had no consultation, mostly with the justification of urgency.[351] While that figure represents a lumping together of law-making, rule-making and other policy proposals, such instances may not be the aberration one might think.[352] Indeed, in 2024, 80 per cent of all EU legislation was not accompanied by an IA.[353] Recent cases of the Asylum and Migration Package and the Omnibus legislation confirm this picture.

It should be kept in mind that there is a crucial distinction to be drawn between impact assessments and participation during the legislative preparatory

European Parliament and Council (n 346), para 43.

[349] *Commission v Czechia* (n 157), paras 82–85.

[350] ibid.

[351] Commission, Taking stock of the Commission's Better Regulation Agenda, COM (2019) 178, 20.

[352] See ch 4, s 4.6.

[353] 'Handling of impact assessments within the Council - Annual report covering the period January–December 2024', https://www.parlament.gv.at/dokument/XXVIII/EU/17052/imfname_11467438.pdf.

work – consultations are, in fact, 'legally embedded'[354] within the IA as evidence supporting rational law-making. It is, therefore, worth considering what role, if any, the principle of participatory democracy plays in such assessment, bringing a different perspective on the importance of consultation. This requires, first, an understanding of how participation as consultation is currently featured in the Court's review.

3.8.3.1. Procedural review and the principle of participatory democracy

In the last decade, the Court has shifted towards focusing on procedural elements in its review; this can, at least in part, be connected to the trend of rationalising the legislative process, and evidence-based law-making, as well as the Court's historical overall deference to the legislator in terms of review.[355] Law-making consultation is, here, featured explicitly in the context of evidence-gathering, and implicitly as an element of IAs, with the latter's appearance in case law drawing the attention of scholars.[356] The prominent feature of consultations in IAs, as well as the rise of IAs as an element of the Court's review, has been seen as a way of legally embedding consultations. If more information is available to courts, they are more likely to use it when they review regulation, and if consultation is combined with IA, courts might raise their evidentiary standards.[357]

The relevant case law begins prior to the insertion of Article 11 TEU but stretches beyond the ratification of the Lisbon Treaty. The EU courts have confirmed that an EU institution can demonstrate the proportionality of its action through providing a reasoned IA. The prominent case is *Spain v Council*, where the Court, after highlighting the lack of an IA by the Community legislature, found a breach of the general principle of proportionality and annulled the regulation in question.[358] The judgment implies that the duty to investigate fully and impartially all aspects of a case prior to taking a decision should include analysis of the potential impact

[354] The term is taken from Meuwese, 'Embedding Consultation Procedures' (n 338).

[355] Koen Lenaerts, 'The European Court of Justice and Process-Oriented Review' (2012) 31 *Yearbook of European Law* 3; Patricia Popelier, 'A Legal Perspective on Regulatory Impact Assessments' (International Symposium: Regulatory Impact Analyses, Luxembourg 23–24 November 2017); Martin Shapiro, 'The Frontiers of Science Doctrine: American Experiences with the Judicial Control of Science-Based Decision-Making' in Christian Joerges, Karl-Heinz Ladeur and Ellen Vos (eds), *Integrating scientific expertise into regulatory decision-making: national traditions and European innovations* (1. Aufl, Nomos-Verl-Ges, 1997).

[356] See, eg David Keyaerts, 'Ex Ante Evaluation of EU Legislation Intertwined with Judicial Review? Comment on Case C-58/08 Vodafone' (2010) 35 *European Law Review* 869; Anne Meuwese and Patricia Popelier, 'Legal Implications of Better Regulation: A Special Issue' (2011) 17 *European Public Law* 455; Alberto Alemanno, 'Courts and Regulatory Impact Assessment' in Claire A Dunlop and Claudio M Radaelli (eds), *Handbook of Regulatory Impact Assessment* (Edward Elgar, 2016); Anne CM Meuwese, 'Regulatory Review of European Commission Impact Assessments: What Kind for Which Better Regulation Scenario?' (2017) 19 *European Journal of Law Reform* 16.

[357] Meuwese, 'Embedding Consultation Procedures' (n 338).

[358] *Spain v Council* (n 258), para 123.

on collateral aspects.[359] Similarly, in *Vodaphone*, the Court emphasised that the Community's legislature must base its choice on objective criteria, explore possible measures, and examine whether objectives pursued by the chosen measure justify negative economic outcomes for a party.[360] In this case, the Court relied on an IA report in its proportionality review. In its substantive assessment of proportionality, it assessed the quality of the decision-making procedure. In the joined cases *Sungro SA and Others v Commission and Council*, the General Court made an implicit argument to uphold the IA as an essential procedural requirement in EU law-making.[361] In *Luxembourg v Parliament and Council*, the ECJ assessed the legality of a measure under the principle of proportionality through establishing whether there was proof of the duty of care by means of an IA report drafted prior to the entry into force of a measure.[362]

Popelier distinguishes between two mechanisms here: formal process review and procedural rationality review.[363] Cases like *Spain v Council* and *Vodaphone* fall under the latter category, as procedural rationality review covers situations in which an act is challenged for failing a substantive check (mostly proportionality), which includes the duty to legislate on the basis of evidence.[364] Formal process review is when an act is challenged directly because of a procedural requirement – in this case, because no IA was conducted, or the IA that was carried out was faulty.[365] The Court has recently confirmed that it must review compliance with not only the substantive but also the procedural safeguards provided for by Protocol No 2 (which demand assessments on subsidiarity and proportionality).[366] Examples of formal process review are, then, *Afton Chemical* and *Pillbox 38*, where the directive in question was challenged on the ground of an absent IA – the legislature had chosen another path from the one proposed by the Commission, and consequently that course of action had not been examined within the context of an IA.[367] Similarly, in *Philip Morris*, and in *Poland v the European Parliament and the Council*, issue was taken directly with the IA.[368]

In *Afton Chemicals*, the Court emphasised that, although its judicial review is limited in scope, the Community institutions must be able to show the Court that, in adopting a legal act, they actually exercised their discretion, which presupposes

[359] ibid.

[360] Case C-58/08, *Vodafone and Others* EU:C:2010:321, para 55.

[361] Joined Cases T-252/07, T-271/07 and T-272/07 *Sungro SA and Others v Commission and Council* EU:T:2010:17; Case C-300/07 *Hans & Christophorus Oymanns* EU:C:2009:358. In *Oymanns*, determinations on the internal coherence in a legal act featured lack of an *ex ante* evaluation.

[362] Case C-176/09 *Luxembourg v Parliament and Council* ECLI:EU:C:2011:290.

[363] Popelier, 'A Legal Perspective on Regulatory Impact Assessments' (n 355) 11–12.

[364] ibid 12.

[365] ibid.

[366] Case C-547/14 *Philip Morris Brands and Others* EU:C:2016:325, para 217; Case C-358/14 *Republic of Poland v European Parliament and the Council of the EU* EU:C:2016:323, para 113.

[367] Case C-343/09 *Afton Chemical Limited v Secretary of State for Transport* EU:C:2010:419, paras 30–40; Case C-477/14 *Pillbox 38 (UK) Limited, trading as Totally Wicked v Secretary of State for Health* EU:C:2016:324, paras 64–66.

[368] *Philip Morris Brands and Others* (n 366), para 226; *Poland v European Parliament and the Council of the EU* (n 366), para 123.

taking into consideration all the relevant factors and circumstances of the situation the act was intended to regulate.[369] The Court here points out that this line of reasoning holds, even though the Court clarified that an IA undertaken by the Commission is not binding on the Parliament or Council.

The specific role of impact assessment and its legal bearing is, however, unclear, and the EU courts' case law is not always consistent.[370] It has been noted that the relatively stringent procedural review in *Spain v Council* has been followed by a more lax overall approach.[371] One relevant observation in this regard is that, in *Vodafone* and *Luxembourg*, as well as subsequent cases *Estonia v Parliament and Council* and the so-called *Tobacco Directive* cases, the IA provided the Court with arguments to support the conclusion that the measure was compliant with proportionality.[372] The IA, therefore, plays a dual role in the review by the courts: it is a procedural requirement in the contexts of gathering evidence (here connected to the administrative principle of duty of care) and also an aid in the substantive element of proportionality review, establishing a 'presumption of legality'.[373] The danger here is that, instead of proper procedural review, IAs and consultations – in particular, justification on subsidiarity and proportionality – become a box-ticking exercise.[374] These reflections align with previous observations that the courts' review may be turning into a drafting guide for practitioners/legislators rather than a real check on discretion.[375] Despite this, the shift towards procedural proportionality has, in certain corners, been defended (provided that the procedural proportionality review is stringent enough), as it poses lesser challenges to the institutional balance of democratic decision-making.[376]

It has been noted that the Court's turn towards procedural proportionality has only strengthened in recent years,[377] with an overall focus on examining the processes by which contested legislation was enacted.[378] The CJEU has been insisting that the EU legislature demonstrate that, when enacting legislation, they actually exercised their discretion; in cases such as *Commission v Czechia*, *Commission v Poland* and *Swedish Match AB v Secretary of State for Health*, the

[369] *Afton Chemical Limited* (n 367).

[370] *Spain v Council* (n 258); compare with Opinion of AG Sharpston: Case C-310/04 *Spain v Council, Opinion of AG Sharpston* EU:C:2006:179, paras 82 and 89.

[371] Jacob Öberg, 'The Rise of the Procedural Paradigm: Judicial Review of EU Legislation in Vertical Competence Disputes' (2017) 13 *European Constitutional Law Review* 248.

[372] Julian Nowag and Xavier Groussot, 'From Better Regulation to Better Adjudication?' in Garben and Govaere, *The EU Better Regulation Agenda* (n 95) 185–202.

[373] ibid.

[374] Schuurmans and Voermans make this case in relation to the IA, while not explicitly discussing consultation: Schuurmans and Voermans, 'Better Regulation by Appeal' (n 338).

[375] Stephen Weatherill, 'The Limits of Legislative Harmonization Ten Years after *Tobacco Advertising*: How the Court's Case Law Has Become a "Drafting Guide"' (2011) 12 *German Law Journal* 827.

[376] See Öberg, 'The Rise of the Procedural Paradigm' (n 371).

[377] Darren Harvey, 'Process-Oriented Federalism in the EU: A (Partial) Response to Critiques of Process Review Advocacy in the EU' (2021) 45 *European Law Review* 460; Darren Harvey, 'Towards Process-Oriented Proportionality Review In The European Union' (2017) 23 *European Public Law* 93; Lenaerts, 'The European Court of Justice and Process-Oriented Review' (n 355).

[378] *Commission v Czechia* (n 157); *Commission v Poland* (n 157), paras 152–53.

IAs have formed an integral part of both demonstrating and subsequently reviewing whether the EU legislature considered all facts and circumstances relevant to the subsidiarity and proportionality principles when legislating.[379] The Court has made clear that the absence of an IA is, in itself, not a breach of the principle of proportionality.

In areas in which the Union institutions, bodies, offices and agencies have a broad discretion, the legality of a measure 'can be affected only if the measure is manifestly or obviously inappropriate having regard to the objective which the competent institution is seeking to pursue'.[380] Despite judicial review being limited in scope, the Court has clarified that the EU institutions which have adopted an act must be able to demonstrate that they actually exercised their discretion.[381] This means that the facts and circumstances of the situation the act aims to regulate need to have been taken into consideration, and that the institutions can clearly demonstrate the basic facts that had to be taken into account as the basis of the contested measures, and on which their discretion depended.[382]

However, the jurisprudence on IAs and the need for careful examination of all facts also does not answer the question of what role or connection there is between evidence-gathering and consultations. While the Commission attempts to draw a line between stakeholder and expert input, demonstrated in its separate guidelines, as well as transparency on reporting in dealings with the two, there is often a large overlap between expert input and 'parties concerned', including those who are affected or have a stated interest in a given issue. The relatively novel references of the courts to the requirements of subsidiarity justifications as enshrined in Protocol No 2 point to a trend which might spill over into the consultation demands in the Protocol.[383]

Considering the current approach of the Court in its subsidiarity and proportionality review, the principle of participatory democracy calls for an amplification of the role of consultation in the Court's review in the following way: within procedural rationality review, it calls for reframing the understanding of 'evidence' as being grounded in links to citizens, including citizens' lived experiences and situated knowledge. This is not only supported by the intrinsic value of participation, which arguably fits less well within the Court's current proportionality review, but also the instrumental value of participation in assessing consequences and impacts of regulation. The legal amplification prescribed by the principle of participatory democracy becomes more acute

[379] *Commission v Czechia* (n 157); *Commission v Poland* (n 157); Case C-151/17 *Swedish Match v Secretary of State for Health* ECLI:EU:C:2018:938.

[380] See *Vodafone and Others* (n 360), para 52; *Afton Chemical Limited* (n 367).

[381] Joined Cases C-541/20 to C-555/20 *Lithuania and Others v Parliament and Council* ECLI:EU:C:2024:818; C-620/18 *Hungary v Parliament and Council* ECLI:EU:C:2020:1001 116; *Commission v Czechia* (n 157), para 81.

[382] ibid.

[383] Nowag and Groussot also take note of the novel mention of Protocol No 2: Nowag and Groussot, 'From Better Regulation to Better Adjudication?' (n 372).

when fundamental rights are impacted by the Commission's proposal, when the Commission is proposing legislation in previously unregulated domains, and when the Commission is proposing legislation which deals with heavy 'ethical balancing', including in areas of complexity. The principle of participatory democracy also informs formal process review through highlighting procedural requirements related to consultation beyond the requirement of its mere existence; notably that the Commission is required to adequately document how participatory input has impacted on its legislative proposal, and that adequate time for consultation has been ensured. The principle of participatory democracy, then, highlights the necessity of participation to ensure that the proposal is in harmony with the legal requirements of subsidiarity and proportionality.

Finally, with regard to the role that the inter-institutional agreements can play in terms of annulment, there is – as has been stated – an important distinction whether the specific obligation outlined in the Interinstitutional Agreement stems from a Treaty provision (for example, consultation) or an IA (primarily self-imposed administrative obligations). Moreover, the Court has indicated that the binding nature of a particular provision in the Interinstitutional Agreement depends on the formulation. Here, *Poland v Parliament and Council II* is indicative. The Court looked at the content and quality of the IA, as well as other information available to the legislators, to draw the conclusion that the Parliament and the Council had taken into account the available scientific data and information in order actually to exercise their discretion.[384] In addition, the Court stated that:

> concerning the Republic of Poland's contention that the Parliament and the Council amended substantial aspects of the proposal for a directive and ought therefore to have updated the impact assessment, in accordance with point 15 of the Interinstitutional Agreement on Better Law-Making, suffice it to note that that provision does not, on any view, contain a definite obligation for the institutions concerned. It provides only for the option to carry out such an update where the Parliament and the Council 'consider this to be appropriate and necessary for the legislative process'.[385]

Following from this statement, *e contrario*, a breach of a provision in the agreement which was framed as a binding obligation could, therefore, possibly lead to annulment.

Having explored direct claims based on the principle of participatory democracy, as well as when they may be embedded (relating to proportionality and subsidiarity) or related to provisions in the Interinstitutional Agreement on Better Law-Making, the issue of compensation is briefly discussed below.

[384] *Poland v European Parliament and Council* (n 346).
[385] ibid, para 43.

3.8.4. Compensation for Damages

Settled case law, in terms of damages, calls for three conditions to be met: the rule of law infringed must be intended to confer rights on individuals; the breach must be sufficiently serious, ie the EU institution or body must have manifestly and gravely disregarded the limits on its discretion; and there must be a direct causal link between the breach of the obligation on the author of the act and the damage sustained by the injured party.[386] Regarding the first requirement, it is, as stated earlier, highly doubtful whether the language of Article 11 TEU supports the establishment of individually enforceable rights.[387] Although the case could be made that, read in combination with Article 10(3) TEU, such a right is implicit, the overall assessment, in line with the textual analysis of Article 11 TEU, is against this claim. The necessary severity of the discretional breach in order for reparations to be granted also means that the types of consultation breaches that could potentially be considered would arguably be limited.[388] This means that the principle of participatory democracy, as it stands, is unlikely to find expression or be ensured through such claims.

3.8.5. Conclusions on the potential for judicial review

The overview of existing jurisprudence demonstrates that there may be distinct pathways through which the principle of participatory democracy in relation to law-making consultation is ensured. The democratising function of consultation has indirectly been touched on in the courts' elaboration of democracy. The ECJ relied on the citizen's right to democratic participation in Article 10(3) TEU in order to strengthen access to the legislative process in its early stages. However, it is also clear that direct challenges based on the principle of participatory democracy face procedural obstacles. Unless the Court shifts its settled law on standing, direct challenges by the privileged actors, and indirect challenges open to the public, would be the avenues potential litigants would have to tread.

Law-making consultation has indirectly surfaced in determinations on subsidiarity and proportionality as IAs have gradually come under the scrutiny of the courts. The analysis highlights the challenge in legally embedding consultations in IAs, because the legal imperative and force of consultation based in Article 11(3)

[386] *Ombudsman v Staelen* (n 247), para 49 and the case law cited there.

[387] ibid.

[388] Speaking in general about the legal redress of Art 11 TEU, Smismans is sceptical that the CJEU would disqualify any type of activity beyond the unlikely scenario that there would be no consultation or participation from affected parties or stakeholders in the law-making process: see Stijn Smismans, 'Regulatory Procedure and Participation in the European Union' in Francesca Bignami and David Zaring (eds), *Comparative Law and Regulation* (Edward Elgar, 2016).

TEU and also Article 10(3) TEU does not necessarily align with the foundations and goals of IAs.[389]

A textual reading of Article 11 TEU and Article 2 Protocol 2 clearly indicates that the presence of consultation in the legislative process is a must, and that it would not be a leap for the courts to explicitly enforce consultation – indirectly, the Court already has.[390] Furthermore, the courts have now clearly begun to engage with the Interinstitutional Agreement on Better Law-Making and have scrutinised whether the institutions have lived up to the standards and provisions set by that agreement. Since the Agreement codifies some of the obligations which flow from the principle of participatory democracy, this makes enforcement more tangible. However, the courts' case law related to impact assessment and participation in the legislative process by non-institutional actors is primarily output-oriented. The legal analysis has, however, demonstrated how the principle of participatory democracy can and should be embedded in the Court's procedural review, to legally amplify the role for consultation and emphasise its democratising function, both through its procedural rationality review and process review.

In sum, a complete lack of consultation constitutes a clear legal breach of the principle of participatory democracy (breach of Treaty) and the outlook for redress in terms of annulment is good – but the procedural path may prove difficult, beyond privileged actors. Furthermore, a claim based on the principle of participatory democracy, in terms of a procedural breach of consultation obligations – for example, not providing enough time to allow for consultation, or not consulting specific groups/individuals, or not being sufficiently transparent in the IA – is unlikely to succeed as a stand-alone annulment claim, although this is not impossible. It has a much stronger chance of success if it is embedded in the proportionality review of the Court (as highlighted above) and is one of several factors which put the disputed legislation in question. What may likely influence the Court's willingness to intervene, in both the case of a stand-alone or an embedded claim based on Article 11(3) TEU, Article 2 Protocol 2, and Article 1(3) TEU (especially for proportionality review), is whether, beyond the Commission's procedural lapse, any substantive harm has occurred because of the lapse. This is likely to be influenced by the nature of the case, and by what happens after the Commission presents its legislative proposal, including whether the Parliament and Council attempt to make up for this lapse.[391]

[389] This distinction is important, as literature on IAs sometimes legally lumps consultation and impact assessments together.

[390] Meuwese noted this already in 2011: see Meuwese, 'Embedding Consultation Procedures' (n 338).

[391] See ch 4.

3.9. The Ombudsman as a guardian of participatory democracy?

While a legal principle, by definition, makes an implicit demand of legal redress in the event of its breach, legal principles, in particular constitutional principles, find expression through many means. Realising the principle of participatory democracy, need not only be achieved through the courts. In recent years, the European Ombudsman has been instrumental in pointing out maladministration while promoting accountability and transparency of the EU institutions. The Ombudsman, with its legal basis in the Treaty dating back to Maastricht, has among its main concerns to deal with cases of maladministration, focusing on transparency and accountability, procedural rights, and the public participation in EU decision-making. In this chapter, the Ombudsman's role in relation to participatory democracy emerged in terms of a guardian role. Through her investigative powers, and in laying out recommendations to be followed by the EU institutions, the Ombudsman has also prompted reforms in several important areas with linkages to the principle of participatory democracy, notably with regard to trilogues, transparency in the Council, and enhancing the regulatory and accountability framework surrounding lobbying and expert groups.[392]

Related particularly to the principle of participatory democracy and consultation is the Ombudsman's work on reforming the Commission's system for advisory and expert groups. Following the Ombudsman's investigation and recommendations, the Commission has reformed its expert-group system through putting in place horizontal binding rules, which included making calls for experts open, as well as transparency requirements of 'complete' minutes, which should also be made accessible to the public,[393] including demonstrating how the expert groups reached their conclusions.[394] The Commission's response to the EU Court of Auditors' recommendations on the Commission's consultation practices were, by comparison, non-committal.[395] Considering the high level of acceptance of the Ombudsman's solutions or recommendations, as well as her insights into EU administration, the Ombudsman's office is well placed to contribute to a realisation of the principle of participatory democracy, including in specific instances when the principle has been breached with regard to consultation design.[396]

[392] See, eg Decision of the European Ombudsman in her strategic inquiry OI/6/2014/NF concerning the composition and transparency of European Commission expert groups; Petia Kostadinova, 'Improving the Transparency and Accountability of EU Institutions: The Impact of the Office of the European Ombudsman' (2015) 53 *Gender, Work And Organization* 1077.

[393] Decision of the European Ombudsman in her strategic inquiry OI/6/2014/NF concerning the composition and transparency of European Commission expert groups; Kostadinova, 'Improving the Transparency and Accountability of EU Institutions' (n 392).

[394] See Kostadinova, 'Improving the Transparency and Accountability of EU Institutions' (n 392) for a detailed account.

[395] See European Court of Auditors, '"Have Your Say!": Commission's Public Consultations Engage Citizens, but Fall Short of Outreach Activities' (Publications Office, 2019) 14, under the title 'Replies of the Commission'.

[396] See, eg Kostadinova, 'Improving the Transparency and Accountability of EU Institutions' (n 392);

This is not to deny the fact that, for politically salient issues, the Ombudsman's recommendations may have lower acceptance rates.[397] Furthermore, the oversight procedure – similar to judicial review – is rather lengthy and usually takes about two years, although the fast-track procedure might be able to address this issue.[398] Although no one-stop-shop remedy, the Ombudsman emerges as an important accountability mechanism for participatory democracy. This is particularly true as it has been observed that litigation, for example in the area of transparency, may have been held back by the requirement that applicants need to demonstrate a direct disadvantage deriving from an access (to document) refusal – which excludes the reliance on a general, societal interest in, for example, improving trilogue transparency – as well as being ordered to pay the costs of the defendant and intervening parties.[399]

Since the Lisbon Treaty, the European Ombudsman's practice has increasingly functioned as a mode of soft enforcement that renders the participatory democracy commitments in Articles 10(3) and 11 TEU operational in everyday governance. The Ombudsman's mandate, anchored in Article 228 TFEU and mirrored as a citizenship right in Article 43 of the Charter, provides a low-threshold channel through which individuals and associations can contest maladministration in ways that are structurally adjacent to, but temporally more agile than, judicial review.[400] This institutional design matters for participatory democracy because many participation deficits arise not as discrete legality questions but as cumulative distortions of informational and procedural conditions (timing, traceability, reason-giving) that determine whether outsiders can meaningfully follow and influence norm production.

The Ombudsman's post-Lisbon contribution is especially visible where participation is mediated through transparency. In the strategic inquiry on trilogues,[401] the Ombudsman treated informal inter-institutional bargaining not as a peripheral technicality but as a decisive stage of legislation that must remain intelligible to the public if participation is to be more than formal rhetoric; the inquiry articulated proposals aimed at improving access to key legislative documents and the overall traceability of compromise-making.[402] Similarly, in the strategic inquiry on the Council legislative process,[403] the Ombudsman explicitly linked preparatory opacity (working party practices, recording of positions, use of 'LIMITÉ') to democratic accountability deficits, and escalated the matter to the European Parliament through a Special Report when resistance persisted – illustrating how

Maarten Hillebrandt and Päivi Leino-Sandberg, 'Administrative and Judicial Oversight of Trilogues' (2021) 28 *Journal of European Public Policy* 53; Hierlemann and others, *Under Construction* (n 85) 110–30.

[397] Hierlemann and others, *Under Construction* (n 85) 115–18.

[398] On this point, see Hillebrandt and Leino-Sandberg (n 396) 67–68.

[399] ibid.

[400] Arts 10(3) and 11 TEU, Art 228 TFEU and Art 43 CFR.

[401] European Ombudsman, 'Decision in OI/8/2015/JAS on the Transparency of Trilogues' (n 197).

[402] ibid.

[403] European Ombudsman, 'Recommendation of the European Ombudsman in Case OI/2/2017/TE on the Transparency of the Council Legislative Process'.

soft enforcement can be paired with political escalation to sustain participatory conditions.[404]

At the same time, the Ombudsman's authority is structured by a self-limiting logic designed to avoid displacing the Court's role. Both the Treaties and the Ombudsman's Statute exclude the Court of Justice acting in its judicial capacity from the Ombudsman's remit, and the post-2021 Statute codifies the Ombudsman's operating conditions within those constitutional boundaries.[405] The boundary is not merely formal: scholarship on the Ombudsman's practice emphasises that the institution seeks to avoid pre-empting judicial determinations, positioning its findings as assessments of maladministration and good administration rather than authoritative legality rulings, even when a dispute overlaps with justiciable transparency questions.[406]

Within an EU legal method, this yields a defensible account of the Ombudsman as a guardian of the principle of participatory democracy in the administrative-constitutional sense: not a substitute for judicial review, but an institutional actor that sustains the practical preconditions of participation where the Court's intervention may be delayed, procedurally costly, or normatively too narrow to address systemic opacity. The controversy about the Ombudsman's 'political' role is, in that light, less an anomaly than a predictable feature of soft enforcement in a polity where participation deficits often track institutional incentives; strategic inquiries and Special Reports inevitably shape governance norms and power relations even when they do not bind in the manner of judgments. The Ombudsman's soft enforcement can be read as structurally connected to Articles 10(3) and 11 TEU, and to the Charter-based right to complain: it reinforces participatory democracy by translating openness, traceability and reason-giving into institution-facing expectations while leaving the Court as the final arbiter of legality.[407]

3.10. Procedural requirements from a democracy theory perspective and summary conclusions

The legal analysis identified several rights and obligations flowing from the principle of participatory democracy. It also revealed a (cumbersome) path for judicial review, in relation to participatory democracy rights and obligations beyond the right 'to know' related to the right of access to documents, as well as rights connected to the ECI. The Commission's obligations to consult were analysed,

[404] ibid.

[405] Regulation (EU, Euratom) 2021/1163 of the European Parliament of 24 June 2021 laying down the regulations and general conditions governing the performance of the Ombudsman's duties (Statute of the European Ombudsman) 2021 (OJ L253).

[406] See, eg Nikos Vogiatzis, 'The European Ombudsman in the EU's Administrative and Institutional Framework' in Gijs J Brandsma (ed), *Handbook on European Union Public Administration* (Edward Elgar, 2024).

[407] ibid and Arts 10(3) and 11 TEU, and Art 43 CFR.

which included both broadly framed obligations such as the obligation to consult widely as well as more specific duties, including to conduct Internet-based consultation.

In order to identify the most important of these obligations, the strength of the legal argument, as well as the insights from democratic theory in the preceding chapter, may serve as a guide. As discussed in the previous chapter, the core complementary drivers of participatory democracy were the intrinsic value of participation; deliberation; and a focus on citizens and civil society as participation protagonists. As regards the inherent value of participation, it connects directly to the Commission's obligations to consult broadly and undergirds the procedural equality of potential participants, including reaching out actively beyond the usual suspects to ensure that such participants are informed of their participation opportunities, thereby reaching the 'parties concerned'.

The constitutional legal interpretation of the principle of participatory democracy, grounded in the telos of the principle to facilitate citizen-grounded participation and legitimise Union action, has prompted a broad interpretation of the right of citizens to participate in the democratic life of the Union. The right is seen as stretching out not only horizontally beyond elections to law-making and rule-making, but also vertically throughout the EU multi-level structure, potentially informing the interpretation of national law. This interpretation of the democratic life of the Union also comports with theorisation of participation in the EU setting and the emphasis, in participatory democracy, on affording those affected by a decision the right to take part in its formation.

In thinking about the deliberative quality of consultations, the analysis highlighted the obligation of the institutions to establish a 'transparent and ethical' framework for interest representation (with related implications) which sets the tone for a deliberative exchange. Furthermore, in consultation settings, enhanced feedback and transparency shift the process in a more deliberative direction. The latter would attend to important procedural qualities that are necessary for deliberation, as well as serving to promote the right of citizens to know about EU action (in order to be able to influence Union actions). While there is no obligation for the Commission to reply individually to consultation replies, the purpose of consultation, as stated in Article 11(3) TEU, to ensure transparency means that it must detail whether and how participation input has been taken on.

The legal analysis in this chapter also directly challenges the argument that Commission consultation activities are a self-imposed obligation or subject to executive discretion. It also clarified that, while they are related, determinations on the legality and necessity of IAs (and related proportionality assessments) cannot be lumped together with determinations on the necessity or legality of participation and consultation. Participation, in the form of consultation, is an element of the principle of participatory democracy; it has a different legislative pedigree, a different telos, and a clear and separate Treaty mention and grounding.

In sum, this chapter has outlined key rights and obligations which flow from the principle of participatory democracy. It has also assessed to what degree the principle of participatory democracy is justiciable and reached the conclusion that judicial review exists for several participatory democracy rights and obligations, even while procedural hurdles often make such review difficult. The Ombudsman, while lacking the full force of judicial review, appears structurally well placed to function as a guardian of the principle of participatory democracy and assess whether the EU institutions are living up to their obligations in their administrative activities.

Justiciability is one part of the puzzle in giving the principle of participatory democracy effect. Another is how the principle of participatory democracy can operate at the national level. The following chapter elaborates on both these elements, as it tests the legal framework against cases of EU law-making and national legal frameworks. provide consultation feedback, and also to actively promote equality of access to consultation opportunities.

4

Testing the legal framework: Case studies

Proceeding from the legal and normative framework flowing from the principle of participatory democracy outlined in the previous chapters, this chapter addresses to what degree current Commission EU law-making consultation practices adhere to or conflict with identified key obligations – as well as how the principle of participatory democracy may inform national legal norms surrounding consultation.

Commission consultations have been increasing over time, with an average of 100 each year over the last 10 years.[1] While participation levels vary widely across exercises, a typical Commission consultation received, on average, 500 responses in 2015–16 and 2,000 responses in each of 2017 and 2018.[2] At the same time, consultation by Member States when they negotiate EU law is scant or uneven, with few Member States having a consistent legal framework for such participation.[3]

Testing four legislative consultations against two key procedural requirements at the EU level, prompted by the principle of participatory democracy, will help to assess to what degree the principle of participatory democracy is given effect in Commission consultation activities and test how the legal framework may be applied to concrete cases. Following this, surveying the legal landscape of three Member States will illustrate how the principle of participatory democracy operates at the national level in relation to participation in EU law-making in a national context.

The chapter is, consequently, divided into two parts. The first part deals with Commission legislative consultation. It begins with a rationale of the two relevant procedural requirements and how they will be measured against the selected cases at the EU level. This part concludes with an in-depth analysis of the four consultation case studies. An analysis of the way in which a constitutional principle finds expression in a multi-level setting must pay attention to the legislative contexts at the different levels. The second part, consequently, explores how the EU principle of participatory democracy relates to EU law-making in a national setting, exploring the legal frameworks in Austria, Sweden and Ireland.

[1] European Court of Auditors, '"Have Your Say!": Commission's Public Consultations Engage Citizens, but Fall Short of Outreach Activities' (Publications Office, 2019) 14.

[2] ibid.

[3] OECD, *Better Regulation Practices across the European Union 2022* (OECD, 2022).

4.1. Key procedural requirements for Commission consultation elicited from the principle of participatory democracy

The consultation processes will be tested against two procedural requirements which have emerged as significant from the congruence between the theoretical foundations of the principle of participatory democracy and the legal analysis of the principle in the previous chapters.[4] These requirements are as follows:

- Transparency as responsiveness: *has the Commission adequately detailed whether, how and why consultation has impacted on the Commission's proposal?*[5]
- Procedural equality: *has the Commission adequately promoted procedural equality?*[6]

The first requirement, on responsiveness, is assessed primarily by how the Commission has detailed in its impact assessment (IA) and/or equivalent document(s) accompanying the legislative proposal whether and how the open and targeted consultations have impacted on the Commission's work on the legislative proposal.

The requirement in Article 11(3) TEU to 'ensure transparency' in the Union's actions through 'broad consultations with parties concerned' implies – as has been argued in the previous chapter – that it should be clear how consultations are impacting on the Commission's legislative work. This interpretation of Article 11 TEU not only finds strong support in the actual wording of Article 11 TEU and the constitutional interpretation developed in chapter three, but also in the overall logic of participatory democracy as a complement to representative democracy in the Union, as elaborated on in chapter two, which highlighted, inter alia, the importance of promoting meaningful exchange,[7] as well as in the established links between transparency and participation in the Treaty,[8] and the confirmation of these links through case law.[9] These features combined provide a strong rationale for this particular form of transparency as a key procedural requirement of the principle of participatory democracy. It also seems a relevant starting point of analysis, as the lack of adequate consultation feedback mechanisms is a recurring critique of the Commission's legislative preparatory work, raised repeatedly by external actors and, notably, civil society over the last decade while also featuring implicitly in the feedback of the Regulatory Scrutiny Board (RSB) to numerous

[4] See ch 3, which grounds these requirements in legal analysis as well as democratic theory.
[5] ibid.
[6] ibid.
[7] See relevant sections of ch 3.
[8] See relevant sections of ch 3.
[9] Case C-57/16 P *ClientEarth v European Commission* [2018] EU:C:2018:660, para 94.

consultation procedures. It is also a main critique of recent EU experimentation with participatory democracy practices, such as EU citizens' consultations, and other participation mechanisms, that they lack a standardised feedback mechanism.[10] Transparency, in this context, also holds promise as a relatively clear legal obligation which may not need to be further fleshed out through additional procedural rules.

The assessment here does not aspire to definitively answer how the legislative proposal actually has been impacted on by the consultations. Notwithstanding that this would prove methodologically cumbersome, as there is no legal requirement for the Commission to follow advice or input from stakeholders, assessing to what degree input has been taken on is legally less relevant. It is the transparency of what the Commission has done with stakeholder input which is the central feedback mechanism in question, not the actual causal link between input and output. It is, therefore, important to distinguish between consultation transparency/design and consultation outcome; while the latter may and should be indicative of the quality of the former, they are not synonymous and causal links may be informed by various factors external to consultation design and the process.

The second dimension which the case studies explore is to what degree the Commission's consultation strategy reflects the legal obligation of procedural equality of participants in order to achieve a diversity of opinions and reach relevant 'parties concerned'.

In assessing whether the Commission's obligations have been met, two elements which span across consultation design and outcome appear specifically legally relevant: the geographical balance of Member States represented, and to what degree there is a balance of economic and non-economic interests, paying attention to whether outreach has occurred for equality purposes, for example to vulnerable groups and citizens. This approach is grounded in the language of Article 11(3) TEU and Article 10(3) TEU, as well as the role that civil society and citizens play in a participatory democracy framework. In deciding on a balance between economic and non-economic interests, inspiration was also drawn from the European Ombudsman's work in issuing recommendations to the Commission on the composition and transparency of its expert groups.[11] The approach is also sensitive to the specific context of EU Commission consultations, where geographical representation is important but has been challenging for the Commission, as well as the noted dominance of market interests.[12]

[10] This theme runs through the assessment of different participation instruments: Dominik Hierlemann and others, *Under Construction: Citizen Participation in the European Union* (Verlag Bertelsmann Stiftung, 2022).

[11] See European Ombudsman, 'Recommendation of the European Ombudsman in her strategic inquiry OI/6/2014/NF concerning the composition of Commission expert groups', 29 January 2016.

[12] Alberto Alemanno, 'Levelling the EU Participatory Playing Field: A Legal and Policy Analysis of the Commission's Public Consultations in Light of the Principle of Political Equality' (2020) 26 *European Law Journal* 114.

4.2. Selection of cases

Four consultation processes have been selected: the Commission's consultation on the Proposal for a Regulation laying down harmonised rules on Artificial Intelligence (the Artificial Intelligence Act); the Proposal for a Directive of the European Parliament and of the Council amending Directive 1999/62/EC on the charging of heavy goods vehicles for the use of certain infrastructures (Revision of the Eurovignette Directive); the Proposal for a new Directive on representative actions for the protection of the collective interests of consumers; and the Regulation on Asylum and Migration Management (New Migration Pact).[13]

This exercise illustrates in what ways concrete current consultation designs or practices may either adhere to or fall short of the legal requirements of participatory democracy, while also testing how well the identified legal obligations can be applied.[14]

The chosen consultations have been selected mainly with a view to capturing the diversity of consultation procedures through diversity as regards policy issues, constellations of interests, and number of consultation responses, in order to allow for a fruitful exploration of their alignment with the relevant legal imperatives, as well as cautiously inferring some broader implications (for elaboration, see chapter one, section 1.4). The four case studies, while all reflecting current practice, cover different thematic policy areas, were organised by different Directorates-Generals (DGs), and deal with legislative issues where different constellations of interests are concerned: diffuse and broad, as well as high-stake and concentrated. The consultation responses in the four case studies vary numerically from between around 100 to several thousand. The various proposals also deal with issues where certain geographical regions in the EU have a specific stake (for example, vignettes), where there is intense lobbying (tech/AI), and where there are clearly defined actors (consumers, business) and broad impacts, as well as minorities impacted that are outsiders to the national democratic process (asylum and migration). Minorities are particularly susceptible to majoritarian bias and vulnerable to the malfunctioning (bias) of the democratic process.

While the cases were selected with diversity in mind, which can give some insight into broader trends and practices, it is clear that such a small sample makes no decisive claim of representativeness of the Commission's consultation practices. However, especially as regards the interplay between EU and national-level frameworks and consultation outcomes, four different legislative consultations should be able to give some indication as to broader trends. The case-study format, however,

[13] Commission, Proposal for a Regulation laying down harmonised rules on Artificial Intelligence COM(2021) 206 final and amending certain union legislative acts; Commission, Proposal for a Directive of the European Parliament and of the Council amending Directive 1999/62/EC on the charging of heavy goods vehicles for the use of certain infrastructures COM(2017) 275 final; Commission, Proposal for a new Directive on representative actions for the Protection of the Collective Interests of Consumers COM(2018) 184 final; Proposal for a regulation of the European Parliament and of the Council on asylum and migration management and amending Council Directive (EC) 2003/109 and the proposed Regulation (EU) XXX/XXX [Asylum and Migration Fund] COM(2020) 610 final.

[14] In fact, testing the robustness of the legal findings in ch 4.

does explore how current consultation practices may be individually and legally evaluated, as well as hinting at trends. This approach highlights opportunities and also challenges with a legal analysis on the lack of more precise procedural rules fleshing out the principle of participatory democracy.

4.3. Case study 1: The Artificial Intelligence Act

By way of background, the proposed Artificial Intelligence Act is the first step of a broader regulatory approach with the stated goal of 'creating EU global leadership in trustworthy AI'.[15] When the Artificial Intelligence Act was proposed by the Commission in April 2021, it was promoted as the first-ever legal framework on artificial intelligence (AI), and was widely acknowledged as an instrument which would use the size of the European market as leverage to propagate the EU approach to the regulation of AI to other markets.[16] With momentum gained from the successful extraterritorial application of the General Data Protection Regulation (GDPR), the upcoming EU AI regulation promised to be the next big 'Brussels Effect'.[17] The proposal advances a risk-based approach, defining areas of intervention for AI systems according to the level of risk they carry: for example, some which cause unbearable risks to fundamental rights, some which constitute high-risk applications (not prohibited, but subject to conditions to manage their risk), and some constituting limited or negligible risk applications.[18]

After the proposal was released, fast-paced development within the AI field, as well as ensuing scandals, generated an enormous amount of interest in AI, and also put into question whether the scope and approach of the proposal was 'tough enough'.[19] These developments, which were also widely reported in the media, included the Dutch benefits scandal in 2021 (which included, inter alia, 1,000 children being taken out of their homes and placed in state custody as a result of false accusations of fraud against their parents driven by algorithmic racial profiling by Dutch authorities),[20] the roll-out of ChatGPT,[21] a UK court ruling that harmful

[15] Commission, White Paper On Artificial Intelligence - A European approach to excellence and trust COM(2020) 65 final.

[16] Mark MacCarthy and Kenneth Propp, 'Machines Learn That Brussels Writes the Rules: The EU's New AI Regulation' (*Brookings*, 4 May 2021), www.brookings.edu/articles/machines-learn-that-brussels-writes-the-rules-the-eus-new-ai-regulation/, accessed 6 February 2026.

[17] On the Brussels Effect, see Anu Bradford, *The Brussels Effect: How the European Union Rules the World* (Oxford University Press, 2020).

[18] Commission, Proposal for a Regulation laying down harmonised rules on Artificial Intelligence COM(2021) 206 final and amending certain union legislative acts.

[19] See, eg 'ChatGPT Broke the EU Plan to Regulate AI' (*POLITICO*, 3 March 2023), www.politico.eu/article/eu-plan-regulate-chatgpt-openai-artificial-intelligence-act/, accessed 6 February 2026.

[20] See, eg Hanneke Sanou, 'Over 1,100 Children of Childcare Benefit Victims Taken into Care' (*DutchNews.nl*, 20 October 2021), www.dutchnews.nl/2021/10/over-1100-children-of-childcare-benefit-victims-taken-into-care/, accessed 6 February 2026; 'AI: Decoded: A Dutch Algorithm Scandal Serves a Warning to Europe — The AI Act Won't Save Us' (*POLITICO*, 30 March 2022), www.politico.eu/newsletter/ai-decoded/a-dutch-algorithm-scandal-serves-a-warning-to-europe-the-ai-act-wont-save-us-2/, accessed 6 February 2026.

[21] See, eg Natali Helberger and Nicholas Diakopoulos, 'ChatGPT and the AI Act' (2023) 12 *Internet Policy Review*.

social media content had contributed to a teenager's death in 2017,[22] and public warning calls by leading AI figures.[23]

In dealing with regulation with wide-ranging implications for numerous actors and sectors, the proposal attracted much attention. The main stakeholder activity of the legislative proposal was the consultation on the Commission's White Paper on AI, where more than 1,200 contributions were received from a wide variety of stakeholders. The White Paper on AI had been preceded by the work of the Commission's High-Level Working Group (HLWG) on AI[24] and the connected European AI Alliance multi-stakeholder platform, with some grumblings of industry capture of the HLWG's recommendations.[25] It was, however, through the publication of the White Paper on AI in February 2020 that a clear intent to legislate was articulated, presenting distinct policy options for a regulatory approach to AI. The White Paper, in addition to presenting regulatory options,[26] discussed the question of liability for potential harms caused by AI, while presenting its overall strategy for promoting 'European excellence in AI'.[27] The public consultation on the White Paper on AI included a set of closed questions that allowed respondents to select one or more options from a list of answers. In addition to the given options, respondents could provide free-text answers to each question of the questionnaire or insert position papers with more detailed feedback.

Following the consultation, the Commission published its IIA, which received 133 responses.[28] Finally, the Commission additionally organised a stakeholder conference and held targeted technical consultations with undisclosed experts, standardisation bodies and experts on biometric data.[29] The results of all consultation activities were somewhat detailed in the main text of the IA, but primarily

[22] 'UK: Court Rules Suicide of 14-Year-Old Girl Attributed to Harmful Posts on Instagram & Pinterest; Incl. Company Statement' (*Business & Human Rights Resource Centre*, 3 October 2002), www.business-humanrights.org/en/latest-news/uk-suicide-of-14-year-old-girl-attributed-to-harmful-posts-on-instagram-and-pinterest/, accessed 6 February 2026.

[23] '"The Godfather of AI" Quits Google and Warns of Danger Ahead' *The New York Times* (New York, 1 May 2023), https://www.nytimes.com/2023/05/01/technology/ai-google-chatbot-engineer-quits-hinton.html, accessed 6 February 2026.

[24] See Commission, 'Shaping Europe's Digital Future: High-Level Expert Group on Artificial Intelligence' (30 June 2023), https://digital-strategy.ec.europa.eu/en/policies/expert-group-ai, accessed 9 August 2023.

[25] Thomas Metzinger, 'EU guidelines: Ethics washing made in Europe' (*Der Tagesspiegel Online*, 8 April 2019, https://www.tagesspiegel.de/politik/ethics-washing-made-in-europe-5937028.html, accessed 9 August 2023.

[26] See Commission, White Paper On Artificial Intelligence - A European approach to excellence and trust COM(2020) 65 final.

[27] ibid.

[28] Commission, Inception Impact Assessment: Proposal for a legal act of the European Parliament and the Council laying down requirements for Artificial Intelligence, Ref Ares(2020)3896535; the feedback received is available on the Commission's consultation web page: see 'Commission, 'Have Your Say AI Initiative' (10 September 2020), https://ec.europa.eu/info/law/better-regulation/have-your-say/initiatives/12527-Artificial-intelligence-ethical-and-legal-requirements_en, accessed 6 February 2026.

[29] As outlined in the IIA: Commission, Inception Impact Assessment: Proposal for a legal act of the European Parliament and the Council laying down requirements for Artificial Intelligence, Ref. Ares(2020)3896535.

featured in the IA Annex.[30] These consultation activities, and their detailing in the IA and IIA, including in the annexed consultation report, form the basis of the analysis below of whether the Commission has aligned its consultation design and reporting according to the main obligations of adequate transparency/responsiveness and promoting procedural equality of potential participants. The raw consultation data, in the form of an Excel file which details all the submissions received, as well as a file with attachments, was posted on the Commission's web page, and has been surveyed as well as subjected to a light check.[31]

4.3.1. Has the Commission adequately detailed whether and how consultations have impacted on the legislative proposal?

The following documents have been screened to assess whether the Commission has lived up to transparency requirements: the IA, the report on the public consultation annexed to the IA, the inception impact assessment (IIA), and published reports of related activities, for example the stakeholder conference report. The stakeholder consultations feature in the IA in four ways. Firstly, the Commission refers to the public consultations, lumped together with other sources, as evidence for its framing of the issue or broader approach, for example:

> The analysed evidence includes results of the public consultation on White Paper on AI, responses to the inception impact assessment, stakeholder consultations carried out within the framework of this impact assessment, European Parliament resolution of 20 October 2020 with recommendations to the Commission on a framework of ethical aspects of artificial intelligence, robotics and related technologies, European Council Presidency Conclusion of 21 October 2020, ongoing work of international organizations, as well as secondary literature.[32]

or

> These requirements have also largely been supported by stakeholders in the consultation the White Paper consultation.[33]

[30] Commission, Impact Assessment Accompanying the Proposal for a Regulation of the European Parliament and of the Council Laying down harmonised rules on artificial intelligence (Artificial Intelligence Act) and amending certain union legislative acts SWD/2021/84 final Part 1/2; Commission, Impact Assessment Accompanying the Proposal for a Regulation of the European Parliament and of the Council Laying down harmonised rules on artificial intelligence (Artificial Intelligence Act) and amending certain union legislative acts SWD/2021/84 final Part 2/2.

[31] The 'light check' refers to whether the detailed reporting in the IA is faithful to the overall outcomes.

[32] Artificial Intelligence Act IA 13.

[33] Artificial Intelligence Act IA 42.

Figure 1 AIA Impact Assessment Excerpt

> **Stakeholders' views:** In the Public consultation on White Paper on AI, 83% of all respondents consider that the fact that AI may endanger safety' is 'important' (28%) or 'very important' (55%). Among SMEs, 72% found safety to be an important or very important concern, whereas only 12% said it was not important or not important at all. This position was even more pronounced among large businesses, with 83% saying that safety was (very) important and only 4% finding the issue unimportant. 80% of academic and other research institutions and 88% of civil society organisations agreed that safety was a (very) important concern. Among EU citizens, 73% found safety to be an important or very important issue. Of those stakeholders who said safety was not a (very) important concern, 43% were EU citizens (which make up 35% of all respondents) and 20% were SMEs (7%).

This occurs in two instances in the IA. Although the relatively early and commendable timing of the Commission's consultations – in this case, preceding the IIA – generally supports the consultations' potential impact on framing the regulation, such statements in the IA do little to further this claim or tease out in what way consultation impacted on the regulation.[34] Also, statements such as 'largely been supported' obscure the fact that the consultations on that very point comprised very diverging views spread out across the various stakeholders.[35]

The second way in which the Commission refers to the stakeholder consultations is through 12 text boxes relaying statistics from the consultation (see Figure 1 below for one such 'box'), as well as two statistical 'figures'. Noting the type of some of the questions asked (for example, 'how important do you think it is that AI may endanger safety?') is telling, in terms of how relevant stakeholder input is expected to be.[36]

None of the 12 boxes or the two figures elaborate on whether or how the breakout of opinions has influenced the legislative proposal, or which input has substantively been taken on. In any case, in a few instances (in relation to the responses on the possible ban of biometric scanning and the definition of AI) it is possible to deduce that there was a diversity of responses, which might indicate that there was no majority view for the Commission to lean on. In general, the link between the statistics presented in the text boxes and relevant chapter of the IA is not clear, perhaps reflecting that the boxes were inserted at a late stage of drafting the IA – likely a direct response to the criticism, by the RSB, that the Commission needed to better use the results of the stakeholder consultation, including better presenting minority views and discussing them in a more balanced way.[37]

It is also not clear how the Commission weighs the presented statistics of the consultations. The Commission has stated, in relation to public consultations

[34] The lack of clarification of the how stakeholder consultations helped shape the framing of the issue may also create the false impression that the responses of the stakeholder opinions were homogenous enough to support the Commission's six-point problem assessment.

[35] *cf* Artificial Intelligence Act IA 42 and Artificial Intelligence Act IA Annex, 14.

[36] For the box retelling consultation outcomes for this question, as demonstrated above, see Artificial Intelligence Act IA 16.

[37] For these comments of the RSB, see Artificial Intelligence Act IA, Annex 2-5.

generally, that it does not consider responses to its consultation activities to be representative, and that the responses to consultations constitute 'a gathering of opinions that tries to ensure everyone gets heard. The influence that public consultations have on evidence-based policy-making depends more on the quality of the contributions than on the number of contributions.'[38]

The Commission at times reiterates this in its consultation reports and IAs, which the Court of Auditors also considers best practice. In light of the responses not being representative (with no such claim or aim), and the mere presentation of statistics with no discussion of how the Commission views the responses or whether and how 'the quality of the responses' has impacted on the outcome, the added transparency to such reporting is low.

The third way in which stakeholder consultation is featured is an actual response or discussion on some of the content of consultation responses. While these discussions are succinct, the IA contains four such instances. The first example surfaces in one paragraph regarding biometric identification systems.[39] Here, the Commission, noting the call from civil society to ban the use of facial recognition, as well as the existence of an European Citizens' Initiative (ECI) with this stated aim, gives a succinct one-sentence rationale for discarding this approach, as a ban would 'prevent [its] use in duly justified limited uses for security purposes'.[40] Second, with regard to the option of not putting further restrictions on remote biometric identification, it 'would not effectively address the high risk to fundamental rights posed by this system and [its] current potential for arbitrary use without an effective oversight mechanism and limitations on their permitted use'.[41] Third, on the issue of prohibition of certain harmful AI practices, the Commission states that it had considered, but eventually discarded, certain prohibitions requested by NGOs regarding, for example, predictive policing and use of AI for allocation of social security benefits, and in border and migration control, as new requirements for trustworthy AI would aim to address 'the problematic uses and ensure that the AI systems used in sensitive contexts would be sufficiently transparent, non-discriminatory, accurate and subjected to meaningful human oversight'.[42]

Fourth, the Commission also discusses that, in contrast to its risk-based approach, an alternative would be to place the assessment of the risk as a burden on the provider of an AI system and foresee in the legislation 'only general criteria for the risk-assessment'.[43] The Commission acknowledges that this could make the risk assessment more dynamic and capture high-risk user cases but mentions that the option was discarded, with the explanation that 'economic operators would

[38] European Court of Auditors, 'Have Your Say!' (n 1) 44.

[39] While this discussion surfaces in the context of presenting the Commission's non-preferred regulatory policy option, Table 7 (on 63) clarifies that the discarding of the relevant approaches is also relevant for the Commission's preferred option.

[40] Artificial Intelligence Act IA 46.

[41] ibid.

[42] ibid 47.

[43] ibid at 51.

face significant legal uncertainty and higher burdens and costs for understanding whether the new rules would apply in their case'.[44] While the Commission does not directly link its discussion here to the consultation input, its rationale is followed by a 'consultation statistic' box which demonstrates that businesses were against putting the risk on the providers, whereas civil society was for it.[45] The Commission, finally, mentions that a fundamental rights IA, which was recommended by other EU institutions and 'some stakeholders', was discarded, as the existing requirement to provide a Data Protection IA for high-risk AI aims at protecting a range of fundamental rights and could be interpreted broadly, meaning that 'new regulatory obligation was considered unnecessary'.[46]

The fourth way in which stakeholder consultation is featured is through the annexed consultation report, which lies outside the general text of the IA. Here, there is a more detailed report on the total outcome of the public consultation. In this report, responses to the survey have been assessed in terms of stakeholder category – business, civil society, academia, public authority, or citizen. In addition, there are two sections summarising the position papers as well as the feedback from the initial IA. The content of the stakeholder consultation report is, all in all, a numerical and statistical breakdown of responses across various themes. A telling example is the following:

> 60.7% of online respondents supported a revision of the existing Product Liability directive to cover particular risks engendered by certain AI applications. 63% of respondents supported that national liability rules should also be adapted for all AI applications (47%) or specific AI applications (16%) to better ensure a proper compensation in case of damage, and a fair allocation of liability.[47]

Further, the stakeholder report covering the position papers, where stakeholders had freely reacted and presented ideas, similarly comprises a head-counting exercise across domains:

> Among business stakeholders, business associations are the ones that mentioned costs the most. Out of all mentions of costs from all stakeholders (75 in total), 56% came from business stakeholders. Academic stakeholders also mentioned costs more often than other types of stakeholders, but also not very often overall.[48]

The report is a detailed, and at times sophisticated, presentation of who said what, in relation to whom. However, there is no analysis or reporting on if or how this made any difference whatsoever to the Commission, what the Commission thought of the responses, and so forth. As in the IA, the Commission also gives no indication of how it weighs its somewhat excessive 'head-counting' on who

[44] ibid.
[45] ibid at 52.
[46] ibid.
[47] Artificial Intelligence Act IA, Annex 55.
[48] Artificial Intelligence Act IA, Annex 18.

preferred what option, in light of the overall response diversity and rate of consultation responses, considering that the Commission itself is very aware that the responses are in no way a representative sample. It is also not possible to deduce whether the noted coalescence of certain responses made any difference, as in some cases the Commission proposal accords with the outcome of certain responses and in some cases it does not.

4.3.1.1. Was there any description of targeted stakeholder consultations?

The consultation report details that, in addition to the open consultation and the IIA feedback, the Commission organised one conference and seven online technical consultations and had undisclosed meetings with stakeholders in some Member States, as well as a few bilateral meetings with countries outside the EU.

Regarding the technical consultations, the report mentions the theme of each consultation, and for each session the date is indicated, as well as the total number of experts participating (except for the children's rights session) and which group of stakeholders was present (for example, 'mainly from academia').[49] For two online sessions, the names of the organisations represented are mentioned.[50] Beyond the theme discussed, there is no mention of the outcome or content of the consultations. The report also details that, due to the pandemic, planned outreach activities in Member States were cancelled or had to move online. The Commission states that it did, however, discuss the approach in meetings with stakeholders in several Member States, including France, Germany and Italy. They also exchanged views with international bodies, in particular the Council of Europe, the G8, and the G20, as well as the OECD. It is also mentioned that the EU approach was also discussed in bilateral meetings with a number of third countries, for example Japan and Canada.

Regarding the conference, which was the Second European AI Alliance Assembly, the themes discussed are mentioned in the Annex, as well as that 1,900 participants across different stakeholder groups participated.[51] Although not mentioned in the IA Annex, a report from the conference was published, which details the content of the panel discussions, which questions were taken from the audience, and the outcome of the two participant polls taken.[52] While there is no mention of how the conference impacted on the proposal of the Commission, one can merely note discussion and elaborations on the implementation of some of the highlighted features of the White Paper, consensus on some of the elements

[49] Artificial Intelligence Act IA, Annex 21.

[50] '[O]nline workshops on standardisation on 29 September 2020 with 27 external participants from UNESCO, OECD, Council of Europe, CEN-CENELEC, ETSI, ISO/IEC, IEEE, ITU' (ibid 24).

[51] Artificial Intelligence Act IA, Annex 6, 21.

[52] 'Second European AI Alliance Assembly, Event Report', https://futurium.ec.europa.eu/sites/default/files/2020-12/Second%20European%20AI%20Alliance%20Assembly%20_%20Event%20Report.pdf, accessed 6 February 2026.

of the Commission's suggested proposal, and diverging views or opposition to the approach on others.[53] Also, the chosen themes of the conference – for example, conformity assessments and standardisation – indicate the direction and shape which the Commission's work at that time was taking.

Finally, the content of the targeted and technical consultations or additional meetings was not further detailed or discussed by the Commission in any of its published or available documents.

4.3.1.2. Overall Assessment

First, it is worth noting that the results of the Commission's public consultation and feedback, as per standard procedure, were published, including the report and all replies and position papers, which were available in zip files on the Commission's website. However, regarding the reporting on the targeted consultation, the Commission was very circumspect. In this respect, the Commission did not report on any of the outcomes of the targeted consultations whatsoever. At least through indicating the number of experts, the designated theme and the date of the respective meetings, the information provided here by the Commission displayed some information while allowing for further inquiry. And, in fact, the initial description of the targeted consultations in the IIA also prompted civil society to request that other targeted consultations should be held.[54]

Setting aside the issue of the targeted consultations, there is no doubt that the Commission has adhered to its own standard practice, and has at times gone beyond it, regarding the publication and presentation of the consultation outcome. However, with regard to the question of how stakeholder feedback and public consultations have impacted on the legislative proposals, transparency is seriously lacking. Considering the extensive consultations of the Commission and the thorough debate initiated, the numerous responses garnered from its consultation activities, and its detailed statistical reporting on the outcome, it is quite remarkable that only a few sentences in the 100-page IA address the consultation responses, providing a brief rationale for why the Commission discarded certain prevalent views presented by stakeholders (and, indeed, by other EU institutions). The breakdown of stakeholder views in the figures and text boxes provides little clarity on their relevance, or lack thereof, to the regulative proposal chosen by the Commission Service, presumably reflecting a late cosmetic add-on in response to the criticism of the RSB.

[53] For example, there was widespread support for regulating high-risk AI, most participants supported horizontal regulation beyond AI, and there were diverging views on biometric identification and standardisation (ibid).

[54] 'The document mentions targeted consultations organised with "technical experts, conformity assessment bodies, standardisation bodies and experts on biometric data." We request that consultations also be arranged with civil society organisations and with representatives of groups likely to be adversely affected by these systems.': 'Access Now, Feedback Response, Consultation Artificial Intelligence Act' (on file with the author).

It is somewhat telling that the RSB requested the Commission Service in question to 'better use the results' and discuss the outcome in a 'more balanced way', whereas the Commission responded by *presenting* a statistical breakdown, with no discussion of these results, including the minority views, nor better 'use' (or statement of how it has used) the results.[55] Considering the combination of the lack of transparency with regard to content and outcome of the targeted consultations and the meagre response of how the Commission viewed the rich stakeholder contributions, the overall assessment, consequently, for the legislative work associated with the Artificial Intelligence Act is that the Commission, in this law-making process, has not lived up to its legal obligation according to the principle of participatory democracy.

It must, however, again be stated that this observed legal lapse is not a judgment on whether the Commission did, in fact, take on the views and inputs of stakeholders. For this very proposal, a close look at the responses to the stakeholder consultations, a comparison between the White Paper and the IA and final proposal, and the discourse surrounding the proposal, including stakeholders' publicised views, indicate a number of areas where the Commission might very well have listened to concerned parties and adjusted the course of its legislative work. For instance, one of the most prevalent concerns from stakeholders in response to the White Paper was the lack of clarity in the definition of high-risk AI applications, which amongst other things, could cause legal uncertainty to business and stifle innovation while also creating loopholes for fundamental rights breaches. It would seem that, taking note of these concerns, the Commission adjusted its framework for determining whether an AI application poses a significant risk. It also included new areas as high-risk per se, corresponding to stakeholder suggestions.

Another area where the Commission seems to have drawn on the consultation is in moving away from language which assumes that AI uptake, in and of itself, is a goal worthy of pursuing, to, rather, stressing that it is the uptake of ethical and trustworthy AI which acts as a force for good in society, which is the goal; that is, the Commission moved away from an innovation-for-innovation's-sake argument. There are also clear indications in the IA that the Commission has drawn on a very high number of 'user cases' provided by various stakeholders and other sources. It is, therefore, possible that the Commission de facto additionally drew on input from numerous citizens and businesses' experiences. The additional lack of transparency here is problematic, as the user cases are not featured in the published responses of the consultation processes nor elaborated on in the IA. The questions of which kinds of user cases were used, how they were selected, and what they demonstrated are, therefore, left unanswered.

[55] For these comments of the RSB, see Artificial Intelligence Act IA, Annex 2-5.

4.3.2. Has the Commission adequately promoted procedural equality?

This question will be addressed through looking at consultation time frames, geographical diversity and the balance of economic and non-economic interests, in particular efforts to reach out to vulnerable groups.

4.3.2.1. Overall diversity

Of the 1,216 contributions received, 353 were from companies or business organisations/associations, 406 from citizens, 152 on behalf of academic/research institutions, and 73 from public authorities.[56] Civil society's voices were represented by 160 respondents, and 72 respondents contributed as 'others'.[57] All Member States were represented through consultation replies (ie from stakeholders who were from those Member States), although 73 per cent of responses came from eight countries, of which seven were Member States.[58] Most of the submitting parties came from Germany (251 responses). Belgium was second, with 162 responses, and many of the respondents were EU-wide organisations with a seat in Brussels, or global companies with a Brussels office.[59]

4.3.2.2. Citizen diversity

Responses from individual citizens amounted to 406, of which 372 were from EU citizens.[60] However, a large number of respondents chose to report their contributions anonymously, in which cases country of residence/citizenship was not published. Cross-referencing the number of citizens who allowed their details to be reported with the number of citizens the Commission reported to have replied demonstrated that 274 citizens preferred to remain anonymous. However, for citizens who allowed their personal details to be published, those respondents (in total, 132) were from 20 Member States[61] and 9 countries outside the EU.[62] 87 per cent of the replies were

[56] Commission, 'Public Consultation on the AI White Paper Final Report' (2020) 3.

[57] ibid.

[58] One of the top countries that responded was the UK, with 60 responses. The UK was officially still an EU Member State at least for part of the consultation period (ibid).

[59] Among the 450 position papers submitted, 72 came from non-governmental organisations, 60 from business associations, 53 from large companies, 49 from academia, 24 from EU citizens, 21 from small and medium enterprises (SMEs), 19 from public authorities, 8 from trade unions, 6 from non-EU citizens, and 2 from consumer organisations (ibid 15–17); 'Consultation Replies, Artificial Intelligence Act Open Consultation' (on file with the author).

[60] Commission, 'Public Consultation' (n 56) 3.

[61] Austria, Belgium, Bulgaria, Denmark, Finland, France, Germany, Greece, Hungary, Italy, Latvia, Luxembourg, Netherlands, Poland, Portugal, Romania, Slovakia, Spain, Sweden, and the UK: see 'Consultation Replies, Artificial Intelligence Act Open Consultation' (n 59).

[62] Albania, Brazil, Canada, Costa Rica, Côte d'Ivoire, India, Japan, Norway, and the United States: see ibid.

Chart 1: Overall interest diversity

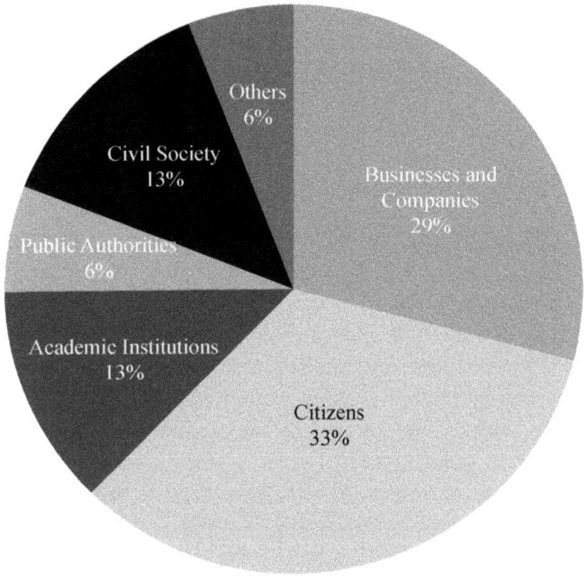

Chart 2: Citizen diversity (geographical, anonymous omitted)

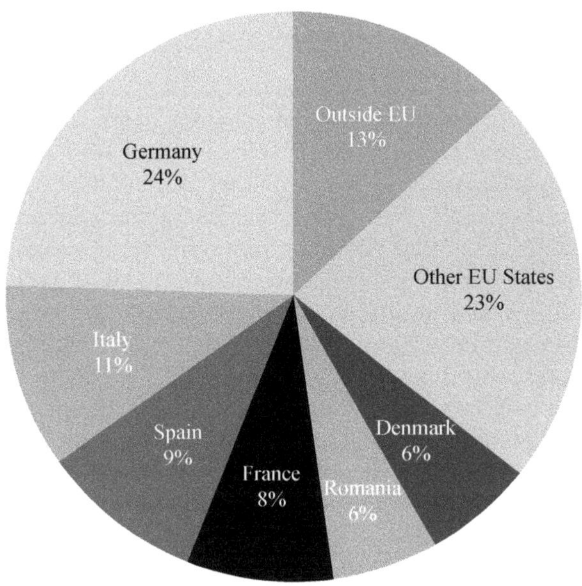

from EU Member States. 24 per cent of the responses came from Germany (32 replies), followed by Italy (14), Spain (12), and France (11). The remaining Member States had between 1 and 8 citizen replies.[63] Information on which survey language anonymous respondents used (published in the raw consultation data) indicates that at least 18 of the other Member States were represented by citizens.[64]

4.3.2.3. Vulnerable groups and affected communities

In terms of specific outreach, the lack of transparency about the Commission's targeted consultation, including its regional outreach in certain Member States, makes it difficult to draw any valid conclusions about whether the Commission made any attempts to alleviate bias and inequality through outreach. What is clear from screening the numerous replies is that many of the citizen replies came from individuals who had been working or publishing in the field of AI. However, many replies from citizens also seem to be concerned with one or another feature, for example biometric identification (perhaps connected to the ECI), as well as other features such as manipulation. For instance, one group which seems to be vulnerable and affected by this proposal is children and families, which find little to no voice in the proposal.[65] There was no visible attempt to reach out to affected communities beyond AI 'insiders', although the Commission has stated that there have been regional consultations in several Member States.

4.3.2.4. Overall assessment

Overall, the consultation drew an impressive amount of citizen responses, and the geographical representation, although not balanced, included all Member States, and citizens from most Member States, as well as citizens from non-EU states and EU citizens living outside the EU. The overall approach of the Commission comes across as outward-oriented. However, in screening consultation replies, much of the participation, including that of citizens, consists of people inside the AI 'bubble' (the lack of transparency on targeted consultations and their outcome, which makes this assessment difficult, is in itself telling). The indication in the IA of a large number of user cases might suggest participation, but again the lack of transparency makes this difficult to assess. While the overall balance, as well as the large number of citizen replies, indicates that the Commission has lived up to its legal duty to promote procedural equality and access to the consultation, there is still much left to improve – in reaching 'parties concerned' – with regard to outreach to potentially affected groups.

[63] Austria 2, Belgium 2, Bulgaria 1, Denmark 8, Finland 2, Greece 2, Hungary 2, Latvia 1, Luxembourg 1, Netherlands 4, Poland 2, Portugal 4, Romania 8, Slovakia 1, Sweden 1, and UK 5 (ibid).

[64] With regard to the following stakeholder feedback of the IIA, the overall geographical diversity of the consultation was quite broad, although citizen response was relatively low (7 EU citizens).

[65] Regarding the exposure to algorithmic-based persuasive design, see Beeban Kidron and others, 'Disrupted Childhood: The Cost of Persuasive Design' (5Rights Foundation, Version 2, 2023), https://5rightsfoundation.com/uploads/Disrupted-Childhood-2023.pdf, accessed 6 February 2026.

4.4. Case study 2: The Revision of the Eurovignette Directive

The revision of the Eurovignette Directive (1999/62/EC) is a part of the 2015 Energy Union Strategy, in which the Commission announced a comprehensive road-transport package promoting, in particular, more efficient pricing of infrastructure, and is also part of the European Green Deal.[66]

The Eurovignette Directive on the charging of heavy goods vehicles for the use of certain infrastructures provides rules to be followed by the Member States which have decided to introduce road charges (tolls or vignettes), although the charges are not mandatory. Together with its two updates, the regulatory framework aims at ensuring that revenues are invested in infrastructure maintenance, that discrimination on the market is prevented, and that some main external costs – such as congestion, noise and air pollution – are internalised.[67]

The revision of the Directive – the legislative proposal in question – would extend the scope of the Directive to cover not only heavy goods vehicles but also heavy-duty vehicles and light-duty vehicles, ie it would encompass passenger cars, minibuses and vans, as well as coaches and buses.[68] The proposal emphasises the application of the 'polluter-pays' and 'user-pays' principles by gradually phasing out the use of time-based user charges (vignettes) and replacing them with distance-based charges.[69] The proposal for revision of the Directive was advanced in tandem with a separate proposal for a Council Directive amending Directive 1999/62/EC as regards certain provisions on vehicle taxation (based on different Treaty provisions), and had been preceded by previous attempts to revise the Directive, which for political reasons were scrapped.[70] The negotiations on the revision of the Eurovignette Directive had been stalled for several years and, finally, after many complex and drawn-out negotiations, reached their conclusion in July 2021 with a text which both the Parliament and Council accepted. The IA report relies on a previous IA prepared in 2013, accompanying a proposal for 'fair and efficient road pricing', which was one of the attempted revisions which were not adopted in view of 'political opportunity reasons'.[71]

In preparing the proposal, a combination of consultation methods were used: a standard 12-week online open public consultation; a targeted consultation through thematic seminars with stakeholders and Member States; a conference on the planned road initiatives, on 19 April 2016; and 21 interviews with stakeholders

[66] Esther Kramer, 'Revision of the Eurovignette Directive PE 603.273' (European Parliamentary Research Service, 2017).

[67] ibid 2.

[68] ibid.

[69] ibid 1.

[70] ibid 2.

[71] Commission, Impact Assessment Accompanying the document Proposal for a Directive of the European Parliament and of the Council amending Directive 1999/62/EC on the charging of heavy goods vehicles for the use of certain infrastructures and Proposal for a Council Directive amending Directive 1999/62/EC2 on the charging of heavy goods vehicles for the use of certain infrastructures, as regards certain provisions on vehicle taxation SWD(2017) 180 final Part 1/2 (Eurovignette IA Part 1/2).

selected on the basis of specific data needs, carried out by the contractor preparing the IA support study.[72]

The open public consultation ran from 8 July to 5 October 2016, with late contributions accepted.[73] It contained two sets of questions: the first, aimed at understanding the perceptions of users, was addressed to the general public, and a second, more technical, one was addressed to experts. Respondents were also given the opportunity to provide any further comments. Some respondents also submitted additional documents providing further relevant information. The questionnaires were based on the issues identified by the evaluation. The issues covered included the quality of road infrastructure, the fairness of road pricing (taxes and charges), the problems of congestion and CO2 emissions, and the scope of EU legislation in the field. There were 135 responses to the questionnaires, as well as 48 additional documents which had been attached to the replies, of which 27 were of relevance.

4.4.1. Has the Commission adequately detailed whether and how consultations have impacted on the legislative proposal?

The following documents have been screened to assess the indicator of transparency: the IA, the report on the public consultation, the report on interviews with SMEs, and the IIA. The consultation replies have also been surveyed, as a light check.

As in the previous case study, the input from the stakeholder and public consultations is presented in an annexed consultation report, as well as throughout the report. The stakeholder report features some basic statistics on the respondents, and then reports on the responses across thematic domains.[74] However, in contrast to the previous case study, the report also contains a dedicated section where the outcomes of the targeted consultations and the conference are reported in detail. For the targeted consultations, contributions are described in terms of content and trends of responses, and according to the specific contributor, for example tolling company, transport SMEs, Member State(s), and so forth (ie not to the broader categories of business, civil society, public authority, and citizens).[75] There is also a dedicated section, of approximately one page, on the 'conclusion and use of the results', which highlights the key takeaway points for the Commission.[76] Here, it is stated that the results of all the consultation activities were used in designing

[72] Commission, Impact Assessment Accompanying the document Proposal for a Directive of the European Parliament and of the Council amending Directive 1999/62/EC on the charging of heavy goods vehicles for the use of certain infrastructures SWD(2017) 180 final Part 2/2 9 (Eurovignette IA Part 2/2).

[73] ibid.

[74] ibid 8–19.

[75] ibid 12–16.

[76] ibid 18.

the policy options, and that, in selecting measures, the 'most rejected ones were discarded after the initial screening and the retained measures were grouped options with increasing level of regulatory intervention, so that decision makers [had] the possibility to judge on the desired level of ambition'.[77] In addition to the consultation report, there is a specific report annexed, on the consultation with small and medium enterprises (SME) representatives (SME test). A detailed stakeholder consultation strategy is also published as part of the IA.[78]

Moving on to the general text of the IA, stakeholder feedback is referenced directly in several instances throughout the IA, here embedded in the text and reasoning. For instance, discussing the phasing-out of vignettes, 'While some Member States that currently apply vignette schemes are not in favour, the majority of stakeholders agree that this is a necessary next step in the harmonization of charges.'[79] Similarly, the result of the feedback is contextualised in light of other available information. Further, the Commission indicates how the consultations have informed the decision to discard certain policy options:

> The most ambitious policy option introducing a full internalization of external costs as suggested by the 2011 White Paper has also been discarded. This option is supported by some environmental NGOs in particular and remains a long-term goal of the European transport policy, but it does not currently appear to be achievable due to excessive implementation costs and for reasons of subsidiarity. Indeed, regarding certain aspects, it appears that Member States are best placed to act. For example, whether or not to apply road charging or congestion charging on a given part of the network can best be assessed at local/regional level.[80]

Regarding the policy option of introducing rules on the liability of the keeper of a toll road to maintain the given road section in sufficiently good/safe condition, the Commission notes:

> Even though the measure received almost as much support from respondents to the on-line public consultation as the monitoring and reporting requirements, it would effectively introduce a legal obligation to ensure that the objective of achieving fair road quality is met.[81]

The Commission indicates that the option has been discarded, as it was considered not to respect subsidiarity requirements, as stakeholders that were interviewed did not support attempting to improve road maintenance by way of rules relating to the potential liabilities, and considered that liability issues were best dealt with at Member State level.[82]

[77] ibid.
[78] ibid 8.
[79] ibid 79.
[80] Eurovignette IA Part 1/2 (n 71) 23.
[81] Eurovignette IA Part 2/2 (n 72) 83.
[82] ibid.

The only area where the Commission's consultation reporting is flawed is regarding the responses from citizens and consumer organisations.[83] The Commission lumps together the two actually distinct groups of 'citizens' and 'consumer organisations', masking the fact that 9 citizens responded to the consultation (of which 6 were from Hungary), and 7 'consumer' organisations, of which 6 were motorists' clubs. This fact is only clear when looking at the raw consultation data.[84] From this data it is also clear that these motorists' clubs often have a very large number of members: for example, the responding German motorists' club had 9 million members, and the Austrian one had 2 million.[85] It is somehow misleading to report on these organisations and the interests they represent together with citizens more broadly. While, in a sense, the motorists' clubs are 'representing' their 2 million members, they are only representing one distinct feature of their members' interests. For instance, in Austria, most individuals who own a car are members of the motorists' club ÖAMTC, as they provide good insurance and exemplary and quick service in the event of a malfunction or accident.[86] However, the idea that those 2 million members actually support the ÖAMTC position in relation to the Commission's piece of legislation is, of course, a very open question, highlighting once again the issue of representativity of actors.

In any case, regardless of whether the responding citizens and consumer organisations are indicative of citizen and consumer positions, the Commission fails to adequately report on the overall oppositions from the responding citizens and consumer organisations to the Commission's proposed line of action.

4.4.1.1. *Overall Assessment*

For this consultation process, it is clear that the targeted and technical consultations have been reported with detail and care, including the responses by interviewees, and while, in cases allowing for anonymity, describing in detail responses which allow the evolution of the Commission's thinking in response to the consultation to be followed. The dedicated section, in the consultation report, of conclusions and use of results, allows for a clearer picture of how participatory input has impacted on the legislation. Further, general statements, in the consultation report, on how consultations have been taken into account are actually accompanied by embedded and clear descriptions of how consultation outcomes correlate to the development of the legislation. A main issue relates to the reporting on citizens and consumer interest organisations. However, considering the overall reporting, the detailed reporting on the outcome of the targeted consultation, and the embedded and clear reasoning on policy choices related to consultation throughout the IA, the Commission has fulfilled the transparency and meaningful-exchange requirements

[83] ibid 16.
[84] 'Commission, Eurovignette Consultation Replies' (on file with the author).
[85] ibid.
[86] Based on the author's experience living in Vienna.

prompted by the principle of participatory democracy. Worth considering is that, in contrast to the Artificial Intelligence Act, this legislative proposal has a much more defined scope. Not only does it revise existing legislation, but the current revision has been reworked, and so not only is there good evidential data, but also drawing up a consultation strategy may be a more straightforward exercise. In addition, considering that one previous attempt at revising the Eurovignette Directive failed for political opportunity reasons, it seems that the Commission has harnessed the consultation to assist in staking out a legislative path which addresses concerns of affected parties while also being politically feasible.

4.4.2. Has the Commission adequately promoted procedural equality?

4.4.2.1. Overall diversity

The Commission received 135 responses to the questionnaires, as well as 48 additional documents, of which 27 were of relevance, covering several stakeholder groups.[87] The breakdown of these categories can be seen below.

The respondents were from 20 different EU Member States, with the highest number of responses received from Belgium (24), Germany (20), Spain (19), Austria (11), and Hungary (8).[88] In addition, a set of targeted interviews received contributions from 21 different stakeholders, including nine Member States (four EU15, and five EU13).[89]

4.4.2.2. Citizen diversity

While the Commission has lumped together citizens/consumer organisations as one group, only nine responses were from citizens (6 from Hungary, 1 from Spain, 1 from the Czech Republic, and 1 from Portugal).[90] The seven organisations which stated that they represented consumers/citizens were from France, Austria, Germany, Spain, Hungary, and Switzerland, and the consumer organisations were mostly motorists' clubs, often representing a large membership (for example, the German motorists' club represented 19 million members, and the Austrian motorists' club represented 2 million users).[91]

[87] The Commission reported on these, including transport undertakings and their representatives; consumers; citizens and their representatives; public authorities; the construction industry; public transport associations; and tolling service/solution providers, also noting that there was a relatively high number of co-ordinated responses (36, ie 27%), indicating standard replies circulated by associations to their members and sent in high numbers: Eurovignette IA Part 2/2 (n 72) 9.

[88] ibid.

[89] ibid 2.3.1.

[90] ibid 2.3.1; compare with 'Commission, Eurovignette Consultation Replies' (n 84).

[91] 'Commission, Eurovignette Consultation Replies' (n 84).

4.4.2.3. *Outreach and balance of economic and non-economic interests*

Specific attempts were made to reach out to SMEs and Member States; however, the environmental associations and citizens which had been targeted in the consultation strategy were largely absent, with no indication that outreach was made. The few consumer organisations which responded represented a large membership base (in the millions) but, all in all, the organisations came from only five Member States and one non-EU country.

4.4.2.4. *Overall assessment*

It is clear that the Commission achieved broad geographical representation throughout the Union, including through its targeted study outreach. However, the response rate from citizens and the geographical representation from citizens and consumer organisations combined were low and seemingly inadequate. That being said, the consumer organisations represented a membership base which was very large, with potential representativity issues noted. While the central aspect of geographical balance of citizens and consumer organisations was lacking, even if one considers that not all EU countries will be affected the same, due to different tolling systems and taxation schemes, it is worth pointing out some crucial strengths of the outreach of the Commission.

One strength of the consultation strategy and outcome, from a legal perspective, is that the Commission has clearly identified which parties it believes are most concerned by this legislation, by targeting and reporting specific groups – for example, 'public transport associations', 'transport undertakings', 'the construction industry', and 'tolling providers' – broad categorisations of 'civil society' or 'business' are avoided, which is helpful and transparent in understanding how the Commission has approached its legislative task of consulting 'parties concerned'. And when certain relevant parties were considered difficult to reach, a special interview study was commissioned which broadened the geographical base. Furthermore, the Commission generally engaged with the consultation input in a very clear and transparent way, allowing the reader to understand how the consultation input impacted on the proposal. However, when looking at the consultation strategy, the targeted 'environmental associations' were completely missing in the consultation outcome. It is unclear whether this lapse was rectified through participation in any of the conferences, but this is highly unlikely, as no environmental association is mentioned in the consultation report or the IA. And the Commission has not attempted to address this through targeted consultations or better outreach to citizens. This lack of action on the Commission's part must, however, also be seen in its legislative context.

The legislative initiative had been proposed several times as a part of the Commission's Green Deal, with the Parliament repeatedly requesting strengthening of the legislation in the field. As an expression of the polluter-pays and user-pays principles, the legislation was intended to incentivise the use of cleaner vehicles and, ultimately, result in a lesser negative impact from transport and a lower level of externalities, including, primarily, reduced CO2 emissions. However, as stated, previous attempts to address this through legislation and revision of the previous Eurovignette Directive had been blocked by the Council. In this context, it is understandable that the consultations are focused on staking out a legislative path, focusing on the obstacles to successfully legislating. While the Commission generally 'targets' citizens, it is not unusual for there to be only a few responses to this type of legislative proposal. All this considered, the lack of geographical representation of a stated consultation target – 'citizens' – and the complete lack of the targeted environmental organisations suggest that the Commission has lapsed in its legal duty. However, the strengths of the Commission's consultation, and the legal context, mitigate this lapse. Clearly, the case study highlights the difficulty in applying the stated indicator in a straightforward way, and how important context is. However, it also resonates with the critique that citizens and environmental organisations, although targeted in theory, are not considered priority stakeholders to listen to.

4.5. Case study 3: Proposal for a new directive on representative actions for the protection of the collective interests of consumers

On 11 April 2018, the Commission published a proposal for a new directive on representative actions for the protection of the collective interests of consumers. Presented as part of the 'New Deal for Consumers' package, the proposal would enable consumers across the EU to use representative actions to collectively demand compensation from companies that infringe their rights. The proposal is a follow-up to the Commission's 2017 fitness check of EU consumer and marketing law, which suggested that, due the rise of cross-border trading and e-commerce, the risk of infringements affecting large numbers of consumers was increasing.[92] It came in the wake of the 2015 Volkswagen emissions scandal (Dieselgate) and the 2017 mass cancellation of Ryanair flights, which signalled that even when faced with mass harm situations, EU consumers were having difficulties accessing efficient remedies.[93] However, beyond these events, the proposal represents efforts over many years to improve and harmonise collective redress in Europe in

[92] Nikolina Šajn, 'Representative Actions to Protect the Collective Interests of Consumers A New Deal for Consumers' (European Parliamentary Research Service, 2021) PE 637.978.
[93] ibid.

the areas of anti-trust and consumer law.[94] The main EU legislation on collective legal actions for consumers, before the current proposal, was the 2009 Injunctions Directive, which requires Member States to put in place procedures for stopping infringements of EU consumer rights.[95] However, the Directive was limited in scope, including that only 'qualified entities' could initiate injunction proceedings.[96] The Commission issued a recommendation, in 2013, on common principles for injunctive and compensatory collective redress mechanisms in the Member States, but a Commission report in 2017 found that Member States had implemented the recommendation only to a limited extent, with large differences in the way representative actions functioned across Member States.[97]

For two years, the Commission proposal went through protracted and difficult negotiations by the Parliament and the Council.[98] Given the complexity of the issues and the diverging views between Member States, inter-institutional discussions were expected to be long and difficult. For Member States where no collective redress instruments were available, the new proposal would mean significant procedural changes in their national systems. For Member States where collective redress was already in place, stakeholders were worried that the new rules could undermine their existing national mechanisms.[99] On top of this, the proposal also faced strong resistance and criticism from business and industry, drawing parallels to the potential for abusive litigation, like in the US system.[100]

In preparing the proposal, the Commission relied on various consultation inputs, including consultation organised in conjunction with its fitness check of related consumer legislation (including the Injunctions Directive); a call for evidence on redress through collective action, running between 22 May 2018 to 15 August 2017; feedback on its IIA; and targeted consultations with the relevant networks of Member State authorities, legal practitioners, consumer organisations, and business associations. [101]

[94] Beate Gsell, 'The New European Directive on Representative Actions for the Protection of the Collective Interests of Consumers – A Huge, but Blurry Step Forward' (2021) 58 *Common Market Law Review* 1365.

[95] Directive 2009/22/EC of 23 April 2009 on injunctions for the protection of consumers' interests [2009] OJ L110/30.

[96] Šajn, 'Representative Actions' (n 92) 2.

[97] Commission, Report on the implementation of the Commission Recommendation of 11 June 2013 on common principles for injunctive and compensatory collective redress mechanisms in the Member States concerning violations of rights granted under Union law (2013/396/EU) COM/2018/040 final.

[98] Šajn, 'Representative Actions' (n 92) 2–4.

[99] ibid.

[100] See, eg US Chamber Institute for legal Reform, 'The Growth of Collective Redress in the EU: A Survey of Developments in 10 Member States' (*ILR*, 21 March 2017).

[101] See Commission, Call for Evidence on the Operation of Collective Redress Arrangements in the Member States of the European Union, https://ec.europa.eu/newsroom/just/items/59539, accessed 6 February 2026; Commission, Public Consultation for the Fitness Check of EU Consumer and Marketing Law', https://ec.europa.eu/newsroom/just/items/31689, accessed 6 February 2026; Commission, A New Deal for Consumers – Revision of the Injunctions Directive (European Commission - Have Your Say, 28 November 2017), https://ec.europa.eu/info/law/better-regulation/have-your-say/initiatives/1170-A-New-Deal-for-Consumers-revision-of-the-Injunctions-Directive_en, accessed 6 February 2026.

4.5.1. Has the Commission adequately detailed whether and how consultations have impacted on the legislative proposal?

The Commission, in its IA, relies on numerous previous consultations, including the 2011 public consultation on collective redress. This raised the question of which consultation exercises should be assessed with regard to the obligation to consult in law-making. The starting point for this assessment is the stated intent to legislate – that is, the IIA. However, an overly formalistic application of this starting point would mean that the large consultations during 2016–17, which culminated in the publication of the IIA, and the stated intent to legislate, would not be included. In the IIA, it is also stated that, considering the broad consultation just concluded, the Commission will only be conducting additional targeted consultations prior to the release of the IA. Considering that, from the relevant consultation documents, it was relatively clear that there was a possibility of a legislative approach to collective action, these activities were included as well. The following documents and consultation activities have, consequently, been screened to assess the indicator of transparency: the IA, including its consultation reports; the consultations on the fitness check; and the Commission's call for evidence on redress through collective action, as well as the published feedback to the IIA, and targeted stakeholder results.[102] Consultation activities carried out in the context of the assessment of the implementation of the 2013 Recommendation on Collective Redress were not included, because of the long amount of time that had passed before the current proposal, and the overall more tenuous link to the current proposal.

Initially, it must be stated that the legislative documents are highly difficult to navigate, for various reasons. For the case-study purposes, this is particularly true, as half of the IA relates to a legislative proposal that was adopted a year earlier than the case studied, and consultations were sometimes on issues overlapping between the different legislative proposals, which were part of the same package, but passed at different stages through different instruments and were consulted on through different, yet sometimes overlapping, means.

Besides the Annex, which contains a consultation report which details the outcome based on stakeholder breakdown, the IA is peppered with consultation outcomes, many of which amount to a reporting of outcomes rather than an understanding of how these have informed the legislative work. The IA, however, also admits transparently when there were diverging opinions and discusses them in depth,[103] as well as when it did not succeed in reaching groups it had hoped to

[102] The 'open consultation' preceding the IA was explicitly not focusing on redress, but on the other legislative proposal covered by the IA. It has been lightly surveyed, as it indirectly serves as a basis for the issue of redress, as it, for example, investigates the digital environment for consumers. However, the Commission explicitly excluded the issue of redress from this consultation and dealt with this separately, in the 'call for evidence'.

[103] Commission, Impact Assessment accompanying proposal for directives (1) amending Council Directive 93/13/EEC, Directive 98/6/EC of the European Parliament and of the Council, Directive

consult.[104] One such example is the fact that business organisations and companies were consistently against the strengthening of collective redress.[105] There are also accounts of which organisations participated in targeted consultations, and some information about the selection process.[106] The IA also cites examples of mass harm situations and ineffective mechanisms to tackle them, citing individual consultation replies.[107] Further, the Commission services indicate where certain consultation replies have contributed to certain conclusions: for example, 'Consumer organizations confirm that the Commission guidance has not led to improvement of transparency of online marketplaces.'[108]

The Commission also notes that, while business organisations observe significant differences in Member State implementation of the relevant EU consumer legislation they prefer adopting further guidelines and recommendations, citing a specific position paper.[109] The Commission, to a certain extent, also responds directly to the concerns and views of large companies:

> There are no viable alternatives to the mechanism for consumer redress under option 3. In order to build redress actions on the existing category of 'measures eliminating the continuing effects of the infringements' in the ID, redress actions would need to follow the existing modalities of the injunction procedure, such as the limitation of representative action to qualified entities.[110]

The report seems to have incorporated the initial appraisal of the RSB that stakeholders' views needed to be better reflected in the assessment.[111] Suggesting, in its final opinion, that the Commission had failed to show significant stakeholder and Member State support for its action, the RSB stated that:

> The revised report does not sufficiently demonstrate the need for legislative action at EU level on collective redress in view of the 2013 Commission Recommendation on this topic. . . . (the) report could expand on the motivation and arguments brought forward by Member States and other stakeholders in favour of an EU legislative initiative on collective redress.[112]

2005/29/EC of the European Parliament and of the Council and Directive 2011/83/EU of the European Parliament and of the Council as regards better enforcement and modernisation of EU consumer protection rules and (2) on representative actions for the protection of the collective interests of consumers, and repealing Directive 2009/22/EC, SWD(2018) 96 final (Representative Action IA) 20–23, 38–43 Part 1/3 (Representative action for consumer protection IA part 1/3).

[104] For example, 'It was challenging to reach specific types of businesses, such as online marketplaces and free digital service providers.' (Representative action for consumer protection IA part 2/3) 7.

[105] ibid 11–12

[106] ibid 16

[107] Representative action for consumer protection IA part 1/3 (n 103) 24.

[108] ibid 31.

[109] ibid 24.

[110] ibid 43–44.

[111] Commission Regulatory Scrutiny Board, Proposal for a Directive as regards better enforcement and modernisation of EU consumer protection rules and Proposal for a Directive on representative actions for the protection of the collective interests of consumers SEC(2018) 185, 1.

[112] ibid 3.

In addition to engaging, in several instances, with the substance of the consultation outcomes, the Commission also details by name which networks it invited to its targeted consultations, as well as what was discussed with which expert groups.[113] However, whereas the content of the main targeted consultation was reported, the consultation with expert groups was not.

4.5.1.1. *Overall Assessment*

Despite the challenges in surveying the IA, as well as the lapse in reporting on the consultation with expert groups, the embedded and detailed discussion of the stakeholder participation indicates that the Commission has lived up to its obligation of providing an account of how participatory input has influenced the legislative proposal. The fact that the targeted consultations were well reported also support this.

4.5.2. Has the Commission adequately promoted procedural equality?

The Commission, in its IA, relies on numerous previous consultations, making it highly difficult to draw up a definitive geographical map of respondents. This is especially so because it sometimes draws on consultation results which raise the question of to what degree the respondents were commenting on the content of the current legislative proposal. In addition, on two questions, the Commission draws on general responses to the public consultation which was targeting another part of the Consumer Deal Package, raising the question whether all those respondents should be incorporated when assessing the geographical reach of the consultations on collective redress. In a similar vein, the Commission also cites results from the 2017 Consumer Scoreboard, which is an EU-wide representative survey of consumer experiences and opinions; for 2017, the number of participants was 26,599, representatively surveyed from all Member States, as well as Norway and Iceland. Although the responses which were drawn upon were relevantly related to assessing the need for collective redress, the question, however, is whether those responses should be seen as participating in law-making (for example, consumers were not commenting on any aspect of a potential legislative approach and, crucially, also not choosing to present their views in the context of a legislative process). In the end, while the use of such surveys can be relevant for a legal obligation to consult, in this context the general-purpose Scoreboard was not included in the impact assessment.[114]

[113] Representative action for consumer protection IA part 2/3 (n 104) 16.

[114] *cf* European Commission, Directorate General for Justice and Consumers, *Consumer Conditions Scoreboard: Consumers at Home in the Single Market*, 2017 edn (Publications Office, 2017).

The fitness check covering six directives, including the Injunctions Directive, saw 436 replies, with an overwhelming 216 replies from Germany, followed by 48 from Belgium, 24 from the UK, and 15 from France.[115] The rest of the replies originated other Member States, with between one and thirteen replies per Member State. In this consultation, there was a predominance of business interests, with 40 per cent companies and 20 per cent business associations, with 22 per cent of the replies being from consumers, 5 per cent from consumer associations, and 6 per cent from public authorities, as well as 7 per cent other.[116]

By contrast, the replies to the call for evidence – less numerous, albeit solely focused on the issues of redress – saw more participation from consumer organisations and public authorities. The call for evidence received 50 replies, spread rather evenly across 17 Member States, comprising 5 per cent consumers, 28 per cent consumer associations, 10 per cent civil society groups, 26 per cent business associations, 3 per cent companies, 15 per cent public authorities or ministries, and 12 per cent other.[117]

In addition, there were 23 responses, across 16 Member States, to the IIA on the revision of the Injunctions Directive, with an even-spread mix of economic and non-economic actors, as well as 3 from citizens.[118] The open public consultation accompanying the IA (with 414 responses spread over 26 Member States, and including 94 individual citizens) was directed at consumer protection rules other than collective redress, while containing one or two questions relevant for redress as well.

Finally, a targeted consultation on the revision of the Injunctions Directive was held, with 90 replies coming in from 26 Member States and three non-EU countries (all Member States were represented except Hungary and France).[119] The respondents were 48 Member States authorities (national consumer protection authorities, European consumer centres, national ministries, national competition authorities), 21 business associations (national and EU-wide), 16 consumer associations (national and EU-wide), and 5 other (chamber of commerce, legal practitioners).

The overall results hardly fit neatly into a pie chart of geographical representation. However, the outcome, as well as the targeted consultation of the Commission, suggest that there has been a strong ambition of the Commission to have broad, sometimes universal, Member States representation, which is reflected in the various consultation outcomes. Citizens' voices were promoted through various means, and there was strong participation from consumer associations, business,

[115] Results available on the consultation website: see Commission, 'Public Consultation for the Fitness Check of EU Consumer and Marketing Law' (n 101). A few additional replies which came in late were not included in the statistics.

[116] ibid.

[117] Replies available at Commission, 'Call for Evidence on the Operation of Collective Redress Arrangements in the Member States of the European Union' (n 101).

[118] Replies available on the consultation website: see Commission, 'A New Deal for Consumers – Revision of the Injunctions Directive' (n 101).

[119] Representative action for consumer protection IA part 2/3 (n 104) 18–19.

and professional circles. Overall, the Commission has adequately promoted procedural equality.

4.6. Case study 4: Regulation on Asylum and Migration Management (New Migration Pact)

Following the large increase of asylum seekers entering the EU in 2015,[120] a substantial number of whom were escaping persecution and unrest as a result of the protracted Syrian war and humanitarian catastrophe, the Commission unveiled a 'European Agenda on Migration' in May 2015, in an effort to develop and co-ordinate policy responses at the EU level.[121] In order to further harmonise the EU asylum acquis and rectify noted shortcomings, the Commission started a comprehensive overhaul of the Common European Asylum System in 2016.[122] One such shortcoming was the 'Dublin system', a mechanism through which Member States establish which nation is in charge of processing an asylum application from a non-EU country or a stateless person. Within the reform framework, on important laws and the overhaul of the Dublin system, Member States were unable to come to an agreement. With the aim of resolving the structural weaknesses in the context of national reception, asylum and return systems of EU Member States, the Commission submitted a 'New Pact on Migration and Asylum' (henceforth, 'the New Pact') in September 2020.[123]

The Pact aimed to 'turn the page' on the years that followed the 2015 migrant wave and Member State clashes.[124] Political tension had ensued between frontline states in the south, who faced the task of processing asylum claims, transit states in central Europe, who criticised ineffective border controls, and destination states in the north, who were ultimately responsible for hosting and integrating refugees.[125] The New Pact consisted of five legal instruments, three recommendations, and one document providing guidance.[126] Pre-entry processes at external borders, responsibility-sharing and solidarity mechanisms, a special mechanism for crises and *force majeure*, and new governance practices in the areas of asylum

[120] The total number of asylum applicants in the EU during that period exceeded 1.3 million. See, eg Wouter van Ballegooij and Cecilia Navarra, 'The Cost of Non-Europe in Asylum Policy' (European Parliamentary Research Service, 2018) PE 627.117.

[121] Commission, Communication from the Commission on a New Pact on Migration and Asylum COM (2020) 609 final.

[122] European Parliamentary Research Service, 'The European Commission's New Pact on Migration and Asylum, Horizontal Substitute Impact Assessment, PE 694.210'.

[123] Commission, 'A Fresh Start on Migration: Building Confidence and Striking a New Balance between Responsibility and Solidarity, Press Release, IP/20/1706'.

[124] ibid.

[125] Jorge Liboreiro, 'EU Gives Fresh Push to Stalled Migration Pact' (*euronews*, 10 June 2022), www.euronews.com/my-europe/2022/06/10/eu-hails-historic-agreement-as-it-gives-fresh-push-to-stalled-migration-pact, accessed 6 February 2026.

[126] See, eg Commission 'New Pact on Migration and Asylum', https://home-affairs.ec.europa.eu/policies/migration-and-asylum/new-pact-migration-and-asylum_en, accessed 6 February 2026.

and migration made up its main components.[127] The centrepiece of the Pact was the proposed Regulation on Asylum and Migration Management, which would replace the current Dublin Regulation and relaunch the reform of the Common European Asylum System.[128]

The Pact drew much attention upon its release and was also criticised by various civil society organisations, who argued that the Pact overly focused on border controls, and that its approach to solidarity mechanisms would allow EU countries to continue to intensify pushbacks at the external borders, with concrete elements of the package breaching fundamental rights and the Refugee Convention, especially non-refoulement.[129] Member States were equally divided and, because of the polarised positions, progress was stalled until new momentum was found in the spring of 2022, when the war on Ukraine had again brought the issue to the fore.[130] By June 2023, both Parliament and Council had adopted their respective common positions and a finish line for the legislation was in sight.

Neither the Regulation on Asylum and Migration Management nor the Pact were accompanied by any IA, and no online public consultation was conducted. The Parliament condemned the lack of IA and commissioned its own substitute IA, the conclusions of which were critical of the substance and overall approach of the legislative package.[131]

From the accompanying staff working document (SWD), it is clear that the Commission did not hold any open public consultation on the legislative proposals.[132] The Commission published a Roadmap on the New Pact on Migration and Asylum, which was available for stakeholders' comments for four weeks, between 30 July and 27 August 2020.[133] It generated, in total, 1,829 replies from 1,753 unique respondents.[134] The feedback on the Roadmap was also summarily noted in the document attached to the proposal.[135] However, the Roadmap clearly stated that it did not aim for any legislative impacts but was a precursor to a pending

[127] ibid.

[128] Commission, Proposal for Regulation of the European Parliament and of the Council, on asylum and migration management and amending Council Directive (EC) 2003/109 and the proposed Regulation (EU) XXX/XXX [Asylum and Migration Fund] COM (2020) 610 final.

[129] See, eg European Economic And Social Committee, 'New EU Pact on Migration and Asylum: A Missed Opportunity for a Much-Needed Fresh Start' (30 November 2020), https://www.eesc.europa.eu/en/news-media/news/new-eu-pact-migration-and-asylum-missed-opportunity-much-needed-fresh-start, accessed 9 August 2023.

[130] Liboreiro, 'EU Gives Fresh Push to Stalled Migration Pact' (n 125).

[131] European Parliamentary Research Service, 'The European Commission's New Pact on Migration and Asylum' (n 122).

[132] 'Commission Staff Working Document, Accompanying the Proposal for a Regulation of the European Parliament and the Council on Asylum and Migration Management and Amending Council Directive (EC) 2003/109 and the Proposed Regulation (EU)XXX/XXX [Asylum and Migration Fund] SWD(2020) 207 final (Commission SWD Asylum and Migration Pact)'.

[133] Commission, Roadmap New Pact on Asylum and Migration Ref Ares(2020)4017751 - 30/07/2020.

[134] ibid.

[135] Commission, 'New Pact on Asylum and Migration, Roadmap Feedback' (*European Commission - Have Your Say*, 27 August 2020), https://ec.europa.eu/info/law/better-regulation/have-your-say/initiatives/12544-New-Pact-on-Migration-and-Asylum_en, accessed 6 February 2026.

'communication on the Migration Pact' and gave very little detail on any direction the Commission was taking with regard to the Pact.[136] As such, it is questionable whether the feedback on the Roadmap can be considered EU law-making consultation.

4.6.1. Has the Commission adequately detailed whether and how consultations have impacted on the legislative proposal?

The SWD provides very little information regarding the substance, outcome or impact of the consultations which did occur. Under the rubric 'consultations with civil society', more than half of the 'consultations' mentioned refer to desk research, which includes publications by civil society or non-state actors, as well as continuous interactions with civil society dating back to 2016.[137] For instance, the document reads:

> Civil society was also engaged through a number of meetings and conferences, since the proposed 2016 CEAS package. The Tampere 2.0 conference, held on 24-25 October 2019 in Helsinki, aimed to facilitate the future negotiations by conducting a series of thematic discussions on why a common system is necessary and on how the current rules should be amended.[138]

The document then continues to mention how the recommendations of the Tampere conference resulted in focusing on the root causes of migration, and issues such as lack of trust between Member States, and so forth. After this listing of broad thematic recommendations, the document then moves on to another topic. There is no information on whether or how these 'recommendations' were put to use, nor anything about who participated in the conference. Overall, these vague and declamatory references to conferences and events, sometimes dating back years, offer little value in terms of transparency and feedback. They may have contributed to the Commission's overall knowledge base, but they cannot be viewed as legislative consultation. Instead, the consultation that seemingly has occurred with regard to the legislative package seems to be the consultation with the Parliament and Member States, the feedback on the Roadmap, and potentially a few targeted consultations during 2020 which are mentioned in the document.[139]

References, in the document, to the targeted consultations basically only include the date and the fact that the Commissioner herself was involved, and in one case the civil society organisation present for that consultation:

[136] Commission, Roadmap New Pact (n 133).
[137] Commission Staff Working Document (n 132) 25–26.
[138] ibid 25.
[139] ibid.

'Commissioner Johansson held targeted consultations with civil society organizations (CSOs) on 14 February 2020', and 'with representatives of the Initiative for Children in Migration on 27 January 2020'.[140] It is also mentioned that, 'during her visits to Member States Commissioner Johansson regularly consulted with relevant local non-governmental organizations'.[141] There is no way to see which issues were discussed, which civil society organisations were involved, and how the discussions impacted on the proposal. One can also question whether these consultations included concrete elements or lines of action related to the Pact, or whether general issues were discussed.

The references to Member States and the Parliament also do not include any detail on the content or outcome of these deliberations.

Finally, there is the feedback on the Roadmap. First, it must be stated it is unclear whether responses to the Roadmap can be considered law-making consultation, when the Commission refers to the Roadmap as preparing a 'Communication' meant not to have any significant impacts:

> The Communication will present the overall context, logic and rationale of various legislative and non-legislative initiatives which the Commission intends to put on the table together with the Communication setting out the New Pact. In line with the Better Regulation Guidelines, an impact assessment will not be prepared as the Communication itself is not intended to have significant direct impacts.[142]

Nevertheless, as the SWD is the only document accompanying the legislative proposals and refers to the Feedback on the Roadmap, it is worth looking at the reporting surrounding the feedback.

With regard to the feedback received, the Commission summarised the outcome of the numerous feedback replies in three paragraphs and a chart detailing which Member States participants in the feedback came from.[143] Notably, the Commission summarily states that, 'in terms of the tone/attitude of the replies towards the New Pact, the largest number were mostly neutral, followed by negative, positive and mixed replies'.[144] From a footnote, the reader can surmise that, in fact, a small sliver of feedback replies were positive towards the initiative and over 700 were negative, with over 800 neutral. Looking at the actual replies, most of these 800 seem to be from citizens (many are noted as anonymous), with many replies not directly commenting on the content of the Pact and others expressing diverse views ranging from relaying strong anti-immigration sentiments, to Black Lives Matter activism, to thoughtful citizen-oriented replies on the wished-for

[140] ibid.
[141] ibid.
[142] Commission, Roadmap New Pact on Asylum and Migration Ref. Ares(2020)4017751 - 30/07/2020.
[143] Commission Staff Working Document (n 132) 27–28.
[144] ibid 28.

approach to asylum and migration.[145] None of these diverse and somewhat disorienting responses are mentioned or dealt with in the SWD.

The Commission, further, makes brief mention of which themes each category of respondent focused on, with little further detail provided, for example:

> Non-governmental organizations and academic research institutes stressed the need to reform the Dublin Regulation and improve the implementation of the rest of the asylum acquis. They also underlined the need for safeguards in the asylum acquis, especially for women, children and other vulnerable groups. Some of them warned against the externalisation of migration policy, the introduction of a screening phase and the extension of the border procedure.[146]

After the end of this paragraph, the Commission moves on from consultation to another chapter in the working document. The phrase 'the Commission has taken into consideration' is repeated several times in the few paragraphs dedicated to consultation in the SWD and introductory paragraphs, with reference to national authorities or organisations, but there is no explanation of how the Commission has taken their views into consideration especially, or even which legislative proposal the Commission is talking about. It is not clear what outcome or insights were derived from the targeted consultations, including whether these consultations related to the legislative package, some of the voluntary recommendations of the Pact, or just broader issues related to migration, for example those brought on by COVID-19. There is no acknowledgment that a vanishingly small portion of the consultation replies were positive on the content of the Pact, or of what implications this has. Finally, the explanatory memorandum embedded in the proposal for a regulation offers no more insight, as it is a condensed form of the already succinct reporting on consultation in the SWD.[147]

It is clear that the Commission has not lived up to its transparency obligations. The vague and sweeping statements offer no clarity on the origin, substance and impact of the ad hoc 'targeted' consultation that did occur, nor the numerous replies to the publication of its Roadmap. As stated above, the explanatory memorandum embedded within the actual proposal for a regulation is a condensed form of the already very succinct reporting in the SWD.[148] While Member States have clearly been consulted, the outcome of these consultations is also not reported. The contrast with the Commission's reporting in all other examined cases, where consultation is reported through reports, statistics, annexes, descriptions, and so forth, is stark.

[145] Compare ibid 27–28 and Commission, 'New Pact on Asylum and Migration, Roadmap Feedback' (n 135).

[146] Commission Staff Working Document (n 132) 28.

[147] Proposal for a regulation of the European Parliament and of the Council on asylum and migration management and amending Council Directive (EC) 2003/109 and the proposed Regulation (EU) XXX/XXX [Asylum and Migration Fund] COM(2020) 610 final 14–16.

[148] ibid.

Overall, the Commission's reporting on consultation is less than forthcoming, seemingly representing a problematic approach in terms of adhering to the principle of participatory democracy and the consultation obligations it entails. At the same time, the legislative process highlighted some of the challenges that occur when citizens are brought into the process in larger numbers, and the kinds of different demands and expectations this places on public institutions, which may well lead to retreat by public institutions rather than engagement. As one of the 'anonymous' (presumably citizen) feedback replies states:

> this is an initiative of profound significance for the future of Europe and its citizens. Yet its existence and this possibility to comment is a well-kept secret, it seems. About 2000 people have commented by today which is the last day, out of a population of 500 million or so. The level of ambition of the EU in this matter appears illustrative of its attitude toward listening to the EU citizens, and is one more reason to question the legitimacy of this whole initiative.[149]

4.6.2. Has the Commission adequately promoted procedural equality?

For the legislative proposal under review, the Commission failed to conduct an open consultation; however, its Roadmap did generate significant reaction. Of the 1,753 unique respondents, 1,657 were citizens, 50 were organisations, 6 were public administrations, and 40 fell under the 'other' category.[150] While replies were numerous, in part due to a campaign activating citizens, replies only originated from 10 Member States, showing little geographical representation.[151] Crucially, countries with a disproportionately strong interest in, and experience with, issues related to asylum and migration and the issue of solidarity – for example, Greece – were not represented at all in the consultation. The four-week deadline and lack of advertising likely contributed to this effect, although the framing of the Roadmap may also have contributed to the lack of replies. The Roadmap's reasoning as to why no IA was necessary is worth recounting:

> The Communication will present the overall context, logic and rationale of various legislative and non-legislative initiatives which the Commission intends to put on the table together with the Communication setting out the New Pact. In line with the Better Regulation Guidelines, an impact assessment will not be prepared as the Communication itself is not intended to have significant direct impacts.[152]

[149] 'Individual Feedback Reply, Roadmap New Pact Asylum and Migration' (on file with author).
[150] See Commission, 'New Pact on Asylum and Migration, Roadmap Feedback' (n 135).
[151] Germany (1,205 EU citizens, 9 non-EU citizens, 3 NGOs, 2 academic research institutes, 2 companies, 27 other respondents), followed by Estonia (165 EU citizens), Austria (101 EU citizens), Hungary (50 EU citizens), Sweden (35 EU citizens), Belgium (23 NGOs, 2 other respondents), the Netherlands (14 EU citizens, 4 NGOs), France (13 EU citizens, 1 academic research institute, 1 other respondent), Italy (13 EU citizens, 1 NGO), and the UK (5 EU citizens, 5 NGOs), see ibid.
[152] ibid.

It is, therefore, unclear what respondents thought they were replying to – which is confirmed after a screening of the replies, especially those of the citizens who accounted for the overwhelming number of replies and would give declamatory feedback related to asylum and migration and the overall role of the EU.

It is clear that the Commission consulted thoroughly with all Member States, and, to some degree, the European Parliament (EP), in order to make progress on the political gridlock. However, with regard to consultation with non-state actors, the Commission made little effort, to the point where it seems as if such engagement was deliberately avoided. Indeed, the introductory statement of the document containing the Proposal for a Regulation is revealing: 'The political profile of migration over recent years and the negotiations on the 2016 proposals mean that there has already been a rich and detailed debate on the issues covered by this Regulation.'[153]

This seems to reflect the view that the substantial consultation had been done before, in relation to previous efforts to legislate in the field of asylum and migration. There may be merit to the argument that the main points of the legislative package had been covered during broad and substantive consultation in contexts other than the specific legislative proposal at hand (reform efforts within the same area). However, such an approach to consultation can, arguably, only make sense if the Commission then clearly states its opinion in this regard and accounts for how such input was taken into account, including where it may have influenced the proposal at hand. Even if that consultation had been properly relayed, there is, furthermore, something inherently problematic, from a legal standpoint, in fulfilling a Treaty obligation to consult through relying on consultations conducted years before the legislative proposal was presented, especially on such a salient topic as migration. This is probably also why the Commission did not explicitly refer to previous rounds of consultations in the document attached to the New Pact on Migration and Asylum.

Overall, while Member State consultation seemed commendable, and there was much feedback to the Roadmap announcing a pending Communication on the Migration Pact, the Commission did not sufficiently promote procedural equality. Indeed, given the failure to have open public consultations, the Commission's framing in the Roadmap, and the lack of established links of the targeted consultations with the legislative proposal at hand, it could be argued that the Commission failed to consult at all, in breach of the principle of participatory democracy and the relevant primary law requirements. In particular, Article 2 of Protocol No 2's statement that, before proposing legislative acts, the Commission shall consult 'widely' can hardly be considered fulfilled through principally only consulting

[153] This statement is followed by: 'In addition, the Commission consulted the European Parliament, Member States, and stakeholders on a number of occasions to gather their views on the New Pact on Migration and Asylum.' However, as reported, the actual description and reporting of such consultation with regard to consultation with non-state actors seems to be highly limited: see Commission, Proposal for a regulation of the European Parliament and of the Council on asylum and migration management and amending Council Directive (EC) 2003/109 and the proposed Regulation (EU) XXX/XXX [Asylum and Migration Fund] COM(2020) 610 final 14.

Member States and the Parliament. Nor is there anything to suggest there is a case of 'exceptional urgency' at hand which would relieve the Commission of its consultation duty according to the Protocol's requirements.

4.7. Reflections on consultation case studies and implications

The assessment of Commission consultations on four legal proposals, against three key legal obligations of the principle of participatory democracy, has demonstrated three things. The first is that the procedural requirement of transparency and responsiveness, ie how participatory input has impacted on a proposal, can be applied effectively. The second is that the obligation of providing procedural equality is difficult to apply in a streamlined and meaningful way, at least as it has been conceived of as a legal threshold and applied in these case studies. However, it remains a key challenge in giving effect to the principle of participatory democracy. Third, egregious violations of the principle of participatory democracy, such as no Commission consultation of parties concerned, persist.

With regard to adequate responsiveness, it is clear that, while the Commission performed admirably across the first three legislative consultations in *presenting* and publishing the results of its open consultation outcomes and replies, reporting on the targeted consultations was less stellar, and for the first, and particularly the last, case was seriously lacking. Meanwhile, as has been argued, merely reporting on consultation outcomes is insufficient. The different outcomes in the cases, however, highlight that the legal obligation can realistically be achieved in different settings through various means. In the case related to the Regulation on Asylum and Migration Management, even the presentation and publication of the results were poorly conducted.

In the first case study, the legal assessment demonstrated that the Commission had failed to provide adequate feedback. Because, as noted, there is a rather strong case to be made that, for this particular law-making process, stakeholder consultations and input actually had a significant impact on the Commission's final proposal in specific instances, it is worthwhile to pause and reflect on a few possible reasons why the Commission consistently refrains from reporting on such impact in any meaningful way.

The first and most obvious reason, which this research seeks to directly address, is that the Commission does not see itself as legally bound to provide such feedback. Absent an understanding of its legal obligation in this regard, such feedback becomes an issue of convenience, and as such, becomes prey to a number of factors.

One such factor may be complexity of attribution. The seeming simplicity of meaningful exchange through 'giving feedback' on how stakeholder and citizen input impacts on a legislative proposal belies the complexity of the various forces which influence the Commission's legislative work and the entry points for such influence. As stated earlier, the multiplicity of entry points does not necessarily fit with a linear chronological narrative of impact. An illustrative example for this very legislative proposal is that the first leaked draft of the Artificial Intelligence Act had a five-year moratorium on biometric identification, which then was scrubbed at a very late stage before release of the Commission proposal for a regulation.[154] Further, many of the concerns or viewpoints of stakeholders in this consultation process are also echoed in research, raised by international organisations such as the Council of Europe, promoted by outside business entities in other spaces, championed through mass citizen mobilization (ECI initiatives), or featured implicitly in discussions during AI conferences and seminars. Attributing developments in the legislative proposal to a specific consultation process, response or stakeholder group may not only be difficult, but often disingenuous.[155] It is often the amalgamation of information, thoughts, experiences, or indeed various co-ordinated lobbying efforts, surfacing in different spaces, which presumably may also evolve and contribute to new perspectives, which engenders impact.

The question then arises of whether this means that adhering to the suggested legal obligation is impossible, or even irrelevant. The answer to this is 'no'. The transparency prompted by the principle of participatory democracy does not require that it is possible to trace impact back to a certain element of a legislative proposal or to a particular stakeholder group or consultation response. Such an obligation would, furthermore, rest on the flawed assumption that preferences and positions are static and best understood as pitted against each other, which runs counter to the very assumptions of interdependence and deliberation which participatory democracy rests on. The obligation does, however, require generosity in sharing how a proposed piece of legislation has evolved in relation to participatory input, and this can foreseeably be achieved despite the complexity of the legislative process. Arguably, such approaches also came through in the case studies: for example, the Commission, in relation to the Eurovignette Directive, was detailed and forthcoming in how it had used the results of the consultation, for example when it disagreed with certain stakeholder or input, and also when it had adjusted course. It would also seem that this kind of transparency not only provides important underpinnings for the participatory democracy, but, perhaps ironically, also for the instrumental arguments for participation concerned with 'evidence-based' regulation.

Another reason is the fear of exposure – here meant to cover a set of concerns which relate to fig-leaf participation and participation fatigue. If participation input is not really having any impact on the Commission's legislative work, or

[154] Michael Veale and Frederik Zuiderveen Borgesius, 'Demystifying the Draft EU Artificial Intelligence Act — Analysing the Good, the Bad, and the Unclear Elements of the Proposed Approach' (2021) 22 *Computer Law Review International* 97, 98.

[155] *ClientEarth* (n 9), para 107.

only participation from certain actors is having an impact (regardless of whether this may be legitimate or not, depending on the quality of those responses), then to adhere to transparency in the context of providing meaningful exchange could arouse fears that this would undermine the Commission's approach and credibility, prompting criticism or participation fatigue. The latest evaluation of the Commission's stocktaking exercise of its Better Regulation Agenda demonstrated that Commission staff felt that consultations were a time-consuming and cumbersome exercise where the outcome generally did not justify the time and energy spent on it, and was often disappointing.[156] If this indeed reflects the general sentiment, or even just a strong current of thought amongst the Commission services, it provides fodder for the hypothesis that a fear of exposure is underlying the reticence to open up the decision-making process. This fear may very well also be a factor in the reluctance to detail the participants and content of targeted consultations. There may be legitimate reasons why the Commission does not take on the input of 'parties concerned', and it is under no legal obligation to do so.

Consideration must also be given to the possibility that 'too much' transparency can have detrimental results on the quality of governance and the very process of learning necessary in complex governance.[157] Naturally, this is related to the overall political climate surrounding the Commission. One important point, however, is that the legal dimension of the Commission's obligation steers the question towards how best to generously share how participatory input is related to the legislative work, and not whether such information should be shared.

The third and final reason, related to a lack of awareness of the legal imperatives to provide meaningful exchange in the consultation context, is that to provide feedback is, of course, a skill that needs to be practised and refined; and it is naturally connected to the thought that was put into drawing up a consultation strategy and the execution of such a strategy.

With regard to the second obligation of procedural equality through promoting diversity and outreach to specifically affected groups or communities, it is clear that there are difficulties in applying the legal threshold in a meaningful way, with the legal assessment on all four cases left vague. The nature of EU law-making consultation and the complexity in achieving procedural equality makes it difficult to define a legal threshold which defines 'parties concerned' without becoming too arbitrary. Consider, for example, the case study on representative actions for the protection of the collective interests of consumers, where the Commission drew on numerous consultations from the previous two years, which, because of the legislative stalemate over the years, were still relevant, making it difficult to establish a threshold for any kind of geographical Member

[156] Commission, Taking stock of the Commission's Better Regulation Agenda, COM (2019) 178, 18.
[157] Deirdre Curtin and Albert Jacob Meijer, 'Does Transparency Strengthen Legitimacy?' (2006) 11 *Information Polity* 109.

State diversity. As regards outreach to vulnerable groups or citizens, the cases also demonstrated how difficult it is to analyse, from a legal perspective, absent profound deficiencies in stakeholder targeting and outcome, whether the 'parties concerned', including citizens, have been reached. At the same time, the first two case studies confirm what observers have long noted: that there is a lack of outreach beyond the well-defined existing networks, with a dominance of corporate interests.

The challenge in achieving sufficient breadth and depth to adequately reach the 'parties concerned' to be consulted is particularly clear when looking at the first two cases. In the first case, the Artificial Intelligence Act is a piece of legislation that has broad and significant impacts across society; however, the legislation is framed in a complex way, sometimes with technical language, and is very difficult for 'outsiders' and ordinary citizens or vulnerable groups to understand.[158] However, the ethical balancing which is reflected in, for example, the liability clause requires an understanding of the potential harm that AI can cause, and the potential costs associated with mitigating or eliminating that harm – as well as the consequences of not regulating.

In an area where legislation is lagging behind technology, citizens have first-hand experience which could prove instructive. It is particularly interesting to see that, for the Artificial Intelligence Act, there were no documented efforts to reach out to groups vulnerable to the adverse effects of AI-driven practices; consider, for example, the exposure to, and effect of, algorithmic-driven persuasive design on children and young people or the negative effects that dependency on algorithmic-driven decision-making in the public sector has had on vulnerable groups.[159]

Overall, it would seem that a meaningful way which gives expression to equality, and which is also more open to review in a straightforward way, is the obligation to have an Internet-based open consultation which is open to the public. This occurred for three of the cases analysed, but not for the New Migration Pact legislative package.

Finally, the case related to the EU Migration Pact demonstrates how the Commission can, for high-profile legislative files for which there is significant political pressure, disregard its constitutional duty to consult, while also setting aside its commitment in the Interinstitutional Agreement on Better Regulation, reflecting a persistent approach to consultation as a discretionary choice. This approach, while legally untenable, is also reflected in similar recent cases discussed in the previous chapter, where the EU Ombudsman critiques, inter alia, lack of Commission consultation during the law-making process.

[158] Indeed, even public authorities may find it difficult to understand. The author's impression when in contact with the Swedish Ombudsman for Children to inquire about their lack of response to the consultation on the Commission's AI proposal was that there was little understanding of the proposal's potential to impact on children.

[159] Although children's rights experts were mentioned as having been consulted through targeted means, there was no reporting on this.

4.8. The right to participate in the democratic life of the Union in the national context – Austria, Sweden and Ireland

Having explored whether and how specific consultation practices live up to the standards which follow from the principle of participatory democracy, this section turns to how the principle operates at the national level. The CJEU states that the 'instruments of participatory democracy' have as their objective 'to encourage the participation of citizens in the democratic process'.[160] The previous chapter highlighted the obligations outlined in Article 11 TEU and Article 10(3) TEU and their implications for EU law-making. Because Article 11(3) TEU solely places a duty on the Commission to consult, presumably the principle's operating article has a limited impact on Member States' actions – in this case, the consultation design and framing which occurs at the national level. However, Article 10(3) TEU prescribes a 'right for citizens to participate' in the democratic life of the Union, which we know from CJEU case law to be a right that goes beyond participating in elections, and which the analysis in the previous chapter demonstrated goes beyond the Brussels 'bubble' and, crucially, extends to EU law-making at the national level.

However, if consultation and participation in law-making is a key element of the principle of participatory democracy, what does this mean for law-making at the national level? How does this understanding inform relevant legal norms operating at the national level? After having explored law-making practices at the EU level, this section explores, based on three case studies, the way that the principle of participatory democracy interacts with national legal norms, informing their interpretation. The section begins with a discussion of the cases selected and the approach to identifying legal norms, followed by a discussion of each Member State – Austria, Sweden and Ireland – and concludes with some reflections.

Most EU countries engage in some form of public consultation or participatory practices when developing laws.[161] However, the legal status of participation and consultation processes differs widely across European countries, ranging from mandatory consultation processes enshrined in the constitution, to legally non-binding guidance, best practices, or internal ministry practice.[162] Furthermore, while there is little overview analysis of the legal status of access and participation of Member States in negotiating EU law, which occurs primarily through participation in Council negotiation, the OECD, for example, note that few Member States systematically consult with non-state actors during the negotiation phase.[163]

[160] Case C-418/18 P *Grégor Puppinck and Others v Commission* EU:C:2019:1113, para 65.
[161] OECD, *Better Regulation Practices across the European Union 2022* (n 3) 50.
[162] ibid, 50, 55; OECD, *Regulatory Policy Outlook 2021* (OECD Publishing, 2021) 202; See also Hanna Hämäläinen and Janne Salminen, 'Inclusive Participation in Law-Making: Good Governance or a Constitutional Obligation?' (2025) 13 *The Theory and Practice of Legislation* 213, 202.
[163] OECD, *Better Regulation Practices across the European Union 2022* (n 3).

Therefore, the approach taken here for each country has been to survey existing legal frameworks which impact on participation in EU law-making during the negotiation phase.[164] The areas of focus will first be on the first-hand legal norms granting participation rights or obliging the government or other relevant Member State body to consult during the negotiation phase, and on the second-hand rules which impact on access to EU law-making negotiation, for example transparency or scrutiny regulation. These two areas correspond to CJEU statements of the right to participate in the democratic life of the Union, exemplified as a right of citizens to know and attempt to influence the legislative process. The existence of such norms, or lack thereof, will determine whether they can serve as relevant legal hooks and contribute to realising Article 10(3) TEU – the right to participate in the democratic life of the Union.

For each Member State, the legal system is briefly framed, the relevant legal frameworks are identified and analysed, and the analysis is concluded with a legal interpretation of the relevant legal norms in light of Article 10(3) TEU. There are two important limitations to the analysis presented. The first is that the aim is not to comprehensively map how Article 10(3) TEU informs the interpretation of national norms. As stated, the application of Article 10(3) TEU refers to both participatory and representative democracy, and would arguably apply to legal norms impacting not only on norm creation, but also on traditional democratic practices such as elections and, potentially, foundational democratic capacities. Instead, the aim is to identify relevant legal hooks for Article 10(3) TEU where Member States function as gatekeepers for the democratic life of the Union – in this case, participation in EU law-making. The second limitation is that the legal analysis is conducted at a rather high level. The ambition has not been to make an exhaustive and detailed legal analysis based on national law where every possible relevant case or legal rule is identified. Rather, the purpose has been to capture how the right of citizens to participate in the democratic life of the Union can fit into a national legal context, and to put forth a legal argument which is persuasive – or at least plausible – from both an EU and national law perspective.[165]

4.8.1. Austria

Austria is a democratic, federal republic comprising nine provinces administered by their own regional governments. After World War II, Austria's constitution, dating back to 1920 and drafted by Hans Kelsen, was re-enacted.[166] Ten years later, Austria's

[164] Following CJEU case law at the EU level, as well as the approach for identifying key procedural requirements for the Commission in the previous section.

[165] While the cases in this book are analysed at a high level, I have made a more exhaustive case for the Swedish setting: see Gloria Golmohammadi, 'I gränslandet mellan rättigheter, skyldigheter och ambitioner – Remissförfarandet ur ett rättsligt perspektiv' (2024) Statsvetenskaplig Tidsskrift Vol 126 Nr 3.

[166] Harald Eberhard and Konrad Lachmayer, 'Constitutional Reform 2008 in Austria' (2008) 2 *Vienna Journal on International Constitutional Law* 112, 113.

sovereignty was re-established by the conclusion of a state treaty between Austria and the Allies.[167] In the same year, Austria declared its permanent neutrality by constitutional law and became a member of the United Nations. In 1995, Austria joined the EU while also becoming a member of the European Monetary Union (EMU), which saw major revisions to the Austrian constitution. The Austrian legal system is based on the civil-law tradition and has its origin in Roman law.[168] As a civil-law system, focus rests on legal text, with no case-law system in Austria. A judge is free to reach his own decision or ruling, although cases from the highest courts carry decisive persuasive authority.[169] Similarly, legal doctrine, while not a legal source per se, carries persuasive authority. *Travaux* are rarely used in order to deduce legislative intent, with the focus resting on the language of the legal text itself.

The Austrian legal order is hierarchical in structure. At the top rests the Austrian Federal Constitution and individual constitutional laws, as well as the EU Acts of Accession. General federal laws and laws of the federal provinces are in the lower tiers. Statutory authorities can enact regulations or individual administrative rulings in accordance with these. Although there is a 'core document', the Federal Constitutional Law, the provisions of the Federal Constitution are scattered over many sources. The Federal Constitution also does not require constitutional amendments to be incorporated into the Federal Constitutional Law. This flexible approach has led to amendments at frequent intervals. Since the renotification of the Federal Constitutional Law in 1929, the Federal Constitution has been amended over 100 times,[170] leading scholars to metaphorically compare the Federal Constitution to a 'ruin'.[171] Austria has a centralised system of judicial review: the Constitutional Court can strike down unconstitutional laws and regulations, mainly through review of laws, with both abstract review (for example, initiated by federal/provincial governments or parliamentary minorities) and case-linked review, triggered from a dispute.[172]

Austria's political system is characterised by a strong corporatist culture. Outside the (legally) institutionalised partnership between government and established interest representation by the Social Partners, other civil society organisations have more circumscribed opportunities to influence the law- and policy-making process.[173] Participation in federal law-making has drawn controversy in relation to the familiar tension between technocratic efficiency and

[167] Josef L Kunz, 'The State Treaty With Austria' (1955) 49 *American Journal of International Law* 535, 535.

[168] Helmut Weichsel, 'A Brief Overview of the Austrian Legal Information System and Laws' [2021] *GlobaLex*, https://www.nyulawglobal.org/globalex/Austria1.html.

[169] ibid.

[170] Theo Öhlinger and Harald Eberhard, *Verfassungsrecht*, 12th edn (Fakultas, 2019) para 6.

[171] Hans Klecatsky, 'Bundes-Verfassungsgesetz Und Bundesverfassungsrecht' in Herbert Schambeck (ed), *Das österreichische Bundesverfassungsgesetz und seine Entwicklung* (Duncker & Humblot, 1980) 83–110, 94 ff.

[172] Constitution of Austria (as amended in 2024): Federal Constitutional Act (Bundes-Verfassungsgesetz) (B-VG) (reinst 1945) See Art 139 B-VG, Art 140 B-VG; 'Verfassungsgerichthof, Functions', https://www.vfgh.gv.at/kompetenzen-und-verfahren/functions.en.html, accessed 3 March 2026.

[173] See, eg Didier Chabanet and Aleksander H Trechsel, 'EU Member States' Consultation with Civil Society on European Policy Matters' (2011) EUDO Report 2011/04, 12.

participatory legitimacy. In this context, the fact that the consultation procedure, the Begutachsverfahren, is a long-standing state practice rather than a codified legal obligation leaves Austrian ministries wide discretion over who is heard and, crucially, how much time they are given. In the last decade, criticism has focused less on the existence of consultation channels than on their tactical compression: draft bills have been circulated with deadlines far before the long-standing recommended six-week benchmark, prompting accusations that consultation becomes performative when time constraints systematically undermine reasoned input.[174]

At the same time, Austria has expanded participatory access in ways that at least partially respond to these concerns. Since 2021, participation has been broadened beyond classic ministerial drafts to parliamentary initiatives, and the formal infrastructure for publishing and receiving submissions has been strengthened through parliamentary procedure – moves that can be read as attempts to align national practice with a thicker understanding of democratic participation in norm creation.[175] Yet the recurring controversy persists, in that consultation is structurally vulnerable to acceleration strategies, especially where political urgency is invoked to narrow the space for deliberation and contestation.[176]

4.8.1.1. What is the legal framework for public participation in law-making?

Zooming in on what the legal norms are, the Austrian constitution has limited regulation of public participation in law-making. The constitution safeguards the prerogatives of the provinces, the Länder, vis-a-vis the federal government, the right of parliament, and the privileged position of the social partners, and provides for certain legislative reforms to require a referendum.

As regards participation and consultation in relation to 'standard' national law-making, there is, as stated, a well-established practice of consultation with interest groups and organisations in addition to authorities and the privileged social partners (Begutachtungverfahren). Consultation can be structured chronologically: ministry consultation during the preparatory stages of legislation (before a draft bill is submitted to the Austrian Council of Ministers); a pre-parliamentary review phase; and a post-parliamentary review phase.[177] As regards the former, the consultation procedure is more state practice than codified law; ministry consultation appears as a requirement in the context of the IA, which is legally mandated by secondary legislation – the Impact assessment bill (WFA-GV).[178] The WFA-GV is a secondary/federal regulation, binding on ministries when preparing draft federal

[174] Jürgen Klatzer, 'Taktieren Mit Begutachtungsfristen' (*Österreichischer Rundfunk (ORF)*, 26 June 2020), https://orf.at/stories/3169772/, accessed 3 March 2026.

[175] Parlament Österreich, 'Das Begutachtungsverfahren', https://www.parlament.gv.at/beteiligen/wissenswertes/begutachtungsverfahren/, accessed 1 February 2026.

[176] Klatzer, 'Taktieren Mit Begutachtungsfristen' (n 174).

[177] Parlament Österreich, 'Das Begutachtungsverfahren' (n 175).

[178] Verordnung des Bundeskanzlers über Grundsätze der wirkungsorientierten Folgenabschätzung bei Regelungsvorhaben und sonstigen Vorhaben, BGBl II Nr 489/2012 zuletzt geändert durch BGBl II Nr 67/2015, § 2, 9§ 3.

laws and ordinances, subordinate to the constitution, and procedural in nature: it specifies what must be assessed, documented and submitted during drafting. The WFA-GV stipulates that, as a rule, consultation should last six weeks, before a draft bill is submitted to the Austrian Council of Ministers.[179] The six-week review period is also recommended by the Constitutional Service in the Federal Chancellery.[180] Other dimensions of consultation are not elaborated on, and accounts indicate that consultation practices vary somewhat from ministry to ministry.[181]

As regards the pre-parliamentary review, this process has relatively recently been opened up to the public, whereby draft bills submitted to parliament are posted to the parliament's website, where interest groups and citizens can comment upon the draft bill while also engaging with comments received.[182] The ministry can then adjust the bill based on input received before formally submitting the bill to parliament. The public then also has the opportunity to comment on the final bill, which is under the parliament's review, also through the parliament website. This procedure is mainly regulated through the Austrian Parliament's rules of procedure.[183] In addition, with the new Austrian Freedom of Information Act (IFG), a strong presumption of publicity exists for documents produced by, or in the hands of, public authorities.[184] According to the IFG, public authorities also have a proactive duty to publish information 'of general interest' on the Internet as soon as possible, in a manner accessible to everyone. The general interest criterion is not clearly defined, but legal commentary suggests a broad understanding of the term. However, noteworthy is that there is little justiciability for these duties and a no opportunity to appeal a decision not to publish information.[185]

While there is a relatively clear and defined framework for non-state and public participation in Austrian national law-making, the scope of existing consultation rules is clearly limited to Austrian legislation. This is clear from the legal text and language, for example, in the WFA-GV and the constitutional provisions. They do not include Austrian participation in EU law-making, and any interpretation in which the obligation to consult encompasses consulting on any kind of dossier or draft negotiation positions does not find support in the legal text.[186]

[179] WFA-GV 9§ 3.

[180] Bundeskanzleramt Österreich, 'Rundschreiben zu Begutachtungen und Konsultationsmechanismen', https://www.bundeskanzleramt.gv.at/agenda/verfassung/legistik/begutachtungs-konsultations-informationsverfahren-bessere-rechtssetzung/rundschreiben-begutachtungen-konsultationsmechanismen.html, accessed 1 February 2026.

[181] See, eg Wanda Tiefenbacher and Markus Möstl, 'Legal Environment and Space of Civil Society Organisations in Supporting Fundamental Rights: Austria' (*European Union Agency for Fundamental Rights*, 2020). Informally, within each ministry there are also lists of organisations to consult.

[182] § 23b Bundesgesetz vom 4 Juli 1975 über die Geschäftsordnung des Nationalrates (Geschäftsordnungsgesetz 1975 – GOG-NR), BGBl Nr 410/1975 (idgF).

[183] 23b GOG-NR; see also §40 and 37a GOG-NR.

[184] Informationsfreiheitsgesetz (IFG), BGBl I Nr 5/2024 (Art 2), idgF.

[185] See Datenschutzbehörde Republik Österreich, 'Leitfaden Zum Informationsfreiheitsgesetz' (30 June 2025), https://dsb.gv.at/sites/site0344/media/downloads/leitfaden_ifg_-_stand_30.6.2025.pdf, accessed 3 March 2026.

[186] *cf* 23b GOG-NR and WFA-GV 9§ 3.

However, the Austrian constitution does provide disclosure obligations on the government in relation to EU matters or projects (*'vorhaben'*, in German). Article 23e BvfG outlines the duty of the federal government to inform the National Council and the Federal Council (the two chambers of the Austrian Parliament) 'of all projects within the framework of the European Union' and afford them the opportunity to express an opinion thereon.[187] This duty, on the part of the federal government, to provide information is incumbent upon the respective federal minister.[188] The duty extends to all so-called 'projects' within the framework of the EU.[189] The term 'project' *('vorhaben')* is an encompassing term and the 'intended duty to provide information is comprehensive in nature'.[190] A broad interpretation is also required in view of the purpose of Article 23e B-VG, which is to enable the National Council and the Federal Council to deal with and discuss EU issues in the relevant committees, and to exercise, inter alia, their right to comment.[191] While the concept of a project is not limited to legal acts, legal acts constitute one of the core 'projects' which the duty encompasses. It has been highlighted that all 'decision-preparatory documents' are covered by the information obligation, and are to be classified as projects.[192]

This constitutional obligation has been fleshed out and crystallised through the Austrian EU Information Act (EU-InfoG).[193] The EU-InfoG regulates how Austrian ministries must provide the parliament with information about ongoing EU legislative and policy-making procedures, including rules on classification, transmission of documents, and access. This is mandated through the establishment of a national EU databank run by the parliamentary administration, to which ministry officials submit documents.

While the EU-InfoG focuses on parliamentary oversight, in line with the constitutional obligation to inform parliament, the aim of the ministry's duty to inform has expanded, through the EU-InfoG, beyond the national council/parliament to include the public: 'The Parliamentary Administration shall provide information to the National Council, the Federal Council, *the public*, the provincial parliaments, and the social partners on projects within the framework of the European Union'.[194] The EU databank is available on the Austrian parliamentary website and contains a wide range of EU-related documents. However, a large part

[187] Art 23e BvfG. This somewhat mirrors the obligation of the federal government to keep the provinces informed of EU matters as well.
[188] In cases of complex matters within the meaning of § 5 BMG 1986, the duty to provide information applies to that member of the federal government who is responsible for leading the negotiations: see Theo Öhlinger and Christoph Konrath, 'Zu Artikel 23d B-VG' in Karl Korinek and Michael Holoubek (eds), *Österreichisches Bundesverfassungsrecht* (Verlag Österreich, 2013) 12.
[189] Without the restrictions comparable in Art 23d (1) B-VG on the 'areas of influence' of the National Council or the Federal Council; Öhlinger and Konrath, 'Zu Artikel 23d B-VG' (n 187).
[190] ibid.
[191] See Art 23e in connection to the rights under Arts 23f and 23g B-VG.
[192] Stefan Griller, 'Verfassungsfragen Der Österreichischen EU-Mitgliedschaft' [1995] ZfRV 89.
[193] Bundesgesetz über Information in EU-Angelegenheiten (EU-Informationsgesetz – EU-InfoG) BGBl I Nr 113/2011, idgF.
[194] 2 § EU-InfoG. Emphasis added.

of the documents in the databank have been classified by the relevant ministry, often because they constitute EU Council 'LIMITÉ' documents, and therefore cannot be accessed, even though they are listed and are technically in the databank. The parliamentary service indicates what documents should be inserted, and the approach is comprehensive. However, if a ministry neglects to insert a document in the databank, this is not resolved through legal appeals, but through contacts with the parliamentary service and the relevant ministry. In rare cases, political pressure is applied through, for example, raising the issue, through the Speaker of the parliament, with a senior ministry official or the minister.

4.8.1.2. How does the 'right to participate in the democratic life of the Union' inform the interpretation of national legal norms?

As has been demonstrated previously, Article 10(3) TEU requires that citizens be placed in a position to 'participate in the democratic life of the Union'; this includes EU law-making, and when Member States act as gatekeepers for this democratic life through negotiating EU law. Considering that existing relevant Austrian legal norms related to participation in EU law-making in the national setting, beyond the parliament and the provinces, are focused on access to information and transparency, the principle of participatory democracy would inform the interpretation of national legal norms in the way described below.

First, the government obligation to publish would encompass not just documents produced by EU institutions, but those produced by the Austrian ministry itself. This could include, inter alia, non-classified negotiation briefs, background documents and consultation documents or minutes in terms of formal and informal consultations which have occurred during the negotiation phase. This would be in line with the language of the obligation as outlined in the EU-InfoG, as well as the stated comprehensive understanding of the duty to inform. This would align participation in EU law-making more with the existing framework for nationally oriented laws. Such information is also shared by ministries with parliament in other Member States.[195] While it would not guide or push officials to consult affected or interested parties during the negotiation phase, it would increase access to the legislative process for parties and, potentially, citizens, providing the foundation for participating in the democratic life of the Union. Second, the EU-InfoG should be interpreted narrowly regarding restrictions classifying documents related to EU law-making, for example in the Council working documents.

Both of these interpretations are reinforced when considering the IFG as working in tandem with the EU-InfoG. The interaction between the legal instruments of the EU-InfoG and the IFG is not clearly commented on in Austrian legal literature, but two possible legal interpretations are, at the outset, possible. The constitutional duty to inform on EU projects, as fleshed out and expanded

[195] As highlighted in the case studies in this section regarding Ireland and Sweden, to name a couple.

in the EU-InfoG would, in light of Article 10(3) TEU, encompass Austrian internal documents related to EU law-making, requiring these to be inserted into the EU document databank. To the extent that such internal documents would be viewed as falling outside the application of the EU-InfoG, they would instead fall under the general freedom of information duties under the IFG, both in terms of a request for access to a document and proactive publication.

Article 10(3) TEU would then inform the understanding of the duties under the Austrian IFG in the way that there is a presumption that the requirement to publish information of 'general interest' applies to documents relating to EU negotiation material and, in particular, consultations during this period.[196] Article 10(3) TEU would here inform the 'necessary and proportionate' test for any exceptions for confidentiality under IFG §6, which include 'for compelling reasons of integration or foreign policy, in particular in accordance with provisions of European Union law that are directly applicable'. Specifically, this would apply for EU legislation with significant impacts on the general public, including on their fundamental rights. Article 10(3) TEU could then be used as a legal tool to undergird arguments in terms of access to documents under the IFG, and be integrated into the judicial review chain for access to documents under § 11 IFG.[197] As there is no review system as regards proactive publication obligations according to the IFG, such appeals would have to be enforced through soft-law appeals or, for example, complaints to the Austrian Ombudsman.

Overall, this interpretive shift would expand transparency and access by the public to documents. It also strengthens access to information of the parliament, making it, overall, coherent with Article 10 TEU (which, as was demonstrated in the previous section, is an overarching democratic right referring to both representative and participatory democracy).

4.8.2. Sweden

Sweden is a constitutional parliamentary democracy with a 'weak' monarch as the head of state.[198] The Swedish constitution – the so-called Basic or Fundamental Laws (Grundlagarna) – form the bedrock of the Swedish legal system. The four Swedish fundamental laws together act as a constitution: the Instrument of Government (RF), the Freedom of the Press Act, the Fundamental Law on the Freedom of Expression, and the Act of Succession.[199] The most prominent of the

[196] §4 IFG; see also §§2,3 IFG.

[197] In addition to §11 IFG, see also §14 IFG.

[198] Bernard Michael II Ortwein, 'The Swedish Legal System: An Introduction' (2003) 13 *Indiana International & Comparative Law Review* 408.

[199] These are: Regeringsformen (Instrument of Government) RF; Successionsordningen (Act of Succession) SO; Tryckfrihetsförordningen (Freedom of the Press Act) TF; and Yttrandefrihetsgrundlagen (Freedom of Expression Act) YGL. The parliament's work is regulated in Riksdagsordningen (The Riksdag Act) (RO).

fundamental laws is the RF, outlining basic principles for governance and political life in Sweden, defining rights and freedoms, and balancing the powers of the state.[200] It is also in the RF that provisions on law-making consultation, as well as judicial review, can be found. Swedish judicial review is uniquely structured; in the absence of a constitutional court, judicial review is available for all levels of courts, administrative and general, and to public authorities as well.[201] Judicial review, in the Swedish case, is directed at two situations: first, instances where a provision does not conform with the constitution or higher-ranking law; and second, where the legally established procedure has been set aside in any significant way during the making of the law.[202] In both cases, the legal rule should not be applied by the Swedish courts.[203] Judicial review in Sweden (and the Nordic countries more broadly) is something of a 'unicorn'. Historically, it has been regarded with caution, as the courts in Sweden have had a relatively limited role.[204]

The formal process of government-facilitated written consultations runs throughout all policy areas and has deep roots in Swedish governance, with a pedigree of over 100 years and a mention in the Swedish constitution. The Swedish consultation 'remiss' procedure is the process whereby legislative or policy proposals are referred to a large number of state or municipal authorities, interest groups, organisations and business interests, who are invited to submit written responses. The procedure is used by various parts of the Swedish government and is particularly institutionalised in the concluding phase of commissions of inquiry that study, prepare and formulate new legislation and policy. An overwhelming majority of commissions of inquiry consult.[205] Nine out of ten government commissions of inquiry have been estimated to consult through the standard procedure.[206] The Swedish procedure is generally a targeted one: a list is compiled of relevant addressees that are asked to submit responses. Other actors and the general public may also respond, even though they are not directly addressed. However, the Swedish practice of publishing the list of specifically selected participants identified and contacted by the executive body makes it more transparent with regard to the consultation strategy.

Over the last two decades it has been observed that the Swedish committee structure[207] – the hub of legislative consultation – is diminishing in importance. Privatisation, de-corporatism and increasing pluralism contribute to shrinking the

[200] Anders Eka, 'Kommentar, Regeringsform (1974:152) 7 Kap. 2 §' [2018] Lexino.

[201] Ortwein, 'The Swedish Legal System' (n 198) 414; while potentially empowering to lower courts, it also arguably dilutes the power of judicial review. Arguing in this vein, see Joakim Nergelius, 'Judicial Review in Swedish Law – A Critical Analysis' (2009) 27 *Nordic Journal of Human Rights* 142.

[202] RF 11 § 14.

[203] ibid.

[204] Nergelius, 'Judicial Review in Swedish Law' (n 200).

[205] Statens Offentliga Utredningar [SOU] SOU 1999:144 Demokrati på remiss [government report series] 56.

[206] ibid.

[207] In Swedish, *'Kommittéväsendet'*.

role for government commissions.[208] Actors are directing their gaze and efforts towards Brussels rather than towards national arenas. Alternative forms of participation and influence, such as lobbying and media engagement, appear more effective and appealing.[209] This is also related to observations that Swedish law-making consultation is not aligned to the EU legislative process and, rather, takes on the role of ex post control.[210] However, a relatively recent survey study with qualitative follow-up interviews of interest groups participating in government consultations in Sweden across a range of policy areas indicates that participation in written consultations remains highly valued.[211] In recent years, controversy has repeatedly emerged when speed and executive discretion compress that deliberative space: during COVID-19, 'quick bills' and extremely short consultation windows were criticised as undermining the quality and inclusiveness of preparation, including by the Council on Legislation (Lagrådet), while also being subjected to judicial review (see below), and in constitutional scrutiny and academic debates around shortened consultation times and urgency as justification for procedural shortcuts.[212]

4.8.2.1. What is the legal framework for public participation in law-making?

The role of consultation is highlighted in the RF, with one constitutional clause being its primary legal foundation. Reference to consultation is found in the chapter of the RF dealing with the work of the government, RF 7:2:

> In preparing Government business, the necessary information and opinions shall be obtained from the public authorities concerned. Information and opinions shall be obtained from local authorities as necessary. Organisations and individuals shall also be given an opportunity to express an opinion as necessary.[213]

[208] Erik Lundberg and Erik Hysing, 'The Value of Participation: Exploring the Role of Public Consultations from the Vantage Point of Interest Groups' (2016) 39 *Scandinavian Political Studies* 1, 1–3; For a contrasting historical perspective, see Olof Ruin, 'Participatory Democracy and Corporativism: The Case of Sweden' (1974) 9 *Scandinavian Political Studies* 171, 171.

[209] It has been argued that this form of consultation has been displaced by other means of influencing policy: lobbying, professional opinion formation/technocrat and media campaigns. See Statens Offentliga Utredningar [SOU] SOU 1999:121 Avkorporativisering och lobbyism – konturerna till en ny politisk modell [government report series]; PerOla Öberg and Torsten Svensson, 'Civil Society and Deliberative Democracy: Have Voluntary Organisations Faded from National Public Politics?: Civil Society and Deliberative Democracy' (2012) 35 *Scandinavian Political Studies* 246, 246.

[210] Jörgen Hettne and Jane Reichel, *Att Göra Rätt Och i Tid – Behövs Nya Metoder För Att Genomföra EU-Rätt i Sverige?*, 2012:4 (Svenska institutet för europapolitiska studier, 2012).

[211] Lundberg and Hysing, 'The Value of Participation' (n 207).

[212] See, eg Rebecca Thorburn Stern, 'When the Ends Justify the Means? Quality of Law-Making in Times of Urgency' (2019) 7 *The Theory and Practice of Legislation* 85.

[213] 'Sveriges Riksdag, The Instrument of Government (Translation Provided by Swedish Parliament)', https://www.riksdagen.se/globalassets/05.-sa-fungerar-riksdagen/demokrati/the-instrument-of-government-2023-eng.pdf, accessed 1 February 2022.

This paragraph expresses that the government should open up for participation in all areas of its mandate, including legislation. The obligation to consult applies in the legislative setting, as well as when the government is the deciding authority in specific individual cases.[214] For organisations and individuals, the constitution prescribes a consultative obligation to the degree that it is 'necessary'. The constitution does not further elaborate on when it is necessary or required to obtain statements, or which considerations should influence who is consulted.

The lack of specificity in this area reflects a conscious choice on the part of the legislator. In conjunction with the birth of this constitutional clause (RF 7:2), *travaux préparatoires* state that the government's investigative preparatory mandate should not be locked down in legislation, so that it may take whatever shape is appropriate in relation to its aims.[215] The *travaux préparatoires* to the RF further state that detailed regulation in this area risks hampering the work of the government, making it unnecessarily bureaucratic and more difficult to adapt to societal change.[216]

The constitutional text clearly attaches a functional role to participation in relation to legislative or policy outcomes: participation in decision-making by external actors is mandated only to the extent necessary or required. However, in deciding on when to consult and which form the consultation should take, the purpose of consultation should be considered. The *travaux préparatoires* highlight that the Swedish consultation procedure aims to secure high-quality legislation as well as to serve as a 'democratic anchor'.[217] The term 'as necessary', according to *travaux préparatoires*, can therefore not exclusively be evaluated from an efficiency or functional perspective. This dual function is also emphasised by the government in communication externally regarding the consultation procedure, as well as in *travaux*.[218] While the main focus of consultation is the quality of the government's work, relevant *travaux* also emphasise consultation with authorities, organisations and other groups as important for the Swedish political process.[219] More recently, the Swedish Supreme Court has confirmed the consultation procedure's constitutional mandate.[220] A consultation lapse, including severely reducing the time frame for the consultation procedure, may lead to a disapplication of a law primarily on procedural grounds – even while it is also

[214] Eka, 'Kommentar' (n 200).

[215] Proposition [Prop] 1973:90 Grundlagsutredningen [government bill] 287.

[216] ibid.

[217] ibid.

[218] Statsrådsberedningen, Svara på Remiss - hur och varför?, SB PM 2003:2 [government memorandum] Stockholm, 2003.

[219] Proposition [Prop] 1973:90 Grundlagsutredningen [government bill] 287. The autonomy of certain Swedish authorities (municipalities, in particular) within Swedish governance explains why public authorities, for the purpose of consultation, legislatively seem to take on the guise of external actors.

[220] Nytt Juridiskt Arkiv [NJA] [Supreme Court Reports] NJA 2018 p 743 (NJA 2018 s 743); See also the Migration Court of Appeal judgment 23 Sep 2018 Miöd UM12649-18.

likely that some kind of substantial harm (beyond the procedural) would need to be identified for a disapplication.

From the legal sources, it is clear that, for implementing EU law, the Swedish constitutional clause operates more or less in the same manner. However, when it comes to negotiating EU law, there is a distinction drawn between the duty to consult for EU law-making at the implementation stage and the possibility to consult in the context of Sweden's participation in the formation of EU law during legislative negotiations. The main reason can be traced back to the standard legal interpretation that the Swedish government's participation in EU law-making, specifically negotiating in the Council, formally does not qualify as 'a government matter' under RF 7:3, as such matters need to be taken by a collegial body.[221] The categorisation of Sweden's participation in the EU law-making process affairs as not being a 'government matter' is not an uncontested view. This interpretation is not reflected in the legal text itself, but in the *travaux* related to Sweden's accession to the EU.[222] At that time, the *travaux* expressed the stated ambition and expectation that the Swedish consultation procedure would keep its central role for the government's work, noting the often lengthy legislative procedures in the EU, which would give ample time to consult nationally.[223] The *travaux préparatoires* to Swedish EU accession furthermore noted, as a positive phenomenon, the double opportunities that would be provided for interest groups to consult: at the national and EU level, through engaging directly with EU institutions.[224] However, the question is whether the standard interpretation of what government business is becomes increasingly untenable as transparency, participation and accountability mechanisms intended for political decision-making – which Swedish positions in EU negotiations, in essence, are – do not apply to decision-making, effectively turning law-making consultation during the negotiation phase, frequently, into a 'black box'. The Committee on the Constitution has touched upon this issue and summarily concluded that the government should clarify that the rules and practices which apply for government matters and decisions also apply for EU matters.[225] Thus far, this has not occurred.[226]

[221] *cf* the travaux to the constitution, clarifying that the government has a collective character (ie Sweden does not have ministerial rule). However, the criteria surfacing in the *travaux* are vague; government matters are all issues which demand a form of decision from someone in the government. Proposition [Prop] 1973:90 Grundlagsutredningen [government bill] 179, 184.

[222] Proposition [Prop] 1994/95:19 Sveriges Medlemskap i Europeiska Unionen [government bill] 458–60.

[223] ibid.

[224] ibid.

[225] Konstitutionsutskottets betänkande 2014/15:KU10 [parliamentary committee report] ch 5; the committee states that the government should clarify that routines and rules applicable to government business and matters also apply to EU matters: Statens Offentliga Utredningar [SOU] 2008:118 Styra och ställa [government report series].

[226] A systematic review of 2,209 memorandums on 'EU proposals' between 2001 and 2019 to which the Swedish government (ministries) were obliged to present the Swedish position to the Swedish Parliament demonstrates that consultation during negotiation is largely absent: Maria Strömvik, 'Hur Väl Förankras Svensk EU Politik?' (Lunds Universitet, 2020).

4.8.2.2. How does the 'right to participate in the democratic life of the Union' inform the interpretation of national legal norms?

In line with the EU principle of consistent interpretation, the principle of participatory democracy would, therefore, influence the interpretation of the Swedish constitution in two crucial ways. The first is that the phrase 'as necessary', in RF 7:2, in the sentence 'Organisations and individuals shall also be given an opportunity to express an opinion *as necessary*' (emphasis added), should be understood and measured against the democratising function of participating in law-making and citizens' rights to participation in the democratic life of the Union. The secondary function of Swedish government consultation highlighted in the *travaux* – its democratic anchor – increases in importance for EU law-making. This statement should, therefore, be interpreted as establishing a general presumption for consulting broadly with non-state actors for EU law-making. This interpretation is possible within the lexical meaning of the constitutional clause. As discussed, it also finds some support in the *travaux* to the RF, emphasising that consultation should serve as a 'democratic anchor', and would simultaneously align to international law obligations with regard to political participation.[227] This interpretation, however, would require a shift in the established practice of focusing heavily on agency consultation, and would also represent a shift away from established legal scholarship on the constitutional provision.

The second way in which the principle of participatory democracy informs the understanding of RF 7:2 is that it extends the duty to consult, not just to the implementation of EU law, but also to the negotiation of EU law. Again, such an interpretation is possible within the lexical formulation of the constitutional clause. It would, however, contradict some statements in the *travaux*, case law and Swedish legal doctrine that participating in EU law-making negotiations does not fall into the definition or category of 'government matters'. At the same time, such an interpretation aligns with some EU accession *travaux* and pre-legislative statements which posit that the Swedish consultation procedure will also maintain its important role post-EU accession.[228]

Crucially, depriving citizens of the opportunity to participate in EU law-making also through national channels would de facto interfere with their right according to Article 10(3) TEU, especially considering that there is no unequivocal right to participate in Commission consultation.

4.8.3. Ireland

The Irish common-law system has been described as an amalgam of the common law, the constitution, the ECHR, and EU law.[229] After Irish independence, in

[227] Note that while the principle of participatory democracy is only applicable to EU law-making, Art 25 ICCPR is applicable to all Swedish law-making. This, however, fall outside of the scope of this book.

[228] Proposition [Prop] 1994/95:19 Sveriges Medlemskap i Europeiska Unionen [government bill] 458–60.

[229] William Binchy, 'The Irish Legal System: An Introduction' (2011) 11 *Legal Information Management* 151.

1921, the system remained modelled on the English system, while the constitution underwent several revisions and established a system of fundamental human rights.

Judicial review, in terms of challenging the legality of a law or regulation, is generally within the jurisdiction of the High Court, which has the authority to determine the validity of any law against the provisions of the constitution.[230] A separate, uniquely Irish route is a form of pre-enactment review: the president may refer legislation to the Supreme Court before it is signed, to test constitutionality.[231] Separately, under the Freedom of Information Act 2014 (FOI Act), access disputes follow an appeal ladder: a public-body decision to deny an access request is first subjected to internal review, then to an Information Commissioner, with further appeal to the High Court on a point of law.[232]

Ireland has seen disputes, comparable to those in Austria and Sweden, relating to participation in national law-making. Even while Ireland has gained recognition for institutionalising citizen participation through citizens' assemblies, over the past decade, civil society and expert criticism have targeted the use of curtailed debate, late-stage technical amendments, and procedural shortcuts that reduce the opportunity for scrutiny, even where formal consultation channels exist. A recurring point of contention has been the ability – under parliamentary rules – to bypass pre-legislative scrutiny where the government asserts urgency, combined with the practice of adding complex provisions late in the process, thereby limiting external actors' capacity to assess what is being enacted – as well as severely curtailed consultation timelines.[233] These concerns have crystallised sharply around legislation during the COVID crisis, and more broadly in the field of planning and housing legislation, where the executive case for 'speed' has collided with participatory expectations embedded in environmental governance and access-to-justice norms.[234]

4.8.3.1. What is the legal framework for public participation in law-making?

Surveying the legal landscape as it pertains to access and participation in national law-making, public or civic participation is guided by guidelines and best practices rather than legal rules. According to the cross-government *Consultation Principles & Guidance*, consultation should be genuine, meaningful, timely and balanced,

[230] Art 34.3.2, Irish Constitution: Bunreacht na hÉireann 1937.

[231] Art 26, Bunreacht na hÉireann, see also Gerard Hogan, *Kelly: The Irish Constitution*, 5th edn (Bloomsbury, 2018) para 26.03.

[232] Freedom of Information Act 2014 (20/2014), s 24.

[233] Civil Liberties Union for Europe, 'Liberties Rule of Law Report 2023', https://www.liberties.eu/f/-3lkvi, accessed 1 February 2026; See also 'President's Warning on Volume of Legislation', https://www.lawsociety.ie/gazette/top-stories/2021/07-july/presidents-warning-on-volume-of-legislation, accessed 1 February 2026.

[234] Mick Clifford and Ciannan Brennan, 'Government under Fire for Rushing through Planning Law with Limited Time for Debate' *Irish Examiner* (Cork, 12 July 2022), https://www.irishexaminer.com/news/politics/arid-40915802.html, accessed 1 February 2026.

targeted, and easily accessible to those with a clear interest or stake, and departments should make systematic efforts to involve interested and affected parties across the full policy cycle, for significant policy and legislative matters.[235] It also pushes for a 'legislative footprint' that publicly records consultation and pre-legislative steps, and says that, where consultation is limited or rushed, the department should explain why.[236] However, considering the lack of legal obligation, consultation consistency across ministries and different legislative files, especially with regard to urgency (real or perceived) remains a matter of executive discretion.

Some statutory scrutiny mechanisms exist as regards negotiating EU law. The European Union (Scrutiny) Act 2002 provides that, '[a]s soon as practicable' after a proposed measure has been presented by the Commission or initiated by a Member State, 'the Minister shall cause a copy of the text concerned to be laid before each House of the Oireachtas', together with a statement outlining the 'content, purpose and likely implications for Ireland'.[237] The Act further provides that the minister 'shall have regard' to recommendations made by either House or relevant committees.[238] It also contains exceptions where, in the minister's view, there is insufficient time, and where measures are considered confidential, with a permissive reporting possibility thereunder.[239]

According to ministry guidelines, Regulatory Impact Analysis (RIA) guidelines should inform the drafting of the note to be presented to parliament.[240] Since RIA guidelines also mandate consultation, this should be taken into consideration for the note as well. However, considering the brief window for presenting the note to the Irish parliament (four weeks), it might be unrealistic to expect participation at this stage, nor to derive a legal obligation to consult in this respect.

4.8.3.2. How does the 'right to participate in the democratic life of the Union' inform the interpretation of national legal norms?

Considering that there is no general Irish legal mandate to consult or include public participation for national legislation, existing scrutiny mechanisms cannot arguably be interpreted to establish such a duty through consistent interpretation in light of Article 10(3) TEU – especially since the scrutiny is strictly framed in terms of parliament.

[235] Department of Public Expenditure and Reform, 'Consultation Principles & Guidance' (2016), https://www.gov.ie/en/department-of-public-expenditure-infrastructure-public-service-reform-and-digitalisation/publications/public-consultation-guidance/, accessed 1 February 2026.

[236] ibid, 4–7.

[237] European Union (Scrutiny) Act 2002 (Acts of the Oireachtas), s 2(1).

[238] ibid, s 2(2).

[239] ibid, s 3 (1)–(3).

[240] Department of Foreign Affairs and Trade, 'Oireachtas Scrutiny: Guidelines for Departments in Relation to the Scrutiny of EU Matters by the Houses of the Oireachtas' (2021), https://www.gov.ie/en/department-of-public-expenditure-infrastructure-public-service-reform-and-digitalisation/publications/public-consultation-guidance/, accessed 1 February 2026.

While there are no national legal hooks in terms of public participation or consultation, Ireland has a well-established legal framework for access and transparency in relation to public documents. The Irish Freedom of Information Act 2014 contains provisions that can be invoked to refuse access to public documents. Section 29(1) allows refusal where: (a) a record contains a 'matter relating to the deliberative processes' of a Freedom of Information (FOI) body (explicitly including 'opinions, advice, recommendations, and the results of consultations'); and (b) granting access would be 'contrary to the public interest'.[241] The Act itself narrows the reach of this deliberation exemption, as the record contains, inter alia, 'factual information' and 'the reasons for the making of a decision'. This internal structure already resists any attempt to convert 'deliberation' into a blanket shield.

Section 30(1)(c), in turn, permits refusal where access could reasonably be expected to 'disclose positions taken, or to be taken, or plans, procedures, criteria or instructions used or followed' for the purpose of 'any negotiations' carried on by or on behalf of the government or an FOI body.[242] But section 30(2) immediately subjects this to a public-interest balancing test: the exemption does not apply where the public interest would, on balance, be better served by granting the request.[243]

In the balancing between the possible harm to deliberations or negotiations, on the one hand, and the public interest, on the other, Article 10(3) TEU would establish a presumption of a weighty public interest in favour of disclosure where records relate to EU legislative negotiations. In this light, relevant Irish documents would not constitute internal administrative materials; they would be elements of EU law-making that shape binding norms for the public. The presumption should, therefore, shift toward disclosure, with refusal requiring specific demonstrable harm rather than general invocations of 'prejudice' or 'confidentiality'.[244]

This also applies to the FOI section on 'international relations', which can also be invoked in EU contexts. The Irish FOI Act permits refusal where access could reasonably be expected to adversely affect 'the international relations of the State' and mandates refusal for certain confidential communications from EU institutions or records relating to negotiations where disclosure is prohibited by the relevant body.[245] The legal point here is, again, interpretive discipline: EU legislative negotiation is not identical to sensitive bilateral diplomacy.[246] The extent to which EU-related records fall within the conditions and subconditions of the section must be applied narrowly and with precision, recognising citizens' right to participate in the democratic life of the Union, with the right to know or be informed as a first step.

[241] Freedom of Information Act (n 232), s 29(1)(a)–(b).
[242] ibid, s 30(1)(c).
[243] ibid, s 30(2).
[244] ibid, s 30(1)(c).
[245] ibid, s 33(1)(d) and s 33(3)(c)(ii).
[246] *cf McKillen v Information Commissioner (and The Minister for Finance, Notice Party)* [2016] IEHC 27.

The case studies have demonstrated how the principle of participatory democracy informs the interpretation of national legal norms in Austria, Ireland and Sweden. Perhaps not unsurprisingly, the pressures that exist at the EU level which work to the detriment of public participation and procedural standards for law- and decision-making are also manifesting themselves at the national level. Surveying the political and legal context in each Member State revealed lapses in consultation as a result of urgency, participation as ex post control rather than informing law-making choices, and a more or less unchecked discretion in terms of whether and how to structure participation – for law-making in general, and for negotiating EU law in particular.

Interpreting existing legal norms connected to participation in law-making in light of citizens' right to participate in the democratic life of the Union functions to open up the legislative process and work towards diversifying participation through consultation. Interpreting the Austrian Freedom of Information Act and EU-InfoG in light of Article 10(3) TEU unveiled an obligation to more openly share ministry documents related to negotiating EU law, partly in the existing EU databank, and partly as a constitutional right of access and proactive publication. In Sweden, the right of citizens to participate in the democratic life of the Union informs the interpretation of the Swedish constitutional clause on the duty of government consultation, to encompass consultation for EU law-making during the negotiation phase. It also shifted the focus of consultation towards non-state actors. And for Ireland, Article 10(3) TEU bolsters existing transparency and access to documents through informing the understanding of required FOI obligations, limiting discretion and disclosure exceptions during ongoing negotiations.

4.8.4. Reflection on Member State Cases

The case studies have demonstrated how Member States, in their role as gatekeepers of the democratic life of the Union, can contribute to the realisation of citizens' right to participate and decision-making as close as possible to citizens. At the same time, in applying the principle of consistent interpretation, the approach and outcome are flexible, and advancements of citizen-oriented participation are context-specific.

That being said, the cases also show that interpreting legal norms in light of the EU principle of participatory democracy is not, in itself, a strong vehicle for participatory practices. Citizens' EU participatory rights in the national context are not stand-alone, but are to a large degree dependent on existing national legal norms and practices. While there need to be existing norms to function as legal hooks, the enforcement framework for an EU-consistent interpretation in this context, for all countries, is weak. Here, the right of citizens to participate in the democratic life of the Union functions not as a stand-alone participation right, but as an instrument in the legal toolbox for practitioners and advocates to advance participation and access, and use in legal argumentation for persuasion, and possibly litigation – in tandem with other legal arguments. The right serves as a tipping point, in conjunction with other legal principles and norms, to advance the participatory practices and to increase access. The analysis has vindicated that the "right to participate in the democratic life of the Union", can be effectively applied in national contexts - not only in relation to the representative democracy element of the Union's democratic life, but also its participatory democracy element. As Member States' democratic practices and legal frameworks evolve, this right will likely gain in importance in interpreting national law and as a strategic asset to promote democratic participation in the multi-level setting.

This chapter moved the content of the principle of participatory democracy outlined in the second and third chapters from the abstract into the concrete. Having concretised key procedural standards required by the principle of participatory democracy, four cases of Commission legislative consultation (or lack thereof) were measured against the principle's standards. The analysis then turned to the principle's import in a multi-level setting, looking at how the principle informs the interpretation of national legal norms across three Member States related to access and influence in the process of negotiating EU law. Having gained this insight, the final chapter now explores how law-making practices can be elevated to align with the principle of participatory democracy.

5

Elevating law-making to a Participatory Democracy Practice

The Commission case studies have confirmed a normative gap between the principle of participatory democracy and consultation practices, for selected key obligations. The Member State case studies, in turn, have revealed implications of the principle of participatory democracy for Member State legislative practices, and how, through consistent interpretation, legal norms at the national level can better situate citizens to participate in the democratic life of the Union. Considering these insights, and the legal mapping of the principle of participatory democracy, how can the principle of participatory democracy then be effectively implemented and the realisation of the principle significantly advanced?

As mentioned in chapter two, the overall approach taken to formulating suggestions is reconstructive, attending to both the moral value and the practice it seeks to reform. The moral value is represented here by the values that undergird the principle of participatory democracy and the key rights and obligations that the principle entails at both the EU and national level (as elaborated in chapters two and three). Being mindful of the practice which the suggestions for reform are directed at means having an awareness of the legal and institutional environment and practices (as exemplified in chapters three and four). This chapter, therefore, begins with a reflection on the insights gained from unpacking the principle of participatory democracy. This leads to suggestions for improvements, clustered around the core complementary elements of participatory democracy in the EU: the inherent value of participation; deliberation; and citizens and civil society.[1] Across these three domains, five lines of action to elevate law-making to a participatory democracy practice are outlined: enhancing procedural equality, feedback through active transparency, drawing on democratic innovation, strengthening multi-level coherence, and consultation as a secondary law strategy. For each line of action, concrete suggestions for how to improve consultation are offered and analysed.[2] The chapter concludes with a discussion of whether, and in what way, the suggestions presented can be realised through existing accountability mechanisms, and whether legal reform is necessary.

[1] Three key elements drawn from the analysis of participatory democracy theory in ch 2, in terms of the inherent value of participation, deliberation, and citizens and civil society

[2] Based on observations from the case studies, the chapter also discusses the imperative of resisting the narrative of episodic crises in EU law-making and concludes with a final reflection.

5.1. Suggestions for improving participation in EU law-making

The suggestions are based in law; that is, they are based on a legal interpretation of the principle of participatory democracy as presented in this book, rooted in legal methods, and particularly in a teleological method of interpretation which is mindful of the normative ideal the principle aims to fulfil.

5.1.1. Attending to the inherent value of participation

In participatory democracy theory, participation has an intrinsic value and is seen as an end in itself. From this follows that the equality of individuals and groups is central to attend to, and that participation is a way of showing respect for, and expressing the dignity of, persons affected. This understanding informs the interpretation of the Commission's obligation to consult 'parties concerned' in light of the principle of equality, which established the equality of all citizens, 'who shall receive equal attention from its institutions'.[3] The congruence of these elements can be construed as an obligation for the Commission to provide procedural equality for its consultation activities, in terms of ensuring equal access to law-making consultation. Insights from democracy theory on the limitations of self-selection procedure in establishing equality strongly suggest that ensuring procedural equality requires positive action. The case studies demonstrated, on the one hand, the difficulty in applying these procedural criteria in an open-ended way, and on the other hand, clear deficiencies in the Commission's consultation practices with regard to procedural equality. The latter confirms what has also been observed at scale.[4] The following line of action is, consequently, focused on procedural equality and how to improve it as featured in EU law-making.

5.1.1.1. Ensuring equal access: Reaching out to the 'unusual' suspects

The case studies explored in the previous chapter support the claim that, at the EU level, there is no clear mechanism or policy to ensure, or even promote, procedural equality and avoiding exacerbating imbalances of access.[5] Neither is there any visible strategy to widely consult beyond those who generally would have information about the consultation exercise, extending, for example, to unorganised civil society, citizens, affected communities or vulnerable groups. Whereas national actors would be better poised to facilitate broader public participation

[3] Art 9 TEU.
[4] Art 9 TEU and Art 11 TEU; see also ch 4, s 4.1.
[5] OECD, *Better Regulation Practices across the European Union* (OECD Publishing, 2019).

(especially for law-making, where there is usually some institutional practice or legal framework to build on)[6] or reaching out beyond the 'usual suspects', it would seem that such grass-roots-level consultation is occurring very sporadically at the national level, with the case studies reflecting a slightly better outcome than that which has been noted in larger quantitative studies. At the national level, the legal analysis and the case studies demonstrated that EU law-making consultation overall (whether it refers to implementing or negotiating EU laws) is not geared towards democratic participation and skews heavily towards inter-governmental agency consultation or parliamentary scrutiny. Specifically with regard to government-facilitated consultations in preparing the government negotiation position, such national-level consultation is frequently not done publicly.

Three concrete suggestions could significantly improve current practice on procedural equality with regard to Commission consultation:[7] the first is to enhance outreach efforts through concrete measures to diversify and expand participation by directly inviting specific stakeholders which are identified as underrepresented to contribute to the consultation. The crucial step to be taken here is that such 'invitation lists' would also be published, for example similarly to the Swedish or Austrian consultation participant lists that are published. If correctly framed, for example, it is clear that a direct invitation to participate in an open or targeted consultation is just one element of an overall consultation outreach strategy – such efforts may serve as a multiplier, triggering participation in previously unreached networks or localities. Increasing the publicity of public consultations, including through social media, so as to attract broader attention, is certainly part of such outreach. Adhering to multilingualism has also been highlighted as having the potential to expand the reach of Commission consultation and mitigating geographical imbalance.[8] Considering the Commission's current penchant for various 'checks' on legislation for specific actors – for example, the SME test,[9] and the more recent 'youth check'[10] – it would be foreseeable to introduce a check for 'procedural equality' or 'equality of access' efforts, to ensure at least that efforts to reach 'parties concerned' or to widely consult have been made. As was demonstrated in the case studies, the obligation to conduct an open Internet-based consultation should also not be taken for granted.

The second suggestion is to focus on capacity-building within the Commission and Member States, to design consultation processes which are more inclusive

[6] OECD, *Better Regulation Practices across the European Union 2022* (OECD, 2022) ch 3.

[7] For a comprehensive scheme of suggestions to improve Commission consultations to align them with the principle of equality in EU law, see Alberto Alemanno, 'Levelling the EU Participatory Playing Field: A Legal and Policy Analysis of the Commission's Public Consultations in Light of the Principle of Political Equality' (2020) 26 *European Law Journal* 114.

[8] European Court of Auditors, '"Have Your Say!": Commission's Public Consultations Engage Citizens, but Fall Short of Outreach Activities' (Publications Office, 2019) 14, 31–33.

[9] See Commission, 'SME Test', https://single-market-economy.ec.europa.eu/smes/sme-strategy/sme-test_en, accessed 6 February 2026.

[10] European Youth Portal, 'Information Session - "EU Youth Test/Check"', https://youth.europa.eu/year-of-youth/activities/15293_en, accessed 6 February 2026.

and do not exacerbate inequalities; this includes thinking about the administrative capacities of the Commission. The overwhelming majority of EU officials, for example, have uniform educational backgrounds.[11] Diversifying and enhancing the epistemic capacities, to include, for example, participatory governance techniques,[12] and the ability to draw on behavioural insights,[13] would be possible factors to consider including in hiring practices.[14] This would also have the advantage of not having to outsource significant participation or consultation activities to private actors.

The third suggestion is to strengthen the infrastructure for national and local consultation through giving visibility to existing national legislative consultation policy and legal frameworks and codifying them. For instance, when the Commission consults on a legislative proposal and Member States are notified accordingly, this would act as a trigger for further consultation at the national/local level.[15] While there are various European networks and ties between regions, cities and municipalities, and the Commission does consult regionally, this is distinct from systematically drawing on national, regional or local state actors acting as consultation multipliers, based on the responsibility of those actors to contribute to the realisation of citizens' rights to contribute to the democratic life of the Union.[16] At the Member State level, some Member State ministerial guidelines recommend that open consultations conducted by the Commission should prompt broader consultations with society, including the general public. Such guidelines could be made more visible, preferably by making them legally binding. The approach of paying attention to legal and institutional frameworks at the national level recognises how the citizens' right to participate in the democratic life of the Union exists in a multi-level context.

5.1.2. Advancing the deliberative nature of participation

One of the key complementary functions of participatory democracy in the EU setting is to advance deliberation. Acknowledgement of, and responsiveness, to difference, the adherence to the principle of justification, transparency, and consequently an emphasis on learning processes, have provided central inputs for theorisation drawing on deliberation for democratic legitimacy in the EU setting. Giving effect to deliberative law-making spaces would also need to include equal

[11] See, eg Alemanno, 'Levelling the EU Participatory Playing Field Equality' (n 7) 126.

[12] Commission, 'Community of Practice of the Competence Centre on Participatory and Deliberative Democracy', https://cop-demos.jrc.ec.europa.eu/, accessed 6 February 2026.

[13] Alemanno, 'Levelling the EU Participatory Playing Field Equality' (n 7) 126.

[14] ibid 129.

[15] This would live up to the requirements of Art 10(3) TEU and international human rights instruments (eg political participation, Art 25 ICCPR).

[16] For existing practices that seemingly take a similar approach, see European Youth Portal, 'Get Involved: EU Youth Dialogue', https://youth.europa.eu/eu-youth-dialogue_en, accessed 6 February 2026.

consideration of potential participants, as well as the discussed equality of access. It would require 'active' transparency of the Commission: to publish more proactively, to be transparent in its consultation strategy, and to adequately provide information on how consultation replies informed the process as a form of meaningful exchange. This obligation is drawn from the stated goal of consultations in Article 11 TEU – of ensuring transparency, as well as the right of citizens to know and attempt to influence directly the EU legislative process. Two lines of action are offered, then, which could enhance the deliberative nature of consultations: feedback through active transparency, and advancing democratic innovations.

5.1.2.1. Feedback through active transparency

The legal duty to transparently demonstrate whether and how consultations have impacted on the proposal, as has been noted, goes beyond publishing consultation contributions and a statistical or summary presentation of consultation replies. For the Commission and Member States in negotiating EU laws, the case studies have highlighted how such feedback is largely lacking, as well as a particular need for more clarity and transparency with regard to targeted consultations. With regard to the Commission, besides the potential negative effects of opaqueness, in terms of participation fatigue and depriving citizens of their democratic rights, it also makes it difficult to understand whether the Commission has lived up to its duty to present legislation in the best interest of the Union.[17] The following practices would, then, need to be adopted to improve consultation practices and align them to the principle of participatory democracy

For the Commission, reporting on the impact (or lack thereof) of consultations on the thinking and process of legislative drafting is central. Although no duty exists to reply individually to each consultation contribution or position, the duty does entail describing how the outcome and substantive contributions have influenced the thinking and drafting of the legislation. This could be achieved through noting it in the impact assessment, or in any document accompanying the legislative proposal. National cases also serve as instructive examples – for example, French and Swedish *travaux* often address, for each element of a law, the positions offered, replying directly as to whether and how this has influenced the final draft, as well as providing justification when the proposal deviates from consultation positions. While such an approach in its entirety may not be feasible or desirable for consultation at the EU level, which often includes several hundred replies, a meaningful narrative or impact which includes how a legislative proposal has evolved in relation to main consultation positions and insights across the spectrum is not only feasible but necessary, in order for law-making consultation 'to ensure that Union action is coherent and transparent' (Article 11(3) TEU), as well as to adhere to 'good governance' and 'ensuring the participation of civil society'

[17] Art 17 TFEU.

according to Article 15 TFEU.[18] This would particularly apply to Commission rule-making.

The legal duty of transparency and feedback, which follows from the principle of participatory democracy and related standards for openness, need not be approached in a formulaic manner. Considering that targeted consultations follow a different format from open public consultations, transparency and feedback requirements may need to align to the mode of such consultations. If such consultation is conducted in an expert group or a smaller deliberative setting, it may, for instance, not be meaningful or desirable to publish the contributions of each member of a targeted group.[19] However, such flexibility depends on the overall transparency of such settings.

For permanent expert committees whose work feeds into the legislative process, the Commission has recently confirmed in a legally binding decision that there is an obligation to disclose who such expert members are and what interests they represent, and to have such experts registered in the Transparency Register.[20] Additionally, as discussed in chapter three, the horizontal rules in the mentioned decision require minutes from such meetings to be 'meaningful and complete' and published in a timely manner.[21] While ad hoc expert groups, as well as expert gatherings for conferences or workshops, are not covered by the Commission decision, transparency requirements are still legally due when such groups or conferences are part of legislative preparation. Publishing minutes or even reporting on the outcome of such targeted consultations is, however, far from established or mainstreamed practice, and in controversial or significant legislation, it would seem often to be eschewed – as the case studies also indicated. The Better Regulation Guidelines now indicate that the Commission itself now has the view that targeted consultation activities should also be reported on.[22] In order to adhere to the legal imperative – similar to the discussed duty for established expert groups – such reporting would not, in all cases, need to attribute responses to any specific expert, but could, rather, follow the Chatham House Rule (which was long the practice of EU expert committees, and is still the frequent practice of, for example, the European Central Bank).[23] Again, such application of transparency requirements demands that there is an overall transparency with regard to members and compositions of targeted consultations.

[18] See ch 4, s 4.3.

[19] See ibid.

[20] See Commission, Decision of 30.5.2016 establishing horizontal rules on the creation and operation of Commission expert groups C (2016) 3301 final.

[21] Decision of the European Ombudsman in her strategic inquiry OI/6/2014/NF concerning the composition and transparency of European Commission expert groups, Annex.

[22] 'In cases where the publication of targeted consultation activities contributions would lead to disproportionate workload, the DG responsible for conducting consultations should contact SG.A2.' Commission, Better Regulation Guidelines' SWD(2021) 305 final (SWD Better Regulation Guidelines) 21.

[23] See the demand by the European Ombudsman for note-taking on meetings of expert committees: European Ombudsman, Decision on how the European Commission applies the rules governing expert groups and other similar entities regarding transparency (case OI/3/2024/KR).

At the national level, the case studies confirmed that, in negotiating EU law, transparency is largely lacking. Reporting on who has been invited to consult, and publishing the contributions to a consultation exercise, are much-needed steps to take at the national level to ensure that procedural requirements flowing from the principle of participatory democracy with regard to EU law-making are met. These transparency requirements, particularly with regard to feedback, might at times need to be balanced against concerns for maintaining the integrity of the national negotiating position. In addition, as the national hearings in the case studies indicated, there may also be the need to be creative in the approach to transparency, to protect the deliberative nature of such hearings.

Overall, however, for other EU countries, such as Finland, whose ministries receive approval of their negotiation mandate from their parliament, and where such mandates are public and are subjected to public consultation,[24] transparency does not seem to have proved a significant obstacle. The force of Article 10(3) TEU in the interpretation of national laws guiding legislative consultation depends, in part, on the content of such laws, and how far the active duty to promote the participation of all citizens in the democratic life of the Union can be extended before crossing the boundary of *e contrario* interpretations.

Even in cases where access to documents could be denied on the basis of legislative exceptions, such information could likely, in an overwhelming number of cases, be released post-negotiation, which would contribute to an overall climate of democratic participation and accountability, if not facilitate participation in that particular law-making process. The Swedish government's publication, on its website, of consultation replies in response to its consultation on the Commission proposal of the Artificial Intelligence Act (AIA) provide a good example of a practice that could be further developed and mainstreamed.[25] The consultation invitees and their responses were published, without commenting on how they might impact on the Swedish position on the legislative proposal.

5.1.2.2. *Advancing democratic experimentation*

Because the Commission's approach to participation in law-making has been through a Better Regulation lens and not a participatory democracy one, it is right to question how much experience has been gained in drawing on the democratising potential of, for example, consultations.

The focus on the deliberative quality of participation is emphasised in participatory democracy in general, and in the EU in particular. Emphasising the democratic quality of law-making consultation aligns with the Commission's work

[24] OECD, *Better Regulation Practices across the European Union 2022* (n 6).

[25] Although publication of consultation replies would need to be complete, as opposed to the Swedish government's practice in that case, where contributions from authorities which were not specifically invited to participate were not published (coincidentally, these unpublished replies also criticised the government for not taking into account the potential impact of the proposal on Swedish consumers and citizens).

to integrate deliberative citizen panels into its pre-legislative work.[26] However, it also means thinking about the deliberative quality of consultations overall. For instance, the deliberative quality of targeted consultations would be one area of learning, while including citizens in structured deliberation would be another. Thus, it is clear that, for certain areas and consultations, sortition to obtain a representative sample of Europeans is a promising path which could lead to the formation of mini-publics. In other instances, the Commission may wish to draw on citizens representing a specific community of interest or experience. Here, gains with regard to the overall quality and effectiveness of legislation could be made. The deliberative quality of consultation conferences and workshops is also an area of learning where there is every indication that the deliberative elements of conferences are often confined to a Q&A. Emphasising the deliberative quality across consultation modalities (to which the above improvement on feedback would also contribute) is important. For, while citizens' panels may provide input for selected legislative proposals, the time and cost of running them makes them unlikely bread-and-butter candidates of Commission law-making. In this regard, organising mini-publics in a decentralised way seems promising, as long as the input is directly fed into the legislative process. Through Article 10(3) TEU and its vertical component, such decentralisation would also have a common legal foundation, which could help shape the discretion in the implementation of such decentralised democratic innovations.

As was noted in the analysis of Article 11 and 10(3) TEU, there are few limits on the modalities for the consultation and participation called for. Informal hearings, which already occur at the national level, in relation to negotiating EU law, seem a good starting point to increase the regularity of such deliberative fora, attending to transparency of participant selection.

5.1.3. Bringing in citizens and civil society

One reason why involving more individuals in democratic participation is crucial, according to participatory democracy, is the broader educative role of participation for citizens. Furthermore, as discussed in chapter three, public participation involving many citizens is tied to the understanding that, when certain groups cannot influence the political agenda or decision-making, or gain relevant information, they are likely to be ill-served by laws and policies.[27]

Citizen participation has also been emphasised because of the epistemic value that it brings to the policy- and law-making process. The legitimising function of engaging citizens can be fulfilled either through direct citizen participation

[26] Commission, 'European Citizens' Panels', https://citizens.ec.europa.eu/index_en, accessed 6 February 2026.

[27] Archon Fung, 'Varieties of Participation in Complex Governance' (2006) 66 *Public Administration Review* 66, 70.

or through (new) forms of representation, prominently through civil society. Article 10(3) TEU, framed as a citizen's right to participate in the democratic life of the Union, constitutes the legal bedrock for a citizen-oriented approach to participation in EU affairs beyond the ballot box. However, as the case studies demonstrated, citizens are either absent from EU law-making consultation or the process is confined to the few initiated. As was discussed in chapter two, empirical research into interest groups shows that consultations are still likely best understood as a form of elite pluralism, with citizens in the back seat. An important step towards making EU law-making more accessible is, consequently, enhancing access at the national level. In this respect, three lines of action are offered: to advance coherence within the multi-level legal framework, to promote consultation requirements in EU secondary law as a democratising strategy, and to not forego participation by citizens and civil society in times of urgency.

5.1.4. Advancing coherence between legal norms and practices at different levels

The case studies confirm how law-making consultation at the national level, during the most meaningful stage in terms of potential impacts, ie the negotiation stage, is sporadic, inscrutable and unevenly practised across ministries, with only a high-level legal framework. This book has argued for a significant reinterpretation of this legal framework, in light of EU law, which still falls within the bounds of consistent interpretation.[28] If this interpretation is applied, it would contribute to the coherence of multi-level law-making consultation. However, even with such an interpretation, the role of law in advancing more meaningful participation is underused, which legal reform could remedy.

5.1.4.1. The national level: Consulting when it is meaningful

Internal ministerial guidelines which demand a consideration of whether open consultations conducted by the Commission should prompt broader consultations should be strengthened, made more visible, and made binding.

5.1.4.2. Better burden sharing and co-ordination

Facilitating timely and meaningful EU law-making consultation at the national and local level includes better institutional linkages between the Commission and national facilitators/initiators of such consultation, and a clearer framing of the shared responsibility. A simple alternative would be for legislative proposals to

[28] As well as within the bounds of international law obligations, primarily according to Art 25 ICCPR.

be signalled by the Commission for national consultation procedures at an early stage. Inter-consultation or joint routines would also be helpful. This could serve as a starting point for the responsible national ministry to make an independent assessment of whether and how national consultation should be conducted.

Another way to facilitate shared responsibility and a co-ordinated approach is to enhance co-operation with regard to public participation in the legislative process. The suggestion, from the Conference on the Future of Europe, of drafting a Charter of EU Citizens' Rights, is one example which could not only include a catalogue of rights (which would include, for example, Article 10(3) TEU) but also how these rights can be accessed by citizens, and not just in relation to EU institutions. This would provide an opportune place to outline more clearly how realising the principle of participatory democracy, and particularly the right to participate in the democratic life of the Union, is a shared agenda, and which (legal) obligations rest with Member States, including for law-making consultation.

5.1.4.3. Consultation requirements in EU secondary law and EU rule-making

Instances where consultation is required per EU secondary legislation, either by EU agencies or Member States or designated national authorities, surfaced in the analysis in chapter three, in the context of elaborating on the reach of the principle of participatory democracy. It is clear how embedding such consultation requirements in secondary law and non-legislative acts, and linking them to Article 10(3) TEU, could give effect to the principle of participatory democracy. The effects of such embedded consultation could potentially be important.[29] For instance, both the Water Framework Directive and the REACH regulation on chemicals include a number of specific consultation obligations for the Commission and relevant agencies.[30] In this context, the practice of the Commission to combine backward- and forward-looking analysis in one consultation round is relevant; that is, the Commission has committed to consulting on the evaluation of the effect of EU legislation and the potential impact of intended legislative reforms in one open consultation round, under its 'call for evidence' (previously, evaluation and impact

[29] The legislative approach taken in the Water Framework Directive is instructive, whereby Member States' obligations in relation to certain documents/information are set out in the following terms: 'Member States shall ensure that, for each river basin district, they publish and make [these] available for comments to the public, including users', also further stipulating relatively detailed procedural obligations for such consultation: Art 14 (1–3) Directive (EC) 2000/60/EC of 23 October 2000 establishing a framework for Community action in the field of water policy [2000] OJ L327.

[30] See ibid; and Art 58(4) and Art 64(3) Regulation (EC) No 1907/2006 of 18 December 2006 concerning the Registration, Evaluation, Authorisation and Restriction of Chemicals (REACH), establishing a European Chemicals Agency, amending Directive 1999/45/EC and repealing Council Regulation (EEC) No 793/93 and Commission Regulation (EC) No 1488/94 as well as Council Directive 76/769/EEC and Commission Directives 91/155/EEC, 93/67/EEC, 93/105/EC and 2000/21/EC [2006] OJ L396/1.

assessment consultation were done separately).[31] Such consultation on the *implementation and application of EU legislation* within Member States (in this case, at the local and regional level) give expression to the principle of participatory democracy in relation to EU law-making in three different ways.

Firstly, such consultation features *indirectly* as EU rule- and law-making consultation, in that the results and outcomes of such consultations are reviewed by the Commission in conjunction with the review of the legislation, and thus feed into evaluation and reforms of EU secondary legislation. Secondly, they build the capacity of Member States and Member State authorities to consult with interested parties. Thirdly, such consultation raises the awareness of citizens and interested parties about the application of EU law, and may well have spillover effects in terms of more direct participation in EU law-making consultation at the national or EU level. The prevalence of legal rules in EU secondary law and non-legislative acts which mandate public participation in the application of EU law, as well as in EU rule-making in general, would build such capacity. There is much to suggest that a holistic approach is helpful, and that such consultation could play an important role in building up and strengthening both citizens' and local and regional capacity – which could be vital to giving effect to the principle of participatory democracy. This approach could be supported by research which could look into the intersection of democratic participation in EU law-making, EU rule-making, and the implementation and application of EU law in local settings, as well as the legal frameworks guiding these processes at the EU and national level.

The strong value attached to participation can also, arguably, be demonstrated in the explicit legal rule that the Commission can only forego its legislative consultation duties in cases of extreme emergency.

5.1.5. Resisting the narrative of crises

The case study on the Migration Pact exemplifies how, in cases of (real or perceived) urgency, combined with politically sensitive or controversial legislation, soft-law or (perceived) self-imposed procedural guarantees are the first to be discarded. In such situations, it is often vulnerable groups and citizens which are deprived of a voice. Some of the statements of the Commission on the Better Regulation Guidelines are illustrative of the approach:

> During the COVID-19 crisis, the Commission has had to propose a number of initiatives as a matter of urgency. . . . The explanatory memoranda set out the underlying rationale for the proposals, but the impacts could not be fully assessed in advance due to the lack of time and the rapidly evolving situation. In such cases, the analysis and all supporting evidence will be set out in a staff working document published with the

[31] See, eg Commission, 'Better Regulation Toolbox, July 2023 Edition' 50, https://commission.europa.eu/system/files/2023-07/BR_toolbox_Jul_2023_en.pdf, accessed 6 February 2026.

> proposal or at the latest within 3 months of its publication. This document will set out clearly how and when the act will subsequently be evaluated.[32]

The Commission further explains in a footnote: 'That is, when an IA should have been prepared according to the provisions of the Better Regulation Guidelines but was not following a discretional decision by the Commission.'[33] When the Commission states that a decision to set aside Better Regulation Guidelines is a matter of Commission discretion, it conveniently fails to mention the CJEU case law, which sets the outer bounds to this discretion in terms of impact assessments' relationship to the proportionality of EU action. More importantly, with regard to the principle of participatory democracy, the Commission fails to mention that its discretion is not self-imposed – and this is one case where the Better Regulation approach contradicts the legal analysis presented in this book, that the Commission's discretion is not just influenced by self-imposed guidelines, but by Treaty articles and primary law on consultation, which is a procedural democratic guarantee. As was highlighted in chapter three, Article 11 TEU demands that the Commission 'shall consult' and, according to Article 2 Protocol No 2, for legislative proposals, only 'exceptional urgency' allows for discounting 'wide consultation'. While certain instances during the COVID-19 pandemic may have qualified under this narrow exception, it is clear that the Commission's misplaced sense of discretion has been applied to several legislative acts over the last couple of years, including the case study on the New Migration Pact in the previous chapter. The fact that the Commission completely refrains from justifying its deviation from this legal obligation with reference to the exception outlined in Article 2 Protocol No 2 or Article 11(3) TEU raises the question of what the Commission's understanding of its legal obligations are in this regard.

Furthermore, understanding 'exceptional urgency' requires a contextual perspective on current times, with political upheaval and crises emerging as a new normal. Consider just a selection of the smorgasbord of crises during the past decade: the financial crises leading up to the Lisbon Treaty; refugee waves framed as crises; the deteriorating rule-of-law situation in a number of Member States, with cascading effects; fiscal upheaval; Brexit; the spread and effects of COVID-19; the ongoing climate crisis; Russia's war on Ukraine; and ongoing tariff disputes with the United States[34] – not to mention the additional domestic political and societal upheavals within Member States, occurring simultaneously. The point here is not to make a definitive statement on how less or more severe these crises are, or on the urgency they place on legislative action. Some of the devastating effects of such crises speak for themselves. The point is, rather, that caution must be applied when interpreting a narrowly framed exception ('exceptional urgency')

[32] Commission, Better Regulation Guidelines (n 22).

[33] ibid.

[34] Erik Jones, R Daniel Kelemen and Sophie Meunier, 'Failing Forward? Crises and Patterns of European Integration' (2021) 28 *Journal of European Public Policy* 1519.

to a constitutionally enshrined democratic and procedural guarantee, and that, in light of evidence, the Commission's view of its unbound discretion in this regard seems particularly unsuited to providing the right frame for this type of judgement. Absent a correct interpretation of such narrow exceptions, considering the times, the question is what procedural or democratic guarantees we would be left with.[35]

Similar patterns are discernible at the national level, as the case studies also demonstrated. Contrary to the inaction on account of the false perception of the Commission's unbound executive discretion with regard to consultation, in Sweden, at least, a few such cases have been subjected to judicial review by Swedish courts, and in other cases addressed publicly through the scrutiny of institutional watchdogs such as the Council on Legislation.

5.2. Ensuring the realisation of improvements

The reconstructive and practicable approach in this chapter implies that the suggestions advanced, if adopted with the understanding that they represent binding legal standards and obligations, offer enough guidance to reform the European Commission and advance government practices to better align them to the EU principle of participatory democracy. However, the Commission's persistent refusal to recognise the existence of a legal framework for public consultations, the inadequate link, in the language for consultations, to their democratising function and the principle of participatory democracy, and the obstacles towards judicial redress combine to shape a distorted perception of the Commission's own discretion. The Commission has, undoubtedly, gradually opened its consultations, in particular its recent commitment to publish the results of targeted consultations (how this will be implemented remains to be seen). However, the Commission's stance on discretion with regard to urgent legislation suggests that reform on procedural equality according to the principle of participatory democracy currently remains elusive. While it seems that the overall trend is moving in the direction of gradual alignment with the standards imposed by the principle of participatory democracy – and an amplification of legal language surrounding consultations would certainly speed up this trend – progress is still slow. To speed up advancements, mechanisms for enforcement would be necessary.

As for the national level, the overlooked EU law (and international law) dimensions suggest a gradual approach. It would seem, then, that a more stringent accountability model is necessary for the realisation of the principle of participatory democracy with regard to law-making. With regard to judicial review, as the

[35] On the risk of misusing the emergency for power-grabbing during COVID, see, eg Jan Petrov, 'The COVID-19 Emergency in the Age of Executive Aggrandizement: What Role for Legislative and Judicial Checks?' (2020) 8 *The Theory and Practice of Legislation* 71; see also Matthias Ruffert and Päivi Leino-Sandberg, 'Next Generation EU and Its Constitutional Ramifications: A Critical Assessment' (2022) 59 *Common Market Law Review* 433.

analysis has demonstrated, judicial review based on the principle of participatory democracy with regard to consultation at the EU level is both weak and narrow. While the CJEU would likely be open to some form of review of procedural requirements for law-making consultation, such litigation has not yet occurred since the Lisbon Treaty came into force. It therefore remains an unreliable enforcement mechanism, even though the analysis in chapter three indicates that strategic litigation would likely bear fruit in this regard.

Judicial review of legislation on the basis of flaws in law-making consultations exists – so far, for one procedural element, i.e. time frames, but others could follow. To what degree legal obligations apply to Member State consultation during the negotiation phase has not been tested in national courts. Neither have the implications of Article 10(3) TEU in tandem with international human rights been debated in the courtroom setting. While these legal arguments deserve to be tested in court, and in my view, it is only a matter of time before Article 10(3) TEU begins to trickle its way down into domestic adjudication on an array of issues, judicial review in many Member States ' context still a rather weak and, for the purpose of participatory democracy, blunt instrument.

At the EU level, a promising existing accountability mechanism which can serve to protect the imperative of the principle of participatory democracy is the European Ombudsman, who, through her investigations and opinions, has contributed to substantial reform in EU governance, including good governance reform of the Commission's expert system and lobbying transparency, and also has recently commented on the performance of the Commission for individual consultation activities.[36] At the national level, similar bodies and institutions could serve this function, as well.

Another potential avenue would be a soft accountability approach, where a spotlight is increasingly placed on participation and consultation practices and their flaws. One challenge at the EU level is that, because the European public sphere remains underdeveloped, EU institutions may be less sensitive to the selective pressure of naming and shaming.[37] The Commission, as it is in many ways ahead of Member States with regard to being in an ongoing dialogue about its own working methods, and on the issues where it has taken a principled stance, may also be less inclined to change its position. However, this is an area where more empirical data would be helpful, to draw any definitive conclusions. At the national level, pointing to those few Member States which are consulting more systematically and transparently during EU law-making, including in the formation of their negotiation positions, could provide helpful pressure at the political level while also encouraging officials to have the 'nerve' to try out different and more open ways to consult.

The final – and most straightforward – avenue is through codifying participatory democracy standards in an EU regulation with clear redress mechanisms

[36] European Ombudsman, Decision on how the European Commission carried out a public consultation concerning the 'Sustainable Corporate Governance initiative' (case 1956/2021/VB).

[37] Case C-280/11 *Council v Access Info Europe*, AG Opinion Cruz Villalón, para 67.

and rules on judicial review. While this would guarantee immediate progress, the strong stance of the Commission against such legislative action makes it an unlikely solution. However, at the national level, legal reform may still provide a possible solution.

In any case, it is clear that the legal framework for EU law-making can and should be significantly reinterpreted in light of the principle of participatory democracy, in order to abide by EU and international law – even though legal reform would be needed to strengthen this aspect.

5.3. Concluding reflections

This book has drawn out the contours of the legal principle of participatory democracy in the Union and explored how its realisation can be advanced. After exploring the theoretical origins of participatory democracy, an inclusive understanding of the concept was adopted which allowed for capture of democracy debates at the European level incorporating contributions in the deliberative and associative traditions. In analysing how 'participatory democracy' emerged in the debates on democracy in the Union, participation in EU governance was viewed from both a functional and a principled perspective, with the latter gaining ascendancy in the events leading up to the drafting of the Constitution. The participatory norm which was constitutionalised did not just represent a functional understanding but an intrinsic one. Links to, and contacts with, citizens were emphasised. Participatory democracy as featured in the EU democracy literature was often articulated in terms of a right of those affected by a decision to be able to participate in its formation. However, in the academic literature, in the documents of the EU institutions, and in the drafting process, it was clear that the role of participatory democracy was complementary to that of representative democracy. And this complementarity would have to play out in a multi-level polity. In order to distil some of these theoretical insights, Rittberger and Kohler-Koch's framework juxtaposing elements of representative democracy in the EU with elements of participatory democracy was drawn upon, emphasising the intrinsic value of participation; deliberation; and an emphasis on citizens and civil society as participation protagonists.

Proceeding from this understanding, I then drew, in chapter three, on legal methods to provide an overview of key instruments, rights and obligations that the principle entails.[38] The legal analysis revealed that the principle of participatory democracy entails a mix of rights and obligations for citizens and EU institutions, respectively, with Article 11 TEU and 10(3)TEU acting as portal paragraphs and legal hubs for rights and duties either flowing from or connected to the principle.

[38] The mapping in this chapter follows the duties of the Commission, ie law-making consultation at the EU level, while ch 4 is concerned with law-making at the national level.

Clearly, the principle of participatory democracy provides a right for citizens to engage in EU governance at various stages and through various means, and case law so far has placed an emphasis on the early stages of decision-making processes when participation is meaningful. The right of citizens to participate in the democratic life of the Union according to Article 10(3) TEU includes the right to be informed of the EU law-making process, in particular for them to effectively make their views known before legislative choices have been definitively adopted, so far as both the Commission's decision to submit a legislative proposal and the content of that proposal are concerned. This means that citizens and interest groups have the right to access pre-legislative documents. The right to know and attempt to inform and influence the EU law-making process applies to all EU institutions acting in a legislative capacity or as 'key players' in the legislative process, notably the Parliament, the Council and the Commission. While there is no overarching general right for citizens to participate in consultations, when consultation opportunities are presented, citizens do, however, have a right to be treated equally, including with regard to access. The right to petition Parliament, in its current modus operandi, while not particularly directed at EU law-making, may still influence the legislative process, and holds potential overall to further realise the principle of participatory democracy in the Union. The right to complain to the Ombudsman, while a citizen's instrument, is connected to both representative and participatory democracy, and is best seen as an overarching 'soft' redress or enforcement mechanism for participatory democracy rights. In addition, the right to participate in legislative agenda-setting through participation in an ECI, as well as related derivative rights, are outlined.

Beyond general obligations for EU institutions to conduct their work as openly as possible in order to ensure the participation of civil society as spelled out in Article 15 TFEU, the duty to promote voice and a regular dialogue finds expression in the institutions' obligation to abide by legally binding commitments in the Interinstitutional Agreement establishing the Transparency Registry, which establishes transparency and accountability for the actors seeking to influence the legislative process.[39] The overall obligation of transparency is connected to the duty enshrined in the Treaty to state the reasons for legislation, and the participatory democracy element of transparency is justiciable with regard to access to legislative documents.

The legal interpretation of Article 11(3) TEU advanced in chapter three demonstrated that the Commission, before adopting a proposal, is under a legal obligation to consult widely, in 'an open and transparent way', ensuring that the modalities and time limits of those public consultations allow for the 'widest possible participation', while taking into account the regional and local dimension of the action envisaged, except for in cases of exceptional urgency, in which case the Commission is obliged to give reasons for its decision to forego consultation. The analysis also demonstrated that the Commission has a duty to communicate the results of public and stakeholder consultations, without delay, to both

[39] See ch 4, s 4.1.

co-legislators and the public. Furthermore, and crucially, the Commission is also obligated to actively promote equality of access to consultation opportunities, and provide consultation feedback. Finally, the legal analysis demonstrated that Member States are under the obligation to interpret national law in light of a citizen's right to participate in the democratic life of the Union (Article 10(3) TEU).

The question then remained of to what degree these rights and obligations are justiciable. The overview of existing jurisprudence demonstrated that there may be distinct pathways through which the principle of participatory democracy is ensured. However, it is also clear that as regards consultation, direct challenges based on the principle of participatory democracy face procedural obstacles. Unless the CJEU shifts its settled law on standing, indirect challenges may be the only avenue open to potential participants. While a complete lack of consultation constitutes a clear legal breach of the principle of participatory democracy (breach of the Treaty) and the prospect for redress, in terms of annulment, is good, the procedural path may prove difficult beyond privileged actors. Furthermore, a claim based on the principle of participatory democracy in terms of a procedural consultation breach, for example not providing enough time to allow for consultation, not consulting specific groups, or not being sufficiently transparent in consultation reporting, is unlikely to succeed as a stand-alone annulment claim.[40] Overall, the analysis in chapter three substantiates the claim that judicial review for EU law-making consultation exists, with procedural hurdles weakening this redress mechanism. Until the procedural path widens, the Ombudsman appears structurally well placed, based on her track record and systematic reviews of EU institutional practices relating to the principle of participatory democracy, to review participatory democracy rights and obligations and contribute to enforcing them.

Having identified and analysed key rights and obligations associated with the principle of participatory democracy, as well as having assessed how they are given effect with regard to justiciability, the following chapter assessed the principle of participatory democracy in practice from two angles. The first was an assessment of to what degree current Commission EU law-making consultation practices adhere to or conflict with identified key obligations and rights, whereas the second was an assessment of how national legal norms in Member States can be interpreted in light of the EU principle of participatory democracy.

The case studies demonstrated that procedural requirements of transparency and responsiveness – ie, how participatory input has impacted on a proposal – can be applied effectively to the Commission's consultations, whereas the obligation of ensuring procedural equality is less straightforward. With regard to adequate responsiveness, it is clear that, while the Commission performed admirably across three out of four legislative consultations in *presenting* and publishing the results of its open consultation outcomes and replies, reporting on the targeted

[40] The criteria of being sufficiently clear, precise and unconditional are unlikely to be granted for more abstract procedural obligations.

consultations was less stellar, and in several cases seriously lacking. Meanwhile, as has been argued, merely reporting on consultation outcomes is insufficient. The case studies also showed that such procedural equality seems to remain a key challenge in giving effect to the principle of participatory democracy. The case related to the EU Migration Pact further demonstrated how the Commission can still, for high-profile legislative files for which there is significant political pressure, disregard its constitutional duty to consult, while also setting aside its commitment in the IIA on Better Regulation.

With regard to the obligation of procedural equality through promoting diversity and outreach to specifically affected groups or communities, it is clear that there are difficulties in applying the legal threshold in a meaningful way, with the legal assessment on all four cases left vague. The nature of EU law-making consultation and the complexity in achieving procedural equality makes it difficult to define a legal threshold which defines 'parties concerned' without becoming too arbitrary. At the same time, the first two case studies confirm what observers have long noted – that there is a lack of outreach beyond the well-defined existing networks, with a dominance of corporate interests.

With regard to the Member State case studies, the analysis demonstrated that, for all countries under study, the legal framework for participation in negotiation of EU law in the national context was predictably weak or incidental. However, the analysis also revealed how the right of citizens to participate in the democratic life of the Union, through consistent interpretation, informs the understanding of national legal norms, raising the bar in terms of access and obligation to consult. While the principle of participatory democracy demands a reinterpretation of the national demands of EU law-making public consultation, the cases revealed that changes based on the current legal toolbox are incremental and modest. Overall, the analysis vindicated that the "right to participate in the democratic life of the Union", can be effectively applied in national contexts - not only in relation to the representative democracy element of the Union's democratic life, but also its participatory democracy element.

Following from the analysis in the previous chapters and the findings of the case studies, this final chapter explored in what ways law-making practices can better be aligned with the principle of participatory democracy. Five lines of action were suggested in order to elevate law-making participation – and, in particular, consultation – to a participatory democracy practice: feedback, procedural equality, democratic innovation, multi-level coherence, and consultation as an EU secondary law strategy. For each line of action, concrete suggestions were explored. Based on observations from the case studies, the chapter also discussed the imperative of resisting the narrative of episodic crises in EU law-making.

The legal analysis developed in this book, and the suggestions to elevate practices to the requirements flowing from the principle of participatory democracy, contribute to the ongoing discourse and learning about how to promote meaningful participation in EU multi-level governance and, ultimately, the evolving understanding and practice of democracy in the EU. The analysis and findings also raise questions and highlight areas for further research: what other practices and legal domains might Article 10(3) TEU be applicable to in Member State legal orders? How does the current generation and application of knowledge impact on citizens' right to participate in the EU at the national level?

Naturally, the realisation of the legal principle of participatory democracy is in no way a panacea to the democracy and governance challenges facing the Union. Indeed, the EU principle of participatory democracy is, in many ways, a very modest formulation of participatory democracy as it features in democratic theory. Giving the principle effect through broad public engagement, characterised by deliberative feedback elements, transparency, and procedural equality with solid links to citizens, is also not straightforward or easy. However, in the words of Advocate General Cruz Villalón, 'it has never been claimed that democracy made legislation easier'.[41] The EU principle of participatory democracy has been formulated to contribute to the underlying purpose of the Union 'to deepen the solidarity' and create 'an ever closer union among the peoples of Europe'.[42] It represents an important evolution of the understanding and tradition of democracy on the European continent. Only when there is a unified and deepened understanding of this constitutional principle, and only when it has been given proper effect, will it be possible to assess whether it adequately serves its role and purpose to this end. The legal dimensions of the principle of participatory democracy, expounded hopefully in this book, demonstrate the potential of law in prompting Member States and national actors to take up a more integral role in facilitating democratic participation in the Union.

[41] *Council v Access Info Europe*, AG Opinion Cruz Villalón (n 37), para 67.
[42] Art 1 TEU.

BIBLIOGRAPHY

Books (in alphabetical order)

Aitamurto, T, *Crowdsourcing for Democracy: A New Era in Policy-Making* (Parliament of Finland, 2012).

Alemanno, A, Sibony, A-L and Sunstein, CR (eds), *Nudge and the Law: A European Perspective* (Hart, 2015).

Alston, P and others, *International Human Rights* (Oxford University Press, 2012).

Arendt, H, *Between Past and Future: Eight Exercises in Political Thought* (Penguin Books, 2006).

Bachrach, P and Botwinick, A, *Power and Empowerment: A Radical Theory of Participatory Democracy* (Temple University Press, 1992).

Barber, BR, *Strong Democracy: Participatory Politics for a New Age*, 20th anniversary edn, with a new preface (University of California Press, 2009).

Benhabib, S, *The Rights of Others: Aliens, Residents, and Citizens* (Cambridge University Press, 2004).

Benz, A and Papadopoulos, Y (eds), *Governance and Democracy: Comparing National, European and International Experiences*, reprint (Routledge, 2007).

Bohman, J, *Public Deliberation: Pluralism, Complexity, and Democracy* (MIT Press, 1996).

Bouza Garcia, L, *Participatory Democracy and Civil Society in the EU: Agenda-Setting and Institutionalisation* (Palgrave Macmillan, 2015).

Bradford, A, *The Brussels Effect: How the European Union Rules the World* (Oxford University Press, 2020).

Brennan, J, *Against Democracy* (Princeton University Press, 2017).

Busschaert, G, *Participatory Democracy, Civil Society and Social Europe: A Legal and Political Perspective*, 1st edn (Intersentia, 2016).

Coen, D, Katsaitis, A and Vannoni, M, *Business Lobbying in the European Union*, 1st edn (Oxford University Press, 2021).

Cole, GDH, *Social Theory*, 1st edn (Routledge, 1920).

Craig, P, *EU Administrative Law* (Oxford University Press, 2012).

Craig, P, *The Lisbon Treaty, Revised Edition: Law, Politics, and Treaty Reform* (Oxford University Press, 2013).

Craig, P and De Búrca, G, *EU Law: Text, Cases, and Materials*, 7th edn (Oxford University Press, 2020).

Curtin, D, *Postnational Democracy: The European Union in Search of a Political Philosophy* (Kluwer Law International, 1997).

Curtin, D, *Executive Power of the European Union: Law, Practices, and the Living Constitution* (Oxford University Press, 2009).

Curtin, D, Mair, P and Papadopoulos, Y (eds), *Accountability and European Governance* (Routledge, 2014).

Dahl, RA, *A Preface to Democratic Theory* (University of Chicago Press, 1956).

Dahl, RA, *Democracy and Its Critics* (Yale University Press, 1989).

Dahl, RA, *After the Revolution? Authority in a Good Society*, rev ed (Yale University Press, 1990).

Dahl, RA, *On Democracy* (Yale University Press, 2020).

Della Porta, D, *Can Democracy Be Saved? Participation, Deliberation and Social Movements* (Polity Press, 2013).

Dür, A and Mateo, G, *Insiders versus Outsiders: Interest Group Politics in Multilevel Europe*, 1st edn (Oxford University Press, 2016).

Dworkin, R, *Taking Rights Seriously* (Harvard University Press, 2001).
Eckes, C, Leino-Sandberg, P, and Ghavanini, AW, *The Dynamics of Power in the European Union*, 1st edn (Bloomsbury, 2024).
Eijken, H van, *EU Citizenship & the Constitutionalisation of the European Union* (Europa Law Publishing, 2015).
Eka, A, *Regeringsformen: Med Kommentarer*, 2:a upplagan, upplaga 2:3 (Karnov Group, 2018).
Eriksen, EO and Fossum, JE (eds), *Democracy in the European Union*, (Routledge, 2002).
Fish, SE, *Is There a Text in This Class? The Authority of Interpretive Communities* (Harvard University Press, 2003).
Fishkin, JS, *When the People Speak: Deliberative Democracy and Public Consultation* (Oxford University Press, 2011).
Geißel B and Joas M (eds), *Participatory Democratic Innovations in Europe: Improving the Quality of Democracy?*, 1st edn (Verlag Barbara Budrich, 2013).
Gest, J and Gray, SWD (eds), *Silent Citizenship: The Politics of Marginality in Unequal Democracies* (Routledge/Taylor & Francis Group, 2018).
Grimonprez, K, *The European Union and Education for Democratic Citizenship: Legal Foundations for EU Learning at School* (*Nomos* Verlagsgesellschaft mbH & Co KG, 2020).
Habermas, J, *Between Facts and Norms: Contributions to a Discourse Theory of Law and Democracy* (MIT Press, 1996).
Harlow, C and Rawlings, R, *Law and Administration*, 3rd edn, (Cambridge University Press, 2009).
Harlow, C and Rawlings, R, *Process and Procedure in EU Administration* (Hart, 2014).
Hersh, E, *Politics Is for Power: How to Move Beyond Political Hobbyism, Take Action, and Make Real Change* (Scribner, 2020).
Hierlemann, D and others, *Under Construction: Citizen Participation in the European Union* (Verlag Bertelsmann Stiftung, 2022).
Hirst, PQ, *Associative Democracy: New Forms of Economic and Social Governance* (Polity Press, 2003).
Hofmann, H, Rowe, GC and Türk, A, *Administrative Law and Policy of the European Union* (Oxford University Press, 2011).
Hogan, G, *Kelly: The Irish Constitution*, 5th edn (Bloomsbury, 2018).
Joerges, C and Dehousse, R (eds), *Good Governance in Europe's Integrated Market* (Oxford University Press, 2002).
Kagan, RA, *Adversarial Legalism: The American Way of Law*, 2nd edn (Harvard University Press, 2019).
Kohler-Koch, B and Quittkat, C, *De-Mystification of Participatory Democracy: EU Governance and Civil Society*, 1st edn (Oxford University Press, 2013).
Komesar, NK, *Imperfect Alternatives: Choosing Institutions in Law, Economics, and Public Policy* (University of Chicago Press, 1997).
Landemore, H, Open *Democracy*: Reinventing Popular Rule for the Twenty-First Century (Princeton University Press, 2020).
Lindberg, LN and Scheingold, SA, *Europe's Would-Be Polity: Patterns of Change in the European Community* (Prentice-Hall, 1970).
Lord, C, *A Democratic Audit of the European Union* (Palgrave Macmillan UK, 2004).
MacCormick N, *Legal Reasoning and Legal Theory* (Oxford University Press, 1994).
Macpherson, CB, *The Life and Times of Liberal Democracy* (OUP Canada, 2012).
Majone, G, *Regulating Europe* (Routledge, 1996).
Mansbridge, JJ, *Beyond Adversary Democracy* (University of Chicago Press, 1983).
Mazey, S and Richardson, JJ (eds), *Lobbying in the European Community*, reprint (Oxford University Press, 1998).
Mendes, J, *Participation in EU Rule-Making: A Rights-Based Approach* (Oxford University Press, 2011).
Mill, JS, *Considerations on Representative Government*, 1st edn (Cambridge University Press, 2010).
Moellers, C, *The Three Branches: A Comparative Model of Separation of Powers* (Oxford University Press, 2013).
Möller, K, *The Global Model of Constitutional Rights* (Oxford University Press, 2015).

Moser, C, *How Open Is 'Open as Possible'? Three Different Approaches to Transparency and Openness in Regulating Access to EU Documents*, vol 80 (Institut für Höhere Studien (IHS), 2001).
Mutz, DC, *Hearing the Other Side: Deliberative versus Participatory Democracy* (Cambridge University Press, 2006).
Nanz, P and Leggewie, C, *No Representation without Consultation: A Citizens' Guide to Participatory Democracy* (Damian Harrison and Stephen Roche trs, Between the Lines, 2019).
OECD, *Better Regulation Practices across the European Union* (OECD Publishing, 2019).
OECD, *Innovative Citizen Participation and New Democratic Institutions: Catching the Deliberative Wave* (OECD Publishing, 2020).
Öhlinger, T and Eberhard, H, *Verfassungsrecht*, 12th edn (Fakultas, 2019).
Pateman, C, *Participation and Democratic Theory* (Cambridge University Press, 1970).
Patton, MQ, *Qualitative Research & Evaluation Methods: Integrating Theory and Practice*, 4th edn (SAGE Publications, 2015).
Pichler, JW, Hinghofer-Szalkay, SG and Pichler, P, *Civil Dialogue and Participatory Democracy in the Practice of the European Union Institutions* (NWV Verlag GmbH, 2016).
Putnam, RD, *Bowling Alone: The Collapse and Revival of American Community*, revised and updated (Simon & Schuster Paperbacks, 2020).
Rose-Ackerman, S, Egidy, S and Fowkes, J, *Due Process of Lawmaking: The United States, South Africa, Germany, and the European Union* (Cambridge University Press, 2015).
Rousseau, J-J, *The Social Contract* (Maurice Cranston tr, Penguin Books, 1968).
Scharpf, F, *Governing in Europe: Effective and Democratic?* (Oxford University Press, 1999).
Schmidt, VA, *Democracy in Europe: The EU and National Polities* (1st edn, Oxford University Press, 2006).
Schumpeter, JA, *Capitalism, Socialism and Democracy* (Routledge, 1976).
Schwarze, J, *European Administrative Law* (Office for Official Publications of the *European* Communities; Sweet & Maxwell, 1992).
Smismans, S, *Law, Legitimacy, and European Governance: Functional Participation in Social Regulation* (Oxford University Press, 2004).
Smith, G, *Democratic Innovations: Designing Institutions for Citizen Participation*, 1st edn (Cambridge University Press, 2009).
Talisse, RB, *Deliberation* (Oxford University Press, 2012).
Tanasescu, I, *The European Commission and Interest Groups: Towards a Deliberative Interpretation of Stakeholder Involvement in EU Policy-Making* (VUB Press/Brussels University Press, 2009).
Tocqueville, A de, *Democracy in America* (Harvey C Mansfield and Delba Winthrop eds, University of Chicago Press, 2002).
Urbinati, N, *Me the People: How Populism Transforms Democracy* (Harvard University Press, 2019).
Weiler, J, *The Constitution of Europe: 'Do the New Clothes Have an Emperor?' And Other Essays on European Integration* (Cambridge University Press, 1999).
Wu, T, *The Attention Merchants: The Epic Scramble to Get Inside Our Heads*, 1st edn (Alfred A Knopf, 2016).
Yin, RK, *Case Study Research: Design and Methods*, 5th edn (SAGE, 2014).
Young, IM, *Inclusion and Democracy* (Oxford University Press, 2000).

Contributions to edited books (in alphabetical order)

Alemanno, A, 'Courts and Regulatory Impact Assessment' in CA Dunlop and CM Radaelli (eds), *Handbook of Regulatory Impact Assessment* (Edward Elgar, 2016).
Argyrou, A, 'An Empirical Investigation of Supportive Legal Frameworks for *Social* Enterprises in Belgium: A Cross-Sectoral Comparison of Case Studies Concerning *Social* Enterprises in the

Social Housing, Finance and Energy Sector' in V Mauerhofer (ed), *Legal Aspects of Sustainable Development* (Springer International Publishing, 2016).
Bache, I, 'Multi-Level Governance in the *European* Union' in D Levi-Faur (ed), *The Oxford Handbook of Governance* (Oxford University Press, 2012).
Bogdandy, A von, 'Founding Principles' in A von Bogdandy and J Bast (eds), *Principles of European Constitutional Law*, 2nd rev ed (Hart; CH Beck, 2010).
Braithwaite, J, '*Democracy*, Community, and Problem Solving' in G Burford and J Hudson (eds), *Family Group Conferencing* (Routledge, 2000).
Cappelletti, M, Seccombe, M and Weiler, JHH, 'Integration Through Law: Europe and the American Federal Experience. A General Introduction' in M Cappelletti, M Seccombe and JH Weiler (eds), *Integration Through Law, Volume 1: Methods, Tools and Institutions, Book 1: A Political, Legal and Economic Overview* (De Gruyter, 1986).
Ceurremans, T and David, E 'Article 10(3) TEU: Unlocking untapped potential to safeguard muted citizens' democratic rights' in D Duez and C Rizcallah (eds), Standing up for the voiceless? Exploring the EU's capacity for rights protection (Presses universitaires Saint-Louis Bruxelles, 2025).
Chalmers, D, 'The Democratic Ambiguity of EU Law Making and Its Enemies' in D Chalmers and A Arnull (eds), *The Oxford Handbook of European Union Law* (Oxford University Press, 2015).
Charnovitz, S, 'The Relevance of Non-State Actors to International Law' in R Wolfrum and V Röben (eds), *Developments of International Law in Treaty Making*, vol 177 (Springer, 2005).
Christiano, T, 'Rational *Deliberation* among Experts and Citizens' in J Parkinson and J Mansbridge (eds), *Deliberative Systems*, 1st edn (Cambridge University Press, 2012).
Closa, C, 'Constitutional prospects of *European* citizenship and new forms of democracy' in G Amato, H Bribosia and B de Witte (eds), *Genèse et destinée de la Constitution européenne: commentaire du traité établissant une constitution pour l'Europe à la lumière des travaux préparatoires et perspectives d'avenir* (Bruylant, 2007).
Cohen, J, '*Deliberation* and Democratic Legitimacy' in J B and W Rehg (eds), *Deliberative Democracy: Essays on Reason and Politics* (MIT Press, 1997).
Cohen, J, 'Reflections on Deliberative *Democracy*' in T Christiano and J Christman (eds), *Contemporary Debates in Political Philosophy* (Wiley-Blackwell, 2009).
Craig, P and De Búrca, G, 'Integration, *Democracy*, and Legitimacy' in P Craig (ed), *The Evolution of EU Law* (Oxford University Press, 2021).
Curtin, DM, 'Betwixt and Between: *Democracy* and Transparency in the Governance of the *European* Union' in AE Kellermann and others (eds), *Reforming the Treaty on European Union* (Brill/Nijhoff, 1996).
Curtin, DM, '"Civil Society" and the *European* Union: Opening Spaces for Deliberative *Democracy*?' in Academy of *European* Law (eds), *Collected Courses of the Academy of European Law*, vol VII, book 1 (Kluwer Law International, 1999).
Dahl, RA, 'Hierarchy, *Democracy* and Bargaining in Politics and Economics' in H Eulau, S Eldersveld and M Janovitz (eds), *Political Behavior: A Reader in Theory and Research* (Free Press of Glencoe, 1956).
Dehousse, R, '*European* Governance in Search of Legitimacy: The Need for a Process-Based Approach' in O De Schutter, N Lebessis and J Paterson (eds), *Governance in the EU* (Office for Official Publications of the *European* Communities, 2001).
Dehousse, R, 'Beyond Representative *Democracy*: Constitutionalism in a Polycentric Polity' in JHH Weiler and M Wind (eds), *European Constitutionalism beyond the State*, 1st edn (Cambridge University Press, 2001).
Elster, J, 'The Market and the Forum: Three Varieties of Political Theory' in D Matravers and J Pike (eds), *Debates in Contemporary Political Philosophy: An Anthology* (Routledge, 2003).
Elstub, S, 'Deliberative and Participatory *Democracy*' in A Bächtiger and others (eds), *The Oxford Handbook of Deliberative Democracy* (Oxford University Press, 2018).
Estlund, D, and Landemore, H, 'The Epistemic Value of Democratic *Deliberation*' in A Bächtiger and others (eds), *The Oxford Handbook of Deliberative Democracy* (Oxford University Press, 2018).

Feldman, D, 'Constitutionalism, Deliberative *Democracy*, and Human Rights' in J Morison, K McEvoy and G Anthony (eds), *Judges, Transition, and Human Rights* (Oxford University Press, 2007).

Floridia, A, 'The Origins of the Deliberative Turn' in A Bächtiger and others (eds), *The Oxford Handbook of Deliberative Democracy* (Oxford University Press, 2018).

Friedrich, D, '*European* Governance and the Deliberative Challenge' in R Kies and P Nanz (eds), Is Europe Listening to Us? Successes and Failures of EU Citizen Consultations (Ashgate, 2013).

Frohnen, B and Grasso, KL, 'Introduction; Rights in a Multicultural Age' in B Frohnen and KL Grasso (eds), *Rethinking Rights: Historical, Political, and Philosophical Perspectives* (University of Missouri Press, 2009).

Garben, S,'The Multi-Faceted *Nature* of *Better Regulation*' in S Garben and I Govaere (eds), The EU *Better Regulation* Agenda: A Critical Assessment (Hart, 2018).

García Macho, RJ, 'Article 11 [Participatory *Democracy*]' in H-J Blanke and S Mangiameli (eds), The Treaty on *European* Union (TEU): A Commentary (Springer, 2013).

Gestel, R van and Micklitz, H-W, 'Revitalising Doctrinal Legal Research in Europe: What about Methodology?' in UB Neergaard, R Nielsen and LM Roseberry (eds), *European Legal Method: Paradoxes and Revitalisation* (DJØF Publishing, 2011).

Grevén, MT, 'Some Considerations on Participation in Participatory Governance' in B Kohler-Koch and B Rittberger (eds), *Debating the Democratic Legitimacy of the European Union* (Rowman & Littlefield, 2007).

Haag, M, 'Art. 10 EUV' in H von der Groeben, J Schwarze, and A Hatje (eds), *Europäisches Unionsrecht*, 7th edn (*Nomos*, 2015).

Halpin, D and McLaverty, P, 'Legitimating INGO Advocacy: The Case of Internal Democracies' in J Steffek and K Hahn (eds), *Evaluating Transnational NGOs: Legitimacy, Accountability, Representation* (Palgrave Macmillan UK, 2010).

Haythornthwaite, R, '*Better Regulation* in Europe' in S Weatherill (ed), *Better Regulation* (Hart, 2007).

Hofmann, HCH, 'Composite Decision Making Procedures in *EU Administrative Law*' in HCH Hofmann and AH Türk (eds), *Legal Challenges in EU Administrative Law* (Edward Elgar, 2009).

Joerges, C, '"Good Governance" Through Comitology?' in C Joerges and E Vos (eds), *EU Committees: Social Regulation, Law and Politics* (Hart, 1999).

Joerges, C and Iverson, M, 'Challenging the Bureaucratic Challenge' in EO Eriksen and JE Fossum (eds), *Democracy in the European Union: Integration through Deliberation* (Routledge, 2000).

Klecatsky, H, 'Bundes-Verfassungsgesetz Und Bundesverfassungsrecht' in H Schambeck (ed), *Das österreichische Bundesverfassungsgesetz und seine Entwicklung* (Duncker & Humblot, 1980).

Kohler-Koch, B, 'The Organization of Interests and *Democracy*' in B Kohler-Koch and B Rittberger (eds), *Debating the Democratic Legitimacy of the European Union* (Rowman & Littlefield, 2007).

Kohler-Koch, B and Rittberger, B, 'Charting Crowded Territory: *Debating the Democratic Legitimacy of the European Union*' in B Kohler-Koch and B Rittberger (eds), *Debating the Democratic Legitimacy of the European Union* (Rowman & Littlefield, 2007).

Kröll, T and Lienbacher, G, *EU-Kommentar*, 4th edn (Ulrich Becker and others (eds); *Nomos*; Facultas; Helbing Lichtenhahn Verlag, 2019).

Leino-Sandberg, P, 'Disruptive *Democracy*: Keeping EU Citizens in a Box' in I Govaere, S Garben and P Nemitz (eds), *Critical Reflections on Constitutional Democracy in the European Union* (Hart, 2019).

Lenaerts, K and Gutiérrez-Fons, JA, 'Epilogue on EU Citizenship: Hopes and Fears' in D Kochenov (ed), *EU Citizenship and Federalism*, 1st edn (Cambridge University Press, 2017).

Lewi-Faur, D, 'Regulation and Regulatory Governance' in D Lewi-Faur (ed), *Handbook on the Politics of Regulation* (Edward Elgar, 2011).

Lock, T, 'Article 11 TEU' in M Kellerbauer, M Klamert and J Tomkin (eds), *The EU Treaties and the Charter of Fundamental Rights: A Commentary* (Oxford University Press, 2019).

Lord, C, 'Parliamentary *Representation* in a Decentered Polity' in B Kohler-Koch and B Rittberger (eds), *Debating the Democratic Legitimacy of the European Union* (Rowman & Littlefield, 2007).

Magnette, P, '*Democracy in the European Union*: Why and How Combine *Representation* and Participation' in S Smismans (ed), *Civil Society and Legitimate European Governance* (Edward Elgar, 2006).
Mansbridge, J and others, 'A Systemic Approach to Deliberative *Democracy*' in J Parkinson and J Mansbridge (eds), *Deliberative Systems*, 1st edn (Cambridge University Press, 2012).
Mendes, J, 'The Democratic Foundations of the Union: Representative *Democracy*, Complementarity and the Legal Challenge of Article 11 TEU' in A Lazowski and S Blockmans (eds), *Research Handbook on EU Institutional Law* (Edward Elgar, 2016).
Nowag, J and Groussot, X, 'From *Better Regulation* to Better
Adjudication?' in S Garben and I Govaere (eds), *The EU*
Better Regulation Agenda: A Critical Assessment (Hart, 2018).
Öhlinger, T, and Konrath C, 'Zu Artikel 23d B-VG' in K Korinek and M Holoubek (eds), *Österreichisches Bundesverfassungsrecht* (Verlag Österreich, 2013).
Parthasarathy, R and Rao, V, 'Deliberative *Democracy* in India' in A Bächtiger and others (eds), *The Oxford Handbook of Deliberative Democracy* (Oxford University Press, 2018).
Peters, BG and Pierre, J, 'Multi-Level *Governance and Democracy*: A Faustian Bargain?' in I Bache and M Flinders (eds), *Multi-level Governance* (Oxford University Press, 2004).
Pollack, MA, 'Theorizing EU Policy-Making' in H Wallace, MA Pollack, and C Roederer-Rynning (eds), *Policy-making in the European Union*, 8th edn (Oxford University Press, 2020).
Quittkat, C and Finke, B, 'The EU Commission Consultation Regime' in B Kohler-Koch, D de Bièvre and W Maloney (eds), *Opening EU-governance to civil society: gains and challenges* (Connex Report Series 05, 2008).
Ruffert M, 'Art. 11 EUV' in C Calliess and M Ruffert (eds), *EU-VERTRAG*, 6th edn (Beck, 2022).
Sabel, CF and Simon, WH, 'Democratic Experimentalism' in J Desautels-Stein and C Tomlins (eds), *Searching for Contemporary Legal Thought* (Cambridge University Press, 2017).
Schmitter, PC, 'Governance in the *European* Union: A Viable Mechanism for Future Legitimation? 1' in A Benz and Y Papadopoulos (eds), *Governance and Democracy* (Routledge, 2006).
Shapiro, M, 'The Frontiers of Science Doctrine: American Experiences with the Judicial Control of Science-Based Decision-Making' in C Joerges, K-H Ladeur and E Vos (eds), *Integrating scientific expertise into regulatory decision-making: national traditions and European innovations*, 1. Aufl (*Nomos*-Verl-Ges, 1997).
Shaw, J, 'Citizenship: Contrasting Dynamics at the Interface of Integration and Constitutionalism' in J Shaw, *The Evolution of EU Law* (Oxford University Press, 2021).
Smismans, S, 'The Constitutional Labelling of "the Democratic Life of the EU": Representative and "participatory" *Democracy*' in L Dobson and A Follesdahl (eds), *Political Theory and the European Constitution* (Routledge, 2006).
Smismans, S, 'Regulatory Procedure and Participation in the *European* Union' in F Bignami and D Zaring (eds), *Comparative Law and Regulation* (Edward Elgar, 2016).
Steffek, J and Nanz, P, 'Emergent Patterns of Civil Society Participation in Global and *European* Governance' in J Steffek, C Kissling and P Nanz (eds), *Civil Society Participation in European and Global Governance* (Palgrave Macmillan UK, 2008).
Tridimas, T and Poli, S, 'Locus Standi of Individuals under Article 230(4): The Return of Euridice?' in A Arnull, P Eeckhout and T Tridimas (eds), *Continuity and Change in EU Law*, 1st edn (Oxford University Press, 2008).
Uhlmann, F and Konrath, C, 'Participation' in U Karpen and H Xanthaki (eds), *Legislation in Europe: A Comprehensive Guide for Scholars and Practitioners* (Hart, 2017).
Vogiatzis, N, 'The *European* Ombudsman in the EU's Administrative and Institutional Framework' in GJ Brandsma (ed), *Handbook on European Union Public Administration* (Edward Elgar, 2024).
Warleigh A, 'Civil Society and Legitimate Governance in a Flexible Europe: Critical Deliberativism as a Way Forward' in S Smismans (ed), *Civil Society and Legitimate European Governance* (Edward Elgar, 2006).
Young, IM, 'Six: Communication and the Other: Beyond Deliberative *Democracy*' in S Benhabib (ed), *Democracy and Difference* (Princeton University Press, 1996).

Zittel, T, 'Participatory *Democracy* and Political Participation' in T Zittel and D Fuchs (eds), *Participatory Democracy and Political Participation: Can participatory engineering bring citizens back in?* (Routledge, 2007).

Articles (in alphabetical order)

Abizadeh, A, 'On the Demos and Its Kin: Nationalism, Democracy, and the Boundary Problem' (2012) 106 *American Political Science Review* 867.

Alemanno, A, 'The Better Regulation Initiative at the Judicial Gate: A Trojan Horse within the Commission's Walls or the Way Forward?' (2009) 15 *European Law Journal* 382.

Alemanno, A, 'Unpacking the Principle of Openness in EU Law: Transparency, Participation and Democracy' (2014) 39 *European Law Review* 72.

Alemanno, A, 'How Much Better Is Better Regulation? Assessing the Impact of the Better Regulation Package on the European Union – A Research Agenda' (2015) 6 *European Journal of Risk Regulation* 344.

Alemanno, A, 'Levelling the EU Participatory Playing Field: A Legal and Policy Analysis of the Commission's Public Consultations in Light of the Principle of Political Equality' (2020) 26 *European Law Journal* 114.

Alemanno, A, 'The Legality of Omnibus Legislation Under EU Law: A Preliminary Analysis of Omnibus I Simplification Directive of CSRD and CSDD and Its Legal Consequences on the EU Legal Order' (*SSRN*, 2025), https://www.ssrn.com/abstract=5727822.

Alemanno, A and Stefan, O, 'Openness at the Court of Justice of the European Union: Toppling a Taboo' (2014) 51 *Common Market Law Review* 97.

Al-Rodhan, N, 'The Wrongs, Harms, and Ineffectiveness of Torture: A Moral Evaluation from Empirical Neuroscience' [2022] *Journal of Social Philosophy* 565.

Argyrou, A, 'Making the Case for Case Studies in Empirical Legal Research' (2017) 13 *Utrecht Law Review* 95.

Armstrong, KA, 'Rediscovering Civil Society: The European Union and the White Paper on Governance' (2002) 8 *European Law Journal* 102.

Arnstein, SR, 'A Ladder Of Citizen Participation' (1969) 35 *Journal of the American Institute of Planners* 216.

Bächtiger, A and others, 'Disentangling Diversity in Deliberative Democracy: Competing Theories, Their Blind Spots and Complementarities' (2010) 18 *Journal of Political Philosophy* 32.

Bächtiger, A and Beauvais, E, 'Taking the Goals of Deliberation Seriously: A Differentiated View on Equality and Equity in Deliberative Designs and Processes' (2020) 12 *Journal of Deliberative Democracy*, Article 2.

Bächtiger, A, Vrydagh, J and Curato, N, 'Democracy without Shortcuts: Introduction to the Special Issue' (2020) 16 *Journal of Deliberative Democracy* 1.

Barnes, M, and others, 'Constituting "the Public" in Public Participation' (2003) 81 *Public Administration* 379.

Bedner, A, 'An Elementary Approach to the Rule of Law' (2010) 2 *Hague Journal on the Rule of Law* 48.

Beger, N, 'Participatory Democracy: Organised Civil Society and the "New" Dialogue' [2004] *Federal Trust Constitutional Online Paper* No 09/04.

Beitz, CR, 'Procedural Equality in Democratic Theory: A Preliminary Examination' (1983) 25 *Nomos* 69.

Binchy, W, 'The Irish Legal System: An Introduction' (2011) 11 *Legal Information Management* 151.

Bogdandy A von, 'The European Lesson for International Democracy: The Significance of Articles 9 to 12 EU Treaty for International Organizations' (2012) 23 *European Journal of International Law* 315.

Bogdandy, A von, and Spieker, LD, 'Transformative Constitutionalism in Luxembourg: How the Court Can Support Democratic Transitions' (2022) 29 *Columbia Journal of European Law* 65.

Bredt, S, 'Prospects and Limits of Democratic Governance in the EU' (2011) 17 *European Law Journal* 35.

Brito-Vieira, MA, and others, 'Critical Exchange: The Nature of Silence and Its Democratic Possibilities' [2019] *Contemporary Political Theory* 424.
Broberg, MP, 'Access to Documents - A General Principle of Community Law?' (2002) 27 *European Law Review* 194.
Broscheid, A, and Coen, D, 'Lobbying Activity and Fora Creation in the EU: Empirically Exploring the Nature of the Policy Good' (2007) 14 *Journal of European Public Policy* 346.
Chambers, S, 'Deliberative Democracy Theory' (2003) 6 *Annual Review of Political Science* 307.
Chambers, S, 'Rhetoric and the Public Sphere: Has Deliberative Democracy Abandoned Mass Democracy?' (2009) 37 *Political Theory* 323.
Christiansen, T, 'Intra-Institutional Politics and Inter-Institutional Relations in the EU: Towards Coherent Governance?' (2001) 8 *Journal of European Public Policy* 747.
Christou, G and Simpson, S, 'The Internet and Public–Private Governance in the European Union' (2006) 26 *Journal of Public Policy* 43.
Closa, C, 'Deliberative Constitutional Politics and the Turn towards a Norms-Based Legitimacy of the EU Constitution' (2005) 11 *European Law Journal* 411.
Coen, D, 'The European Business Lobby' (1997) 8 *Business Strategy Review* 17.
Coen, D, and Katsaitis, A, 'Chameleon Pluralism in the EU: An Empirical Study of the European Commission Interest Group Density and Diversity across Policy Domains' (2013) 20 *Journal of European Public Policy* 1104.
Cohen, J, 'An Epistemic Conception of Democracy' (1986) 97 *Ethics* 26.
Cohen, J, and Sabel, C, 'Directly-Deliberative Polyarchy' (1997) 3 *European Law Journal* 313.
Cotter, J, 'To Everything There Is a Season: Instrumentalising Article 10 TEU to Exclude Undemocratic Member State Representatives from the European Council and the Council' (2022) 47 *European Law Review* 69.
Cuesta Lopez V, 'The Lisbon Treaty's Provisions on Democratic Principles: A Legal Framework for Participatory Democracy' (2010) 16 *European Public Law* 123.
Curato, N and others, 'Twelve Key Findings in Deliberative Democracy Research' (2017) 146 *Daedalus* 28.
Curtin, D, 'Citizens' Fundamental Right of Access to EU Information: An Evolving Digital Passepartout' (2000) 37 *Common Market Law Review* 7.
Curtin D, Hofmann H, and Mendes J, 'Constitutionalising EU Executive Rule-Making Procedures: A Research Agenda' (2013) 19 *European Law Journal* 1.
Curtin, D, and Leino-Sandberg, P, 'Openness, Transparency and the Right of Access to Documents in the EU' (2016) No RSCAS 2016/63 *Robert Schuman Centre for Advanced Studies.*
Curtin, D, and Leino-Sandberg, P, 'In Search of Transparency for EU Law-Making: Trilogues on the Cusp of Dawn' (2017) 54 *Common Market Law Review* 1673.
Curtin, D, and Meijer, AJ, 'Does Transparency Strengthen Legitimacy?' (2006) 11 *Information Polity* 109.
Dacombe, R and Parvin, P, 'Participatory Democracy in an Age of Inequality' (2021) 57 *Representation* 145.
Dahl, V and others, 'Apathy or Alienation? Political Passivity among Youths across Eight European Union Countries' (2018) 15 *European Journal of Developmental Psychology* 284.
Daly, TG, 'Democratic Decay: Conceptualising an Emerging Research Field' (2019) 11 *Hague Journal on the Rule of Law* 9.
Dawson, M, 'Better Regulation and the Future of EU Regulatory Law and Politics' (2016) 53 *Common Market Law Review* 1209.
De Schutter, O, 'Europe in Search of Its Civil Society' (2002) 8 *European Law Journal* 198.
Dehousse, R, 'Comitology: Who Watches the Watchmen?' (2003) 10 *Journal of European Public Policy* 798.
Delfino, M, 'The Court and the Charter: A "Consistent" Interpretation of Fundamental Social Rights and Principles' (2015) 6 *European Labour Law Journal* 86.
Downs, A, 'An Economic Theory of Political Action in a Democracy' (1957) 65 *Journal of Political Economy* 135.
Dryzek, JS, and Niemeyer, S, 'Discursive Representation' (2008) 102 *American Political Science Review* 481.

Dür, A, Bernhagen, P, and Marshall, D, 'Interest Group Success in the European Union: When (and Why) Does Business Lose?' (2015) 48 *Comparative Political Studies* 951.
Eberhard, H, and Lachmayer, K, 'Constitutional Reform 2008 in Austria' (2008) 2 *Vienna Journal on International Constitutional Law* 112.
Eckes, C, and D'Ambrosio, R, 'Composite Administrative Procedures in the European Union' (1 November 2020), https://papers.ssrn.com/abstract=3742384.
Egeberg, M, Schaefer, G, and Trondal, J, 'The Many Faces of EU Committee Governance' (2003) 26 *West European Politics* 19.
Eka A, 'Kommentar, Regeringsform (1974:152) 7 Kap. 2 §' [2018] *Lexino.*
Eriksen, A, and Katsaitis, A, 'Accountability through Mutual Attunement: How Can Parliamentary Hearings Connect the Elected and the Unelected?' (2023) 38 *Public Policy and Administration* 352.
Featherstone, K, 'Jean Monnet and the "Democratic Deficit" in the European Union' (1994) 32 *Journal of Common Market Studies* 149.
Feezell, JT, 'Predicting Online Political Participation' (2016) 69 *Political Research Quarterly* 495.
Fishkin, JS, 'Consulting the Public through Deliberative Polling' (2003) 22 *Journal of Policy Analysis and Management* 128.
Follesdal, A and Hix, S, 'Why There Is a Democratic Deficit in the EU: A Response to Majone and Moravcsik' (2006) 44 *Journal of Common Market Studies* 533.
Franklin, CN, 'The Burgeoning Principle of Consistency in EU Law' (2011) 30 *Yearbook of European Law* 42.
Friedrich, D, 'Old Wine in New Bottles? The Actual and Potential Contribution of Civil Society Organisations to Democratic Governance in Europe' *RECON Online Working Paper 2007/08.*
Friess, D and others, 'Political Online Participation and Its Effects: Theory, Measurement, and Results' (2021) 13 *Policy & Internet* 345.
Fung, A, 'Deliberation before the Revolution: Toward an Ethics of Deliberative Democracy in an Unjust World' (2005) 33 *Political Theory* 397.
Fung, A, 'Varieties of Participation in Complex Governance' (2006) 66 *Public Administration Review* 66.
Fung, A, 'Putting the Public Back into Governance: The Challenges of Citizen Participation and Its Future' (2015) 75 *Public Administration Review* 513.
Fung, A, and Wright, EO, 'Deepening Democracy: Innovations in Empowered Participatory Governance' (2001) 29 *Politics & Society* 5.
Fyhr, K, 'The Reform of the EU Transparency Register' (2021) 17 *Croatian Yearbook of European Law and Policy* 177.
Garzón Clariana, G, 'Les droits politiques des citoyens de l'Europe: les vingt premières années' (2013) 13 *ERA Forum* 545.
Gjaldbæk-Sverdrup, E, Nicolaïdis, K, and Palomo Hernández, N, '"Technocratic Democratisation": What Can We Learn from the European Commission's New Generation European Citizens' Panels?' (European University Institute) *RSC Working Paper 2023/65.*
Golmohammadi, G, 'I gränslandet mellan rättigheter, skyldigheter och ambitioner – Remissförfarandet ur ett rättsligt perspektiv' (2024) *Statsvetenskaplig Tidsskrift* Vol 126 Nr 3.
Goodin, RE, 'Enfranchising All Affected Interests, and Its Alternatives' (2007) 35 *Philosophy & Public Affairs* 40.
Greenwood, J, and Dreger, J, 'The Transparency Register: A European Vanguard of Strong Lobby Regulation?' (2013) 2 *Interest Groups and Advocacy* 139.
Griller, S, 'Verfassungsfragen Der Österreichischen EU-Mitgliedschaft' [1995] *ZfRV* 89.
Gsell, B, 'The New European Directive on Representative Actions for the Protection of the Collective Interests of Consumers – A Huge, but Blurry Step Forward' (2021) 58 *Common Market Law Review* 1365.
Habermas, J, Lennox, S and Lennox, F, 'The Public Sphere: An Encyclopedia Article (1964)' [1974] *New German Critique* 49.
Hämäläinen, H, and Salminen, J, 'Inclusive Participation in Law-Making: Good Governance or a Constitutional Obligation?' (2025) 13 *The Theory and Practice of Legislation* 213.

Harlow, C, 'Accountability in the European Union' (2002), https://cadmus.eui.eu/handle/1814/2895 .Harvey, D, 'Towards Process-Oriented Proportionality Review In The European Union' (2017) 23 *European Public Law* 93.
Harvey, D, 'Process-Oriented Federalism in the EU: A (Partial) Response to Critiques of Process Review Advocacy in the EU' (2021) 45 *European Law Review* 460.
Hatzisavvidou, S, 'Disturbing Binaries in Political Thought: Silence as Political Activism' (2015) 14 *Social Movement Studies* 509.
Hauser, H (ed), 'European Union Lobbying Post-Lisbon: An Economic Analysis' [2011] *Berkeley Journal of International Law* 694.
Heidbreder, EG, 'Civil Society Participation in EU Governance' (2012) 7 *Living Reviews in European Governance* 8.
Helberger, N, and Diakopoulos, N, 'ChatGPT and the AI Act' (2023) 12 *Internet Policy Review*.
Heritier, A, 'Elements of Democratic Legitimation in Europe: An Alternative Perspective' (1999) 6 *Journal of European Public Policy* 269.
Héritier, A, 'Composite Democracy in Europe: The Role of Transparency and Access to Information' (2003) 10 *Journal of European Public Policy* 814.
Herlin-Karnell, E, and Konstadinides, T, 'The Rise and Expressions of Consistency in EU Law: Legal and Strategic Implications for European Integration' (2013) 15 *Cambridge Yearbook of European Legal Studies* 139.
Hettne, J, and Reichel, J, *Att Göra Rätt Och i Tid – Behövs Nya Metoder För Att Genomföra EU-Rätt i Sverige?*, 2012:4 (Svenska institutet för europapolitiska studier, 2012).
Hickey, E, and Weimer, M, 'The Transparency of EU Agency Science: Towards a New Proactive Approach' (2022) 59 *Common Market Law Review* 673.
Hillebrandt, M, 'EU Transparency as "Documents": Still Fit for Purpose?' (2021) 9 *Politics and Governance* 292.
Hillebrandt, M, and Leino-Sandberg, P, 'Administrative and Judicial Oversight of Trilogues' (2021) 28 *Journal of European Public Policy* 53.
Hix, S, 'The Study of the European Union II: The "New Governance" Agenda and Its Rival' (1998) 5 *Journal of European Public Policy* 38.
Hix, S, 'When Optimism Fails: Liberal Intergovernmentalism and Citizen Representation' (2018) 56 *Journal of Common Market Studies* 1595, https://onlinelibrary.wiley.com/doi/abs/10.1111 /jcms.12785. Hojnacki, M, and others, 'Assessing Business Advantage in Washington Lobbying' (2015) 4 *Interest Groups and Advocacy* 205.
Holst, C, and Molander, A, 'Public Deliberation and the Fact of Expertise: Making Experts Accountable' (2017) 31 *Social Epistemology* 235.
Houge, AB, and Lohne, K, 'End Impunity! Reducing Conflict-Related Sexual Violence to a Problem of Law' (2017) 51 *Law & Society Review* 755.
Howe, P, 'Eroding Norms and Democratic Deconsolidation' (2017) 28 *Journal of Democracy* 15.
Irvin, RA, and Stansbury, J, 'Citizen Participation in Decision Making: Is It Worth the Effort?' (2004) 64 *Public Administration Review* 55.
Jakab, A, 'Three Misconceptions about the EU Rule of Law Crisis' [2022] *Verfassungsblog: On Matters Constitutional*.
Joerges, C, and Neyer, J, 'From Intergovernmental Bargaining to Deliberative Political Processes: The Constitutionalisation of Comitology' (1997) 3 *European Law Journal* 273.
Jungkunz, V, 'The Promise of Democratic Silences' (2012) 34 *New Political Science* 127.
Kessler, F, 'Natural Law, Justice and Democracy—Some Reflections on Three Types of Thinking about Law and Justice' (1944) 19 *Tulane Law Review* 32.
Keyaerts, D, 'Ex Ante Evaluation of EU Legislation Intertwined with Judicial Review? Comment on Case C-58/08 Vodafone' (2010) 35 *European Law Review* 869.
Kielmansegg, PG, 'Legitimität Als Analytische Kategorie.' (1971) 3 *Politische Vierteljahresschrift* 12 367.
Kohler-Koch B, 'The Three Worlds of European Civil Society—What Role for Civil Society for What Kind of Europe?' (2009) 28 *Policy and Society* 47.

Kohler-Koch B, 'Civil Society and EU Democracy: "Astroturf" Representation?' (2010) 17 *Journal of European Public Policy* 100.

Kohler-Koch, B, and Finke, B, 'The Institutional Shaping of EU–Society Relations: A Contribution to Democracy via Participation?' (2007) 3 *Journal of Civil Society* 205.

Kohler-Koch, B, and Rittberger, B, 'Review Article: The "Governance Turn" in EU Studies' (2006) 44 *Journal of Common Market Studies* 27.

Korkea-Aho, E, '"Mr Smith Goes To Brussels": Third Country Lobbying and the Making of EU Law and Policy' (2016) 18 *Cambridge Yearbook of European Legal Studies* 45.

Koskenniemi, M, 'Constitutionalism as Mindset: Reflections on Kantian Themes About International Law and Globalization' (2006) 8 *Theoretical Inquiries in Law* 9.

Kostadinova, P, 'Improving the Transparency and Accountability of EU Institutions: The Impact of the Office of the European Ombudsman' (2015) 53 *Gender, Work And Organization* 1077.

Kunz, JL, 'The State Treaty With Austria' (1955) 49 *American Journal of International Law* 535.

Kutay, A, 'Limits of Participatory Democracy in European Governance: Participatory Democracy in Lisbon Treaty' (2015) 21 *European Law Journal* 803.

Lafont, C, 'Deliberation, Participation, and Democratic Legitimacy: Should Deliberative Mini-Publics Shape Public Policy?' (2015) 23 *Journal of Political Philosophy* 40.

Landemore, H, 'Deliberation, Cognitive Diversity, and Democratic Inclusiveness: An Epistemic Argument for the Random Selection of Representatives' (2013) 190 *Synthese* 1209.

Leino-Sandberg P, 'Transparency, Participation, and EU Institutional Practice: An Inquiry into the Limits of the "widest Possible"' *EUI Dept of Law Research Paper* No 2014/03.

Lenaerts, K, 'The European Court of Justice and Process-Oriented Review' (2012) 31 *Yearbook of European Law* 3.

Lenaerts, K, 'The Principle of Democracy in the Case Law of the European Court of Justice' (2013) 62 *International and Comparative Law Quarterly* 271.

Levitt, M, 'Access to the File: The Commission's Administrative Procedures in Cases Under Articles 85 and 86' (1997) 34 *Common Market Law Review* 1413.

Lodge, J, 'Transparency and EU Governance: Balancing Openness with Security' (2003) 11 *Journal of Contemporary European Studies* 95.

Lombardo, E, 'The Participation of Civil Society in the Constitution-Making Process' (*CIDEL Workshop Constitution Making and Democratic Legitimacy in the EU*, 2004).

Lord, C, and Beetham, D, 'Legitimizing the EU: Is There a "Post-Parliamentary Basis" for Its Legitimation?' (2001) 39 *Journal of Common Market Studies* 443.

Lundberg, E, and Hysing E, 'The Value of Participation: Exploring the Role of Public Consultations from the Vantage Point of Interest Groups' (2016) 39 *Scandinavian Political Studies* 1.

Maggetti, M, and Gilardi, F, 'The Policy-Making Structure of European Regulatory Networks and the Domestic Adoption of Standards' (2011) 18 *Journal of European Public Policy* 830.

Magnette, P, 'European Governance and Civic Participation: Beyond Elitist Citizenship?' (2003) 51 *Political Studies* 144.

Majone, G, 'Europe's "Democratic Deficit": The Question of Standards' (1998) 4 *European Law Journal* 5.

Marks, G, Hooghe, L, and Blank, K, 'European Integration from the 1980s: State-Centric v. Multi-Level Governance' (1996) 34 *Journal of Common Market Studies* 341.

Marxsen, C, 'Open Stakeholder Consultations at the European Level—Voice of the Citizens?' (2015) 21 *European Law Journal* 257.

Mayoral, JA, 'Democratic Improvements in the European Union under the Lisbon Treaty: Institutional Changes Regarding Democratic Government in the EU' [2011] *SSRN Electronic Journal*.

Mendes, J, 'Participation and the Role of Law after Lisbon: A Legal View on Article 11 TEU' (2011) 48 *Common Market Law Review* 1849.

Meuwese, A, 'Embedding Consultation Procedures: Law or Institutionalization?' (2011) 17 *European Public Law* 527.

Meuwese, A, 'Regulatory Review of European Commission Impact Assessments: What Kind for Which Better Regulation Scenario?' (2017) 19 *European Journal of Law Reform* 16.

Meuwese, A, and Popelier, P, 'Legal Implications of Better Regulation: A Special Issue' (2011) 17 *European Public Law* 455.

Monaghan, E, 'Assessing Participation and Democracy in the EU: The Case of the European Citizens' Initiative' (2012) 13 *Perspectives on European Politics and Society* 285.

Moravcsik, A, 'Reassessing Legitimacy in the European Union' (2002) 40 *Journal of Common Market Studies* 603.

Mouffe, C, 'Deliberative Democracy or Agonistic Pluralism?' (1999) 66 *Social Research* 745.

Mousmouti, M, 'Making Legislative Effectiveness an Operational Concept: Unfolding the Effectiveness Test as a Conceptual Tool for Lawmaking' (2018) 9 *European Journal of Risk Regulation* 445.

Näsström, S, 'The Challenge of the All-Affected Principle' (2011) 59 *Political Studies* 116.

Nentwich, M, 'Opportunity Structures for Citizens' Participation: The Case of the European Union' *European Community Studies Association Austria*, vol 0 (1996)

Nergelius, J, 'Judicial Review in Swedish Law – A Critical Analysis' (2009) 27 *Nordic Journal of Human Rights* 142.

Novak, S, and Hillebrandt, M, 'Analysing the Trade-off between Transparency and Efficiency in the Council of the European Union' (2020) 27 *Journal of European Public Policy* 141.

Öberg, J, 'The Rise of the Procedural Paradigm: Judicial Review of EU Legislation in Vertical Competence Disputes' (2017) 13 *European Constitutional Law Review* 248.

Öberg, P, and Svensson, T, 'Civil Society and Deliberative Democracy: Have Voluntary Organisations Faded from National Public Politics?' (2012) 35 *Scandinavian Political Studies* 246.

Obradovic, D, and Alonso Vizcaino, JM, 'Good Governance Requirements Concerning the Participation of Interest Groups in EU Consultations' (2006) 43 *Common Market Law Review* 1049.

Ortwein BMI, 'The Swedish Legal System: An Introduction' (2003) 13 *Indiana International & Comparative Law Review* 405.

Ouyang J, 'The Omnibus Comeback of the Neoliberal EU' [2025] *Verfassungsblog: On Matters Constitutional*, https://intrechtdok.de/receive/mir_mods_00021446. Oxenham, S, 'The Rise of Political Apathy in Two Charts' [2020] *Nature*.

Pansardi, P, 'Democracy, Domination and the Distribution of Power: Substantive Political Equality as a Procedural Requirement' (2016) 275 *Revue internationale de philosophie* 91.

Pateman, C, 'Participatory Democracy Revisited' (2012) 10 *Perspectives on Politics* 7.

Pech, L, and Scheppele, KL, 'Illiberalism Within: Rule of Law Backsliding in the EU' (2017) 19 *Cambridge Yearbook of European Legal Studies* 3.

Peers, S, and Costa, M, 'Court of Justice of the European Union (General Chamber), Judicial Review of EU Acts after the Treaty of Lisbon; Order of 6 September 2011, Case T-18/10 *Inuit Tapiriit Kanatami and Others v. Commission* & Judgment of 25 October 2011, Case T-262/10 *Microban v. Commission*' (2012) 8 *European Constitutional Law Review* 82.

Petrov, J, 'The COVID-19 Emergency in the Age of Executive Aggrandizement: What Role for Legislative and Judicial Checks?' (2020) 8 *The Theory and Practice of Legislation* 71.

Pogrebinschi, T, and Samuels, D, 'The Impact of Participatory Democracy: Evidence from Brazil's National Public Policy Conferences' (2014) 46 *Comparative Politics* 313.

Popelier, P, 'A Legal Perspective on Regulatory Impact Assessments' (*International Symposium: Regulatory Impact Analyses, Luxembourg* 23–24 November 2017).

Rabinovici, I, 'The Right to Be Heard in the Charter of Fundamental Rights of the European Union' (2012) 18 *European Public Law* 149.

Ranchordás, S, 'Consultations, Citizen Narratives and Evidence-Based Regulation: The Strange Case of the Consultation on the Collaborative Economy' (2017) 19 *European Journal of Law Reform* 52.

Rittberger, B, and Wonka, A, 'Introduction: Agency Governance in the European Union' (2011) 18 *Journal of European Public Policy* 780.

Ruffert, M, and Leino-Sandberg, P, 'Next Generation EU and Its Constitutional Ramifications: A Critical Assessment' (2022) 59 *Common Market Law Review* 433.

Ruin, O, 'Participatory Democracy and Corporativism: The Case of Sweden' (1974) 9 *Scandinavian Political Studies* 171.

Sabel, CF, and Zeitlin, J, 'Experimentalism in the EU: Common Ground and Persistent Differences: Experimentalism in the EU' (2012) 6 *Regulation & Governance* 410.
Saurugger, S, 'Interest Groups and Democracy in the European Union' (2008) 31 *West European Politics* 1274.
Saurugger, S, 'The Social Construction of the Participatory Turn: The Emergence of a Norm in the European Union' (2010) 49 *European Journal of Political Research* 471.
Schmidt, V, and Wood, M, 'Conceptualizing Throughput Legitimacy: Procedural Mechanisms of Accountability, Transparency, Inclusiveness and Openness in EU Governance' (2019) 97 *Public Administration* 727.
Schmidt, VA, 'Democracy and Legitimacy in the European Union Revisited: Input, Output, and "Throughput"' (2013) 61 *Political Studies* 2.
Schrauwen, A, 'European Union Citizenship in the Treaty of Lisbon: Any Change at All?' (2007) 15 *Maastricht Journal of European and Comparative Law* 55.
Schuurmans, Y, and Voermans, W, 'Better Regulation by Appeal' (2011) 17 *European Public Law* 507.
Scott, J, and Trubek, DM, 'Mind the Gap: Law and New Approaches to Governance in the European Union' (2002) 8 *European Law Journal* 1.
Sieberson, SC, 'The Treaty of Lisbon and its Impact on the European Union's Democratic Deficit' (2007), available at SSRN: https://ssrn.com/abstract=1628869.Sloam, J, 'Diversity and Voice: The Political Participation of Young People in the European Union' (2016) 18 *The British Journal of Politics and International Relations* 521.
Smismans, S, 'New Modes of Governance and the Participatory Myth' (2008) 31 *West European Politics* 874.
Stasavage, D, 'Open-Door or Closed-Door? Transparency in Domestic and International Bargaining' (2004) 58 *International Organization* 667.
Steiner, HJ, 'Political Participation as a Human Right' (1988) 1 *Harvard Human Rights Yearbook* 77.
Stern, RT, 'When the Ends Justify the Means? Quality of Law-Making in Times of Urgency' (2019) 7 *The Theory and Practice of Legislation* 85.
Strömvik, M, 'Hur Väl Förankras Svensk EU Politik?' (Lunds Universitet, 2020).
Sunstein, CR, 'Cost-Benefit Analysis, Who's Your Daddy?' (2016) 7 *Journal of Benefit-Cost Analysis* 107.
Terpan, F, 'Soft Law in the European Union–The Changing Nature of EU Law: Soft Law in the European Union' (2015) 21 *European Law Journal* 68.
Tiefenbacher, W, and Möstl, M, 'Legal Environment and Space of Civil Society Organisations in Supporting Fundamental Rights: Austria' (*European Union Agency for Fundamental Rights*, 2020).
Türk, AH, 'Oversight of Administrative Rulemaking: Judicial Review' (2013) 19 *European Law Journal* 126.
Urbinati, N, and Warren, ME, 'The Concept of Representation in Contemporary Democratic Theory' (2008) 11 *Annual Review of Political Science* 387.
Van Der Meer, TWG (Tom), and Van Ingen, EJ (Erik), 'Schools of Democracy? Disentangling the Relationship between Civic Participation and Political Action in 17 European Countries' (2009) 48 *European Journal of Political Research* 281.
Veale, M, and Zuiderveen Borgesius, F, 'Demystifying the Draft EU Artificial Intelligence Act — Analysing the Good, the Bad, and the Unclear Elements of the Proposed Approach' (2021) 22 *Computer Law Review International* 97.
Vieira, MB, 'Silence in Political Theory and Practice' (2021) 24 *Critical Review of International Social and Political Philosophy* 289.
Vitale, D, 'Between Deliberative and Participatory Democracy: A Contribution on Habermas' (2006) 32 *Philosophy & Social Criticism* 739.
Walker, N, 'The White Paper in Constitutional Context' [2001] *Jean Monnet Chair, Jean Monnet Working Papers*.
Ward, AF and others, 'Brain Drain: The Mere Presence of One's Own Smartphone Reduces Available Cognitive Capacity' (2017) 2 *Journal of the Association for Consumer Research* 140.
Warren, ME, 'The All Affected Interests Principle in Democratic Theory and Practice' (*Institut für Höheren Studien – Insitute for Advanced Studies (IHS)*, 2017).

Weatherill, S, 'The Limits of Legislative Harmonization Ten Years after *Tobacco Advertising*: How the Court's Case Law Has Become a "Drafting Guide"' (2011) 12 *German Law Journal* 827.
Weichsel, H, 'A Brief Overview of the Austrian Legal Information System and Laws' [2021] *GlobaLex*, https://www.nyulawglobal.org/globalex/Austria1.html.
Weiler, JHH, 'The Transformation of Europe' (1991) 100 *Yale Law Journal* 2403.
Weiler, JHH, 'Does Europe Need a Constitution? Demos, Telos and the German Maastricht Decision' (2010) 1 *European Law Journal* 219.
Weiler, JHH, Haltern, U, and Mayer, F, 'European Democracy and Its Critique Five Uneasy Pieces' EUI Working Paper RSC No 95/11.Werner, F, 'Verwaltungsrecht Als Konkretisiertes Verfassungsrecht' [1963] *Mensch und Verwaltung*.
Wolfe, JD, 'A Defense of Participatory Democracy' (1985) 47 *The Review of Politics* 370.

EU documents, guidelines, and communications

European Commission

Commission, 'A New Deal for Consumers – Revision of the Injunctions Directive' (*European Commission - Have your say*, 28 November 2017), https://ec.europa.eu/info/law/better-regulation/have-your-say/initiatives/1170-A-New-Deal-for-Consumers-revision-of-the-Injunctions-Directive_en.
Commission, 'A Simpler and Faster Europe: Communication on Implementation and Simplification' COM (2025) 46 final.
Commission, 'Better Regulation Toolbox, July 2023 Edition', https://commission.europa.eu/system/files/2023-07/BR_toolbox_Jul_2023_en.pdf.
Commission, 'Call for Evidence on the Operation of Collective Redress Arrangements in the Member States of the European Union', https://ec.europa.eu/newsroom/just/items/59539.
Commission, 'Commission Proposes to Cut Red Tape and Simplify Business Environment' (26 February 2025), https://commission.europa.eu/news/commission-proposes-cut-red-tape-and-simplify-business-environment-2025-02-26_en.
Commission 'Commission Work Programme 2026: Europe's Independence Moment' COM (2025) 870 final.
Commission, 'Competitiveness of the European Economy: Annual Competitiveness Report 2025 - The Competitiveness Compass' COM (2025) 30 final.
Commission, 'Better Regulation Guidelines' SWD(2021) 305 final (SWD Better Regulation Guidelines).
Commission, 'Commission discussion paper "The Commission and non-governmental organisations: building a stronger partnership"' COM/2000/0011 final.
Commission, 'Communication from the Commission on a New Pact on Migration and Asylum' COM (2020) 609 final
Commission, 'Communication from the Commission to the European Parliament, the Council, The European Economic and Social Committee and the Committee of Regions: A Union of equality: EU anti-racism action plan 2020–2025' COM (2020) 565 final, 18 September 2020.
Commission, 'Communication from the Commission - Towards a reinforced culture of consultation and dialogue - General principles and minimum standards for consultation of interested parties by the Commission' COM (2002) 704 final, 11 December 2002.
Commission, 'Communication from the Commission to the European Parliament, The Council, The European Economic and Social Committee and the Committee of the Regions, Better Regulation: Joining Forces to Make Better Laws' COM (2021) 219 final.
Commission, 'Community of Practice of the Competence Centre on Participatory and Deliberative Democracy', https://cop-demos.jrc.ec.europa.eu/.

Commission, 'Conference on the Future of Europe: Putting Vision into Concrete Action' (2022) COM (2022) 404 final.

Commission, 'European Citizens' Panels', https://citizens.ec.europa.eu/index_en.

Commission, 'European Citizens' Panels' (Factsheet, 2023), https://citizens.ec.europa.eu/european-citizens-panels_en.

Commission, 'European Governance: A White Paper' COM (2001) 428 final, 25 July 2001.

Commission, 'Have Your Say AI Intiative' (10 September 2020), https://ec.europa.eu/info/law/better-regulation/have-your-say/initiatives/12527-Artificial-intelligence-ethical-and-legal-requirements_en.

Commission, 'Impact Assessment accompanying proposal for directives (1) amending Council Directive 93/13/EEC, Directive 98/6/EC of the European Parliament and of the Council, Directive 2005/29/EC of the European Parliament and of the Council and Directive 2011/83/EU of the European Parliament and of the Council as regards better enforcement and modernisation of EU consumer protection rules and (2) on representative actions for the protection of the collective interests of consumers, and repealing Directive 2009/22/EC, SWD(2018) 96 final (Representative Action IA)'.

Commission, 'Impact Assessment Accompanying the document Proposal for a Directive of the European Parliament and of the Council amending Directive 1999/62/EC on the charging of heavy goods vehicles for the use of certain infrastructures and Proposal for a Council Directive amending Directive 1999/62/EC2 on the charging of heavy goods vehicles for the use of certain infrastructures, as regards certain provisions on vehicle taxation' SWD(2017) 180 final Part 1/2.

Commission, 'Impact Assessment Accompanying the document, Proposal for a Directive of the European Parliament and of the Council amending Directive 1999/62/EC on the charging of heavy goods vehicles for the use of certain infrastructures' SWD(2017) 180 final Part 2/2.

Commission, 'Impact Assessment Accompanying the Proposal for a Regulation of the European Parliament and of the Council Laying down harmonised rules on artificial intelligence (Artificial Intelligence Act) and amending certain union legislative acts' SWD/2021/84 final Part 1/2.

Commission, 'Impact Assessment Accompanying the Proposal for a Regulation of the European Parliament and of the Council Laying down harmonised rules on artificial intelligence (Artificial Intelligence Act) and amending certain union legislative acts' SWD/2021/84 final Part 2/2

Commission, 'Inception Impact Assessment: Proposal for a legal act of the European Parliament and the Council laying down requirements for Artificial Intelligence', Ref Ares(2020)3896535.

Commission, 'New Pact on Migration and Asylum', https://home-affairs.ec.europa.eu/policies/migration-and-asylum/new-pact-migration-and-asylum_en.Commission 'Proposal for a Directive of the European Parliament and of the Council Amending Directive 2008/98/EC on Waste' (2023) COM(2023) 420 final

Commission, 'Proposal for a Directive of the European Parliament and of the Council amending Directive 1999/62/EC on the charging of heavy goods vehicles for the use of certain infrastructures' COM (2017) 275 final.

Commission, 'Proposal for a new Directive on representative actions for the Protection of the Collective Interests of Consumers' COM (2018) 184 final.

Commission, 'Proposal for a Regulation laying down harmonised rules on Artificial Intelligence' COM (2021) 206 final and amending certain union legislative acts.

Commission, 'Proposal for a Regulation of the European Parliament and of the Council, on asylum and migration management and amending Council Directive (EC) 2003/109 and the proposed Regulation (EU) XXX/XXX [Asylum and Migration Fund]' COM (2020) 610 final.

Commission, 'Public Consultation for the Fitness Check of EU Consumer and Marketing Law', https://ec.europa.eu/newsroom/just/items/31689.

Commission, 'Report on the implementation of the Commission Recommendation of 11 June 2013 on common principles for injunctive and compensatory collective redress mechanisms in the Member States concerning violations of rights granted under Union law' (2013/396/EU) COM (2018) 040 final.

Commission, 'Roadmap New Pact on Asylum and Migration Ref Ares(2020)4017751 - 30/07/2020'.

Commission 'Selection of Civil Dialogue Groups' (13 April 2023), https://agriculture.ec.europa.eu/common-agricultural-policy/cap-overview/committees-and-expert-groups/civil-dialogue-groups/2014-22-agricultural-cdgs/selection-civil-dialogue-groups_en.
Commission, 'Study on the Citizens' Panels as Part of the Conference on the Future of Europe' (Technopolis Group).
Commission, 'Taking stock of the Commission's Better Regulation Agenda' COM (2019) 178.
Commission, 'White Paper On Artificial Intelligence - A European approach to excellence and trust' COM(2020) 65 final.
Commission, Directorate General for Justice and Consumers, *Consumer Conditions Scoreboard: Consumers at Home in the Single Market: 2017 Edition* (Publications Office, 2017).
Commission Regulatory Scrutiny Board, 'Proposal for a Directive as regards better enforcement and modernisation of EU consumer protection rules and Proposal for a Directive on representative actions for the protection of the collective interests of consumers' SEC(2018) 185.
Commission Regulatory Scrutiny Board, 'Regulatory Scrutiny Board: Annual Report 2022', https://commission.europa.eu/system/files/2023-05/RSB_2022_1.pdf.

European Parliament

Ballegooij, W van, and Navarra C, 'The Cost of Non-Europe in Asylum Policy' (European Parliamentary Research Service, 2018) PE 627.117.
European Parliament resolution of 9 June 2016 for an open, efficient and independent European Union administration OJ 2018/C086/19.
European Parliament, Resolution of 11 November 2015 on the reform of the electoral law of the European Union [2017] OJ C366/7.
European Parliament resolution of 14 March 2023 on the annual report on the activities of the European Ombudsman in 2021 (2022/2141(INI), P9_TA(2023)0070.
European Parliament resolution of 26 November 2020 on stocktaking of European elections (2020/2088(INI)) OJ L C425/11.
European Parliament, 'Rules of Procedure' 9th parliamentary term, July 2023.
European Parliament, 'Simplified Sustainability Reporting and Due Diligence Rules for Business', https://www.europarl.europa.eu/pdfs/news/expert/2025/12/press_release/20251211IPR32164/20251211IPR32164_en.pdf.
European Parliamentary Research Service, 'The European Commission's New Pact on Migration and Asylum, Horizontal Substitute Impact Assessment, PE 694.210'.
Kramer E, 'Revision of the Eurovignette Directive' (European Parliamentary Research Service, 2017) PE 603.273.
Šajn N, 'Representative Actions to Protect the Collective Interests of Consumers A New Deal for Consumers' (European Parliamentary Research Service, 2021) PE 637.978.

European Ombudsman

European Ombudsman, 'Decision in OI/8/2015/JAS on the Transparency of Trilogues'.
European Ombudsman, 'Decision of the European Ombudsman in her strategic inquiry OI/6/2014/NF concerning the composition and transparency of European Commission expert groups'.
European Ombudsman, 'Decision on how the European Commission carried out a public consultation concerning the "Sustainable Corporate Governance initiative"' (case 1956/2021/VB).
European Ombudsman, 'Decision on how the European Commission applies the rules governing expert groups and other similar entities regarding transparency' (case OI/3/2024/KR).

European Ombudsman, 'European Ombudsman Strategic Inquiry on the Transparency of Trilogues: Follow-up and First Results', www.ombudsman.europa.eu/en/doc/correspondence/en/88698.
European Ombudsman, 'Recommendation of the European Ombudsman in Case OI/2/2017/TE on the Transparency of the Council Legislative Process'.
European Ombudsman, 'Recommendation on the European Commission's Failure to Comply with Its Better Regulation Guidelines in Preparing Several Legislative Proposals'.
European Ombudsman, 'Recommendation of the European Ombudsman in her strategic inquiry OI/6/2014/NF concerning the composition of Commission expert groups', 29 January 2016.
European Ombudsman, '25 Years of the European Ombudsman. Strengthening the role of the European Ombudsman in challenging times for citizens' (Speech, Brussels, 25 October 2020, https://www.ombudsman.europa.eu/en/speech/en/134202.

European Economic and Social Committee

European Economic and Social Committee, 'Action Plan for the implementation of Articles 11(1) and 11(2) of the Treaty on European Union' (4 July 2018), https://www.eesc.europa.eu/en/documents/action-plan-implementation-articles-111-and-112-treaty-european-union.
European Economic And Social Committee, 'European Economic and Social Committee', https://european-union.europa.eu/institutions-law-budget/institutions-and-bodies/search-all-eu-institutions-and-bodies/european-economic-and-social-committee-eesc_en.
European Economic And Social Committee, 'New EU Pact on Migration and Asylum: A Missed Opportunity for a Much-Needed Fresh Start' (2020), https://www.eesc.europa.eu/en/news-media/news/new-eu-pact-migration-and-asylum-missed-opportunity-much-needed-fresh-start.
European Economic and Social Committee, Opinion of the Economic and Social Committee on 'Organised civil society and European governance: the Committee's contribution to the drafting of the White Paper' (2001/C 193/21).

European Court of Auditors

European Court of Auditors, '"Have Your Say!": Commission's Public Consultations Engage Citizens, but Fall Short of Outreach Activities' (Publications Office, 2019) 14.

Other

Presidency Conclusions of the Laeken European Council (14 and 15 December 2001) SN 300/1/01 REV 1.
Secretariat of the Convention, 'Cover Note from Praesidium to the Convention', Conv 369/02, Brussels, 28 October 2002.
Document from the Praesidium: Draft Title VI of the Constitutional Treaty relating to the democratic life of the Union (2 April 2003).
European Convention, 'Report from the Presidency of the Convention to the President of the European Council', CONV 851/2003, 3.
Joint Declaration (EC) on Practical Arrangements for the Co-decision Procedure (Art 251 EC Treaty) [2007] OJ C145/2.
'State of the Union Address by President von Der Leyen' (*European Commission*), https://ec.europa.eu/commission/presscorner/detail/en/speech_22_5493.
European Union, 'EUR-Lex - Civil_society_organisation', https://eur-lex.europa.eu/EN/legal-content/glossary/civil-society-organisation.html.

UN documents

Office of the United Nations High Commissioner for Human Rights, 'Promotion, Protection and Implementation of the Right to Participate in Public Affairs in the Context of the Existing Human Rights Law: Best Practices, Experiences, Challenges and Ways to Overcome Them' [2015] UN Doc A/HRC/30/26.

Special Rapporteur on extreme poverty and human rights, 'Report of the Special Rapporteur on extreme poverty and human rights', UN Doc A/HRC/23/36 (2013).

United Nations Human Rights Committee, General Comments article 25: The right to participate in public affairs, voting rights and the right to equal access to public service, UN Doc CCPR/C/21/Rev.1/Add.7 (1996).

National legislative and official documents

Bundeskanzleramt Österreich, 'Rundschreiben zu Begutachtungen und Konsultationsmechanismen', https://www.bundeskanzleramt.gv.at/agenda/verfassung/legistik/begutachtungs-konsultations-informationsverfahren-bessere-rechtssetzung/rundschreiben-begutachtungen-konsultationsmechanismen.html.

Datenschutzbehörde Republik Österreich, 'Leitfaden Zum Informationsfreiheitsgesetz' (30 June 2025), https://dsb.gv.at/sites/site0344/media/downloads/leitfaden_ifg_-_stand_30.6.2025.pdf.

Department of Foreign Affairs and Trade, 'Oireachtas Scrutiny: Guidelines for Departments in Relation to the Scrutiny of EU Matters by the Houses of the Oireachtas' (2021), https://www.gov.ie/en/department-of-public-expenditure-infrastructure-public-service-reform-and-digitalisation/publications/public-consultation-guidance/.

Department of Public Expenditure and Reform, 'Consultation Principles & Guidance' (2016), https://www.gov.ie/en/department-of-public-expenditure-infrastructure-public-service-reform-and-digitalisation/publications/public-consultation-guidance/.

Konstitutionsutskottets betänkande 2014/15:KU10 [parliamentary committee report].

Parlament Österreich, 'Das Begutachtungsverfahren', https://www.parlament.gv.at/beteiligen/wissenswertes/begutachtungsverfahren/.

Proposition [Prop] 1973:90 Grundlagsutredningen [government bill].

Proposition [Prop] 1994/95:19 Sveriges Medlemskap i Europeiska Unionen [government bill].

Proposition [Prop] 2002/03:35 Mål for folkhälsan [government bill].

Statens Offentliga Utredningar [SOU] SOU 1999:121 Avkorporativisering och lobbyism – konturerna till en ny politisk modell [government report series].

Statens Offentliga Utredningar [SOU] SOU 1999:144 Demokrati på remiss [government report series].

Statens Offentliga Utredningar [SOU] 2008:118 Styra och ställa [government report series].

Statsrådsberedningen, Svara på Remiss - hur och varför?, SB PM 2003:2 [government memorandum] Stockholm, 2003.

Reports

Alemanno, A, 'Strengthening the Role and Impact of Petitions as an Instrument of Participatory Democracy, Study Commissioned by the European Parliament's Policy Department for Citizens' Rights and Constitutional Affairs' PE 694.837.

Alemanno, A, 'Towards a Permanent Citizens Participatory Mechanism in the EU, Study Commissioned by the Policy Department for Citizens' Rights and Constitutional Affairs, European Parliament' (2022) PE 735.927.

Aparajita, A and others, 'A Comparative Survey of Procedures for Public Participation in the Lawmaking Process' (Oxford Pro Bono Publico, 2011).

Chabanet, D. and Trechsel, AH, 'EU Member States' Consultation with Civil Society on European Policy Matters' (2011) EUDO Report 2011/04.

Civil Liberties Union for Europea, 'Liberties Rule of Law Report 2023', https://www.liberties.eu/f/-3lkvi.

Civil Society Europe, 'A Roadmap to Civil Dialogue in the EU' (20 June 2019)', https://civilsocietyeurope.eu/a-roadmap-to-civil-dialogue-in-the-eu/.

Demidov, A, Greubel, J and Petit, P, 'Assessing the European Citizens' Panels: Greater Ambition Needed' Observatory Report (EU Democracy Reform Observatory, 2023). Eriksen, EO, Joerges, C, and Neyer, J (eds), 'European Governance, Deliberation and the Quest for Democratisation' ARENA Report 2/03 (2003).

Fazi, E, and Smith, J, 'Civil Dialogue: Making It Work Better, Study Commissioned by the Civil Society Contact Group' (Civil Society Contact Group, 2006).

Kohler-Koch, B, 'Does Participatory Democracy Hold Its Promises?' in B Kohler-Koch and F Larat (eds), 'Efficient and Democratic Governance in the European Union' (Connex Report Series 09, 2008).

Kidron, B, and others, 'Disrupted Childhood: The Cost of Persuasive Design' (*5Rights Foundation, Version 2*, 2023), https://5rightsfoundation.com/uploads/Disrupted-Childhood-2023.pdf.

Kværk, GO, 'Organised Civil Society in the EU Constitution-Making Process' in JE Fossum, P Schlesigner and GO Kværk (eds), Public Sphere and Civil Society? Transformations of the European Union (ARENA Report 2/2007: 141–223).

OECD, *Best Practice Principles on Stakeholder Engagement in Regulatory Policy Draft* (OECD, 2008).

OECD, *Better Regulation Practices across the European Union 2022* (OECD, 2022).

OECD, *Lobbying in the 21st Century: Transparency, Integrity and Access* (OECD, 2021), https://www.oecd-ilibrary.org/governance/lobbying-in-the-21st-century_c6d8eff8-en.

OECD, *Regulatory Policy Outlook 2021* (OECD Publishing, 2021).

US Chamber Institute for legal Reform, 'The Growth of Collective Redress in the EU: A Survey of Developments in 10 Member States' (*ILR*, 21 March 2017).

Newspaper Articles, Press releases, and Blog Posts

Abnett, K, 'EU Commission Faces Complaint over Easing of Sustainability Rules' (*Reuters*, 18 April 2025), https://www.reuters.com/sustainability/climate-energy/eu-commission-faces-complaint-over-easing-sustainability-rules-2025-04-17/.

'AI: Decoded: A Dutch Algorithm Scandal Serves a Warning to Europe — The AI Act Won't Save Us' (*POLITICO*, 30 March 2022), https://www.politico.eu/newsletter/ai-decoded/a-dutch-algorithm-scandal-serves-a-warning-to-europe-the-ai-act-wont-save-us-2/.

Blenkinsop, P, and Abnett, K, 'EU Points Way to Competitive Future to Catch US, China Rivals' (*Reuters*, 29 January 2025), https://www.reuters.com/business/eu-points-way-competitive-future-catch-us-china-rivals-2025-01-29/.

'ChatGPT Broke the EU Plan to Regulate AI' (*POLITICO*, 3 March 2023), https://www.politico.eu/article/eu-plan-regulate-chatgpt-openai-artificial-intelligence-act/.

Clifford, M, and Brennan, C, 'Government under Fire for Rushing through Planning Law with Limited Time for Debate' *Irish Examiner* (Cork, 12 July 2022), https://www.irishexaminer.com/news/politics/arid-40915802.html.

Corporate Europe Observatory, 'Big Tech Takes EU Lobby Spending to an All Time High', https://corporateeurope.org/en/2021/08/big-tech-takes-eu-lobby-spending-all-time-high.

European Commission, 'SME Test', https://single-market-economy.ec.europa.eu/smes/sme-strategy/sme-test_en.

European Commission, 'A Fresh Start on Migration: Building Confidence and Striking a New Balance between Responsibility and Solidarity, Press Release, IP/20/1706'.

Klatzer, J, 'Taktieren Mit Begutachtungsfristen' (*Österreichischer Rundfunk (ORF)*, 26 June 2020), https://orf.at/stories/3169772/.

Liboreiro, J, 'EU Gives Fresh Push to Stalled Migration Pact' (*euronews*, 10 June 2022), https://www.euronews.com/my-europe/2022/06/10/eu-hails-historic-agreement-as-it-gives-fresh-push-to-stalled-migration-pact.

Lih, A, 'Opinion: Can Wikipedia Survive?' *The New York Times* (New York, 20 June 2015), https://www.nytimes.com/2015/06/21/opinion/can-wikipedia-survive.html.

MacCarthy, M, and Propp, K, 'Machines Learn That Brussels Writes the Rules: The EU's New AI Regulation' (*Brookings*, 4 May 2021), https://www.brookings.edu/articles/machines-learn-that-brussels-writes-the-rules-the-eus-new-ai-regulation/.

Metzinger, T, 'EU guidelines: Ethics washing made in Europe' (*Der Tagesspiegel Online*, 8 April 2019, https://www.tagesspiegel.de/politik/ethics-washing-made-in-europe-5937028.html

'President's Warning on Volume of Legislation', https://www.lawsociety.ie/gazette/top-stories/2021/07-july/presidents-warning-on-volume-of-legislation.

Sanou, H, 'Over 1,100 Children of Childcare Benefit Victims Taken into Care' (*DutchNews.nl*, 20 October 2021), https://www.dutchnews.nl/2021/10/over-1100-children-of-childcare-benefit-victims-taken-into-care/.

Satariano, A, and Stevis-Gridneff, M, 'Big Tech Turns Its Lobbyists Loose on Europe, Alarming Regulators' *The New York Times* (New York, 14 December 2020), https://www.nytimes.com/2020/12/14/technology/big-tech-lobbying-europe.html.

'"The Godfather of AI" Quits Google and Warns of Danger Ahead' *The New York Times* (New York, 1 May 2023), https://www.nytimes.com/2023/05/01/technology/ai-google-chatbot-engineer-quits-hinton.html.

'UK: Court Rules Suicide of 14-Year-Old Girl Attributed to Harmful Posts on Instagram & Pinterest; Incl. Company Statement' (*Business & Human Rights Resource Centre*, 3 October 2022), https://www.business-humanrights.org/en/latest-news/uk-suicide-of-14-year-old-girl-attributed-to-harmful-posts-on-instagram-and-pinterest/.

Web pages

'ALTER-EU – Europe's Campaign for Lobbying Transparency', https://www.alter-eu.org/.

Commission, 'Shaping Europe's Digital Future: High-Level Expert Group on Artificial Intelligence' (30 June 2023), https://digital-strategy.ec.europa.eu/en/policies/expert-group-ai.

Corporate Europe Observatory, https://corporateeurope.org/en.

European Youth Portal, 'Get Involved: EU Youth Dialogue', https://youth.europa.eu/eu-youth-dialogue_en.

European Youth Portal, 'Information Session - "EU Youth Test/Check"', https://youth.europa.eu/year-of-youth/activities/15293_en.

'LATINNO: Innovations for Democracy in Latin America', https://www.latinno.net/en/.

World Health Organization, 'Mental Health: Strengthening Our Response', https://www.who.int/news-room/fact-sheets/detail/mental-health-strengthening-our-response.

'Participatory Research in Asia', https://www.pria.org/.

'Participedia', https://participedia.net/.

'ReNEUAL – the Research Network on EU Administrative Law', http://www.reneual.eu/.

'Second European AI Alliance Assembly, Event Report', https://futurium.ec.europa.eu/sites/default/files/2020-12/Second%20European%20AI%20Alliance%20Assembly%20_%20Event%20Report.pdf.

'SILE, Silent Agents Affected by Legislation: From an Insufficient Knowledge Base to Inclusive Solutions' (*Hiljaiset toimijat*), https://www.hiljaisettoimijat.fi/?lang=en.

'Transparency Register', https://ec.europa.eu/transparencyregister/public/homePage.do.
'Verfassungsgerichthof, Functions', https://www.vfgh.gv.at/kompetenzen-und-verfahren/functions.en.html.

Consultation documents, on file with the author

'Access Now, Feedback Response, Consultation Artificial Intelligence Act' (on file with the author).
'Commission, Eurovignette Consultation Replies' (on file with the author).
'Individual Feedback Reply, Roadmap New Pact Asylum and Migration' (on file with the author).

INDEX

www.ingramcontent.com/pod-product-compliance
Ingram Content Group UK Ltd.
Pitfield, Milton Keynes, MK11 3LW, UK
UKHW021826230926
475688UK00003BC/127

9 781509 995943